A VIRTUE LESS CLOISTERED

A Virtue Less Cloistered

Courts, Speech and Constitutions

IAN CRAM

·HART·
PUBLISHING

HART PUBLISHING
OXFORD AND PORTLAND, OREGON
2002

Published in North America (US and Canada) by
Hart Publishing
c/o International Specialized Book Services
5804 NE Hassalo Street
Portland, Oregon
97213-3644
USA

Distributed in Netherlands, Belgium and Luxembourg by
Intersentia, Churchillaan 108
B2900 Schoten
Antwerpen
Belgium

Hart Publishing is a specialist legal publisher based in Oxford, England.
To order further copies of this book or to request a list of other publications
please write to:

Hart Publishing,
Salters Boatyard, Folly Bridge, Abingdon Rd,
Oxford, OX1 4LB
Telephone: +44(0)1865 245533 Fax: +44(0)1865 794882
email: mail@hartpub.co.uk
WEBSITE: http//:www.hartpub.co.uk

British Library Cataloguing in Publication Data
Data Available

ISBN 1–84113–038–9 (hardback)

Typeset by J&L Composition Ltd, Filey, North Yorkshire
Printed and bound in Great Britain by
TJ International Ltd, Padstow, Cornwall

Some degree of abuse is inseparable from the proper use of every thing: and in no instance is more true than that of the press.

James Madison, 4 *Elliot's Debates on the Federal Constitution* (1876) at 571.

Acknowledgements

I owe a number of people considerable debts of gratitude for various forms of help received during the writing of this book.

Over the years, gatherings of the SPTL Media Law Group provided a supportive and constructive environment in which to test out some early ideas and drafts. I am grateful for the feedback which these sessions generated.

Two colleagues who read through a draft of the completed manuscript are deserving of special acknowledgement. Professor Eric Barendt of the Faculty of Laws, University College London and Dr Mario Oetheimer of the Media Division of the Council of Europe, provided detailed critical commentaries and helpful suggestions on the text. I consider myself extremely fortunate to have had the benefit of their respective inputs. Inevitably, ultimate responsibility for any book rests with the author, nonetheless I am certain that their efforts resulted in improvements to the final product.

The chapter on freedom of expression under the Spanish Constitution could not have been written without the support and active assistance of a number of academic colleagues in Spain. Through Professor Marc Carrillo of the Faculty of Law, Pompeu Fabra University, Barcelona, I was fortunate enough to be given access to the resources of the University's law library. My period of study in Barcelona was funded by a grant from the SPTL's Academic Purposes Fund which I happily acknowledge. Professor Rafael Bustos Gisbert of the Faculty of Law, Salamanca University also gave me considerable help in tracking down useful materials. Associate Professor Carmen Camba Constenla of the Faculty of Law, Santiago de Compostela University was kind enough to read an earlier draft of this chapter and offer thoughtful amendments.

I would also like to thank the staff of the Louis Brandeis School of Law, Louisville University, Kentucky for providing me with an intellectually productive and socially congenial atmosphere during the all too brief time spent as a Visiting Professor in the Summer of 2001. Particular thanks are due to Don Burnett, Linda Ewald, Mike Fowler, Jim Jones, Susan Kosse, Sam Marcosson, Bob Stenger, and Russ Weaver.

Hannah Young at Hart Publishing saw this work through to completion and to her go my sincere thanks.

Finally, I want to record my thanks to my wife Aurora and children Seumas and Fiona for their love and support during work on this book.

Ian Cram

Human Rights Research Unit
Department of Law
Leeds
July 2002

Contents

Table of Cases xiii
Table of Legislation xxv
Table of Conventions and Treaties xxxv

Introduction 1

1 Free Speech Rationales and Constitutional Landscapes 5

I Introduction 5
II Rationales for Speech and their Relation to Court Reporting/ Comment 6
III Conclusion: An Argument From Government Incompetence 19
IV Constitutional Landscapes 21
V Judicial Review and Constitutional Freedoms: Some Concluding Thoughts 39

2 More or Less Different? The First Amendment and Article 10 43

I Introduction 43
II Some Structural Differences 43
III Free Speech Jurisprudence Compared—Rationales and Key Features of First Amendment and Article 10 Thinking 45
IV US Regulation of Speech Impacting upon Judicial Proceedings—An Overview 59
V The Regulation of Court-Related Speech Under Articles 6 and 10 of the European Convention on Human Rights—An Overview 66
VI A Moral Reading of Article 10 68
VII Conclusion 74

3 Speech and Criminal Jury Trials 77

I Introduction—Two Models of Court-Related Speech Regulation 77
II The Jury in Anglo-American Legal Systems 78
III Scots and English Approaches to Prejudicial Media Comment: From Divergence to Rapprochement? 80
IV Free Press and Fair Trial in the United States 93

V Canada—Reconciling Free Speech and Fair Trial Concerns Under The Charter 98
VI Australia 105
VII Taking Speech Too Seriously? 115
VIII The Empirical Evidence Considered 116
IX Conclusion: Return to Era of Jury as Persons with Knowledge of Matters at Issue in the Trial 121

4 For the Sake of the Children? Young Persons, Reporting Restrictions and Open Justice 123

I Introduction 123
II Domestic Provisions Governing Access to and Reporting of Criminal Proceedings Involving Young Persons in England and Wales 125
III Prior Restraints—A Freeze on Speech? Bickel and his Critics 128
IV Young Persons' Privacy Interests—Arguments and Counter-arguments 134
V The Advancement of Children and Young Persons' Privacy Interests in International Law 142
VI National Legal Systems' Treatment of Privacy Claims 145
VII Lessons from Europe—(I) Access to Crown Court Proceedings Post *T v United Kingdom; V v United Kingdom* and (II) The (In)Compatibility of Reporting Restrictions under the Youth Justice and Criminal Evidence Act With Article 10 of the European Convention on Human Rights 157
VIII Conclusion 160

5 The English Foolishness: Scandalising the Courts and the Limits of Constitutionally Protected Expression 161

I Introduction 161
II The Offence Outlined 163
III The English Foolishness Abroad—the Constitutionality of Scandalising in the United States, Australia, Canada and Under The European Convention on Human Rights 168
IV Conclusion 178

6 A Civil Law Comparison: Freedom of Expression and the Administration of Justice in Spain 183

I Introduction 183
II Burgos 1970 and After 184
III The 1978 Constitution—Human Rights in a Modern Social Democracy 189

IV Freedom of Expression Jurisprudence of the Tribunal Constitutional: Some General Features 192
V Media Freedom and Impartial Trials 202
VI Conclusion 207

7 Conclusion: Court-Related Speech in the Electronic Age and some Emergent Themes 209

I Internet Speech—An Introduction 209
II The Internet—Definition and Characteristics 210
III Threats to the Administration of Justice 212
IV Conclusion 217

Index 223

Table of Cases

EUROPEAN COMMISSION AND COURT OF HUMAN RIGHTS CASES

AG v Channel 4 (1989) 61 DR 285 92
Barfod v Denmark 162, 175–77
Barthold v Germany (1985) 7 EHRR 383 ....55–56, 174
Bergens Tidende and others v Norway (2001) 31 EHRR 16 53
Casado Coca v Spain (1994) 18 EHRR 1 ....55–56, 114, 174
Castells v Spain (1992) 14 EHRR 445 ....52, 55, 174–75, 195
Chorherr v Austria (1994) 17 EHRR 358...67
Crociani et al v Italy App nos 8603, 8723, 8729/79 (1981) 22 D & R 147 66–67
De Haes & Gisjels v Belgium (1998) 25 EHRR 1 ....162, 176–77
Dorsen v Netherlands (1996) 22 EHRR 330...39
Fey v Austria (1994) 16 EHRR 387 67
Goodwin v UK (1996) 22 EHRR 123..58
Grigoriades v Greece (1999) 27 EHRR 464 54
Handyside v UK (1979–80) 1 EHRR 737..................17, 51, 53, 56, 71, 174, 194
Jacubowski v Germany (1995) 19 EHRR 64 ....55–56, 174
Jersild v Denmark (1995) 19 EHRR 1..52–53
Kostovski v Netherlands (1989) 12 EHRR 434..39
Leander v Sweden (1987) 9 EHRR 59 71
Lingens v Austria (1986) 8 EHRR 407 ....51–52, 54–55, 114, 174–76, 195–96
Markt Intern Verlag & Beerman v Germany (1990) 12 EHRR 161 ....55, 174
Moreira de Azevedo v Portugal (1990) 13 EHRR 721....................................66
Muller v Switzerland (1988) 13 EHRR 212 174
News Verlags GmbH v Austria (2001) 31 EHRR 8................52–53, 67–68, 196
Nortier v Netherlands Series A no 267 (1993) 158
Oberschlick v Austria (1995) 19 EHRR 389.............................52–55, 174, 194
Observer & Guardian Newspapers v UK (1992) 14 EHRR 153 ....54, 56–57, 129, 174, 197
Open Door Counselling and Dublin Well Woman v Ireland (1993) 15 EHRR 244 59
Otto-Preminger Institut v Austria (1995) 19 EHRR 34 ....53, 56, 174
Prager & Oberschlick v Austria (1996) 2 EHRR 1 ....55, 162, 175–79, 218
Schopfer v Switzerland [1998] HRCD 560 175
Schwabe v Austria Series A no 242-B 54
Sporrong and Lonnroth, 23 Sept 1982 58
Stanford v UK Series A no 282 (1994) 144

Sunday Times v UK (1979) 2 EHRR 245 ....12, 33, 52, 56, 59, 67, 70, 73, 80, 82, 174, 206
T v UK (2000) 30 EHRR 121 ....124, 125, 139, 143, 157–59
Thorgeir Thorgeirson v Iceland (1992) 14 EHRR 843................52, 55, 175, 195
V v UK (2000) 30 EHRR 121 ....124, 135, 139, 144, 157–59
Wingrove v UK (1997) 24 EHRR 1...56, 174
Wloch v Poland ECtHR Information Note No 16 (March 2000) 67
Worm v Austria (1998) 25 EHRR 454......43, 52, 67, 71–75, 80, 196, 205–7, 218
X v Austria (1963) 11 Coll 31 66
X v Norway (1970) XIII Yearbook 302 66

NATIONAL CASES

AUSTRALIA

Adelaide Company of Jehovah's Witnesses v Commonwealth (1943) 67 CLR 116 32
AG (Cth): Ex rel McKinlay v Commonwealth (1975) 135 CLR 1..................34
AG NSW v Mundey [1972] 2 NSWLR 887 163
AG NSW v Willesee (No 1) [1980] 2 NSWLR 143 108
AG NSW v Willesee (No 2)...108
Amalgamated Society of Engineers v Adelaide Steamship Co Ltd (1920) 28 CLR 129...32
Australian Broadcasting Commission v Parish (1980) 29 ALR 228 147
Australian Capital Television Pty Ltd v Commonwealth (ACTV) (1992) 177 CLR 106..34, 114, 149, 170
Australian Capital Territory v Commonwealth (1992) 177 CLR 106......113–14
Bread Manufacturers Ltd, ex parte; Re Truth and Sportsman Ltd (1937) 37 SR (NSW) 242 ....33–34, 107–10
Civil Aviation Authority v Australian Broadcasting Commission (1995) 39 NSWLR 540 112
Colina ex parte Torney, Re (1998)..162
David Syne & Co Ltd v General Motors-Holden's Ltd [1984] 2 NSWLR 294 145
Davis v Baillie [1946] VLR 486 105
Dietrich v R (1992) 177 CLR 292 79
DPP v Wran (1986) 7 NSWLR 616...117
F, Re (1989) 51 SASR 141 148
G v The Queen (1984) SASR 349...148
Gallagher v Durack (1983) 152 CLR 238 ....105, 161
Herald Weekly and Weekly Times Ltd v Levine (1996) (SC Vic, CA) (LEXIS) 147
Hinch v AG (Vic) (1987) 164 CLR 15 ....34, 105–6, 108–10, 117

Hoffnung (S) & Co Ltd v Hesky [1977] 2 NSWLR 669 145
James v Robinson (1963) 109 CLR 593 106
John Fairfax & Sons Ltd v McRae (1955) 93 CLR 351 ....33, 107
John Fairfax & Sons Ltd v Police Tribunal of New South Wales (1986) 5 NSWLR 465 106
Kruger and Others v Commonwealth of Australia and Others (1997) 190 CLR 1 ....113, 170
Lange v Australian Broadcasting Corporation (1997) 145 ALR 96, (1997) 189 CLR 520..............................35–36, 113–14, 170
Levy v State of Victoria (1997) 189 CLR 579 114
Mann v O'Neill (1997) 191 CLR 204 181
Miller v TCN Channel Nine Pty Ltd (1986) 161 CLR 556 34
Nationwide News Pty Ltd v Wills (1992) 177 CLR 1 ....34, 164, 170–71
Packer v Peacock (1912) 13 CLR 577 ....105, 106
R v Archdall (1928) 41 CLR 128 32
R v Dunbabin ex parte Williams (1935) 53 CLR 434 106
R v Fletcher ex parte Kisch (1935) 52 CLR 248 164
R v Glennon (1992) 173 CLR 592 110–11
Raybos Australia Pty Ltd v Jones [1986] 2 NSWLR 47..............................106, 141, 145, 148
Registrar, Court of Appeal v Willesee (1985) 3 NSWLR 650 107
Registrar of the Supreme Court of Equity Division v McPherson [1980] 1 NSWLR 688..............................107
Russell v Russell (1976) 134 CLR 495 ....106, 145, 148
Scott v Scott [1913] AC 417 ....105, 145
Stephens v West Australian Newspapers Ltd (1994) 182 CLR 211..............................35, 149
Theophanous v The Herald & Weekly Times Ltd (1994) 182 CLR 104, [1994] 3 LRC 369..............................35–36, 55, 113, 149
Tuckiar v R (1934) 52 CLR 335 110–11
Victoria v Australia Building Construction Employees' and Builders Labourers' Federation (1982) 152 CLR 25 34

CANADA

AG of Alberta and Interwest Publications Ltd, Re (1991) 73 DLR (4th) 83 100
AG Canada and Dupond v Montreal [1978] 2 SCR 770..............................25
AG for Manitoba v Groupe Quebecor Inc (1988) 45 DLR (4th) 80..............................100
AG for Manitoba and Radio OB Ltd, Re (1977) 70 DLR (3d) 311 99
Alberta Statutes, Reference re [1938] SCR 100..............................25
BCGEU v AG (British Columbia) [1988] 2 SCR 214 28
Canada (Human Rights Commission) v Taylor (1990) 75 DLR (4th) 577 132
Canadian Newspaper Co v Attorney General (1985) OR (2d) 557 51
CBC v AG (New Brunswick) [1996] 3 SCR 480..............................28, 150–51, 172

CBC v Keegstra (1986) 36 DLR (4th) 76 104
Dagenais v Canadian Broadcasting Corp [1994] 3 SCR 835; (1995) 120 DLR (4th) 12 ....11, 30, 101–4, 172, 218
Edmonton Journal v Alberta (1989) 64 DLR (4th) 577; [1990] 1 WWR 577 ....11, 28, 30, 100, 172
Ford v AG (Quebec) [1988] 2 SCR 712..27–28
Guest v Knowles (1908) 17 OLR 416..100
Homolka case (1993) 14 *Journal of Media Law and Policy* 157 214–15
Irwin Toy v Quebec [1989] 1 SCR 927..28
L'Imprimerie Populaire Ltee et al v Leclerc [1960] Que QB 923 98
McKinney v University of Guelph [1990] 3 SCR 229....................................27
Murphy and Southam Press Ltd, Re (1972) 9 CCC (2d) 330..........................99
Ouellet, Re (1976) 72 DLR (3d) 95 163
Phillips v Nova Scotia (Westray Inquiry) (1995) 124 DLR (4th) 129......104, 121
R v Big M Drug Mart [1985] 1 SCR 295 27
R v Bryan (1954) 108 CCC 209 99
R v Carrochia (1973) 43 DLR (3d) 427 99
R v CHBC Television et al (1998) 121 CCC (3d) 266 102–4
R v Corbett [1988] 1 SCR 670..104
R v Drybones [1970] SCR 282..26
R v Horsham JJ ex parte Farquharson [1982] 1 QB 762................................65
R v Hubbert (1975) 29 CCC (2d) 279 104
R v Keegstra [1990] 3 SCR 697 28
R v Kopyto [1987] OR (2d) 449; (1987) 47 DLR (4th) 213 ....28, 172–73, 179
R v Kray (1969) 53 Cr App R 412..65, 92, 117
R v Mills [1986] 1 SCR 863..26
R v O'Connor [1995] 4 SCR 411..28
R v Oakes [1986] 1 SCR 103 ....27–29, 102, 172–73
R v P (1978) 43 CCC (2d) 197 151
R v Robinson-Blackmore Printing and Publishing Co Ltd (1989) 47 CCC (3d) 366..102
R v Therens et al [1985] 1 SCR 613 26
R v Vairo and CFCF Inc (1982) 4 CCC (3d) 274..100
R v Vandervelde (1994) 89 CCC (3d) 161..150
R v Vermette (1988) 50 DLR (4th) 385..104
R v Zundel (1992) 95 DLR (4th) 202..29
RJR MacDonald Inc v AG (Canada) (1995) 127 DLR (4th) 1 27
RWDSU v Dolphin Delivery [1986] 2 SCR 573 ....26, 30, 172
Scott v Scott 29
Southam Inc and The Queen (No 1), Re (1983) 41 OR (2d) 113, (1983) 70 CCC (2d) 264 ....29, 99–100, 149–50
Southam Inc and The Queen, Re (1984) 48 OR (2d) 678 28
Steiner v Toronto Star Ltd (1955) 114 CCC 117..99

Stoffman v Vancouver General Hospital [1990] 3 SCR 483 27
Teale (Bernardo) case (1993) 14 *Journal of Media Law & Policy* 157 214–15
Telegraph, Ex parte [1993] 1 WLR 980 65
Thomson Newspapers Co v Canada (AG) [1998] 1 SCR 887 28
Westray Inquiry, see *Phillips v Nova Scotia*

ENGLAND AND WALES

Abnee v DPP [1999] 2 AC 295 161
AG v BBC [1997] EMLR 76 84
AG v Birmingham Post and Mail Ltd [1998] 4 All ER 49 ....84, 86
AG v Channel 4, unreported 92
AG v English [1983] 1 AC 116 ....88–90, 93
AG v Guardian Newspapers (No 3) [1992] 1 WLR 874 134
AG v Guardian Newspapers [1999] EMLR 904 86
AG v ITN [1995] 1 Cr App R 204 73
AG v ITN & others [1995] 2 All ER 370 ....82, 84
AG v Leveller [1979] AC 440 148
AG v MGN Ltd [1997] 1 All ER 456......................73, 83–84, 92, 112, 121, 133
AG v Newspaper Publishing Ltd [1987] 3 All ER 276 82
AG v Sport Newspapers Ltd [1991] 1 WLR 1194...81
AG v Sunday Newspapers Ltd & others (1998) January 20 (LAWTEL) ....
82–84
AG v Sunday Times [1974] AC 273 92
AG v Times Newspapers Ltd [1974] AC 273..................................106–7, 117
AG v Times Newspapers & others (1983) *The Times* 12 Feb 89–90
AG v TVS and Southey...90
AG v Unger [1998] 1 Cr App R 308 ....84, 86
Almon's case (1765) Wilm 243 164–65
Ambard v AG for Trinidad & Tobago [1936] AC 322........................1, 12, 163
Bingley (William) case (1768) 164–65
Crook, Re (1991) 93 Cr App R 17 125
General Medical Council v BBC [1998] 3 All ER 426 87–88
Godfrey v Demon Internet Ltd [1999] 4 All ER 342 ....211, 213, 217
Hellewell v Chief Constable of Derbyshire [1995] 1 WLR 804 137
Hulbert case 221
Leary v BBC (1989) LEXIS 29 Sept 88
Lewis v Daily Telegraph [1963] 2 All ER 151 141
Lonhro, In re [1990] 2 AC 154...92
Marbury v Madison (1803) 1 Cranch 137 23
Onslow and Whalley (1873) LR 9 QB 219 165
P, ex parte The Times 31 Mar 1999 148
Pepper v Hart [1993] AC 59 38

Practice Note on safeguarding the right of young persons to effective participation in trials [2000] 2 All ER 285 ....124, 157–59
R v Central Criminal Court ex parte Plummer The Times 28 Oct 1998 136
R v Central Criminal Court ex parte Simpkins The Times 28 Oct 1998 136
R v Central Criminal Court ex parte W, B & C (2001) 1 Cr App R 7 127
R v Chief Constable of North Wales and others ex parte AB and another [1998] 3 All ER 310 138
R v City of London Magistrates' Court ex parte Cropper The Times 7 Dec 1999 140
R v Clement 165
R v Clerkenwell Metropolitan Stipendiary Magistrate ex parte The Telegraph [1993] QB 462 134
R v Colsey The Times 9 May 1931 166
R v Commissioner of Police of the Metropolis ex parte Blackburn (No2) [1968] 2 QB 150 ....163–64, 166
R v Editor of New Statesman ex parte DPP (1928) 44 TLR 301 ....163, 166
R v Evening Standard Co [1954] 1 QB 578 99
R v Evesham JJ ex parte McDonagh [1988] 2 WLR 227 ....139, 148
R v Felixstowe JJ ex parte Leigh [1987] 1 All ER 551 12
R v Gray [1900] 2 QB 36 ....163, 166
R v Lee [1993] 1 WLR 103 ....136, 159
R v McCann, Cullen & Shanahan (1991) 92 Cr App R 239....81, 86, 206
R v Savundranayagan and Walker [1968] 3 All ER 439 107
R v Secretary of State for Home Dept ex parte Brind [1991] 1 AC 696....37
R v Solicitor-General ex parte Taylor [1995] COD 61 87
R v Taylor and Taylor (1994) 98 Cr App R 361 86
R v Uxbridge Magistrates' Court ex parte Patel The Times 7 Dec 1999 140
R v Waterfield [1975] 1 WLR 711 125
R v Wilkinson The Times 16 July 1930 166
Roach v Garvan (St James Evening Post case) (1742) 2 Atk 468 164
Skipworth and Castro (1873) LR 9 QB 230 165
Steare case (1768) *State Trials* viii, 60 165
Thompson v News Group Newspapers Ltd and others [2001] 2 WLR 1038....216, 221
Venables v News Group Newspapers Ltd and others [2001] 2 WLR 1038 ....216, 221

HONG KONG

Secretary of State for Justice v The Oriental Press Group Ltd and others [1998] 2 HKLRD 123 ....162, 172
Wong Yueng Ng v Secretary for Justice [1999] 3 HKC 143 162

NEW ZEALAND

Solicitor General v Radio Avon Ltd and another [1978] 1 NZLR 225 ....161, 163

SCOTLAND

Al Megrahi (Abdelbasset Ali Mohamed) and another v Times Newspapers Ltd and others 1999 SLT 466 ....91, 93
Atkins v London Weekend Television Ltd 1978 SLT 76....84, 89, 92
Cox & Griffiths Petrs 1998 SCCR 561 ....87, 91–92
Ellis (Walter Scott) unreported 167
HMA v Caledonian Newspapers Ltd 1995 SLT 926 84–85
HMA v Carr (1854) 1 Irv 464 166
HMA v Daily Record (1997) Part 9 Media Lawyer 28 84
HMA v News Group Newspapers Ltd and Scottish Express Newspapers Ltd 1989 SCCR 156....93
HMA v Scotsman Publications Ltd 1989 SLT 705 ....87, 89, 92
HMA v Scottish Media Newspapers Ltd and others http://194.128.11.201/opinions/84_99.html....85, 92
HMA v Whaldon and others (1998) 3 Communications Law 155 ....84, 87
Kaur (Surjit) v Lord Advocate [1980] 3 CMLR 79 91
Lord Advocate v Hay (1822) 1 S 288 (N E 267) 167
Magistrates of Kirkaldy v Dougal (1679) Mor 1984....167
Milburn 1946 SC 301 167
Muir v BBC 1997 SLT 425....88, 90
Robb v Caledonian Newspapers Ltd 1995 SLT 631 87
Robertson (Alex) (1870) 1 Couper 404....167
Smith v Ritchie (1892) 20 R (J) 52....89
Stirling v Associated Newspapers Ltd 1960 SLT 5 ....79, 84
Stuurman [1980] JC 111 86–87

SOUTH AFRICA

S v Van Niekerk 1970 (3) SA 655 (T) 163

SPAIN

STC 6/1981 (periodistas de San Sebastián) 195–96
STC 30/1982 (Diario 16)....196, 203–4
STC 62/1982 ....194, 200

STC 52/1983 196
STC 36/1984 192
STC 13/1985 (Última Hora) 197
STC 168/86 (Tiempo) 196
STC 165/1987 ....198, 200
STC 6/1988 (Crespo) 195
STC 107/1988 (Objetor Navazo) 195, 199–200
STC 145/1988 191
STC 51/1989 (capitán de Caballería) 193
STC 121/1989 193
STC 20/1990 (Punto y Hora) 193
STC 105/1990 198
STC 171/1990 (Patino-El País) 195
STC 20/1992 (Baleares) 200
STC 40/1992 (Televisión Española) 195
STC 65/1992 203
STC 85/1992 (concejal de Palencia) 198, 200
STC 223/1992 ....195, 199
STC 240/1992 194
STC 15/1993 (Igualada) 195, 199–200
STC 52/95 (Correos) 201
STC 60/1995 191
STC 76/1995 198–200
STC 46/1998 (El Mundo del País Vasco) 199–200
STC 136/99 (La Mesa de Herri Batasuna) 201, 205–6, 220
STC 146/1999 204

UNITED STATES

Abrams v US 250 US 616 (1919) 10, 45, 61
Aldridge v US 283 US 308 (1931) 65
Alexander v US 509 US 544 (1993) 124
American Communications Association v Douds 339 US 382 (1950) 62
Baldwin v New York 399 US 66 (1970) 79
Bates v State Bar of Arizona 433 US 350 (1977) 49
Beauharnais v Illinois 343 US 250 (1950) 45
Bigelow v Virginia 421 US 809 (1975) 49
Bolger v Youngs Drugs Products Corp 463 US 60 (1983) 49, 56
Brandenburg v Ohio 395 US 444 (1969) 61
Branzberg v Hayes 408 US 665 (1972) 46
Breed v US 421 US 519 (1975) 154
Bridges v California 314 US 252 (1941) 60–63, 161, 168–69, 173, 178
Broadrick v Oklahoma 413 US 601 (1973) 50

Cable News Network, In re 18 *Media Law Reporter* 1358 (11 Cir 10 Nov 1990) 129
Cantwell v Connecticut 310 US 296 (1940) 61
Central Hudson Gas and Electricity v Public Service Commission 447 US 557(1980) 49
Chaplinsky v New Hampshire 315 US 568 (1942) 47
Coats v City of Cincinnati 402 US 611 (1971) 51
Cohen v California 403 US 15 (1971) 47, 60
Collin v Smith 578 F 2d 1197 (1978) 45, 53
Cox v Louisiana 379 US 536 (1965) 48, 155
Cox v New Hampshire 312 US 569 (1941) 155
Cox Broadcasting Corporation v Cohn 420 US 469 (1975) 152
Craig v Harney 331 US 367 (1947) 61–63, 168–69
Curtis Publishing Co v Butts 338 US 130 (1967) 49
Debs v US 249 US 211 (1919) 10
Dennis v US 341 US 494 (1951) 62
Estes v Texas 366 US 717 (1961) 64, 98
FCC v Pacifica Foundation 438 US 726 (1978) 48, 156
Frohwerk v US 249 US 204 (1919) 10
Gannett Co v De Pasquale 443 US 368 (1979) 23
Garrison v Louisiana 379 US 64 (1964) 168
Gault, In re 387 US 1 (1967) 136, 154
Gentile v State Bar of Nevada 501 US 1030 (1991) 63, 65–66, 116
Gertz v Robert Welch Inc 418 US 323 (1974) 48
Gitlow v New York 268 US 652 (1925) 22, 61
Globe Newspapers Co v Superior Court for the County of Norfolk 457 US 596 (1982) 12, 50–51, 155, 157
Groppi v Wisconsin 400 US 505 (1971) 97
Hague v CIO 307 US 496 (1939) 48
Herald Co, Re Application of 734 F2d 93 (1984) 50
Hudgens v NRLB 424 US 507 (1976) 48
Irwin v Dowd 366 US 717 (1960) 96–97
Irwin v Dowd 381 US 532 (1965) 64
Kent v US 383 US 541 (1966) 154
Kingsley Books Inc v Brown 354 US 436 (1957) 130
Landmark Communications v Virginia 425 US 829 (1978) 57
Maryland v Baltimore Radio Show Inc 338 US 912 (1950) 63, 96
Miller v California 413 US 15 (1973) 48–49
Mu'Min v Virginia 500 US 415 (1990) 64, 96
NAACP v Alabama 357 US 449 (1964) 50, 62
Near v Minnesota 283 US 697 (1931) 49, 124, 128
Nebraska Press Association v Stuart 427 US 539 (1976) 49, 57, 97, 128, 131

New York v Ferber 458 US 747 (1982) 49, 156
New York Times v Sullivan 376 US 254 (1964) 35, 48–49, 55, 168, 180
New York Times v US (Pentagon Papers) 403 US 713 (1971) 57, 128
Nye v US 313 US 33 (1941) 60
Oklahoma Publishing Co v District Court 430 US 308 (1977) 131, 152
Osborne v Ohio 495 US 103 (1990) 156
Palko v Connecticut 302 US 319 (1937) 62
Pennekamp v Florida 328 US 331 (1946)....................61, 63, 168–69, 219
Pentagon Papers case, see *New York Times v US*
Press-Enterprise Co v Superior Court of California 464 US 501 (1984) 28, 50, 154–55
Providence Journal Company, Matter of 820 F 2d 1342 (1986) 131
RAV v City of St Paul, Minnesota 120 LEd 305 (1992) 45, 47, 53
Richmond Newspapers Inc v Virginia 448 US 555 (1980) 11, 46, 154–56
Rideau v Louisiana 373 US 723 (1962)....................98
RLK, In re 269 NW 2d 367 (1978) 153
Rosales-Lopez v US 451 US 182 (1981) 65
Rosenfeld v New Jersey 408 US 901 (1972) 47
Saia v New York 334 US 558 (1948)....................62
Schaumberg v Citizens for a Better Environment 444 US 620 (1980)..............50
Schenk v US 249 US 357 (1919) 10, 61
Sheppard v Maxwell 384 US 333 (1966) 64–65, 96, 98
Silverthorne v US 400 F2d 627 (9th Cir 1968) 96
Southeastern Promotions Ltd v US 403 US 713 (1975) 128
Street v New York 394 US 576 (1969) 54
Texas v Johnson 491 US 397 (1989) 47, 54
Thomas v Collins 323 US 516 (1945) 62
Thornhill v Alabama 310 US 88 (1940) 61
Toledo Newspaper Co v US 247 US 402 (1918) 60, 168
US v Abello-Silva (10th Cir) 96
US v AD (PG Publishing) 28 F 3d 1353 (3rd Cir 1994) 153
US v Brooklier 685 F2d 1162 (1982)....................50
US v Carolene Products Co 304 US 144 (1937)....................62
US v Dickinson 465 F 2d 496 (1972) 131
US v Eichman 496 US 310 (1990)....................54
US v The Progressive 486 F Supp 990 (1979) 57
US v Three Juveniles 61 F 3d 86 (1st Circ 1995); 862 F Supp 651 ....136, 153
US ex rel Darcy v Handy 351 US 454 (1956) 97
Valentine v Chrestensen 316 US 52 (1942) 49
Walker v City of Birmingham 388 US 307 (1967)....................131
Whitney v California 274 US 357 (1927) 17, 46–47, 61
Winship, In re 397 US 358 (1970) 154

Wood v Georgia 370 US 375 (1962)..63, 168–69
Worcester Telegram and Gazette Inc v Commonwealth 238 NE 2d 861
(1968) 63, 96
Zwickler v Koota 389 US 241 (1967) 51

Table of Legislation

EUROPEAN COMMUNITY LEGISLATION

DIRECTIVES

Dir 89/552 201
Dir 97/36/EU Television Without Frontiers Directive [1997] OJ L202/60 210

RECOMMENDATIONS

Recommendation R (87) 20 1987 143
para 5 143
para 8 143
Recommendation 98/560/EC [1998] OJ L270/48 212

NATIONAL LEGISLATION

AUSTRALIA

Australia Act 1986 31
Child Welfare Act 1960 (Tas)
s 17 146
(1) 146
s 18(1) 146
Children (Care and Protection) Act 1987 (NSW)
s 67(1) 146
s 68(1) 146
Children and Young Persons Act 1989 (Vic)
s 19(1) 146
s 26(1)(a) 147
(b) 147
Children's Court of Western Australia Act 1988
s 31(1) 146
s 35(1) 146
s 36A 147

Children's Services Act 1965
s 138(2)(a) 147
(b) 147
Children's Services Act 1986 (ACT), s 169(1)(h) 146
Constitution 1901 .... 31–32, 35–36, 79
s 7 .... 31, 34
s 24 .... 31, 34
s 51 31–32
s 71 33
s 75 33
s 80 .... 31, 79
s 92 31
s 116 31
s 128 32
Evidence Act 1929 (SA), s 69(1)(b) 148
Evidence Amendment Act 1989 (SA) 148
Family Court Act 1975 (Cth)
s 97(1) 145
(2) 145
Family Law Amendment Act 1983 (Cth), s 52 145
Federal Court of Australia Act 1976
s 17(4) 147
s 50 147–48
First Offenders (Women) Repeal Act 1976 145
Industrial Relations Act 1988 170–71
s 299(1)(d)(ii) 170
Juvenile Justice Act 1983 (NT)
s 22(1) 146
s 23(1) 133, 147
s 62 147
Magistrates' Court Act 1989 (Vic), s 126 147
New South Wales Constitution Act 1902, s 5 32
Supreme Court Act 1986 (Vic), s 19 147
Western Australia Constitution Act 1889 35
Youth Court Act 1993 (SA)
s 24(1)(f)(ii) 146
s 25(1)(b)(ii) 146–47
(2) 147

AUSTRIA

Media Act, s 23 71–73

BURMA

Constitution 1948 191

CANADA

Act to amend the Charter of the French Language SQ 1983..........................27
Alberta Press Bill 25
Bill of Rights 1960...25–27
s 1(d) 25
(f) 25
s 2...25
(f) 25
Canada Act 1982..24, 26
Sch B (Constitution Act 1982) 24
Pt 1...24
Charter of Rights and Freedoms 1982 ....2, 24, 26–30, 98–104, 132, 149, 151–52, 171–74, 217–18
s 1 ....27–28, 51, 102, 150, 171–72
s 2 ....27, 29, 51, 171
(a) 29, 171
(b)..28–30, 101, 171
(c) 29
(d) 101
s 7...27
s 8...27
s 9...27
s 10...27
s 11...27
(d)...30, 79, 101, 104
(f) 79
s 12...27
s 13...27
s 14...27
s 15...27
s 24(1) 26, 104
s 26...27
s 32...26
s 33...27
(3) 27
(4) 27
s 52(1)...26

Constitution 24–26, 30, 39, 79, 172
Criminal Code RSC 1985 C–46 ....133–34, 150–52
s 442(3) 51
s 486(1) 150
(1.1) 150
(3) 151
(4) 151
(a) 152
(4.1) 134, 152
(4.7) 152
s 542(2) 102, 104
s 599(1)(a) 104
s 638(1)(b) 104
s 648 ....102, 104
Juvenile Delinquents Act 1970, s 12(1) 149
Young Offenders Act 150
s 38(1)(a) 151
(b) 151
(1.2) 151
(1.3) 151
Youth Criminal Justice Bill, cl 110 151
Youth Offenders Act SC 1980–81–82, c 110 150
s 5(1) 150
s 16(1) 150
(1.01) 150
s 39(1)(a)(i)–(iii) 150
(b) 150

DENMARK

Constitution, Art 62 176

GREENLAND

Penal Code 176

ITALY

Constitution 1948 189

SPAIN

Código Penal (Penal Code) 194, 202, 208
Art 1 202
Art 7(7) 198
Art 161 (1983) 194
Art 174 (1973) 205–6
Art 463 204
Art 464 204
Art 571 205
Art 573 205
Constitution 1931 190
Constitution 1936, Art 18 186
Constitution 1978 (CE) 189–94, 196–99, 204, 206, 217–18
Art 1 189
(1) 189, 193
(2) 189, 196
(3) 189
Art 9 189
(1) 189
Art 10(2) 192
Art 14 190
Art 15 190
Art 16 190
(1) 193
Art 17 190
Art 18 ....190, 198
(1) 194
Art 19 190
Art 20 ....190, 193, 198
(1) 193–96, 199–200
(a) 193
(d) 193, 195, 202–3
(2) 193, 196–98
(4) 193, 195, 198
Art 21 190
Art 22 190
Art 23 ....190, 195–96
Art 24 190
(2) 190, 206–7
Art 25 190
(1) 205
Art 26 190

Art 27 190
Art 28 190
Art 29 190
Art 30 191
(2) 191
Arts 31–38 191
Art 53(2) 191
(3) 191
Art 55 193
(1) 193
Art 56(1) 189
Art 62 189
Art 81 191
Art 82 190
Art 86(1) 190
Art 93 192
Art 94(1) 192
Art 95 192
(2) 192
Art 96 192
(1) 192
Art 116(1) 193
(3) 193
(4) 193
Art 120 203
(1) 197, 203
(3) 203
Art 159 190
Art 160 190
Art 161(1)(b) 191
Title 1 ....190, 198
Ch 2 190
s 1 191
s 2 191
Ch 3 191
Constitution of Cádiz 1812 208
La Ley 4/1980 (del Estatuto de la Radio 7 Televisión), Art 4 201
Ley de Enjuiciamento Criminal (LECr - Law of Criminal Procedure) 197, 202–3
Art 301 197–8
Art 680(1) 203
(2) 203
(3) 203

Ley 14/1966 de Prensa e Imprenta (Press Law) 184, 196–97
Art 12 197
Art 64 197
Ley de 25/1994 201
LO 2/1979 Oct 12 191
LO 1/1982 198
LO 5/95 (del Tribunal del Jurado) 203, 208
Art 1 208
LO 10/1995 ....198, 202

UNITED KINGDOM

Australia Act 1986 31
British North America Act 1867 24–25
Preamble 25
s 91 25
s 92 25
Children and Young Persons Act 1933 138
s 37 138
s 39 ....127, 158
(1) 124
s 46(1) 126
s 47(2) 125
s 49 ....123, 125, 134, 139, 141–42
(1)(a) 126
(b) 126
(2) 126
(4) 126
(A) 123, 126
(B) 123
(5) 126, 138
(6) 126
(7) 126
s 53(2) 126
Children and Young Persons Act 1969
s 10(2) 125
s 15 125–26
s 16 125–26
Colonial Laws Validity Act 1865 24
Commonwealth of Australia Constitution Act 1900 31
Contempt of Court Act 1981 ....33, 80–82, 84, 88–89, 91, 213, 218
s 1 92
s 2 92

(2) 73, 88, 91, 93, 121, 133
s 3(1) 107, 213
(3) 213
s 4(2) 9, 133–34
s 5 ......88–91, 109
s 7......87
s 11......139
Sch 1......107
para 4 81
para 5 ......82, 107
para 15 107
Crime and Punishment (Scotland) Act 1997
Sch 1, para 21 85
Crime Sentences Act 1997 ......123, 125–26, 135, 137
s 45 ......123, 125
Criminal Appeals Act 1995, s 2 86
Criminal Justice Act 1988, s 32A 138
Criminal Justice and Public Order Act 1994 41
s 49......125
(5) 126
s 84(4) 211
Criminal Procedure and Investigations Act 1996, s 73 85
Criminal Procedure (Scotland) Act 1995
s 65(1)......85
(4)(b) 84
(7)......84
Crown Court Rules 1982
r 23C 138
Habeas Corpus Act......164
Human Rights Act 1998 ......2, 36–39, 41, 79, 91, 129, 218
Preamble......36
s 1......37
(1)(a)......38
s 2(1)......38, 80
(2) 81–87
s 3......38
(1)......37
s 4(5) 38
(6)......38
s 6(2) 38
s 10......38
s 12(3)......129
s 19......38

(1) 159
(b) 38
Judges Act 1540 167
Kilmuir Rules 180
Magistrates' Courts Act 1980 79
s 24(1) 126
Police Act 1997 136
Pt V 136
Protection of Children Act 1978, s 7(4) 211
Public Order Act 1986, s 19 211
Scotland Act 1998 ....91, 218
Sexual Offences (Amendment) Act 1976 141
Sexual Offences (Amendment) Act 1992, s 1 128
Statute Law (Repeals) Act 1973 167
Statute of Westminster 1931 24
Youth Justice and Criminal Evidence Act 1999 ....124–25, 127–28, 157–59
s 44 ....139–42, 159
(2) 124, 127
(3) 127
(6) 127
(7) 127, 142
(8) 127
s 45 ....124, 138, 158–59
(3) 127
(4) 127
(5) 127
(6) 127
s 49 128
(2) 128
(3) 128
(5) 128
s 50(2)(b) 128
(3) 128
(b)(ii) 128
(4)(b)(ii) 128
(5) 128
(6) 128
(8) 128
s 68(6) 128
Pt II Ch V 124
Sch 2, para 3 125

UNITED STATES

Bill of Rights 1791 ......22, 60–61
28 CFR 50.9 50
(1) 50
(2) 50
(3) 50
Constitution 10, 22–24, 45, 69, 79, 218
Art III, s 2 78
First Amendment....1, 3, 5–6, 10–11, 23, 43–51, 53–54, 56, 58–63, 65, 68, 70, 75, 93, 96–97, 115–16, 128–30, 152, 155–57, 160, 168–69, 172, 178
Second Amendment 22
Third Amendment 22, 68
Fourth Amendment 22
Fifth Amendment 22, 154
Sixth Amendment 22–23, 63–66, 78–79, 97–98, 116, 153
Seventh Amendment 22
Eighth Amendment 22
Ninth Amendment 22
Tenth Amendment 22
Fourteenth Amendment 22, 93, 98, 116, 168
Federal Rules of Criminal Procedure 64, 96–97
r 21(a) 97
Judiciary Act 1789, s 13 23–24
Juvenile Court Statute 1899 (Illinois) 154
Juvenile Delinquency Act 1988 (18 USC 5031–5042) 153
Public Nuisance Law (Minnesota) 49
Sedition Act 1798 ......46, 59
Smith Act 62
Taft-Hartley Act 129

WEST GERMANY

Constitution 1949 189

Table of Conventions and Treaties

EUROPEAN COMMUNITY

Convention on Transfrontier Television 4, 210
Art 7 210
IP Protocol 210
TCP Protocol 210
Draft Convention on Cybercrime
<http://conventions.coe.int/Treaty/EN/projets/FinalCybercrime.htm> 212
European Convention on Human Rights and Fundamental Freedoms....27, 36–39, 51–55, 57–59, 66, 69–70, 74, 80, 91, 114, 125, 129, 157, 159, 168–78, 184, 192, 217–18
Art 1 74
Art 2 37
Art 3 ....37, 144
Art 4 37
Art 5 ....37, 58
Art 6 ....37–39, 43, 66–68, 124, 144, 158
(1) 66–68, 79, 139, 144, 178, 207
(2) 67
Art 7 37
Art 8 ....36, 57–58
(2) 27
Art 9 ....37, 57–58
(2) 27
Art 10 ....3, 37–39, 43–44, 51–59, 66–75, 80, 92, 140, 157–59, 162, 174–78, 194, 218
(1) 44, 52, 66
(2) 27, 44, 52, 54, 56, 66, 70
Art 11 ....37, 57–58
(2) 27
Art 12 37
Art 14 58
First Protocol
Art 1 ....37, 54, 58
Art 2 37
Art 3 37
Sixth Protocol
Art 1 37
Art 2 37

OTHER TREATIES AND CONVENTIONS

Declaration on the Rights of the Child 1924 142
Declaration on the Rights of the Child 1959 142
International Covenant on Civil and Political Rights 1966 ....27, 142
Art 10(2)(b)....................142
Art 14(4) 142
Philadelphia Convention 1787....................22
Resolution 40/33 UN Standard Minimum Rules for the Administration of Juvenile Justice (Beijing Rules) 1985 142
r 8....................143
(1) 143
(2) 143
UN Convention on the Rights of the Child 1989 143
Art 40 143
(1) 143
(2)(b)p(vii)....................143
Universal Declaration of Human Rights 192

Introduction

The path of criticism is a public way: the wrong headed are permitted to err therein: provided that members of the public abstain from imputing improper motives to those taking part in the administration of justice, and are genuinely exercising a right of criticism, and not acting in malice or attempting to impair the administration of justice, they are immune. Justice is not a cloistered virtue: she must be allowed to suffer the scrutiny and respectful, even though outspoken, comments of ordinary men.

Ambard v Attorney-General for Trinidad and Tobago [1936] AC 322, 335 per Lord Atkin.

WHILST LIP SERVICE has often been paid by judges and politicians to the importance of public access to court proceedings and its corollary of free media reporting, a trawl through common law jurisdictions reveals in reality a heavily circumscribed notion of open justice. Outside the United States where the media enjoy a considerable degree of freedom under the First Amendment to publish material relating to legal proceedings, judges and legislators elsewhere in common law jurisdictions have long subordinated media freedom to report and comment upon matters relating to the administration of justice in order to safeguard the fairness of individual proceedings and/or the more general interest of maintaining public confidence in the administration of justice. In the context of individual criminal proceedings for example, a number of judges continue to invoke powerful rhetoric in support of the protection of fair trials, pointing to the dire consequences of 'descent into trial by media' and showing a readiness to halt criminal jury proceedings. Indeed, at times, it has seemed that the rule of law no less was under threat from the activities of journalists, editors and broadcasters. In such circumstances, it is commonly said that a choice must be made between 'a free press or fair trials.' This characterisation may be queried in two respects however. First, in so far as it neglects the important functions served by the media in *ensuring* that trials are fair and that public confidence in the courts is maintained, it constitutes a gross simplification of the issues raised by media coverage of legal proceedings. Second, the dichotomy assumes rather than establishes a causal connection between media coverage and unfair trials. It does not seem unreasonable in these circumstances to ask those who would limit speech about the working of the courts to support their claims by way of empirical evidence.

The origins of this comparative examination of speech restraints lie in a concern previously expressed by the South African lawyer Barend van Niekerk that, across a number of common law jurisdictions, judicial and legislative curtailment of media reporting and comment occurs too readily.[1] Apart from promoting fair trials and public confidence in the judiciary, other legitimate interests advanced by a system of free reporting include informed scrutiny of the exercise of state powers and the actions of public office holders as well as the education of the public in matters legal. Just as these benefits have often been overlooked or easily overridden, so conversely have dangers posed by the media to the unimpeded administration of justice been frequently exaggerated. A central theme in this book is that a more critical approach to the imposition of restraints is overdue. In adopting this position, the book is informed by and draws upon the 'constitutionalisation' of speech/expression entitlements more generally. By constitutionalisation is meant the lifting of speech/expression out from its status as a residual freedom to one given more formal recognition in a constitutional document (such as the Canadian Charter of Rights and Freedoms or the United Kingdom's Human Rights Act) or, as occurred in Australia in respect of the narrower concept of political communication, one given greater judicial protection against legislative incursion. The enhanced level of constitutional protection accorded to expression interests in these distinct processes raises the possibility that previously established boundary lines between speech and administration of justice interests which prioritised the latter may now be constitutionally dubious. That speech interests must now be given weightier consideration also hints at the prospect referred to in the title of this book, namely that the workings of the judicial system might emerge more fully from the cloisters and become more freely discussed.

At the outset, the book's first chapter looks at theories of freedom of speech and seeks to show how these might support media freedom to report and comment upon court proceedings. Instrumental accounts of free speech such as Mill's argument from truth and the argument from democracy are considered here. Later, deontological accounts such as Scanlon's notion of self-fulfilment and Dworkin's constitutive theory of speech are discussed. One way of exploring speech rationales is to consider whether the interests of speakers or listeners are stressed. Where the beneficiary of speech is the audience (as is the case for example in the argument from democracy or the argument from truth) speech claims rest upon what Dworkin has called an argument of 'policy' in which the long term interests of the community determine whether the particular exercise of speech is worth protecting. Here, opposing and weightier concerns (eg national security, public confidence in the judiciary or personal reputation) may prevail against speech. Where, by contrast, the beneficiary of the freedom is the speaker himself, the argument is said to be one of 'princi-

[1] B van Niekerk *The Cloistered Virtue* (Praeger, New York, 1987).

ple' whereby the speaker would suffer in some unacceptable way if he/she were prevented from speaking. If it is important to protect the interests of the speaker, this may mean permitting speech even where some actual harm is inflicted on community interests. The second part of the chapter outlines the respective constitutional frameworks of the United States, Canada, Australia and the United Kingdom and the status of claims to freedom of expression and fair trials. The material described here will set the legal context for the discussion of substantive laws which follows elsewhere in the book. Of course, one difference between the UK and the other national legal systems considered in this book is the absence of judicial review of primary legislation in the UK (outside of EU law). Chapter one concludes with a summary of some of the central arguments surrounding the appropriateness of judicial review of legislative action.

One consequence of the trend towards more formal constitutional protection for speech claims is enhanced levels of judicial and academic interest in other jurisdictions' attempts to resolve difficult questions about the outer limits of protected speech. The case for domestic incorporation of aspects of US First Amendment jurisprudence was considered by academics and judges in a collection of essays edited by Loveland in 1997. In contrast to the predominantly unreceptive tone of contributions in that collection, Chapters two and five of this book—whilst acknowledging obvious structural differences between the protection of speech/expression interests under the First Amendment and Article 10 of the European Convention on Human Rights—make the argument that common underlying concerns in the realm of political speech may require the Strasbourg Court to re-examine its deference to national authorities' restrictions in the field of contempt/criminal defamation.

Chapter three looks at the application of *sub judice* rules to criminal proceedings before juries in the legal systems of England and Wales, Scotland, Canada and Australia. Contrasts are drawn with the relative immunity enjoyed by the US media to report on matters pending before the courts under First Amendment standards and the emphasis there upon remedial devices to correct any resultant prejudice. The same chapter also surveys the state of empirical research into the prejudicial impact of publicity (including a recent study in New Zealand which analysed the impact of media reporting upon actual jurors) and asks whether assumptions of media influence which underpin laws of criminal contempt are, in fact, soundly based.

Aside from the limits on media reporting imposed via *sub judice* rules, sets of statutory prior restraints further curtail media freedom. These restraints may apply automatically or require a judicial order to be operative. Chapter four examines prior restraints which limit the reporting of children and young persons' involvement with the criminal courts out of a concern to protect minors' privacy interests. The chapter details privacy-based reporting restraints in a number of jurisdictions, noting the role played by international norms in their creation and considers some constitutional and empirical arguments to which they have given rise.

Civil law jurisdictions too have rules which safeguard the administration of justice from outside interference. Whilst something is known of French laws after Chesterman's work,[2] little work appears to have been published in English about Spanish materials in this area. Chapter six attempts to make good this gap. After describing Spain's emergence as a social democracy under the rule of law committed to the underlying values of political pluralism and fundamental rights (including the right to freedom of expression), the chapter explores some general themes to have emerged in freedom of expression jurisprudence before looking at specific limits placed in the context of court reporting and comment. High profile proceedings against figures in the Basque conflict and corruption scandals involving senior public officials have led the *Tribunal Constitucional* to articulate its understanding of the purposes behind the constitutional protection of speech and its outer limits. An account is also provided of the recent re-introduction of jury trials in selected criminal proceedings.

Finally, the electronic age has generated newer and less easily regulated forms of speech. Each one of us is arguably a potential broadcaster of news and opinion via the Internet, using web sites, newsgroups and e-mail. In most discussions of the dangers of virtually unregulated expression through the Internet, threats to the administration of justice have not featured prominently. Instead, the literature has focused on issues such as digital pornography, privacy and libel. Chapter seven addresses this lacuna by detailing specific examples of problematic electronic expression and official responses to it. I argue that, in the absence of internationally enforceable rules, the practical difficulties which ensue at the domestic level from seeking to control the content of expression on the Internet may force a re-evaluation of the basis of some current restrictions. For all the attention the Internet has generated, it remains true that transborder flows of broadcast material existed and were regulated well before the era of Internet-based communications. In Europe for example, the Convention on Transfrontier Television may be seen as an early attempt to limit the cross-border broadcast of certain material deemed harmful. In this final section of materials, internet expression forms causing prejudice to trials, undermining confidence injunctions or disparaging judges are all considered.

[2] 'Contempt: In the Common Law, but not the Civil Law' (1997) 46 *International and Comparative Law Quarterly* 521.

1

Free Speech Rationales and Constitutional Landscapes

I INTRODUCTION

DEBATES OVER THE extent of media freedom in modern liberal democracies have a tendency to fall back on cliches about the importance of a free press/media in a democracy. In the United States for example, there are some fine examples of First Amendment scholarship which chronicle the rise and fall of freedom of speech and the press which nonetheless manage to avoid addressing the philosophical bases upon which these freedoms are predicated.[1] In his important comparative analysis of speech restraints prompted by administration of justice concerns, Barend van Niekerk criticised accounts of UK contempt law because of the paucity of engagement with these deeper level issues.[2]

Taking as its starting point liberal arguments for free speech, the first part of this chapter concerns itself with the application of those arguments to media freedom to report and comment upon court proceedings. Drawing upon materials from a variety of jurisdictions, it will show that, whilst arguments for unfettered reporting are multi-stranded, instrumental rationales have been to the fore in judicial reasoning. Some of the free speech theories considered in this section have as their objective the protection of the rights of the speaker whilst others prioritise those of the audience. If, as has been suggested, the right of the media to report court proceedings is inextricably linked to the interests of the audience, the implications of this finding need to be explored. Of particular concern here is the susceptibility of an audience-interest-based account of media freedom to weightier societal interests which argue for restrictions on speech.

After sketching out some of the more philosophical aspects of media freedom debates, the second part of the chapter sets down the varying constitutional landscapes in which potentially conflicting interests in free speech and the unimpeded administration of justice are played out. In addition to setting the context

[1] See A Lewis, *Make No Law: The Sullivan Case and the First Amendment* (Random House, New York NY, 1991) and N Hentoff, *The First Freedom:The Tumultous History of Free Speech in America* (Delacourt, New York NY, 1979)

[2] B van Niekerk, *The Cloistered Virtue* (Praeger, New York NY, 1987).

for the discussion of substantive law which follows in the rest of the book, the discussion here focuses upon the constitutionalisation of speech claims. By constitutionalisation is meant the formal recognition of speech/expression as a fundamental principle of democratic society. The mechanisms by which this constitutionalisation has occurred across a number of jurisdictions and the implications for court-related speech will be outlined before consideration is given to some objections to the judicial role it usually implies.

II RATIONALES FOR SPEECH AND THEIR RELATION TO COURT REPORTING/COMMENT

Intuitively, freedom of speech/expression is thought by many to have a special status among the cherished liberties of individuals. This belief may be related to the fact that a number of constitutions single out speech/expression (accompanied in some cases by specific reference to the press/media) as worthy of protection from governmental interference in its own right, prompting in turn the suggestion that there is a self-standing or independent principle of free speech which is distinct from claims for a more general liberty. According to Schauer, if the case for an independent free speech principle can be successfully asserted, it follows that where speech is restricted, the reasons for restriction must be more compelling than those we ordinarily accept as a basis for government restraint of conduct generally.[3] Thus, if a restraint on other conduct is deemed legitimate where, on balance, it yields a slight gain in total welfare, the regulation of speech would have to be premissed on an overall welfare gain which was more than slight to support the existence of an independent free speech principle. If, by contrast, the State needs no stronger a justification for regulating speech than is needed for regulating other forms of conduct, the notion of an independent principle is an illusion.

The major theories which have been advanced in support of an independent free speech principle may be seen as either consequentialist or deontological in character. Consequentialist arguments for speech treat speech as valuable because it serves another value or interest such as the pursuit of truth or democratic self-governance. Deontological arguments by contrast disregard the consequences of the exercise of free speech, stressing instead the intrinsic importance of speech to each individual. One of the first great scholars of the First Amendment, Zechariah Chafee identified strands of both consequentialist and deontological arguments in his survey of the sorts of interest protected under the First Amendment. There was, he claimed, first a social interest in the attainment of truth so that the nation could choose the wisest course of action and implement the same wisely. A second argument for free speech comprised

[3] F Schauer, *Free Speech: A Philosophical Enquiry* (Cambridge University Press, Cambridge, 1982).

the individual interest of men and women to express their opinions on matters which mattered to them.[4] Bollinger has since observed that the individual interest in speech has figured less prominently than the social interest and that the latter has come to comprise a political interest related more to the specific aim of enhancing democratic self-government than the more general pursuit of truth.[5] Following Barendt's typology of free speech rationales,[6] the two sections which follow outline some salient features of the major consequentialist and deontological theories of speech and consider some implications for court-related speech.

Some Instrumentalist Arguments for Freedom and Their Relation to Court Reporting and Comment

(i) Argument fromTruth

The Millian argument from truth can be broken down into two connected arguments both of which proceed from the assumption that human judgement is fallible. On the first argument, which Ten has labelled the avoidance of mistake argument,[7] we should be slow to suppress what is purportedly a false opinion in case it turns out to be true. After all the decision to suppress may be based on inaccurate information, display unsound reasoning or be informed by prejudice. If truth about the world is to be attained, all individuals must have unrestricted access to the views and opinions of others and enjoy freedom of self-expression so that established opinion may be tested. In turn, newly accepted opinion must be subject to the possibility of displacement/refinement by other views. In the long run, the argument from truth holds out the prospect that false knowledge claims will be exposed for what they are in unfettered public discussion and that society will be the beneficiary of that exposure as truthful claims emerge freshly vindicated. An objection to the avoidance of mistake argument asserts however that it may be right to suppress an opinion which turns out to be true if there is a genuine mistaken belief that it is false and that its publication will have harmful consequences. Mill's response is to advance his second argument—the assumption of infallibility argument—which states that we can have no rational assurance that the opinion which is sought to be censored is false unless there is freedom to discuss it. The 'silencing of discussion' entailed in the objection thus constitutes an unwarranted assumption of infallibility on the part of the censor. Even if we could be certain that an opinion is false, it would still be wrong to

4 Z Chafee, *Free Speech in the United States* (Harvard University Press, Cambridge Mass, 1941).

5 L Bollinger, *The Tolerant Society* (Clarendon Press, Oxford, 1986) ch 2. Bollinger himself offers a further justification for free speech namely in helping to control the impulse towards intolerance.

6 E Barendt, *Freedom of Speech* (Clarendon Press, Oxford, 1985).

7 CL Ten, *Mill on Liberty* (Clarendon Press Oxford, 1980) ch 8.

suppress that viewpoint since, by being forced to defend the true belief, the latter's supporters are challenged to examine the grounds for holding the true belief and if need be adapt it to changing circumstances. The benefits of rigorous thinking which follow from having to defend the true belief disappear if the false opinion is suppressed and the belief is held instead as a 'dead dogma.' In this way, Mill's theory is audience-led although it is worth noting that the argument has the interests of future speakers in mind too. Members of the recipient audience are after all rational and thinking individuals who can be expected to express their own beliefs in due course.

Applying the foregoing to court-related speech we can see that Mill's account confers a very wide degree of immunity upon speakers in general and the media in particular. We cannot interfere with speech which is possibly true but highly prejudicial ('the defendant is a racist') nor with the plainly ill-informed and intemperate ('all judges are fascist bastards'). Statements such as these which would be subject to criminal penalty under the contempt laws of a number of common law jurisdictions considered in this book would have to remain protected speech in the Millian account.[8] Although the emphasis in Mill is the theoretical ground for freedom of expression, he does acknowledge *en passant* circumstances in which speech might properly be limited. This occurs when an opinion amounts to a positive instigation to do a 'mischievious act.' The examples he gives are the statements that corn dealers are starvers of the poor and that private property is theft. Where these are delivered orally to an impassioned crowd gathered close to a corn-dealer's house or handed around the crowd in leaflet form, they may justly incur punishment. On the other hand, where the same opinions are expressed in a newspaper article, they should go uncensored and unpunished. Ten explains the distinction on the following basis. In the case of the orally delivered remarks, there is an immediately inflicted harm which is causally related to the words whereas the quality of immediacy is absent in the case of publication in a newspaper.

Criticisms of the argument from truth are well known[9] and it is proposed here to deal only with those points that have some bearing on the issue of court-related speech. One general criticism of Mill's position centres upon the objectivist assumptions behind the search for 'truth' which is placed beyond personal opinion or community standards. Even assuming that freedom of speech might be utilised by many persons eager to engage in rational discourse (and capable of the same), the view that there is an objective truth to be discovered (even if it can be shown to be shared by many) on issues relating to morality, politics and the organisation of society (including its legal institutions) is highly contestable.

[8] As Ten has pointed out, Mill's theory would also reject the suppression of views regarded as blasphemous or obscene: *ibid*.

[9] Among the vast literature see Barendt, *Freedom of Speech*, n 6 above, ch 2 and T Campbell, 'Rationales for Freedom of Communication' in T Campbell and W Sadurski (eds) *Freedom of Communication* (Dartmouth, Aldershot, 1994).

Even if the validity of an objectivist account of truth is conceded, it does not follow (and remains empirically undemonstrated) that truth will result from unregulated expression since whether an idea becomes accepted depends upon factors other than its rational force. This is not to say however that rational discourse is not possible. Free speech does have a role in fostering enlightened debate about the merits and defects of competing beliefs.[10]

Mill's primary focus is to offer a justification for freedom of expression in matters of morals, religion, politics, social relations and something which Mill called 'the business of life' in respect of possibly true and almost certainly false claims. A major question which arises in the context of court reporting centres upon the application of Mill's theory to factual disclosures. Can it be that Mill intended the dissemination of most factual information to be outside the scope of his free speech principle as Barendt has suggested?[11] Clearly there will be factual information which is deployed as a basis upon which moral, religious and political beliefs are advanced and, believing as he did in the rational thinking capacities of persons, it would be odd indeed if Mill intended that the expression of this sort of information to be outside the scope of protection. For example, in order to convince an audience of the correctness of a claim that the judicial system is corrupt, a speaker might cite evidence which purports to show individual instances of bias on the part of judges. In different circumstances however, it may be imagined that the speaker (such as a court reporter) has no particular opinion to advance but merely wishes to convey some factual information to the audience. Under other free speech arguments considered later in this chapter such expression may be protected, but what is the position under Mill's account? As Barendt has remarked,[12] restrictions placed on the dissemination of true information cannot by definition offend the assumption of infallibility argument which only prevents governmental restrictions on speech believed to be false. Rather, it is precisely because the information is true and that disclosure is harmful to another purportedly more valuable societal/individual interest that publication is in fact prohibited. For example, an order under section 4(2) of the Contempt of Court Act 1981 postponing the publication of certain evidence in criminal proceedings might be justified by reference to the societal and individual interests in the fairness of any subsequent proceedings. The lack of protection for accurate communications reveals Mill's account to be ill-suited to the task of defending the freedom to report court proceedings.

As advanced by Mill, the courts have infrequently relied upon the argument from truth to ground claims to free speech in case law. More commonly invoked

[10] See T Campbell, *ibid.*

[11] Barendt, *Freedom of Speech,* n 6 above, at 12. Although a clear division between statements of opinion and fact may not always exist. Greenawalt has disputed the claim that Mill did not intend his argument to cover the expression of factual information. See RK Greenawalt, *Speech, Crime and the Uses of Language* (Oxford University Press, New York NY, 1989) at 17.

[12] *Ibid.*

is the related 'marketplace of ideas' argument associated with Justice Holmes dissent in *Abrams v US*.

> [W]hen men have realised that time has upset many fighting faiths, they may come to believe even more than they believe the very foundations of their own conduct that the ultimate good desired is better reached by free trade in ideas—that the best test of truth is the power of the thought to get itself accepted in the competition of the market, and that truth is the only ground upon which their wishes safely can be carried out. That at any rate is the theory of our Constitution.[13]

This shares with Mill the view that the censorship of opinions by government is wrong since, until it has been examined by others, the truthfulness of an opinion may not be known. Like Mill, it is primarily concerned with ideas and beliefs rather than the freedom to impart factual information and like Mill it looks to the interests of both speakers and audience. It departs from the Millian account thereafter however with its rejection of an objectivist version of truth, resting instead upon moral scepticism and a faith in unregulated markets and customer choice to be the ultimate determinant between rival versions of the truth (including the acceptability of political and moral arguments). It is not clear however that the market success of an idea can be compelling evidence either of its truth or the rationality of its 'purchasers'.[14] What is clear nevertheless is the grip of Holmes' argument on First Amendment jurisprudence as reflected in the hostility to contents-based speech restrictions.[15] Holmes formulated his views during the 'subversive advocacy' cases which came before the Supreme Court in the early part of the twentieth century[16] and his marketplace defence of speech recognised that the state might nonetheless lawfully restrict speech where it posed a 'clear and present danger of substantive evil' such as encouraging military desertion during wartime. Significantly, the test of 'clear and present danger' remains the standard by which the constitutionality of restrictions on media speech about court proceedings is judged in the US today. The process by which it was grafted onto contempt law is described in chapter two. For the time being, we can note that the strictness of the standard means that, in practice, the US media may publish highly prejudicial material without facing a threat of contempt proceedings.

(ii) Argument from Democracy

Of all the arguments for free speech surveyed in this chapter, it is the argument from democracy that seems to speak most directly to the matter of court-related

[13] (1919) 250 US 616, 630.

[14] See E Barendt 'The First Amendment and the Media', in I Loveland (ed), *Importing the First Amendment: Freedom of Speech and Expression in Britain, Europe and the USA* (Hart Publishing, Oxford, 1998) at 43.

[15] European jurisprudence, by contrast, has tended to stress other rationales for protecting expression interests. See ch 2 below.

[16] *Schenk v US* (1919) 249 US 357; *Frohwerk v US* (1919) 249 US 204; *Debs v US* (1919) 249 US 211.

speech in liberal democracies and is either implicit or explicit in judicial defences of media reporting across a variety of jurisidictions. The argument is associated with the First Amendment scholarship of Alexander Mieklejohn although it may be traced back further to James Madison, the author of the First Amendment. Like Mill's account, it is a consequentialist theory of the importance of speech in which the benefits to the audience (electors) are stressed, this time in terms of democratic self-governance. Indeed, as Schauer has pointed out, the argument from democracy may be seen as a sub set of the argument from truth in which the pursuit of *political* truth provides the rationale for free speech.

The link between governmental design and free speech is made clear in the writings of James Madison. The deliberate vesting of sovereignty in the people placed a high value on a deliberative democracy and unencumbered political discussion among equals. Free speech is thus valued as a means by which the citizens of a democratic state can acquire information about the functioning of government and through which different points of view can be expressed. Mieklejohn's easily imagined notion of a town hall meeting of rational New England people listening to and participating in debates about how best to govern their affairs has a resonance which is attractive to many and may explain its continuing appeal. In addition, informed town hall discussion renders government accountable and responsive to the electorate who thereby retain their sovereignty over government.

In the judicial sphere, Justice Brennan has been a prominent defender of the structural role played by freedom of speech in securing a republican system of self-government.[17] Free speech on this account is needed for meaningful communication and well informed debate which in turn is a pre-condition of effective participation by citizens in governmental affairs. The argument accords prime importance to political speech defined by Barendt as including speech which is:

> relevant to the development of public opinion on the whole range of public issues which an intelligent citizen should think about.[18]

Whilst this definition excludes certain speech/expression types from protection (such as art, pornography or commercial speech), these need not therefore detain us here.[19] In supporting, as a matter of principle, media freedom to

[17] See his opinion in *Richmond Newspapers Inc v Virginia* (1980) 448 US 555, 587 and further (1979) 32 *Rutgers Law Review* 173. For Canadian Supreme Court authority stressing the fundamental role played by freedom expression in democratic society, see *Dagenais v Canadian Broadcasting Corp* (1995) 120 DLR 12, 36–37; and *Edmonton Journal v Alberta* (1989) 64 DLR (4th) 577, 607–08.

[18] E Barendt, *Freedom of Speech*, n 6 above, at 152.

[19] Mieklejohn denied that artistic expression was precluded from protection for 'political speech' arguing that knowledge of Shakespeare was essential for wisdom in political matters. See his article 'The First Amendment is an Absolute' [1961] *Supreme Court Review* 245. For a view that the First

report and temperate comment upon judicial proceedings, judges across a variety of common law jurisdictions have implicitly or explicitly drawn from the argument from democracy. In particular, the scrutinising and disciplining tendencies of media reporting have been stressed. Lord Atkin's remarks which were cited in the preface to this book point up the legitimate scrutinising function of speech concerning the legal process:

> Justice is not a cloistered virtue: she must be allowed to suffer the scrutiny and respectful, even though outspoken, comments of ordinary man.[20]

For Justice Brennan in *Globe Newspapers v Superior Court for the County of Norfolk*, the link between public access on the one hand and informed scrutiny of governmental institutions and the maintenance of public confidence in the administration of justice on the other were quite obvious:

> Public scrutiny of a criminal trial enhances the quality and safeguards the integrity of the factfinding process, with benefits to both the defendant and to society as a whole. Moreover public access to the criminal trial fosters an appearance of fairness, thereby heightening public respect for the judicial system. And in the broadest terms, public access to criminal trials permits the public to participate in and serve as a check upon the judicial process—an essential component in our structure of self-government.[21]

The particular role of the media in keeping justice out of the cloisters has received attention on occasions. In *R v Felixstow JJ ex parte Leigh* Lord Justice Watkins described the court-reporter as the 'watchdog of justice, a person of vital significance' in opening up the administration of justice to public scrutiny and comment.[22] The European Court of Human Rights has likewise defended media reporting and comment within certain limits on matters before the courts in the following terms:

> whilst the mass media must not overstep the bounds imposed in the interests of the proper administration of justice, it is incumbent upon them to impart information and ideas concerning matters that come before the courts just as in other areas of public interest.[23]

In passing however, it is important to remember the social and commercial realities behind media reporting of court cases. Typically, media reports concentrate on those proceedings involving extreme violence, such as murder or sexual offences, or those concerning well-known persons or those with bizarre facts.

Amendment applies in relation to political speech only, see R Bork 'Neutral Principles and the Some First Amendment Problems' (1971) 47 *Indiana Law Journal* 1. For a contemporary academic defence of a Madisonian free speech principle, see CR Sunstein, *Democracy and the Problem of Free Speech* (Macmillan, New York NY, 1993).

[20] *Ambard v Attorney-General for Trinidad and Tobago* [1936] AC 322, 335.

[21] (1982) 457 US 596, 606.

[22] [1987] 1 All ER 551,

[23] *Sunday Times v UK* (1979–80) 2 EHRR 245, 280.

Those cases which attract media attention may in the event be covered selectively because of the perceived news value of the proceedings, pressure from competing stories and the broader commercial interests of the proprietor. Notwithstanding these imperfections, the physical constraints of courtrooms mean that for the overwhelming majority of persons the media remain their principal source of information about the functioning of the courts.

Grounded as it is in an appeal to the sovereign powers of the people, the argument from democracy is however made vulnerable to decisions of the majority to restrict speech. Schauer has put this point in the following way:

> If the people collectively are in fact sovereign, and if that sovereign has unlimited powers normally associated with sovereignty, then acceptance of this view of democracy compels acceptance of the power of the sovereign to restrict the liberty of speech just as that sovereign may restrict any other liberty.[24]

Thus a decision by the majority (or their elected representatives) to close all criminal courts to the media and members of the public alike could not be resisted by appeal to the argument from democracy. In Britain for example, democratically elected legislatures have sanctioned closure or partial closure in order to safeguard a variety of interests including the fair trial rights of defendants, the privacy interests of certain crime victims (alleged and actual), particular classes of witnesses, cases involving national security issues.[25] In response, it may be claimed that, if it is to mean anything, democratic self government has to recognise certain limits beyond which the majority may not tread. Thus it may be asserted that the legitimacy of majoritarian political processes depend upon electors having unimpeded access to political information and opinion and that without such free access, the very legitimacy of majoritarian processes is called into question.[26]

One way around the difficulty of majoritarian-backed speech restrictions in practice is to entrench freedom of speech alongside other core values in a constitutional settlement so as to be beyond the reach of temporary majorities. Of course, in so doing, the argument from democracy justification for free speech ceases to be relevant and another rationale for speech protection must be articulated. Some issues which arise from counter-majoritarian strategies of entrenchment are considered in the second part of this chapter.

A separate difficulty which is thrown up by the argument from democracy is apparent on closer inspection of the specific claim of journalists to be able to attend and report court proceedings. It is frequently argued that the presence of journalists advances the public interest in subjecting court processes and officials

[24] Schauer, *Free Speech,* n 3 above, 41.

[25] See I Cram, 'Automatic Reporting Restrictions in Criminal Proceedings and Article 10 of the ECHR' [1998] *European Human Rights Law Review* 742.

[26] See further TM Scanlon, 'Freedom of Expression and Categories of Expression' (1979) 40 *University of Pittsburgh Law Review* 519, 544–45.

to a degree of scrutiny and furthers the cause of informed public debate. Using the distinction made by Dworkin between free speech claims based on an argument of principle on the one hand and arguments of policy on the other, the scrutiny argument is revealed as an audience or policy-based rationale for journalist access which renders it prone to weightier, competing societal interests.[27]

Dworkin's argument of principle maintains that free speech is needed to protect the rights of speakers who would suffer some unacceptable injury if prevented from speaking. Considerations about the community's welfare are largely irrelevant to the exercise of the speaker's rights under this argument. Where a clash exists between the rights of a speaker and community welfare, then, in the absence of an especially compelling community interest, the speaker's rights should prevail. This, for Dworkin, is what it means to claim that the speaker has the right to free speech. Arguments of policy by contrast stress the benefits to the audience and society in general of free speech. These benefits must however be weighed against other competing social interests and a balance arrived at. Where it can be shown that a community will be worse off as a result of the exercise of free speech because it is believed to undermine a weightier, competing policy consideration such as perhaps national security or public order, then the claim to free speech is lost. The claim by journalists to act, in Lord Justice Watkin's words, as the public's watchdog plainly makes a policy type argument for free speech. The claim does not rest upon the interests of journalist *qua* speakers wishing to express a particular viewpoint on a matter of political importance.[28] Rather, it is being said that the ability of the community to exercise effective self-governance is strengthened by virtue of the audience being given access to court proceedings via media reports.[29] The weakness inherent in an audience-based rationale is that the appeal to the public interest or welfare in receiving information *invites* the discovery of a weightier public interest such as the interests of justice or the privacy interests of participants which would point in favour of closure in an individual trial. Proponents of closure could then argue that the damage caused to democratic self-governance which may result from the public in not learning about the details of any particular trial would be relatively slight in comparison to the threatened damage to the administration of justice/individual privacy interests were a trial to proceed in public.

Dworkin's analysis also helps to make sense of oft-invoked claims made by media representatives (echoed by some judges) that their news gathering activities are undertaken on behalf of the public's *right to know*. This is, on reflection, a curious claim with its suggestion of a correlative duty on the part of

[27] RM Dworkin, *Taking Rights Seriously* (Duckworth, London, 1977) ch 4.

[28] Although where a journalist voices an opinion about the functioning of the courts, it would be important on the argument from democracy to protect the journalist's freedom to do so.

[29] Where, by contrast, a journalist wishes to pass comment on legal matters, this looks more like a speaker-based claim for free speech even though the audience share an interest in receiving that opinion.

news agencies to investigate and report, or in the event of deriliction of this duty, an action for compensation for non-investigation/reporting. In fact, the 'right to know' claim is more plausibly framed as a public interest in having more, not less information about government and public affairs. It is thus derived from an argument of policy and, as such, vulnerable to other, public welfare-based claims.

Deontological Arguments for Media Freedom to Report Court Proceedings

Non-instrumentalist arguments for free speech share at their core the contention that free speech is valuable/good for each individual in an intrinsic sense, irrespective of the gains/losses such freedom brings to wider society such as the generation of truthful knowledge claims and progress or ensuring proper democratic structures of governance. Speech on these accounts has a special place in the intellectual development of the individual tending as it does to promote the autonomy and/or dignity of each person both in his/her capacity as a listener to receive information as well in the more active sense of speaking. In the following section, the arguments of Thomas Scanlon and Ronald Dworkin are considered.

(i) Argument from Self-determination or Fulfilment

Most closely associated with Thomas Scanlon,[30] the argument from self-determination or fulfilment holds that free speech is valuable because it is needed if individuals are to develop their capacities and realise their potential. Expression is stated to be an integral part of the self. Without the freedom to express beliefs and opinions and to have access to the beliefs and opinions of others in order to shape his/her own views, the individual is unable to develop fully and, instead, intellectual growth becomes stunted.[31] Scanlon's account serves to protect both the interests of speakers and of the audience.[32] The speaker's interest in expression is in being able to call something to the attention of a wide audience. This might include speech aimed at increasing the speaker's reputation, sales of his product, urging a change in government or in simply amusing or shocking people. The audience interest in freedom of expression is in having a good environment for the

[30] Scanlon, 'Freedom of Expression and Categories of Expression' n 26 above and 'A Theory of Freedom of Expression' in RM Dworkin (ed), *The Philosophy of Law* (Oxford University Press, Oxford, 1977).

[31] See T Emerson, 'Towards a General Theory of the First Amendment' (1963) 72 *Yale Law Journal* 877, 879. As Lichtenberg puts it, 'A person cannot think freely if he cannot speak; and he cannot think freely if others cannot speak, for it is in hearing the thoughts of others and being able to communicate that we develop our thoughts.' J Lichtenberg (ed), *Democracy and Mass Media* (Cambridge University Press, Cambridge, 1990) 108.

[32] Scanlon, 'Freedom of Expression and Categories of Expression', n 26 above, 520–28.

formation of beliefs, although, as Scanlon recognised, other factors (such as access to education) will also be relevant here. Under his notion of 'justified paternalism', speech might only be curtailed after taking into account:

> such factors as the value attached to being able to make one's decisions, as well as the costs of so doing and the risks of empowering government to make them on one's behalf.[33]

This cost/benefit analysis will reveal whether additional information is worth the costs entailed in acquiring it. Thus Scanlon can support a restriction on information concerning the making of nerve gas but not one relating to political agitation which could lead to social unrest. In the case of the former, the serious public safety considerations raised by such information outweigh the insignificant losses endured by speakers and audience if a restriction is imposed. Deceptive advertising might also be curtailed since it hinders the audience's decision-making abilities which require truthful information to be able to evaluate the worth of products. By contrast, the regulation of socially inflammatory speech is not legitimate not just because of the difficulty of predicting the likelihood of social unrest but more importantly because of the 'notoriously partisan and unreliable' nature of government responses to political speech.

What implications does Scanlon's argument have for court-related expression? At the outset, expression about the courts, their functioning and personnel clearly relates to a form of governmental activity understood broadly. It follows that state restraints upon court-related speech (whether by judicial order or legislative enactment) may be viewed as 'partisan and unreliable' and, although this is not conclusive, it is sufficient for restraints on court-related speech to be treated with suspicion. Beyond this point however, it is difficult to predict how Scanlon's formula plays out in specific settings. Thus, despite its obvious interest in suppression, the State may nevertheless have good grounds for restricting speech. But how are these situations distinguished from others where restrictions are less justified? It is not clear for example whether the prejudgment of criminal cases in the popular press with any resultant loss of confidence in the judicial system would be deemed a sufficiently high cost to overcome initial suspicions of state regulation. Would the difficulty of predicting the likely adverse impact on trial fairness put *sub judice* rules on a par with socially inflammatory speech as an unjustified restraint on expression? What if *actual* harm to a defendant's interest in a fair trial could be demonstrated, would this afford a legitimate ground for restricting or penalising expression?

Another way of examining Scanlon's argument is from the perspective of audience interests. If audience interests in learning about factual matters concerning court proceedings are considered first, it may be claimed that this information is useful to individuals in developing their ideas about the legal system

[33] Scanlon, 'Freedom of Expression and Categories of Expression', n 26 above, 532.

and whether to act on those beliefs (for example the decision to join a group seeking better treatment for crime victims and witnesses). It is interesting to note in this regard that one of the arguments made by supporters of recent legislation which allows for the naming of young persistent offenders has been that their public identification allows other community members to make a more informed decision about the threat posed by the offenders. The costs of discovering certain factual matters however may prove in the long run to work against audience interests. An example concerns the disclosure of the identities of complainants in rape, other serious sexual assault cases and blackmail cases. Any (presumably very marginal) gains in terms of producing a better environment for taking decisions which might result from learning the identity of the rape/assault/blackmail victim might be thought outweighed by the future disinclination of victims to inform the police with the result that more perpetrators would remain at large. Elsewhere, the disclosure of certain types of information in proceedings involving issues of national security may be damaging to the effective operation of state security and thereby also to public safety.

Aside from difficulties inherent in allocating weight to factors in Scanlon's cost/benefit analysis, the central weakness in the claim for speech as essential for individual self-development is that the latter notion is apt to include making the most out of oneself or making oneself as wise as possible and therefore becomes so open-ended as to fail to mark out speech in particular and confer on it the status of an independent principle.[34] Thus, in terms of self-fulfilment, other interests apart from speech are important too. It might be conceded that individual privacy, religious freedom and freedom of association are all relevant to individual development. On what basis, if any, might speech be regulated when its exercise infringes these other freedoms?

Whatever the strength of these various observations and criticisms, it remains the case that the argument from self-fulfilment has secured a level of judicial recognition in free speech/expression disputes. Thus, Justice Brandeis in *Whitney v California* famously remarked:

> Those who won our independence believed that the final end of the state was to make men free to develop their faculties.[35]

The European Court of Human Rights in one of the earliest landmark rulings on freedom of expression *Handyside v UK*, noted that freedom of expression was 'one of the basic conditions for the progress of democratic societies and *for the development of each individual*.[36] [Emphasis added].

[34] J Lichtenberg, 'Foundations and limits of freedom of the press' in J Lichtenberg (ed), *Democracy and Mass Media* (Cambridge University Press, Cambridge, 1990) at 109. Other constitutional writers in the US have expressed much the same point: see G Gunther, *Constitutional Law* (Foundation Press, Westbury NY, 1985) ch 11.

[35] *Whitney v California* (1927) 274 US 357, 374.

[36] (1979–80) 1 EHRR 737.

(ii) Dworkin's Constitutive Basis of Speech

Dworkin has advanced a similar non-consequentialist justification for free speech for both listeners and speakers alike which proceeds from the demand that government treat all its adult members as responsible moral agents. Government, he asserts,

> insults its citizens and denies their moral responsibility, when it decrees that they cannot be trusted to hear opinions that might persuade them to dangerous or offensive opinions. We retain our dignity, as individuals, only by insisting that no-one—no official and no majority has the right to withold an opinion from us on the ground that we are not fit to hear and consider it.'[37]

In addition to the right of listeners to hear all opinions, the constitutive theory of speech asserts that the right of speakers to express their convictions must not be frustrated by government no matter how hateful the opinion in question. To suppress is to assert the unworthiness of the idea and its speaker. By discriminating between permitted speech and suppressed speech the Government treats its members unequally.

Dworkin has two motivations in advancing his rationale. The first is to protect speech from the fragility inherent in instrumental accounts when faced by a majoritarian preference for speech restriction. The second is to expand the narrow kinds of speech afforded protection under instrumental rationales to other kinds of speech including pornography and speech that is generally loathed such as race-hate speech. On this account restrictions on comment or opinion about administration of justice issues would plainly amount to an insult to the dignity of both media-based speakers and their audience. Although phrased in terms of opinionated speech, it is clear from elsewhere in Dworkin's account that it extends to speech with an informational content. It follows that the factual reporting of court proceedings and other administration of justice issues would also be protected.

Earlier, it was noted that a major problem with Scanlon's argument was its inability to mark out speech as specially valuable in protecting individuals from the paternalistic and censorial activities of government. It is not clear that Dworkin's account is free of this difficulty either. If the reason for not suppressing speech is that it infringes an equality of respect for the dignity of each citizen, does this not draw on a broader, more inclusive liberty-based argument against state interference? Moreover, if, as most would agree, this more inclusive general liberty justification extends to the protection of privacy type interests, talk of a speaker's (or listener's) dignity being offended by a speech restriction imposed to protect another from harm appears most odd. Consider for example the limitations placed on newspapers and broadcasters preventing the iden-

[37] RM Dworkin, *Freedom's Law: The Moral Reading of the American Constitution* (Oxford University Press, Oxford, 1996) 200.

tification say of rape complainants. It is difficult to see how these limitations might be construed as an insult to the dignity of a newspaper or its readers. Paradoxically, it is more obviously the dignity of the rape complainant which stands to suffer injury if the speech in question is not restricted.

III CONCLUSION: AN ARGUMENT FROM GOVERNMENT INCOMPETENCE

The summary of free speech theories considered above has shown that free speech is desired for a number of reasons in which the interests of society, the individual, speakers and audience are variously engaged.[38] Each theory attempts in its own way to suggest some individual or collective good that is uniquely promoted by speech or identify some individual harm which suppression of that speech uniquely causes. Each account however seems prone to objections.[39] Initially, the argument from democracy looks the most promising. It is directly relevant to the reporting of factual matters (such as legal proceedings) and opinion and is concerned to protect the audience interest in receiving that information and comment. Nonetheless, in common with other consequentialist arguments for speech, it is vulnerable to being traded off against competing values. Crucially, speech on this account is unable to resist the demands of a censorious majority. Deontological arguments seem more promising because, outside of wholly exceptional circumstances, they are not susceptible to these shortcomings. Significantly however, it has proved difficult to disentangle speech claims from more general liberty claims and establish that speech by itself is an activity which is worthy of a special degree of protection.

Before leaving the discussion of free speech rationales, it is important to consider a further attempt to establish speech as an independent principle deserving of special protection in its own right from state regulation. The arguments for free speech which have been canvasssed thus far have made positive claims about the benefits of conferring special protection on speech. Schauer has sought to establish an independent free speech principle by means of a negative justification, that is by pointing to the special dangers which exist in allowing the state to regulate speech.[40] On this account, the fact that there may be nothing especially or distinctly valuable about speech as compared to other conduct does not matter. Instead, what is emphasised is the state's lesser

[38] See further Lichtenberg (ed) *Democracy and Mass Media* n 31 above, who has argued on this basis that the search for a 'monistic' theory of speech is misguided as it fails to do justice to the variety and richness of our interests in speech.
[39] L Alexander and P Horton, 'The Impossibility of a Free Speech Principle' (1984) 78 *Northwestern University Law Review* 1319, 1328.
[40] See Schauer, *Free Speech*, n 3 above, 86.

ability to regulate speech (when compared to other forms of conduct) or the special dangers in speech regulation not present in the regulation of other forms of conduct. If it can be shown either that the state is an especially inefficient regulator of speech or that state regulation of speech causes greater damage than its regulation of other conduct, then Schauer asserts, a free speech principle will have emerged by negative implication under which speech may rightly be made the beneficiary of special protection to counteract inefficient/especially harmful regulation. Citing variously the condemnation of Galileo, religious persecution in the Counter-Reformation and prosecutions for sedition and obscenity, he argues that, historically speaking, states have made some fairly plain errors in speech regulation and that this unhappy record persists to the present day. The explanation which is offered for this poor performance is the regulators' self-interest which has produced overly aggressive regulation.[41] Those who have most to lose from the exercise of political forms of speech such as sedition are those entrusted with its regulation. The emphasis upon biased regulation has obvious similarities with the work of Scanlon and his observation that where political issues are involved, governments are notoriously partisan and unreliable.[42] Moreover, the account has a clear application to *sub judice* contempt laws developed by the courts themselves and statutory restrictions on media reporting. It is certainly plausible to claim that the undoubted interest in maintaining public confidence in the courts and the desire not to give convicted criminals an additional ground of appeal on account of a prejudiced trial has led, at times, to an overly restrictive stance on the part of the judges about what may or may not be published about pending criminal trials.

Leaving aside the empirical issue about whether speech *uniquely* constitutes an area of conduct where the state has shown itself to be an inefficient regulator, Schauer's argument leaves unclear other questions about the circumstances in which speech may legitimately be restrained.[43] Suppose it is conceded that the state's censorious inclinations should be viewed with suspicion, by what values can it be decided whether certain forms of speech may nonetheless be regulated. Schauer proposes the construction of a balance on which to weigh speech interests against state interests in prohibiting expressive conduct. The distrust of governmental regulation requires that, for the balance to come down in favour of suppression, a convincing and substantial benefit must result from the imposition of any restraint. Consider the case of speech

[41] Although Schauer is careful to qualify his claim by observing that no empirical data exists to support this point.
[42] Scanlon, 'Freedom of Expression and Catgories of Expression', n 26 above, 534—a point which Scanlon himself acknowledged marked out political speech as a distinctively important category of speech.
[43] This point is made forcefully by Alexander and Horton, 'The Impossibility of a Free Speech Principle', n 39 above.

which is critical of the performance of a judge. It would be important to establish at the outset the value to be attached to protecting judicial reputations and the harm which results from critical speech. Then, the probability that the critical speech in question would cause the harm previously identified would have to be factored in. On the other side of the balance, we might legitimately enquire into how much value or weight should be attached to speech which criticises judicial figures. We would need to know whether the value varied depending upon the tone of criticism, the place of publication, the prominence of the individuals attacked. As Alexander and Horton have argued, to answer all such questions we need a positive theory of speech in which values are assigned to a range of communicative activities such as political and commercial expression. Unfortunately, Schauer's argument stops short of equipping us to do the necessary balancing.

In the final analysis, it may be that no one theory can offer a wholly convincing basis for the widely held belief that free speech is especially worth having. From a legal perspective, a major difficulty arises from the fact that the accounts outlined above are primarily treatises in political philosophy rather than attempts at constitution building. They do not as a consequence offer much insight into complex practical issues raised in the legal regulation of speech. Nothwithstanding this difficulty, it is important to acknowledge two common themes which are yielded up by these philosophical accounts, namely that speech about the way society is organised is valuable and that the institutional bias which government (understood broadly) brings to its regulation of political speech ought to make us distrustful of such regulation. Both themes will recur throughout this book.

IV CONSTITUTIONAL LANDSCAPES

Whatever difficulties lie in the way of constructing an independent speech principle, liberal democracies continue to profess their commitment to free speech/expression as a core human right. The second part of this chapter considers the status of protection for claims to freedom of speech and expression in the constitutions of the United States, Canada, Australia and the United Kingdom, as well as the framework in which conflicts between claims to freedom of expression and the entitlement to fair trials are managed. Three of the legal systems looked at in this section provide for judicial review of primary legislation restricting core freedoms. Standing somewhat isolated in this regard, the UK Constitution confers (outside of challenges involving European Union law) upon the legislature ultimate authority to decide the proper bounds of state power and individual liberty. Towards the end of the chapter, some arguments concerning the appropriateness of judicial review in liberal democracies are addressed.

United States

Unlike other nations' more evolutionary transitions from colonial territory to sovereign state, the sudden overthrow of their British oppressors offered the drafters of the US Constitution an opportunity to design political and judicial institutions anew. The initial concerns of those attending the Philadelphia Convention of 1787 did not however lie primarily in the area protecting individual liberties against federal or state interference. Delegates were faced by more urgent economic problems posed by the chaotic nature of inter-state relations in which the 13 independent states imposed trade tariffs on each other and possessed their own coinage. No single national currency existed because no central government existed to issue one. It was thus for largely economic reasons that the argument for an effective central authority prevailed in Philadelphia. At the same time, delegates were wary of creating a new concentrated central power after the experience of British rule. The Convention therefore conferred on the federal authorities certain specified powers only (such as those relating to inter-state commerce), leaving much power at state level. In addition, the division of federal government into three branches; legislative, executive and judiciary was intended to create a natural competition for power and prevent one branch becoming all powerful.

The Bill of Rights was added to the original constitution in 1791 as a means of placating those who believed the safeguards built in to the new federal powers might not be enough to prevent a return of tyranny, albeit in a new guise. Specific sets of limitations on central authority were agreed to by Conventions in Massachusetts, New York and Virginia. The first Congress then met and approved the first ten amendments (including speech and fair trials) which became part of the Constitution.[44] The First Amendment states:

> Congress shall make no law respecting an establishment of religion, or prohibiting the free exercise thereof; abridging the freedom of speech or of the press; or the right of the people peaceably to assemble and to petition the government for a redress of grievances.

an apparently absolutist command to Congress and, as subsequently interpreted by the Supreme Court, applied to the states via the due process clause of the Fourteenth Amendment.[45]

The Sixth Amendment requires that:

> In all criminal prosecutions, the accused shall enjoy the right to a speedy and public trial, by an impartial jury of the State.

To the extent that the Sixth Amendment protects an accused's right to a *public* trial, this guarantee would seem to be entirely consistent with (or perhaps more

[44] The states had given their approval separately.
[45] *Gitlow v New York* (1925) 268 US 652, *per* Stanford J at 666.

accurately assume) press freedom under the First Amendment. There is an issue however about whether the right to a public trial belongs exclusively to the parties before the court so that where they wish to exclude the public and media representatives a court should accede to this request automatically.[46]

The major themes which inform First Amendment jurisprudence and the ordering of the potentially conflicting constitutional values represented in the First and Sixth Amendments are considered in more detail in chapters two and three. For the time being, three features of US speech regulation may be noted. First, whilst free speech has been valued for a variety of reasons which reflect the influence of rationales associated with Mill, Madison/Mieklejohn and Scanlon, it is also correct to say that, in relation to court reporting and comment, the argument from democracy has figured most prominently. Second, the primacy of First Amendment interests over those encompassed by the Sixth Amendment distinguishes the US system from other jurisdictions examined in this book, requiring that the constitutional guarantee of fair trials be safeguarded by measures other than those which impinge upon media freedom. These remedial measures range from the *voir dire* and warnings from the bench through to jury sequestration and re-trials. Finally, there is the more general issue of judicial supremacy over legislative and executive action. The absence of express authorisation in the Constitution for judicial review of the Acts of Congress, state legislatures and executive agencies has long raised nagging questions about the legitimacy of review.[47] Indeed, one of the founding fathers—James Madison—rejected the idea of a judicial veto over Acts of Congress as something which could never be proper.[48] In the landmark ruling of the Supreme Court in *Marbury v Madison* however, the improper happened.[49] In an application brought by Marbury for formal delivery of his commission as a justice of the peace against Secretary of State Madison, Marshall CJ held that section 13 of the Judiciary Act 1789 which purportedly authorised the Court to issue a writ of mandamus against persons holding public office was itself unconstitutional since the Court's jurisdiction was fixed exclusively by the Constitution and

[46] See the distinct opinions in *Gannett Co v De Pasquale* (1979) 443 US 368 of Justice Stewart (for the majority) who held that the public interest in a public trial under the Sixth Amendment was fully encompassed by participants to the litigation who had all agreed to a closure order and Justice Blackmun (partially dissenting and joined Brennan, White and Marshall JJ) who declared that the societal interest in public trials existed independently of, and sometimes in opposition to the interests of the accused.

[47] L Fisher, *Constitutional Rights: Civil Rights and Civil Liberties (American Constitutional Law vol 2)*, 2nd edn (McGraw-Hill, New York NY, 1995) at xxv. See the debate between Judge Learned Hand, *The Bill of Rights* (Harvard University Press, Cambridge Mass, 1958) and Professor H Wechsler, *Principles, Politics and Fundamental Law* (Harvard University Press, Cambridge Mass, 1961).

[48] G Hunt (ed), *The Writings of James Madison* (Putnam's, New York NY, 1904) Vol 5, 294 although it should be remembered that Madison did support judicial review of state legislation. For a statement of support of judicial review of acts of Congress, see A Hamilton, 'The Judiciary Department', *The Federalist No.78*, 14 June 1788.

[49] (1803) 1 Cranch 137.

could not later be enlarged by ordinary statute. The Court accordingly lacked authority to order delivery of the commission.[50] The ruling may be broken into two key stages. First, the Constitution which lays down limits on the powers of the departments of government provides the paramount source of rules. Ordinary acts of the legislature must therefore conform to the Constitution. Second, any legislative act which is contrary to the Constitution is void and need not be given effect in a court. Marshall's assertion of judicial supremacy in matters of constitutional interpretation was condemned by the Jefferson administration. The President himself was quoted as saying that the Chief Justice 'would make the judiciary a despotic branch.'[51] The doctrine remains to this day highly controversial, especially as the repugnancy of an Act to the Constitution is seldom self-evident, a fact which may draw the Court into evaluation of legislative policy and a task to which some believe it is ill-suited.

Canada

The framework within which rights to freedom of expression and fair trial are currently given constitutional status is provided by the Charter of Rights and Freedoms in Part 1 of Schedule B of the Canada Act 1982.[52] The 1982 Act marked diminished British influence over Canadian constitutional development and may be seen as an attempt to unite a nation hitherto characterised by the forces of provincialism.[53] Key features of the 1982 Charter and judicial interpretation of its provisions are considered shortly. To begin with however, it is necessary to say something about the protection of speech claims before 1982.

(i) Pre-Charter Constitutional Setting

Prior to 1982, the Canadian Constitution had in the main been a product of three statutes enacted by the UK Parliament namely; the Colonial Laws Validity Act 1865, the British North America Act 1867 and the Statute of Westminster 1931. Of these, the British North America Act was the most important component of

[50] It seems clear however that had Marshall upheld the constitutionality of s 13 of the 1789 Act, any resulting order would have been ignored by Jefferson's Cabinet, L Fisher, *Constitutional Rights*, n 47 above, xxvi.

[51] Quote taken from A Lewis, *Make No Law*, n 1 above, at 48. Jefferson remained of this opinion saying in 1819 that Marshall's ruling had made the Constitution a 'mere thing of wax in the hands of the judiciary, which they may twist and shape into any form they please.' *The Writings of Thomas Jefferson* (Ford, New York NY, 1899) Vol 10.

[52] Schedule B of that Act is the Constitution Act 1982.

[53] For the background to the Charter and the key role played by Pierre Trudeau see I Greene, *The Charter of Rights* (James Lorimer & Co, Toronto, 1989) 37–44 and more generally see E McWhinney, *Canada and the Constitution 1979–1982: Patriation and the Charter of Rights* (University of Toronto Press, Toronto, 1982). For general discussion of the Canadian Constitution see P Hogg, *Constitutional Law of Canada*, 4th edn (Carswell, Toronto, 1996).

the written part of the Constitution and provided that any statute passed by the Canadian Parliament[54] or provincial legislatures[55] must be within the respective jurisdictions conferred by that Act. The preamble to the 1867 Act stated that Canada would have a constitution 'similar in principle to that of the United Kingdom' a phrase understood to mean that Canada had adopted the principle of legislative sovereignty, albeit qualified by the fact that a federal structure of government was established in which no single legislature in Canada was supreme over all matters and further that the UK Parliament retained legal authority to amend the Canadian Constitution. [56] The words of the preamble were also taken by some to mean that civil liberties principles developed in the United Kingdom by 1867 such as freedom of speech and the press were also to be part of the new Canadian Constitution. A pressing issue here was how far these principles might stand up to apparently conflicting legislative provisions. An indication of judicial willingness to review provincial legislation emerged in *Reference re Alberta Statutes*[57] when the Supreme Court unanimously found that the Alberta Press Bill—a measure which conferred on an administrative agency in Alberta wide powers of press censorship—was beyond the powers of provincial legislatures under the 1867 Act. In a judgment which anticipated the Australian doctrine of implied freedom of political communication by over half a century, Duff CJ declared that the Bill was unconstitutional because it infringed freedom of the press and with it free discussion of public affairs which were essential for the proper working of representative legislatures envisaged by the Constitution. The 'Duff Doctrine' as it came to be known was never however endorsed by a majority of the Supreme Court and was effectively laid to rest in 1978.[58]

A further attempt to limit incursions by the Canadian Parliament and federal administrative authorities into individual freedoms including freedom of speech and the press[59] was enacted in 1960 as the Canadian Bill of Rights and, although this measure did not achieve superior status via incorporation into the British North America Act, it did attempt to protect certain enumerated rights against implied repeal with its declaration in section 2 that:

> Every law of Canada shall, unless it is expressly declared by an Act of Parliament of Canada that it shall operate notwithstanding the Canadian Bill of Rights, be so construed and applied as not to abrogate, abridge or infringe . . . any of the rights or freedoms herein recognized . . .

One of the rights expressly recognised in section 2(f) was the right of a person charged with a criminal offence:

[54] British North America Act 1867, s 91.
[55] BNA 1867, s 92.
[56] This formula is also taken to have incorporated the doctrines of the rule of law and responsible government into Canadian law.
[57] [1938] SCR 100.
[58] *AG Canada and Dupond v Montreal* [1978] 2 SCR 770.
[59] S 1(d), (f).

to be presumed innocent until proved guilty according to the law in a fair and public hearing by an independent and impartial tribunal.

The major constitutional issue to arise from this Bill was whether the 'notwithstanding' clause would successfully protect the enumerated rights against implied repeal by later inconsistent legislation in a legal system purportedly based upon the idea of legislative supremacy. With some exceptions,[60] the Supreme Court refused to strike down later inconsistent legislation referring to what Le Dain J stated was the absence of:

a clear constitutional mandate to make judicial decisions having the effect of limiting or qualifying the traditional sovereignty of Parliament.[61]

Despite this cautious approach, parliamentary support for human rights legislation grew. The provincial legislatures in Alberta, Quebec and Saskatchewan pressed ahead with their own statutory bills of rights. Discrimination and other human rights violations in the private sphere by employers, landlords etc. were also addressed in Human Rights Codes at provincial and federal level.

(ii) *The Canadian Charter of Rights and Freedoms*[62]

By virtue of its incorporation in the Canada Act 1982, the Charter of Rights and Freedoms is part of the Canadian Constitution. Under section 52(1), any law which is inconsistent with the provisions of the Constitution is, 'to the extent of the inconsistency of no force or effect.' Responsibility for determining whether a breach of Charter rights and freedoms has occurred rests with a court of 'competent jurisdiction' under section 24(1) of the Charter.[63]

The Charter applies to the federal Parliament and Government as well as provincial legislatures and governments.[64]A power of express override in respect

[60] The most notable being *R v Drybones* [1970] SCR 282.

[61] *R v Therens et al* [1985] 1 SCR 613, 639.

[62] There is needless to say a vast amount of literature on the Charter including, in addition to works already cited in this section, CP Manfredi, *Judicial Poer and the Charter*, 2nd edn (Oxford University Press, Canada, 2001); DC McDonald, *Legal Rights in the Canadian Charter of Rights and Freedoms: A Manual of Issues and Sources* (The Carswell Company, Toronto, 1982); J Black-Branch, 'Entrenching Human Rights Legislation under Constitutional Law' [1998] *European Human Rights Law Review* 312. For a useful discussion of the protection of freedom of expression under the Charter, see R Burns, *An Overview of the Protection of Freedom of Expression under Canadian Constitutional Law and Section 2(b) of the Canadian Charter of Rights and Freedoms* (Research Paper No 3, Centre for Media, Communications and Information Technology Law, Melbourne University, 1996). See also chapter by D Beatty 'The Canadian Charter of Rights: Lessons and Laments' in GW Anderson (ed), *Rights and Democracy: Essays in UK–Canada Constitutionalism* (Blackstone Press, London, 1999) for a critical review of the Supreme Court record in human rights cases.

[63] On the meaning of a 'court of competent jurisdiction' see *R v Mills* [1986] 1 SCR 863.

[64] S 32 of the Charter. There must be some form of 'governmental action' for the Charter provisions to apply, *RWDSU v Dolphin Delivery* [1986] 2 SCR 573, 602. The adoption of a 'control' test to determine whether there is 'governmental action' has meant that public agencies answerable to min-

of the rights and freedoms referred to in section 2 and sections 7 to 15 of the Charter is given to the federal and provincial Parliaments in section 33 of the Charter although any such override ceases to have effect five years from the date it comes into force.[65] In as far as its provisions do not conflict with those in the Charter, the provisions of the Canadian Bill of Rights continue to apply to the federal Parliament and governmental bodies.[66] Importantly, the rights and freedoms enumerated in the Charter are made subject in section 1 to 'such reasonable limits prescribed by law as can be demonstrably justified in a free and democratic society',[67] reflecting the fundamental tension in liberal society between individual rights and wider societal goals.

The leading interpretation of section 1 remains that advanced by Dickson CJ in *R v Oakes*[68]where it was stated that for a limit on a Charter right to be valid, a two part test must be satisified.[69] Under the first part, the objective behind a restriction must be considered of 'sufficient importance.' Trivial or discordant objectives are thus excluded from the category of lawful restraints on Charter rights. Instead, only those limitations based upon pressing and substantial concerns in a democratic society are legitimate. Sometimes however, the identification of the objective behind a restriction of a Charter freedom has not proved straightforward, particularly as regards the level of generality at which it is to be stated.[70] Moreover, the failure of the Charter to spell out permissible purposes of derogation under section 1 (as occurs for example in Articles 8(2), 9(2),10(2) and 11(2) of the European Convention on Human Rights) has required the Court to articulate these purposes on a case by case basis, although it is rare for a limitation to be challenged successfully at this stage.[71] Examples of objectives deemed sufficiently important to limit

isters are subject to the Charter, whereas public service providers with a degree of autonomy from governmental control such as universities and hospitals (*McKinney v University of Guelph* [1990] 3 SCR 229; *Stoffman v Vancouver General Hospital* [1990] 3 SCR 483) are not.

[65] S 33(3). The override may be expressed to endure for a shorter period. Under s 33(4) an override may be renewed. For an example of a valid override, see, An Act to amend the Charter of the French Language SQ 1983 in *Ford v Quebec* [1988] 2 SCR 712 and for a defence of the override clause, see PH Russell, 'Standing Up for Notwithstanding' (1991) 29 *Alberta Law Review* 293.

[66] S 26 of the Charter.

[67] See further S Woolman, 'Riding the Push-Me Pull-You; Constructing a Test that Reconciles the Conflicting Interests which Animate the Limitation Clause' (1994) 10 *South African Journal of Human Rights* 60. Burns has noted the debt owed by the framers of s 1 to international human rights instruments such as the International Convention on Civil and Political Rights and the European Convention on Human Rights, see Burns, *An Overview of the Protection of Freedom*, n 62 above, 26.

[68] [1986] 1 SCR 103.

[69] Once an infringement of a Charter right has been established, the burden of proof lies on the government or other party to establish on a balance of probabilities the constitutional validity of the restriction.

[70] Consider for example the different judicial interpretations of statutory objective in *RJR MacDonald v AG (Canada)* (1995) 127 DLR (4th) 1 between La Forest and McLachlin JJ.

[71] For such a rare example see *R v Big M Drug Mart* [1985] 1 SCR 295 concerning compulsory religious observance.

freedom of expression include preventing hate speech directed at an identifiable group,[72] ensuring unimpeded access to the courts,[73] preventing the distortion of votes resulting from inaccurate opinion surveys in the period immediately before an election,[74] and the promotion of the French language in Quebec.[75] In respect of restrictions on media reports of court proceedings, sufficiently important objectives have included safeguarding fair trials and the administration of justice,[76] the protection and rehabilitation of young persons caught up in the criminal justice system,[77] and the privacy interests of sexual offence complainants.[78]

The second part of the *Oakes* test relates to the requirement in section 1 that a limit is reasonably and demonstrably justified. This is usually referred to as the proportionality test and is sub-divided into three parts. In the first place a limitation must be rationally connected to its objective. In *R v Kopyto* the federal offence of scandalising the court was held by the Ontario Court of Appeal to lack a rational connection with the lawful objective of protecting the administration of justice because the federal law did not require the offending remarks to constitute a serious threat to the administration of justice.[79] Secondly, the limitation should impair the right as little as is necessary to meet the objective. As Burns notes, this would appear to offer the courts a wide power to strike down legislative enactments wherever a less intrusive means of achieving the same end was available, even where this less intrusive alternative was more costly in financial or other terms to implement.[80] In *Irwin Toy v Quebec* however the Supreme Court indicated that it would not follow US jurisprudence with its strict requirement of narrowly tailored infringements of constitutional rights,[81] preferring instead to allow legislatures a 'margin of appreciation' in devising solutions to particular problems.[82] The precise extent of the margin of appreciation varies from context to context reflecting greater or lesser judicial deference to the judgment of legislatures. On occa-

[72] *R v Keegstra* [1990] 3 SCR 697.

[73] *BCGEU v AG (British Columbia)*[1988] 2 SCR 214 where picketing at the entrance to a courthouse was held to be a form of expression under s 2(b).

[74] *Thomson Newspapers Co v Canada (AG)* [1998] 1 SCR 887.

[75] *Ford v AG (Quebec)* [1988] 2 SCR 712 where a law prohibiting the use of English for commercial signs was nonetheless held to be a disproportionate means of securing this objective.

[76] *Edmonton Journal v Alberta* (1990) 64 DLR (4th) 577; *Canadian Broadcasting Corp v AG (New Brunswick)* [1996] 3 SCR 480.

[77] *Re Southam Inc and The Queen* (1984) 48 OR (2d) 678.

[78] *R v O'Connor* [1995] 4 SCR 411; *Canadian Broadcasting Corp v AG (New Brunswick)* [1996] 3 SCR 480.

[79] [1987] OR (2d) 449. Issues concerning the constitutionality of the offence of scandalising will be explored more fully in chapter five.

[80] Burns, *An Overview of the Protection of Freedom*, n 62 above.

[81] [1989] 1 SCR 927. For US approach see for example *Press-Enterprise Co v Superior Court of California* (1984) 464 US 501.

[82] See also the remarks of McLachlin J in *Committee for the Commonwealth of Canada v Canada* [1991] 1 SCR 139.

sion, this issue has thrown up sharp differences of opinion among the Supreme Court Justices.[83]

The final part of the *Oakes* test requires that the effect of the measures must not be out of all proportion to that which is gained by securing the government objective. Whether this limb imposes a further obstacle to the constitutional validity of a law already deemed to serve an objective of sufficient importance, rationally connected to that objective and infringing a Charter right as little as possible, is open to doubt. The view that the third limb requires merely a proportionate relationship between the objective and its deleterious effects was rejected by Lamer CJ in *Dagenais v Canadian Broadcasting Company*. He recast the third limb more widely to permit in addition judicial assessment of the proportionality *between the deleterious and salutory effects of the limiting measures*.[84] It was possible after all for a measure's deleterious effects to be proportionate to its objectives (especially where those objectives were of the most pressing and substantial nature) whilst these same deleterious effects were out of all proportion to the few salutary or beneficial effects of the measure.

(iii) Free Expression

Section 2 of the Charter states that:

> Everyone has the following fundamental freedoms:
> (a) . . .
> (b) freedom of thought, belief, opinion and expression, including freedom of the press and other media of communication;
> (c) . . .

In section 2(b) freedom of expression cases to come before it, the Supreme Court has consistently stressed the multi-stranded nature of underlying values served by freedom of expression, embracing both individual and collective interests, deontological and consequentialist arguments. Thus, the Millian argument from truth and the arguments from individual autonomy and democracy have all been invoked (sometimes simultaneously) in judicial analyses. Typical is the remark of McLachlin J in *R v Zundel* that section 2(b) served the interests of 'truth, political or social participation, and self-fulfilment.'[85]

In relation to the dissemination of court proceedings, the principle of open justice enunciated in *Scott v Scott* has been described as 'one of the hallmarks of a democratic society'.[86] The linkage between freely reportable proceedings

[83] Note the contrasting rulings in *RJR MacDonald Inc v Canada* (1995) 127 DLR (4th) 1 of La Forest J favouring a relatively wide margin of appreciation and that McLachlin J cautioning against the same.
[84] [1994] 3 SCR 835.
[85] (1992) 95 DLR (4th) 202, 206.
[86] *Re Southam Inc and The Queen (No.1)* (1983) 41 OR (2d) 113, 119

and democratic self-governance through informed public comment is a central feature of section 2(b) jurisprudence. The courts, as Cory J remarked in *Edmonton Journal v Alberta*,

> are the forum not only for the resolution of disputes between citizens, but for the resolution of disputes between the citizens and the state in all its manifestations. The more complex society becomes, the more important the function of the courts. As a result of their significance, the courts must be open to public scrutiny and to public criticism of their operation by the public.[87]

(iv) Fair Trial and Free Expression Interests Under the Charter

The respective entitlements to a fair trial and freedom of expression enjoy paramount constitutional status under the 1982 consitutional settlement. According to Lamer CJ in *Dagenais v Canadian Broadcasting Company*:

> Like the right of an accused to a fair trial, a fundamental principle of our justice which is now protected by s.11(d) of the Charter, freedom of expression, including freedom of the press is now recognised as a paramount value in Canadian society by its enshrinement as a constitutionally protected right in s.2(b) of the Charter.[88]

It is beyond dispute that the Charter has produced a sea-change in judicial attitudes towards the constitutionality of laws restricting media freedom. Previously, the pre-Charter common law of discretionary publication bans designed to safeguard particular legal proceedings from interference had prioritised fair trial interests over those of free expression. In order to reflect the enhanced status of expression interests under the Charter, the majority in *Dagenais* used its power to reformulate the common law rule in a manner consistent with the fundamental values of the Constitution.[89] Consequently, before issuing a publication ban at common law, a judge must respect the equal status of the free expression interests at issue—an obligation which would entail *inter alia* consideration of alternative means by which the fairness of any proceedings might be assured. Finally, it is worth noting that, far from being considered a threat to the fairness of proceedings, openness in criminal trials is perceived in the 1982 Charter to be a core element of the fair trial guarantee in section 11(d). Anyone charged with an offence has the right:

> to be presumed innocent until proven guilty according to law in a fair and *public* hearing by an independent and impartial tribunal. (emphasis added)

A more detailed assessment of the impact of the Charter upon specific sets of restraints on court-related speech will be offered in later chapters of this book.

[87] (1990) 64 DLR (4th) 577, 610.
[88] (1994) 120 DLR (4th) 12, 36.
[89] For recognition of this power, see *RWDSU v Dolphin Delivery* [1986] 2 SCR 573.

Australia

The 1901 Australian Constitution was the product of gradual evolution in relations with the United Kingdom.[90] The values of representative and responsible parliamentary government which had been brought by the British into colonial governance during the nineteenth century were carried forward into the new constitutional settlement.[91] No place was found in the new Constitution for a comprehensive statement of individual human rights guarantees,[92] a fact usually attributed to the absence of a violent struggle against the colonial power (which had characterised American experience),[93] although a Diceyean preference for common law regulation of individual liberty (and an accompanying hostility towards broad declarations of rights) may also have been significant. The Constitution contains a few, eclectic rights including the right to a jury trial for indictable offences against the Commonwealth,[94] the right to enjoy private property secure from compulsory acquisition by the Commonwealth,[95] the freedom to cross state borders,[96] freedom of religion[97] and the prevention of discrimination against any subject of the Queen on the basis of residence.[98] In addition, the right to vote in elections for the Senate and House of Representatives is provided for in sections 7 and 24 of the Constitution respectively. In contrast however, freedom of speech/expression is not expressly protected. It has been suggested that the real safeguard for individual rights derives from the share in the government granted to each Australian under these rights to

[90] The 1901 Constitution was created by an Act of the Westminster Parliament. The process was completed in 1986 when the Australia Act passed by both the United Kingdom and Commonwealth Parliaments removed the last vestiges of colonial rule. The Act prevented the UK Parliament from legislating for the Commonwealth, abolished the legislative override of State laws by UK laws and removed the system of appeals from State courts to the Privy Council. It remains the case however that the Queen is still the Head of State.

[91] See PH Bailey, *Human Rights: Australia in an International Context* (Butterworths, Sydney, 1990); PD Finn, *Law and government in colonial Australia* (Oxford University Press, Melbourne, 1987). The Constitution was given formal legal status by an Act of the UK Parliament—the Commonwealth of Australia Constitution Act 1900.

[92] This has been described as a 'stark omission' by Hanks in *Constitutional Law in Australia* (1996, 2nd edn Butterworths, Sydney). See further his chapter 'Constitutional Guarantees' in HP Lee and G Winterton (eds), *Australian Constitutional Perspectives* (The Law Book Company, Sydney, 1992). It is argued by some that the framers deliberately chose not to enshrine individual rights fearing the likely outlawing of certain discriminatory practices. See JA La Nauze, *The Making of the Australian Constitution* (Melbourne University Press, Melbourne, 1972). For analysis of the Conventions' treatment of rights see the discussion by H Patapan.,'The Dead Hand of the Founders: Original Intent and the Constitutional Protection of Rights and Freedoms in Australia' [1997] 25 *Federal Law Review* 211.

[93] See RCL Moffatt, 'Philosophical Foundations of the Australian Constitutional Tradition' (1965) 5 *Sydney Law Review* 59.

[94] S 80.

[95] S 51.

[96] S 92.

[97] S 116.

[98] S 117.

exercise the franchise.[99] Amendments to the Constitution must take the form of a Bill passed by one House of the Parliament and approved by a majority of electors nationally and majorities in at least four out of the six states in a referendum. The effect of such a hurdle has been to make constitutional change infrequent.[100] Consequently, the task of modernising the Constitution has fallen to the High Court with its power of judicial review over federal and state legislation. For much of its history however, the Court has shown limited enthusiasm for this task. Nowhere is this more clearly demonstrated than in respect of its record in cases involving individual civil rights claims. Under the literalist approach adopted by the judiciary to the interpretation of formal protections for individual freedom under the Constitution, individual rights were narrowly construed and in some cases actually diminished as a consequence of High Court rulings.[101] Thus Hanks points to the example of the right to jury trial which was reduced to a formality and evaded by resort to a device other than an indictment for commencing a prosecution.[102] In *Adelaide Company of Jehovah's Witnesses v Commonwealth*, the provision guaranteeing freedom of religion did not prevent the proscription of a religious organisation in wartime.[103] As will shortly be seen, a more activist approach to policing constitutional freedoms has lately come to replace literalism with the result that freedom of political expression at least has been strengthened.

Although it may not have featured in the guarantees of individual rights, the influence of US constitutional design is apparent in the division of powers between the federal or Commonwealth power and state powers. Onto this otherwise essentially British model, a federal division of powers was grafted under which the federal or Commonwealth government was granted certain enumerated powers[104] while the States retained general law-making powers in other areas.[105] The Constitution Act of each State defines the competences of the institutions of state government—the parliaments, executive bodies and the State supreme courts. These Acts, however, do not contain a statement of individual rights or fundamental values.

[99] WH Moore, *The Constitution of the Commonwealth of Australia*, 2nd edn (1910) cited by T Jones, 'Legal Protection for Fundamental Rights and Freedoms: European Lessons for Australia?' (1994) 22 *Federal Law Review* 57.

[100] S 128. See further G Sawer, *Australian Federalism in the Courts* (Melbourne University Press, Melbourne, 1967) and HP Lee, 'Reforming the Australian Constitution: The Frozen Continent Refuses to Thaw' [1988] *Public Law* 535.

[101] The classic literalist interpretation which reflects adherence to a model of judicial self-restraint is the High Court ruling in *Amalgamated Society of Engineers v Adelaide Steamship Co Ltd* (1920) 28 CLR 129.

[102] *R v Archdall* (1928) 41 CLR 128.

[103] (1943) 67 CLR 116.

[104] Commonwealth Constitution s 51.

[105] For example, the New South Wales Parliament was empowered under s 5 of its Constitution Act 1902 to 'make laws for the peace, welfare and good government of new South Wales in all cases whatsoever.'

The judicial power vested by section 71 of the Constitution in the High Court of Australia grants original jurisdiction in matters arising under treaties, disputes between States, residents of different States or between a State and a resident of another State.[106]Appellate jurisdiction exists in relation to decisions of State Supreme Courts and lower federal courts. Although no express power of review of the validity of Commonwealth and State legislation was conferred upon it, the High Court has assumed this function in line with views expressed at constitutional conventions in the 1890s where adherents of the US model of judicial review played an influential role.[107]

(i) A Residual Liberty No Longer: The Emergence of the Implied Freedom of Political Communication

Outside those few constitutional guarantees detailed earlier, the content of individual liberty in Australia reflected standards at English common law, derived as in England from the absence of a prohibition. Freedom of expression was what remained after laws relating to defamation, contempt, public order etc, had been taken into account.[108] Moreover, as in other federal jurisdictions, the laws of each State with their variations on the laws of defamation, contempt and so on merely complicated the matter further. Writing in 1983 Michael Kirby described the permutations arising from the interplay between federal and state laws as being 'as depressing as they are dazzling.'[109] In relation to contempt law, he noted that the pre-eminent position of fair trial interests under English *sub judice* rules given effect in cases such as *Ex parte Bread Manufacturers Ltd*[110] and *John Fairfax & Sons v McRae*[111] had placed the media under a 'much more restrictive' legal regime than that found in most parts of Europe, including the United Kingdom where defeat in the European Court of Human Rights in the *Sunday Times*[112] case had prompted the Westminster Government to push reforming legislation through Parliament in the shape of the Contempt of Court Act 1981.[113]

106 S 75.

107 *Convention Debates* (Sydney, 1898) and see D Galligan, 'Judicial Review in the Australian Federal System: Its Origin and Function' (1979) 10 *Federal Law Review* 367.

108 M Kirby, *Reform the Law* (Oxford University Press, Melbourne, 1983) 171. For analysis of the case for and against the constitutionalisation of individual rights in Australia, see MR Wilcox, *An Australian Charter of Rights?* (The Law Book Company, Sydney, 1993).

109 *Ibid.*

110 (1937) 37 SR (NSW) 242. See further S Walker, 'Freedom of Speech and Contempt of Court: The English and Australian Approaches Compared' (1991) 40 *International and Comparative Law Quarterly* 583.

111 (1955) 93 CLR 351. Interestingly, the right to a fair trial is not expressly protected in either the Commonwealth or any State Constitutions. Instead, an argument for a constitutional right to a fair trial has had to made by implication. See further J Hope 'A Constitutional Right to a Fair Trial?' (1996) 24 *Federal Law Review* 173.

112 (1979) 2 EHRR 245.

113 See also Australian Law Reform Commission, *Contempt*, Report No 35 (Government Publishing Service, Canberra, 1987) which recommended the abolition of common law contempt rules and

Subsequently however, the High Court ruling in *Hinch v Attorney General (Vic)*[114] appeared to relax aspects of the earlier test laid down in *Ex parte Bread Manufacturers Ltd*.[115] A detailed consideration of this common law-led regulation of court-related speech is to be found in chapter three of this book.[116]

Since *Hinch* however, a fundamental shift away from dependence upon common law notions of residual freedom in the area of political expression occurred in a series of High Court rulings in the 1990s presaging an era of greater judicial activism in the protection of a core aspect of freedom of expression, namely political communication. Although an in-depth treatment of the background to these decisions is beyond the scope of this book, it is important to set out the reasoning upon which the Court has conferred enhanced protection for political speech against curtailment by statute and the common law.

The first unequivocal signs of a more activist Court emerged in *Nationwide News Pty Ltd v Wills*[117] and *Australian Capital Television Pty Ltd v Commonwealth (ACTV)*.[118] *Nationwide* concerned the validity of a Commonwealth statute which made it an offence to use words calculated to bring the Industrial Relations Commission or its members into disrepute. *ACTV* raised questions about the legality of statutory restrictions on political advertising. The Court commenced its analysis by declaring that sections 7 and 24 of the 1901 Constitution not only establish but, crucially, entrench Australia as a representative democracy.[119] Where a representative democracy is constitutionally entrenched, it is an 'essential'[120] element of such a society that there be freedom of political communication of an on-going nature rather than periodically at election time. Mason CJ noted that freedom to criticise governmental action in modern representative democracies had been recognised in England, the United States and Canada as well as the European Court of Human Rights. He drew particularly on Canadian jurisprudence which had declared freedom of expression to be 'indispensable to the efficacious working of Canadian representative democracy' to bolster his view that the legislative power of the Commonwealth Parliament

their replacement by statutory rules. Note however that limitations on the Commonwealth Parliament's legislative power would mean that, at State and Territory level, separate, equivalent legislation would also have had to be passed in all the States and Territories for any reform to have been effective.

114 (1987) 164 CLR 15.

115 (1937) 37 SR (NSW) 242. See further S Walker, 'Freedom of Speech and Contempt of Court' n 110 above.

116 A useful background is to be found in Australian Law Reform Commission, *Contempt*, n 113 above.

117 (1992) 177 CLR 1.

118 (1992) 177 CLR 106.

119 For anticipation of this development and the implication of other constitutional freedom see the judgments of Murphy J in cases such as *Miller v TCN Channel Nine Pty Ltd* (1986) 161 CLR 556 and *Victoria v Australia Building Construction Employees' and Builders Labourers' Federation* (1982) 152 CLR 25; and Stephen J in *Attorney General (Cth): Ex rel McKinlay v Commonwealth* (1975) 135 CLR 1.

120 *Per* Brennan and Gaudron JJ or 'indispensable' *per* Mason CJ.

was constrained to the extent that it might not infringe the entrenched freedom of political expression.

The scope of the judicially implied freedom was further considered in *Theophanous v The Herald & Weekly Times Ltd*[121] and *Stephens v West Australian Newspapers Ltd*[122] where a majority held that the common law of defamation applicable throughout Australia was incompatible with the implied freedom as it 'chilled' political speech in respect of both Federal and State politicians excessively. Out of these actions, a new constitutionalised version of the defence of qualified privilege emerged.[123] Subsequently, the High Court in *Lange v Australian Broadcasting Corporation* indicated its support for the extended category of qualified privilege, reiterating the interest each citizen has in disseminating and receiving information, opinions and arguments concerning government and political matters affecting the people of Australia.[124] Significantly however, *Lange* adopted a different methodology to protect the implied freedom to that invoked previously in *Theophanous*. In its earlier ruling, the majority in the High Court held that the common law rules of defamation were affected and reformulated by the constitutional principle.[125] The Constitution thus superimposed the overriding constitutional principle upon common law and statutory rules of defamation. In *Lange*, the High Court started with the common law defence of qualified privilege and reformulated it to meet the requirements of the implied constitutional freedom.[126] *Theophanous* may thus be said to operate in a 'top-down' manner whereby the judgments articulate a theory about how the Australian Constitution limits the power of laws to interfere with representative government, and then consider the actual dispute before the court by reference to this controlling idea.[127] *Lange* takes conversely a 'bottom-up' approach in which common law rules emerge from individual disputes and are refined, distinguished or overruled.[128] Whilst

[121] (1994) 182 CLR 104.

[122] (1994) 182 CLR 211 and see further I Loveland, *Political Libels: A Comparative Study* (Hart Publishing, Oxford, 2000) ch 8.

[123] For comment, see Loveland, *ibid*. and G Williams, '*Engineers* is Dead, Long Live the Engineers!' [1995] 17 *Sydney Law Review* 62; S Walker, 'The Impact of the High Court's Free Speech Cases on Defamation Law' [1995] 17 *Sydney Law Review* 43. The majority also held that an implied freedom of political communication existed at State level in Western Australia under the Constitution Act 1889.

[124] (1997) 145 ALR 96, 115 citing in support remarks of McHugh J in *Stephens* (1994) 182 CLR 211, 264.

[125] As per *Sullivan v New York Times* (1964) 376 US 254. See further A Stone 'Freedom of Political Communication, the Constitution and the Common Law' (1998) 26 *Federal Law Review* 219.

[126] See further M Chesterman, *Freedom of Speech in Australian Law: A Delicate Plant* (Ashgate, Aldershot, 2000) ch 2.

[127] RA Posner, 'Legal Reasoning From the Top Down and From the Bottom Up' (1992) 59 *University of Chicago Law Review* 433.

[128] A Stone 'Freedom of Political Communication, the Constitution and the Common Law', n 125 above, argues that a court should generally favour 'a construction of the common law that is consistent with the Constitution, rather than the enunciation of a constitutional standard to replace an unconstitutional common law standard.'

raising important issues, these methodological differences are beyond the scope of the present discussion.

(ii) The Scope of the Implied Freedom

The High Court in *Theophanous* adopted Barendt's broad definition of political speech as that which is:

> relevant to the development of public opinion on the whole range of public issues which an intelligent citizen should think about.[129]

This is a definition which clearly encompasses court-related speech including court reporting, analysis and comment. Shortly afterwards however, a differently constituted High Court in *Lange v Australian Broadcasting Corporation* preferred a narrower definition which limited the scope of the implied freedom to expressive activity which enables the people to make informed choices as electors and facilitates the effective functioning of responsible government. Cast thus, *Lange* may be seen as an attempt to tie the new found freedom of political communication more closely to the text and structure of the Australian Constitution, and in particular to the demands resulting from periodic elections and accountable executive government. It is probably premature however to conclude that the scope of the implied freedom has been authoritatively settled.

United Kingdom[130]

The passage into law of the Human Rights Act 1998 is rightly seen as a major element of the Labour Government's constitutional reforms. Insofar as the Act enshrines a set of rights requiring UK judges to balance statements of individual freedoms against competing individual and state interests, it represents a fundamental shift away from the previous piecemeal and residual approach to individual liberty.[131] The Preamble to the Human Rights Act 1998 declares that the measure is intended to 'give further effect to rights and freedoms guaranteed under the European Convention on Human Rights'.

[129] Barendt, *Freedom of Speech*, n 6 above, 152. Barendt's definition was adopted by the High Court of Australia in *Theophanous v The Herald and Weekly Times Limited* [1994] 3 LRC 369, 382.

[130] It is important to mention that the Human Rights Act 1998 will impact upon different constitutional contexts across the separate legal systems in the UK and that developments in one part might not be mirrored elsewhere.

[131] It should be remembered however that the rights incorporated fall short of a comprehensive set of entitlements. The European Convention does not for example contain rights to fair trial in respect of the extradition process or prohibit expressly discrimination on grounds of disability or sexual orientation. The Convention also omits to refer specifically to the rights of children.

Prior to this Act, Convention standards were taken account of where domestic law was ambiguous[132] although some have argued that the range of circumstances where human rights treaties generally might be taken into account was broader than mere ambiguity.[133]Today, the 1998 Act offers protection against decisions/acts of public authorities in the United Kingdom which violate core civil and political freedoms,[134] albeit via mechanisms which do not ultimately challenge the notion of parliamentary sovereignty.

The decision not to seek entrenched status for Convention rights amounted to a retreat from the Labour Party's commitment whilst in opposition in the mid 1990's to Canadian-style incorporation by means of a 'notwithstanding' clause.[135] In October 1997 the White Paper *Rights Brought Home: The Human Rights Bill* announced that:

> The government has reached the conclusion that the courts should not have the power to set aside primary legislation past or future, on the ground of incompatibility with the Convention. This conclusion arises from the importance which the Government attaches to Parliamentary sovereignty.[136]

Somewhat late in the day, the Government appears to have realised that judicial review of primary legislation would be out of keeping with the UK's constitutional traditions.[137] Its preferred method for giving effect to Convention rights in domestic law which did not offend the doctrine of parliamentary sovereignty was the imposition of an interpretative duty on the courts by section 3(1) of the 1998 Act to read and give effect to primary and subordinate legislation (whether enacted before or after the commencement of the Human Rights Act) in a way which is consistent with the Convention in 'so far as it is possible to do so'. The significance of this formulation is that the courts will be required to prefer a possible intepretation of legislation which is consistent with Convention rights to any alternative, inconsistent interpretation. It is expected that the meaning of words may occasionally have to be strained in order to achieve a possible interpretation which is consistent with Convention rights.[138] As

[132] *R v Secretary of State for Home Dept ex parte Brind* [1991] 1 AC 696.
[133] M Hunt, *Using Human Rights Law in English Courts* (Hart Publishing, Oxford, 1997).
[134] S 1 of the 1998 Act incorporates Arts 2–12 of the European Convention on Human Rights together with Arts 1–3 of the First and Arts 1 and 2 of the Sixth Protocol. There is a vast and growing body of work on the 1998 Act, see, inter alia, J Wadham and H Mountfield, *Blackstone's Guide to the Human Rights Act 1998* (Blackstone Press, London, 1999); R Clayton and H Tomlinson, *The Law of Human Rights* (Oxford University Press, Oxford, 2000);
[135] See the comments of Tony Blair MP, *The Guardian*, 16 July 1994.
[136] (1997) Cm 3782 para 2.13.
[137] Judicial review of primary legislation in matters relating to European Union law seems to have been conveniently forgotten here.
[138] Lord Lester, 'The Art of the Possible—Interpreting Statutes under the Human Rights Act' [1998] *European Human Rights Law Review*. For an argument that the search for consistency will lead to the Convention having a lesser impact see, G Marshall, 'Interpreting Interpretation in the Human Rights Bill' [1998] *Public Law* 167. See also F Bennion, 'What Interpretation is "Possible"

commentators have pointed out, this will encourage a purposive form of statutory interpretation.[139]

The judicial task of ascertaining the purpose of new legislation is considerably assisted by section 19 of the 1998 Act which requires Ministers, prior to the Second Reading stage of a Bill, to state whether the Bill's provisions are compatible with Convention rights.[140] Under the rule of interpretation from *Pepper v Hart*,[141] any such statement may be used by the courts to construe a statute consistently with Convention rights. Section 2(1) of the 1998 Act further interweaves Convention Rights into domestic law by requiring that courts and tribunals 'must take account' of relevant judgments, decisions, declarations or advisory opinions of the European Court of Human Rights. Significantly however, section 2(1) does not however require a court to follow Convention jurisprudence. An amendment to make Strasbourg rulings binding on domestic courts was rejected in the House of Lords on the basis that this would unduly hamper UK courts' flexibility to adapt European jurisprudence to domestic circumstances.[142] Nothing in the Act prevents a court from taking account of other jurisdictions' human rights jurisprudence and it is thought that resort to such material will become more frequent.[143]

In those cases where a conflict between Convention rights and a statutory provison has been identified, a declaration of incompatability may be granted by the High Court.[144] Consistently with prevailing notions of parliamentary sovereignty, this declaration does not affect the continuing validity of a statutory provision[145] although a Minister may make a remedial order to remove this incompatibility.[146]

(i) Free Speech and Fair Trial Interests Under the Human Rights Act 1998

Section 1(1)(a) of the 1998 Act incorporates both the freedom of expression (Article 10) and fair trial provisions (Article 6) of the European Convention. It is predicted that Article 6 type claims will feature prominently in criminal liti-

Under section 3(1) of the Human Rights Act 1998' [2000] *Public Law* 77; Lord Cooke of Thorndon, 'The British Embracement of Human Rights' [1999] *European Human Rights Law Review* 243.

139 Wadham and Mountfield, *Blackstone's Guide to the Human Rights Act 1998*, n 134 above, 28–29.

140 The Government anticipated that a positive statement would be forthcoming 'whenever possible' see the speech of Home Secretary Jack Straw MP at HC Debs (1997–98) Vol 306 col 780.

141 [1993] AC 59.

142 The converse position whereby ECHR case law is binding on UK courts would seem in any event to conflict with retention of the doctrine of parliamentary sovereignty as reflected in ss 3, 6(2) and 19(1)(b).

143 Clayton and Tomlinson, *The Law of Human Rights,* n 134 above, 133–34.

144 S 4(5).

145 S 4(6) raising the question why a self-financing litigant (other than a pressure group wishing to cause political embarassment) would wish to pay a barrister to argue for a declaration.

146 S 10.

gation, offering a means of challenge to the compatibility of *inter alia* domestic rules of evidence and decisions concerning legal aid. Clayton and Tomlinson have also suggested that the grant of witness anonymity in exceptional circumstances might breach Convention fair trial standards where the evidence of the witness is deemed decisive.[147] It is less likely however that Article 6 will add to existing domestic protection for defendants in respect of prejudicial publicity. Harris, O'Boyle and Warbrick have commented that although Article 6 might be pleaded where criminal proceedings had been surrounded by considerable publicity, no case has been admitted on the merits by the Strasbourg authorities on this basis, indicating that a degree of media comment on matters pending before the courts is tolerated.[148]

In respect of media freedom to report or comment upon court-related matters, *sub judice* rules, various sets of prior restraints and the archaic offence of scandalising might now all be considered vulnerable to close judicial scrutiny. The impact of Convention jurisprudence on these restraints is returned to in later chapters of this book. For the time being, it is sufficient to comment that whilst reasonable grounds exist to suppose that some sets of prior restraints might well be declared incompatible with Article 10, the enhanced status of expression claims in domestic law is unlikely to signal the wholesale demise of media restraints.

VI JUDICIAL REVIEW AND CONSTITUTIONAL FREEDOMS: SOME CONCLUDING THOUGHTS

> *The root difficulty is that judicial review is a counter-majoritarian force in our system . . . When the Supreme Court declares unconstitutional a legislative act or the action of an elected executive, it thwarts the will of the representatives of the actual people of the here and now, it exercises control, not on behalf of the prevailing majority, but against it.*[149]
>
> *Alexander Bickel, The Least Dangerous Branch*

In three of the national legal systems considered above, the courts enjoy the ultimate power to decide whether legislative measures regulating speech in general (in the case of Canada and the US) or political expression (Australia) conform to entrenched constitutional norms. How, if at all, might this seemingly anti-democratic state of affairs be defended? One response is to point to the founding documents of the Constitution and ascertain whether, as is the case in Canada, judicial review of primary legislation was expressly authorised as part

[147] *Kostovski v Netherlands* (1989) 12 EHRR 434; *Dorsen v Netherlands* (1996) 22 EHRR 330. See further Clayton and Tomlinson, *The Law of Human Rights,* n 134 above, 712.

[148] DJ Harris, K O'Boyle and C Warbrick, *The Law of the European Convention* (Butterworths, London, 1995) at 216 where they also state that if a national appeal court does not consider that a trial has been unfair, Strasbourg is unlikely to do so either.

[149] AM Bickel, *The Least Dangerous Branch: The Supreme Court at the Bar of Politics* (Bobbs-Merrill, Indianapolis Ind, 1962) 16–17.

of the new constitutional settlement. There, judicial review enjoys some constitutional legitimacy. Even then, it cannot be assumed that this preference for judicial oversight in 1982 is shared by the current set of Canadian electors. Of course, in those constitutions where judicial review is not expressly authorised, US experience shows that a defence of judicial review may be even more problematic.

Alexander Bickel's enquiry into judicial review of legislative acts in *The Least Dangerous Branch* considered the case against judicial oversight. The 'root difficulty' he conceded consisted in the fact that control over key issues of political morality was wrested away from the people (acting via their elected representatives) and placed with an elite and unaccountable group. Thus stated, judicial review constituted an improper encroachment into the policy-making function of legislature and seemed 'grotesquely to constrict the moral sovereignty of the people themselves'.[150] Sympathetic to this objection one commentor John Hart Ely has argued that, at its broadest, judicial review should be confined to questions of ensuring the informed participation of all members of society in political debate and not transgress into evaluation of the substantive merits of political choices.[151]

Bickel also considered another objection whose origin he ascribed to James Bradley Thayer, an American constitutional lawyer writing at the beginning of the twentieth century. Thayer feared the long term weakening of the democratic process brought about by reliance upon outsiders (ie unelected judges) to correct legislative mistakes.[152] He argued that this produced a diminished political capacity on the part of the people to govern themselves and deadened their sense of moral responsibility. Likewise, Levy considered that judicial resolution of such issues lulled the people 'into apathy on matters that are fundamentally their concern.'[153]

In response, Bickel argued that whilst the US system of government did call upon the legislature and the executive to serve enduring constitutional values by articulating and defending them, too often in the past these bodies had acted out of expediency, rather than principle.[154] The courts on the other hand enjoyed certain advantages in dealing with matters of principle, including their insulation from daily political affairs and their training to give expression to enduring values in actual disputes to come before them. Moreover, in addition

[150] Dworkin, *Freedom's Law*, n 37 above, 4.

[151] JH Ely, *Democracy and Distrust: A Theory of Judicial Review* (Harvard University Press, Cambridge Mass, 1980) chs 5 and 6.

[152] JB Thayer, 'The Origin and Scope of the American Doctrine of Constitutional Law' in *Legal Essays* (The Boston Book Co, Boston Mass, 1908) Thayer supported an extremely limited form of judicial review in those instances where the legislature had made a very clear mistake, one which was not open to rational question. For Bickel's criticism of this approach, see *The Least Dangerous Branch*, n 149 above, at ch 2.

[153] L Levy, *Original Intent and the Framers' Constitution* (MacMillan, New York NY, 1988) 362–63.

[154] For criticism of this view as historically shaky, see Ely, *Democracy and Distrust*, n 151 above.

to its checking function, the Supreme Court performed a valuable legitimating role when it confirmed legislative action as within the scope of Congress' powers. This function would be meaningless if the court had no power to strike down ultra vires measures.[155]

A further defence of the vesting of ultimate constitutional authority beyond the reach of temporary political majorities and into the hands of the judiciary is to be found in the writing of Ronald Dworkin. Tackling the root difficulty head-on, Dworkin argues that it is misconceived to see judicial review as anti-democratic. On the contrary, for Dworkin it is majoritarian institutions which have at times conspiciously failed to adhere to the 'democratic conditions' such as treating all members of the community including minority groups with equal concern and respect.[156] Judicial review, by contrast, is 'practically indispensable to democracy' as it holds out the prospect that issues of political morality will be decided by an institution whose structure, composition and practice respect the democratic conditions and which may be trusted to apply the best conception of constitutional principles which fits with a 'moral reading of a constitution.' The latter phrase refers to a reading of a constitution which reflects an understanding of the constitutional heritage of a nation and yields up an application of the Constitution which is consistent with that heritage. It does not however permit judges to impose their own personal values. Dworkin should not however be understood as claiming that majoritarian institutions can never be relied upon to respect the democratic conditions, it is just that, with Bickel, he does not find the historical record particularly encouraging.

It will be clear by now that much of this dispute has hinged upon the respective records of legislatures and courts and which has shown more respect for the democratic conditions. Those who oppose judicial review of primary legislation doubt the ability of the courts to give effect to the values of society.[157] For supporters such as Bickel and Dworkin, while the judges may not always get it right, temporary majorities in the legislature have shown themselves unable to resist interference with minority rights and there is no reason to suppose that they will resist the temptation to do so again.

UK readers coming across Dworkin's description of the US judiciary as an institution whose composition and practice has respected the 'democratic conditions' including according equal respect and concern to all members of the community might not recognise an equivalent on this side of the Atlantic—a fact which may constitute a powerful home-grown objection to judicial review and suggest why the failure to entrench the Human Rights Act

[155] See CL Black Jnr, *The People and the Court* (Macmillan, New York, 1960) and also D Rostow, 'The Democratic Character of Judicial Review' (1952) 66 *Harvard Law Review* 193.

[156] A recent example close to home is surely provided by the passage of the Criminal Justice and Public Order Act 1994, provisions of which appear to show clear antipathy towards certain kinds of lifestyle choices.

[157] Ely, *Democracy and Distrust*, n 151 above, ch 3.

caused so few ripples. Certainly, if appointment procedures for senior judicial figures are compared, the UK cannot point to anything approximating to the elements of openness and elected representative involvement which characterise the structure of Senate confirmation hearings.[158] Until domestic reform is forthcoming, resistance to judicial review of primary legislation is unlikely to diminish.

[158] See D Beatty 'The Canadian Charter of Rights: Lessons and Laments' n 62 above, for criticisms of the appointment of Supreme Court judges in Canada.

2

More or Less Different? The First Amendment and Article 10[1]

I INTRODUCTION

THE PURPOSE OF this chapter is to explore the extent of congruencies and dissimilarities between the jurisprudence of the First Amendment and that developed under Article 10 of the European Convention on Human Rights. Its theme will be that, notwithstanding clear differences in terms of the constitutional structure of speech/expression guarantees (a fact stressed in Ameri-sceptic writings) and the prioritisation of speech interests ahead of fair trial claims in the United States, a closer look at the underlying rationales for expression protection and other established features of Article 10 jurisprudence does in fact reveal a number of points of overlap. Using Ronald Dworkin's notion of the moral reading of constitutions[2] and the distinction he advances between concepts and conceptions as aids to an interpretative strategy for Articles 10 and 6,[3] it will be argued that the 'best fit' reading of European free speech/fair trial regulation requires a distinctive reading of the Article 10 freedom in the context of court-related speech in which robust protection for such expression might nonetheless be reconciled with legitimate administration of justice concerns. The chapter concludes by taking a critical look at the width of discretion afforded to the national authorities in *Worm v Austria* and argues that the Court's deference to the Austrian authorities sits uneasily alongside a vigorous commitment to the protection of court-related expression.

II SOME STRUCTURAL DIFFERENCES

At first glance, the differences between the respective guarantees of free speech in the First Amendment and Article 10 are so marked as to call into question the feasibility of any comparative analysis of free speech jurisprudence. The seemingly absolutist nature of the First Amendment imperative:

1 An earlier version of this chapter appeared in (2000) 7 *Maastricht Journal of European and Comparative Law* 244.

2 *Freedom's Law—The Moral Reading of the American Constitution* (Oxford University Press, Oxford, 1996) esp Introduction.

3 *Taking Rights Seriously* (Duckworth, London, 1977) ch 5.

> Congress shall make no law respecting an establishment of religion, or prohibiting the free exercise thereof; abridging the freedom of speech or of the press; or the right of the people peaceably to assemble and to petition the government for a redress of grievances.

stands in stark contrast to the heavily circumscribed notion of free expression in Article 10:

> 1. Everyone has the right to freedom of expression. This right shall include the freedom to hold opinions and to receive and impart information and ideas . . . 2. The exercise of these freedoms . . . may be subject to . . . restrictions . . . as are prescribed by law and are necessary in a democratic society in the interests of national security, territorial integrity or public safety, for the prevention of disorder or crime, for the protection of health or morals, for the protection of the reputation or rights of others, for the preventing the disclosure of information given in confidence, or for maintaining the authority and impartiality of the judiciary.

One commentator has observed that the terms of the First Amendment have fostered a tendency:

> to treat free speech as a fundamental right, without reference to the social responsibilities which under a less absolutist European . . . jurisprudence, exemplified by Article 10(2) of the European Convention on Human Rights . . . would accompany it.[4]

Article 10 jurisprudence is thus said to be characterised by a search for the appropriate balance between a particular expression interest and the countervailing societal/individual interest in its curtailment. For example, it will be seen below that the European Court has been quite prepared to uphold the legality of state interferences with expression on content grounds in order to promote the goal of social harmony. By contrast, individual speech interests have enjoyed protection under the First Amendment in accordance with prevailing notions of content neutrality even where identifiable social harms may result. In another clear difference, the Supreme Court has had to deal with questions about what constitutes 'speech', whereas, the more inclusive notion of 'expression' in the Convention has shifted attention onto states' justification for interference with expression. Beneath such structual differences however, a consideration of underlying rationales for speech/expression in the United States and Europe and established features of their respective jurisprudence suggests that certain shared attributes have been overlooked. In the next section, bare outlines of First Amendment and Article 10 jurisprudence are sketched in the course of which an attempt is made to identify common themes and outstanding differences.

[4] See chapter by D Feldman in I Loveland (ed), *Incorporating the First Amendment* (Hart Publishing, Oxford, 1998) at 162.

III FREE SPEECH JURISPRUDENCE COMPARED—RATIONALES AND KEY FEATURES OF FIRST AMENDMENT AND ARTICLE 10 THINKING

The First Amendment

Free Speech Rationales

As was seen in chapter one, judicial pronouncements on the nature and limits of First Amendment freedoms reveal attachment to a variety of philosophical bases for free speech of a mainly instrumentalist nature. On one prominent view most famously associated with Justice Holmes, free speech is valuable because it enhances individuals' ability to think for themselves (based on what they do as recipients of others' free speech) and enables the individual to communicate the product of this process with others. The state's ability to determine what is true and what is false is doubted—(a Millian rejection of the assumption of infallibility upon which such regulation is predicated) and, in its place, is substituted the notion of a 'marketplace of ideas' in which rival versions of the truth battle to achieve widespread acceptance. As Holmes J put it in *Abrams v US:*

> [W]hen men have realised that time has upset many fighting faiths, they may come to believe even more than they believe the very foundations of their own conduct that the ultimate good desired is better reached by free trade in ideas—that the best test of truth is the power of the thought to get itself accepted in the competition of the market, and that truth is the only ground upon which their wishes safely can be carried out. That at any rate is the theory of our Constitution.[5]

This famous dictum may go some way to explaining the particular dislike of contents-based restrictions encountered in the United States. Once a society confers on government the power to restrict individuals' speech which is generally recognised to be harmful, the fear is that the power might next be used against less obviously harmful types of speech. As decisions such as *Collin v Smith*[6] (permitting Nazi sympathisers to march through an area with a sizeable Jewish community) and *RAV v City of St Paul, Minnesota*[7] (outlawing of state ordinance prohibiting Ku Klux Klan burning of crosses) show, individuals' speech entitlements may then prevail in the face of identifiable social and community harms.

Alongside this essentially individual interest-driven account of speech and its promotion of intellectual values such as truth, Lichtenberg has rightly observed that an equally prominent rationale for free speech in US political thinking is the furtherance of democratic self-government, a fact evidenced by

[5] (1919) 250 US 616, 630.
[6] (1978) 578 F 2d 1197 Cf *Beauharnais v Illinois* (1950) 343 US 250.
[7] (1992) 120 LEd 2d 305. See further chapter by Feldman in Loveland at n 4 above.

the respective writings of the First Amendment author James Madison,[8] Alexander Mieklejohn[9] and, in the judicial sphere, most forcefully by Justice Brennan.[10] This view holds that the essential purpose of the First Amendment is to allow citizens to exercise informed political choices and thus participate effectively in societal decision-making processes.[11] The central importance of the media in ensuring the free flow of ideas and information so that informed political choices may be made by the citizens is accordingly recognised.[12]

Chapter one also brought out a further justification for free speech in US judicial thought namely to safeguard and promote individual autonomy and self-development. As Gunther notes, the emphasis on individual realisation in this rationale would extend speech protection beyond the purely political to artistic and literary forms of speech.[13]

The different rationales for free speech overlap and it is not uncommon to find elements of all three conjoined. Consider the remarks of Justice Brandeis in *Whitney v California*:

> Those who won our independence believed that the final end of the state was to make men free to develop their faculties; and that in its government the deliberative forces should prevail over the arbitrary. They valued liberty both as an end and as a means. They believed liberty to be the secret of happiness and courage to be the secret of liberty. They believed that freedom to think as you will and to speak as you think are indispensable to the discovery and spread of political truth; that without free speech and assembly discussion would be futile; that with them discussion affords ordinarily adequate protection against the dissemination of noxious doctrine, that the greatest menace to freedom is an inert people and that public discussion is a political duty and that this should be a fundamental principle of the American government.[14]

Apart from these various justifications for free speech, Dworkin has argued for a different kind of free speech justification which he calls 'constitutive' and which upholds free speech in the following way. It is an essential feature of a just political society, he argues, that government treat competent adults as responsible moral agents. Being a responsible moral agent requires that a person must be free to make up his/her own mind about politics, justice and faith and to

[8] Madison opposed for example the Sedition Act of 1798 because it prevented the free examination of public characters and measures.

[9] *Free Speech and Its Relation to Self-Government* (Harper, New York, 1948).

[10] *Richmond Newspapers Inc v Virginia* (1980) 448 US 555, 587 'the First Amendment embodies more than a commitment to free expression and communicative interchange for their own sakes; it has a *structural* role to play in securing and fostering our republican system of self government.'

[11] For a discussion of the distinctions and tensions between the 'market' model of Holmes and 'self-governing republicanism' see C Sunstein, 'The First Amendment in Cyberspace' (1995) 104 *Yale Law Journal* 1757.

[12] *Branzberg v Hayes* (1972) 408 US 665; *Richmond Newspapers v Virginia* (1980) 448 US 555.

[13] G Gunther, *Constitutional Law* (The Foundation Press Inc, New York NY, 1985) ch 11. For a leading academic exposition see T Scanlon, 'A Theory of Freedom of Expression' (1972) 1 *Philosophy and Public Affairs* 204. See further ch 1 above.

[14] *Whitney v California* (1927) 274 US 357, 374–377.

express his/her views to others.[15] He too relies on the passage from *Whitney v California* quoted above to demonstrate support for the constitutive view of free speech at the point where Brandeis says that free speech is valuable as an end as well as a means. Cast thus, it does not share the vulnerability in the Madisonian/Mieklejohn argument to restrictions on speech when voted for by a majority acting through their representatives in the legislature.[16]

Right to Shock/Offend

> If there is a bedrock principle underlying the First Amendment, it is that the Government may not prohibit the expression of an idea simply because society finds the idea itself offensive or disagreeable.[17]

Reflecting an established hostility to speech regulation on contents grounds, the Supreme Court has, outside of a few exceptional categories, struck down state laws which purport to limit speech on the grounds of causing offence to others. Thus in *Cohen v California* where the defendant was convicted for offensive conduct after wearing a jacket at the Municipal Court on which was written 'Fuck the Draft', the Supreme Court held that the conviction violated Cohen's First Amendment rights.[18] While the language used was 'more distasteful than most others of its genre', this alone was insufficient to justify its restraint. The importance of the emotive function of Cohen's 'speech' and the underlying fear that state bans on the use of particular words would act as a guise for censorship of unpopular views demanded that his conviction be quashed.[19] Offensive speech may however be lawfully regulated under the 'fighting words' doctrine where the speaker's words are likely to provoke the average person to retaliation and therefore cause a breach of the peace.[20] After the majority ruling in *RAV v Minnesota* however, it is not possible to regulate 'fighting words' in a way which is contents-based, that is which is based on state hostility to the speaker's underlying message. On the facts in *RAV*, an Ordinance which was designed to combat expressive activity of the Ku Klux (including the burning of crosses which aroused anger, alarm or resentment on the basis of race, colour, creed etc) was struck down by the Court on the basis that it was aimed at a particular kind of offensive speech.[21]

[15] *Freedom's Law* (Oxford University Press, Oxford, 1996) 200–01.
[16] For an application of this rationale to censorship laws *see ibid* at ch 8.
[17] *Texas v Johnson* (1989) 491 US 397, 414 per Brennan J.
[18] (1971) 403 US 15.
[19] See further *Rosenfeld v New Jersey* (1972) 408 US 901.
[20] *Chaplinsky v New Hampshire* (1942) 315 US 568 although Justice Murphy's ruling went further than this and found that speech which was 'lewd and obscene', 'profane' and 'libellous' might be curtailed without any infringement of First Amendment rights. This list has not survived to the present day.
[21] For an unpacking of the various senses in which 'content-neutrality' has arisen in US case law see the chapter by D Feldman in I Loveland (ed), *Importing the First Amendment* (Hart Publishing, Oxford, 1998).

At other times however, the Court has plainly upheld the regulation of speech on contents grounds where it is of limited or no social value. Thus, speech which is libellous,[22] obscene[23] or contrary to the state's interest in the well-being of its youth[24] can be lawfully restricted. In each of these lawfully regulated categories, state restrictions will nevertheless be constitutionally invalid if formulated in vague language or in terms which go beyond that which is needed to advance the relevant compelling state interest. This is a matter which will be returned to below.

Location-based Speech Distinctions

The scope of free speech under First Amendment jurisprudence has also depended upon location. Restrictions on speech which occurs in a traditional public forum such as a public park or at a public forum so designated by the state such as a state university are subject to stricter scrutiny than speech at other kinds of public property and private spaces (eg private homes).[25] Nonetheless, even in respect of public spaces, the Supreme Court has long recognised the validity of 'time, place or manner' regulation on speech to limit their use.[26]

Variable Levels of Scrutiny According to Speech Type

As was noted above, notwithstanding its avowedly content-neutral stance, the Supreme Court's supervision of speech restrictions has reflected an ordering of the relative social value of distinct speech types.[27] Given the centrality of the republican ideal of self-government in First Amendment jurisprudence, it is unsurprising to see that regulation of speech about public affairs attracts the strictest standard of supervision. Consider for example the distinctions in the US defamation laws between speech concerning public officials on the one hand and that relating to private persons. In *New York Times v Sullivan*,[28] the Supreme Court held that criticism of public servants in respect of their official conduct was entitled to First Amendment protection unless it could be shown to have been made with actual malice or reckless disregard for the truth. By con-

[22] But note the difference in approach between cases involving public figures *New York Times v Sullivan* (1964) 376 US 254 and private figures *Gertz v Robert Welch Inc* (1974) 418 US 323.
[23] *Miller v California* (1973) 413 US 15.
[24] *FCC v Pacifica* (1978) 438 US 726.
[25] Contrast *Hague v CIO* (1939) 307 US 496 and *Cox v Louisiana* (1965) 379 US 536 with *Hudgens v NRLB* (1976) 424 US 507.
[26] There is thus no constitutional right to 'insist on a street meeting in the middle of Times Square at the rush hour as form of free speech or assembly.' *Cox v Louisiana* (1965) 379 US 536, 554.
[27] See further Brennan J writing extra-judicially 'The Supreme Court and the Meiklejohn Interpretation of the First Amendment' (1965) 79 *Harvard Law Review* 1, 11.
[28] (1964) 376 US 254.

trast, First Amendment protection is not available to someone who defames a private citizen.[29]

In the case of commercial speech, a less strict standard of court supervision of state regulation is apparent.[30] In *Central Hudson Gas & Electricity v Public Service Commission*, it was held that there must be a reasonable fit between the purpose behind a restriction on commercial speech and the means chosen to achieve that purpose.[31] The informational content of certain forms of commerial speech which have allowed readers to make more informed choices has however forced the court to invalidate state laws prohibiting the unsolicited mailing of contraceptive advertisements,[32] the advertising of abortion services,[33] and routine legal services.[34]

Other speech types have been treated as having little or no redeeming social value and have accordingly been denied First Amendment protection altogether. Thus, the distribution of child pornography[35] and obscene materials generally[36] are outside of First Amendment protection.

Hostility to Prior Restraints

One measure of the commitment to press freedom in the United States is the special hostility with which the courts have traditionally viewed prior restraints.[37] This owes much to the influence of Blackstone's *Commentaries* which were widely referred to in state courts and which famously declared that:

> The liberty of the press . . . consists in laying no previous restraints upon publications . . .[38]

More recently, Alexander Bickel famously described prior restraints as falling on speech

> with a brutality and a finality all their own. Even if they are ultimately lifted they cause irremediable loss—a loss in the immediacy, the impact, of speech. They differ

[29] *Curtis Publishing Co v Butts* (1967) 338 US 130. It is fair to say however, that the distinction between public and private relied upon in *New York Times* has not been problem-free. See further H Abraham and B Perry, in *Freedom and the Court* 7th edn (Oxford University Press, New York, 1998) 217–18.

[30] Earlier cases from the 1940's onwards had assumed that most types of commercial speech were outside First Amendment protection, see *Valentine v Chrestensen* (1942) 316 US 52.

[31] (1980) 447 US 557.

[32] *Bolger v Youngs Drugs Products Corp* (1983) 463 US 60.

[33] *Bigelow v Virginia* (1975) 421 US 809.

[34] *Bates v State Bar of Arizona* (1977) 433 US 350.

[35] *New York v Ferber* (1982) 458 US 747.

[36] *Miller v California* (1973) 413 US 15.

[37] Eg *Near v Minnesota* (1931) 283 US 697 although note the dissenting view of Butler J that Minnesota's Public Nuisance Law did not constitute a prior restraint in the sense intended by Blackstone. For a commentary on prior retraint after *Nebraska Press Association v Stuart* 427 US 539 (1976) see S Barnett, 'The Puzzle of Prior Restraint' (1977) 29 *Stanford Law Review* 539.

[38] Blackstone, 4 *Commentaries on the Laws of England* 151–52. Blackstone's principal target was the system of state licensing of the presses imposed in seventeenth century England.

> from the imposition of criminal liability in significant procedural respects as well, which in turn have their substantive consequences. The violator of a prior restraint may be assured of being held in contempt; the violator of a statute punishing speech criminally knows that he will go before a jury, and may be willing to take his chance, counting on a possible acquittal. A prior restraint, therefore, stops speech more effectively.[39]

In the context of media reporting of criminal proceedings, hostility is evidenced in both federal statute and in Supreme Court rulings both of which place a heavy emphasis on the advantages of open judicial proceedings. The Justice Department's policy on the matter is stated in 28 CFR 50.9 which refers to the 'vital public interest in open judicial proceedings . . .' Government attorneys are restrained from seeking or consenting to closure of federal trials, pre-trial evidentiary or plea proceedings unless:

1. No reasonable alternative exists for protecting the interests at stake; and
2. Closure is clearly likely to prevent the harm sought to be avoided; and
3. The degree of closure is minimised to the greatest extent possible.

Relying upon the First Amendment, the Supreme Court and several Federal Courts of Appeal have upheld press and public access rights to a variety of pre-trial proceedings in criminal cases including the *voir dire* examination of potential jurors[40] and hearings to determine the admissability of evidence.[41] In those instances where the press and public have been denied access under a statute authorising automatic closure, the exclusion may violate First Amendment standards either because of the failure to make express factual findings in the instant case which support closure or because the means chosen to protect the compelling interest has not been tailored narrowly to serve that interest.[42] This latter point is considered further in the next section.

Overbreadth

Under the overbreadth doctrine, an entire statute which regulates speech may be invalidated despite having a lawful objective, if the means chosen by the legislature to achieve that object 'sweep(s) unnecessarily broadly and thereby invade(s) the area of protected freedoms.'[43] Thus, in *Globe Newspapers v Superior Court*

[39] *The Morality of Consent* (Yale University Press, New Haven, 1975) at 61.
[40] *Press-Enterprise Co v Superior Court of California* (1984) 464 US 501. (*Press-Enterprise No 1)*
[41] *Re Application of Herald Co* (1984) 734 F2d 93; *United States v Brooklier* (1982) 685 F2d 1162. See further I Cram, 'Automatic reporting restrictions in criminal proceedings and Article 10 of the ECHR' [1998] *European Human Reports Law Review* 742.
[42] *Globe Newspapers v Superior Court for the County of Norfolk* (1983) 457 US 596.
[43] *NAACP v Alabama* (1964) 357 US 449 per Harlan J. See also *Schaumberg v Citizens for a Better Environment* (1980) 444 US 620 and *Broadrick v Oklahoma* (1973) 413 US 601. There is however an issue about how far the Court should strain to find potential applications of a statute which may invade the area of protected freedoms.

for the County of Norfolk a Massachusetts statute automatically excluded press and public from the courtroom during the testimony of a minor victim in a sex offence trial.[44] Although the court could agree that closure might be necessary in a particular case to protect the welfare of the victim having regard to factors including the latter's age and psychological maturity, automatic closure in every case could not be justified and the provision in question was struck down.[45] Where overbreadth is invoked by the court, the Congress may re-enact legislation which provides a more narrowly defined means of securing its chosen objective.

Vagueness

In addition to overbreadth, a further ground for impugning the validity of a statute regulating speech is that of vagueness. Here, it is asserted that the statute in question is lacking in clarity and that, in the words of Justice Brennan, persons 'of common intelligence must necessarily guess at its meaning and differ as to its application.'[46] Thus, a prohibition on three or more persons meeting on the pavement and acting in a manner 'annoying' to persons passing by was held in *Coates v City of Cincinnati* to be constitutionally invalid on vagueness grounds.[47]

Key Themes in Article10 Jurisprudence and the Extent of Reliance Upon First Amendment Reasoning

Rationales for Freedom of Expression in European Convention Jurisprudence

In one of its earliest landmark rulings *Handyside v UK*, the Court stressed a dual instrumentalist rationale for freedom of expression stating that it was:

> one of the basic conditions for the progress of democratic societies and for the development of each individual.[48]

The democracy-enhancing and individual development functions of freedom of expression have since been reiterated on numerous occasions notably in *Lingens*

[44] (1983) 457 US 596

[45] See the similar conclusion by the Ontario Court of Appeal in *Canadian Newspaper Co v Attorney General* (1985) O.R. (2d) 557 where a mandatory publication ban in respect of the identity of a sexual offence complainant imposed by s 442(3) of the Canadian Criminal Code violated ss 1 and 2 of the Canadian Charter of Rights and Freedoms.

[46] *Zwickler v Koota* (1967) 389 US 241.

[47] (1971) 402 US 611.

[48] (1979–80) 1 EHRR 737. For some interesting insights into the dynamics of Article 10 jurisprudence, see M Oetheimer, *L'Harmonisation de la Liberté d'Expression en Europe* (Editions A Pedone, Paris, 2001).

v Austria[49] and *Oberschlick v Austria*.[50] There is thus some considerable overlap with US free speech rationales although it should be noted that the Holmesian notion of a marketplace of ideas and the search for truth has not been a prominent feature of Article 10 jurisprudence. Articulation of the link between freedom of expression and the democratically governed society is found in *Sunday Times v UK*,[51] where it was stated that:

> [F]reedom of expression constitutes one of the essential foundations of a democratic society.

Just as in the United States, the especial importance attached to the role played by the press/media in imparting political information and ideas and the public's interest in receiving such material in a democracy has been stressed. In *Castells v Spain*, the Court observed that

> Freedom of the press affords the public one of the best means of discovering and forming an opinion on the ideas and attitudes of their political leaders. In particular, it gives politicians the opportunity to reflect and comment upon the preoccupations of public opinion; it thus enables everyone to participate in the free political debate which is at the core of the concept of a democratic society.[52]

Similar declarations linking the nature of democratic society, media freedom and the right of the public to receive information and ideas are to be found in *Thorgeir Thorgierson v Iceland* and *Jersild v Denmark*.[53] In *Lingens v Austria* the Court declared that:

> Whilst the press must not overstep the bounds set, inter alia, for the 'protection of others', it is nevertheless incumbent on it to impart information and ideas on political issues just as on those in other areas of public interest. Not only does the press have the task of imparting such information and ideas: the public also has a right to receive them.[54]

The notion of a duty on the media to impart information and ideas is consistent with the reference to 'duties and responsibilities' imposed by paragraph 2 of Article 10 on those exercising freedom of expression under paragraph 1. Van Dijk and Van Hoof have suggested that the general rule in Article 10 requiring exceptions to freedom of expression to be interpreted narrowly is of 'particular importance to the press.'[55] A further essential element of the free-

[49] (1986) 8 EHRR 407, 418.
[50] (1995) 19 EHRR 389, 421.
[51] (1979) 2 EHRR 245, 280.
[52] (1992) 14 EHRR 445.
[53] *Thorgier Thorgierson v Iceland* (1992) 14 EHRR 843; *Jersild v Denmark* (1995) 19 EHRR 1, 25–26.
[54] (1986) 8 EHRR 407 at para 41. See also *Worm v Austria* (1998) 25 EHRR 454 and *News Verlags GmbH v Austria* (2001) 31 EHRR 8.
[55] P Van Dijk and G J H Van Hoof, *Theory and Practice of the European Convention on Human Rights* 3rd edn (Kluwer, The Hague, 1998) at 576.

dom in Article 10 is that media organisations must be left to decide for themselves the forms and means of communication. It is not for the Court or national authorities to specify how information and opinions are to be conveyed.[56] This latitude extends as far as recourse to a degree of exaggeration or provocation.[57]

Right to Shock/Offend

The European Court has also emphasised that the freedom conferred in Article 10 is not to be seen as confined to information or ideas that are favourably received or deemed inoffensive. On the contrary, to be meaningful, the freedom must extend to those forms of expression that offend, shock or disturb the State or any sector of the population[58] Allowing such expression was said in *Oberschlick v Austria* to follow from the demands of pluralism, tolerance and broadmindedness 'without which there is no democratic society.'[59] At the same time however, the Court is less tolerant of offensive speech than the US Supreme Court in a way which has left doubt about its true commitment to this type of speech.[60] Thus, in stark contrast to the latter's general hostility towards speech regulation on content grounds, European jurisprudence has accepted the case for limiting certain forms of harmful speech on contents-based grounds and thereby prioritised countervailing societal interests such as the religious sensibilities of others. In *Otto-Preminger Institut v Austria* the majority of the Court upheld the seizure and forfeiture of a film which it deemed was 'gratuitiously offensive' to the religious feelings of others (including Roman Catholics) as a lawful restraint on the applicant film institute even though it was only shown to a paying audience with an interest in 'art cinema' type films who had been given prior warning of the nature of the film.[61] Whether based on the 'rights of others' or 'the protection of morals', the scope for offensive expression under the Convention was consequently considerably narrowed. The tolerance of racist speech/conduct found in the First Amendment cases of *Collin v Smith* and *RAV v Minnesota* offers a sharp contrast in this regard. Moreover, the enactment in most European jurisdictions of incitement to racial hatred laws provides further evidence of a greater preparedness to intervene on contents grounds than is apparent across the Atlantic. By way of explanation, Barendt has commented that the US was:

[56] *Jersild v Denmark* (1995) 19 EHRR 1; *News Verlags GmbH v Austria* (2001) 31 EHRR 8.
[57] *Bergens Tidende and others v Norway* (2001) 31 EHRR 16.
[58] (1979–80) 1 EHRR 737.
[59] (1995) 19 EHRR 389, 421.
[60] As the minority noted in *Otto-Preminger Institute v Austria* (1995) 19 EHRR 34, 61, 'There is no point in guaranteeing this freedom only as long as it is used in accordance with accepted opinion.'
[61] *Ibid*. The joint dissent from Judges Palm, Pekkanen and Makarczyk held that the forfeiture was a disproportionate means of protecting the sensibilities of those likely to be offended.

> geographically and psychologically far removed from any experience of the totalitarian regimes of the late 1920's and 1930's.[62]

Recently, members of the European Court have signalled a greater willingness to align the Court with First Amendment jurisprudence on offensive speech. In *Grigoriades v Greece*,[63]Judge Jambrek observed that both European and US jurisdictions extended protection to speech (whether symbolic or otherwise) which was calculated to cause offence to national values. The applicant's critical remarks about the Greek Army were likened to cases such as *Street v New York*[64], *Texas v Johnson*[65] and *United States v Eichman*[66] (where the public burning of the US flag was held to be protected speech under the First Amendment) and were likewise held to enjoy the protection afforded by Article 10.

Approach to Construction of Derogations from Freedom of Expression

When national authorities seek to rely upon the enumerated exceptions to this freedom in Article 10(2), the Court has said that these exceptions,

> must be narrowly interpreted and the necessity for (them) . . . convincingly established.[67]

—a position which contrasts with relatively wide discretion accorded to States where restrictions on property rights under Article 1 of Protocol 1 are concerned.[68] Within freedom of expression, further distinctions in terms of the appropriate level of scrutiny are made which draw in part upon speech type (political, commercial etc) and the precise purpose behind the curtailment of expression (protection of morals, maintenance of the authority and impartiality of the judiciary). These are further examined below. A more general point underpinning Convention jurisprudence in this area is the fact/value distinction, the assessment of which has proved crucial to the intensity of the Court's supervision of national authorities' punishment of untrue statements. From *Lingens* onwards, the Court has made it clear that requirements in national law on journalists and others to prove the truth of value judgements in order avoid criminal liability will violate the speaker's Article 10 freedoms where the factual basis upon which the value judgement is based is not disputed.[69] By contrast, a similar

[62] In (eds T Campbell and W Sadurski, *Freedom of Communication* (Dartmouth, Aldershot, 1994) at 65. Barendt also comments upon the resistance to the regulation of broadcast speech in the US (and attempts to confer access opportunities in particular) which stands in marked contrast to the imposition of contents restrictions and guarantees of pluralism found in Europe.

[63] (1999) 27 EHRR 464, 487.

[64] (1969) 394 US 576.

[65] (1989) 491 US 397.

[66] (1990) 496 US 310.

[67] *Observer and Guardian v UK* (1992) 14 EHRR 153, 191.

[68] Van Dijk and Van Hoof, at n 55 above 88.

[69] *Lingens v Austria* (1986) 8 EHRR 407; *Oberschlick v Austria* (1995) 19 EHRR 389; *Schwabe v Austria*, (A/242-B) 1992 August 28.

requirement in respect of alleged statements of fact would not by itself amount to a breach. It follows therefore that the willingness of the Court in cases of general political interest to categorise a statement as a 'value-judgement' expands rather than contracts the scope of the speaker's freedom.[70] Disappointingly however, in the context of an article critical of judges sitting in the Austrian courts, the Court in *Prager and Oberschlick* opted for a less intensive look at national authorities' punishments of what were plainly value-judgements by leaving it to the national authorities to categorise the statement in question.[71]

Special Position of Political Speech and the Variable Intensity of Review

A further theme in Convention jurisprudence is that the level of protection enjoyed by forms of expression may vary according to subject matter. Given the democracy enhancing function of political expression, it is unsurprising to find that political speech enjoys special status within the core category of freedom of expression. Political speech has been defined by Barendt as including speech which is:

> relevant to the development of public opinion on the whole range of public issues which an intelligent citizen should think about.[72]

The special status of political speech under the Convention is reflected in a variable margin of appreciation doctrine where restraints on political expression have been subjected to closer scrutiny than restraints on commercial or artistic expression. The requirement to ensure the open discussion of political issues such as the conduct of politicians has led the Court to find in both *Lingens v Austria*[73] and *Oberschlick v Austria*[74] that the convictions of journalists in the national courts for the defamation of politicians violated Article 10. Whilst not expressly adopting the US 'public figure' doctrine advanced in *New York Times v Sullivan*, the European Court has stressed that the limits of acceptable criticism of politicians were wider than those where the reputation of a private citizen was attacked. In *Castells v Spain* the Court was prepared to confer an even wider scope upon criticism made of government per se than countenanced in *Lingens* in respect of individual politicians.

A less strict standard of supervision of national authorities' actions exists in respect of restrictions on commercial[75] and artistic expression. In the case of

[70] See for example *Thorgier Thorgeirson v Iceland* (1992) 14 EHRR 843.
[71] See further Van Dijk and Van Hoof, at n 55 above at 573.
[72] *Freedom of Speech* (Clarendon Press, Oxford, 1985) 152. Barendt's definition was adopted by the High Court of Australia in *Theophanous v The Herald and Weekly Times Limited* (1994) 182 CLR 104.
[73] (1986) 8 EHRR 407.
[74] (1995) 19 EHRR 389.
[75] *Markt Intern Verlag and Beerman v Germany* (1990) 12 EHRR 161; *Casado Coca v Spain* (1994) 18 EHRR 1. *Jacubowski v Germany* (1995) 19 EHRR 64. The boundary between commercial and non-commercial expression was discussed in *Barthold v Germany* (1985) 7 EHRR 383.

restrictions placed upon commercial speech for example, the Court in the *Casado Coca* example deferred to the views of national authorities in setting the boundaries of permissible speech in the advertising of lawyers' professional services. Restrictions placed by national authorities on denigratory comments made by one business about a competitor in order to draw clients away from the latter were deemed in *Jacubowski* to be within the margin of appreciation. Likewise, a broad discretion is accorded to national authorities in cases involving artistic expression. The confiscation of the film *Das Liebeskonzil* by an Austrian court in *Otto-Preminger Institut* was held not to have exceeded the margin of appreciation enjoyed by national authorities to protect the religious beliefs of citizens from insult.[76] One factor which is relevant to the standard of supervision of national authorities' actions is the existence or otherwise of consensus in law and practice among States. Where no such consensus is said to exist, such as on matters relating to the protection of morals,[77] the Court has tended to accord a wider margin of appreciation to national authorities deeming the latter better placed to strike the appropriate balance. Where however the Court finds a fairly substantial measure of common ground across States, the latter will be afforded a lesser margin of appreciation. An example of this stricter level of scrutiny is provided by an analysis of the restriction on freedom of expression in Article 10(2) imposed in order to maintain the authority and impartiality of the judiciary. The *Sunday Times* case makes clear that the common ground in this area allows the Court to treat this category of restriction as an objectively determinable interest.[78] Consequently, States' contempt restrictions will be subject to a more searching review than would occur where the restriction is justified say for the protection of morals.[79] As was seen earlier, differential levels of judicial scrutiny according to speech type are also to be found in the United States. Thus, commercial speech enjoys lesser protection under the First Amendment than political speech,[80] a point noted by Judge Pettiti in *Barthold*.[81]

Hostility to Prior Restraints

Specifically, in the case of prior restraints affecting news coverage, the Court reminded national authorities in *The Observer and the Guardian v UK* that

[76] *Otto-Preminger Institut v Austria* (1995) 19 EHRR 34. See also *Wingrove v UK* (1997) 24 EHRR 1.
[77] Eg *Handyside v UK* (1979–80) 1 EHRR 737.
[78] (1979) 2 EHRR 245, 276.
[79] Reflecting the fact that, in the absence of uniform moral codes, and with diverse cultures across Europe, national authorities are best placed in the first instance to determine what restrictions should be imposed on expression. See also *Wingrove v UK* (1997) 24 EHRR 1.
[80] *Bolger v Youngs Drugs Products Ltd* (1983) 463 US 60. For a comment on the difficulties faced by the US courts in distinguishing between the sub-categories of commercial speech (eg pure advertisements and information about services/products) see E Barendt., *Freedom of Speech* (Clarendon Press, Oxford, 1985) at 54–63.
[81] *Barthold v Germany* (1985) 7 EHRR 383, 408.

these were to be viewed with the most careful scrutiny.[82] Echoing the remarks of Bickel cited earlier, the Court considered news to be a:

> perishable commodity and to delay its publication, even for a short period, may well deprive it of all its value and interest.[83]

a stance which, as was seen above, bears comparison with the special hostility reserved for prior restraints in the US. Indeed, a number of the minority judgements in *The Observer and the Guardian v UK*, which arose from the original interlocutory injunctions in the Spycatcher litigation, made detailed reference to US case law.[84] Judge de Meyer who was joined by Judges Pettiti, Russo, Foighel and Bigi cited Justice Black in *New York Times v US* (the Pentagon Papers case) in support of his conclusion that, other than in war or times of public emergency, there could be no room for prior restraints.[85] A less extreme position was adopted by Judge Morenilla who relied upon authorities such as *Landmark Communications v Virginia*[86], *Nebraska v Stuart*[87] and *US v The Progressive*[88] to assert that very strict conditions must be present for prior restraints to be lawful. In particular, he drew the court's attention to the test laid down by Justice Brennan in *Nebraska* that prior restraints would only be constitutional where publication:

> will surely result in direct, immediate and irreparable damage to our nation or its people.[89]

Proportionality

The notion of proportionality—by which it is sought to strike a fair balance between the demands of the wider community and an individual's fundamental rights—ranks as a general principle in the Convention system.[90] The principal areas of its application occur in respect of Articles 8–11 where derogations from the enumerated freedoms must be 'necessary in a democratic society.' In this type of case, the principle has been interpreted in a strict manner to require national authorities to show firstly that the derogation in question does not represent a disproportionate or excessive means of achieving a legitimate aim,

[82] *Observer and Guardian v UK* at n 67 above.
[83] *Ibid.* See further Cram at n 41 above.
[84] The majority found that the national authorities were entitled to think that the interference complained of in the initial period covered by the Millet injunctions was necessary in a democratic society. All members of the Court agreed however that their continuation after publication of Peter Wright's memoirs in the United States did violate Article 10.
[85] (1992) 14 EHRR 153, 206.
[86] (1978) 425 US 829.
[87] (1976) 427 US 539.
[88] (1979) 486 F Supp 990.
[89] (1976) 427 US 539.
[90] P Van Dijk and G J H Van Hoof, *Theory and Practice of the European Convention on Human Rights* 3rd edn (Kluwer, The Hague, 1998) at 80–81.

then that there is a pressing social need for the restriction in question and finally that the reasons for the measure are both relevant and sufficient. In *Goodwin v UK*, it was held that an order requiring a journalist to disclose the name of his source within a company who had supplied him with sensitive financial information was not sufficient to outweigh the vital public interest in the protection of journalists' sources.[91] Crucial to this finding was the fact that an injunction had already been issued to prevent publication of the confidential financial information in the national media which rendered a disclosure order unnecessary and hence an excessive means of safeguarding the company's rights. The concern to avoid excessive interference with individual rights has, of course, parallels with the doctrine of overbreadth in First Amendment jurisprudence outlined earlier in this chapter.

Outside the context of restrictions in Articles 8–11 which must be shown to be 'necessary in a democratic society', the Court has adopted a more relaxed proportionality test. Thus, in relation to scrutiny of restrictions on property rights under Article 1 of Protocol 1, the Court has required merely that there be a 'reasonable relationship of proportionality between the means employed and the aim sought to be realised'.[92]

The precise level of scrutiny engaged in by the Court when assessing the proportionality of a restriction will also depend upon the margin of appreciation. The latter concept affords to domestic authorities—as those authorities with direct and continuous contact with the competing interests at stake—a variable degree of latitude in assessing the basis of the pressing social need for restriction on the basis that they are best placed to balance conflicting interests. As was seen earlier, where restraints are placed on political speech, the especial status of this form of expression in Article 10 jurisprudence has led Strasbourg to concede a relatively narrow margin of appreciation to domestic authorities.

Certainty

A recurrent theme in rule of law discourse is the need for laws to be accessible and clearly stated. Where laws lack clarity, unpredictability of application ensues with damaging effects for the exercise of individual liberties.[93] The requirement of certainty described earlier in US law has a counterpart in Convetion jurisprudence in respect of the criterion in Articles 5 and 8–11 that any derogation from an enumerated right must be prescribed by 'law'. This has been interpreted as requiring that restrictions are both recognisable as law and of a

[91] (1996) 22 EHRR 123.

[92] See judgment of 23 September 1982, *Sporring and Lonnroth*, A 52 (cited in Van Dijk and Van Hoof where they note that the less strict formulation has also been used in the context of the non-discrimination provisions of Article 14).

[93] Reflecting adherence to the principle '*Nulla poena sine lege*', Article 7 of the Convention prohibits retrospective criminal legislation.

sufficient quality. On the latter point, the Court in *Sunday Times* stated that a norm constituted 'law' only when formulated with sufficient precision for the citizen (appropriately advised if need be) to forsee to a reasonable degree the consequences which certain actions may have and to regulate his conduct accordingly.[94] There is moreover a view in Convention jurisprudence that the Court will take a strict view of the obligation to frame rules precisely where the state seeks to limit particularly vital Convention rights.[95]

IV US REGULATION OF SPEECH IMPACTING UPON JUDICIAL PROCEEDINGS—AN OVERVIEW

Outside of a few brief periods in its history, the jurisprudence of the United States has tended to attach great weight to the notion of a free press.[96] Even during one of the most restricted periods—after the passing of the Sedition Act 1798 which was intended by the Federalist supporters of President Adams to silence domestic opposition—the available evidence indicates that the state presses operated as if the Act was not in force.[97] Madison and Vice President Jefferson were active in arousing opposition to the Act in state legislatures.[98] Once Jefferson was elected President in 1800, he used his executive powers to pardon those convicted of sedition. To gain a proper understanding of the current extent of media freedom to publish on matters pending before the courts, it is important to trace developments in First Amendment jurisprudence from their Blackstonian origins to the emergence of a robust standard of speech protection under the 'preferred freedom' doctrine.

Post-publication Contempt—the Emergence of 'Clear and Present Danger'

Beyond the early Blackstonian consensus around the rejection of prior restraints, opinion in the United States was far from settled as to the appropriate extent of constitutional protection for speech. Some claim that the First Amendment was never intended to confer immunity from punishment for matters already published. Blackstone himself expressly endorsed criminal sanctions upon publications which endangered the fairness and impartiality of trials. Commentators such as Corwin have argued that there was no intention on the part of the framers to revise English common law as set down by

[94] (1979) 2 EHRR 245.

[95] *Open Door Counselling and Dublin Well Woman v Ireland* (1993) 15 EHRR 244.

[96] L Fisher, *Constitutional Rights: Civil Rights and Civil Liberties* (vol 2 *American Constitutional Law*) 2nd edn (McGraw-Hill, New York, 1995) 642.

[97] L Levy, *Emergence of a Free Press* (Oxford University Press, Oxford, 1985).

[98] A Lewis, *Make No Law—The Sullivan Case and the First Amendment* (Random House, New York, 1991) ch 7.

Blackstone.[99] Lewis supports this interpretation, pointing to the degree of reliance placed by state courts on English common law and the *Commentaries*.[100] Others, conversely, argue that circumstances surrounding the ratification of the First Amendment indicate that English common law restraints on the press were expressly rejected. Mr Justice Black in the Supreme Court ruling *Bridges v California* cited Madison on the First Amendment:

> the state of the press . . . under the common law cannot . . . be the standard of its freedom in the United States.[101]

In the absence of contrary indications at the time of the framing and adoption of the First Amendment and noting the fact that memories of what he termed 'oppressive English restrictions' on many of the enumerated liberties were still fresh, Black J claimed that:

> No purpose in ratifying the Bill of Rights was clearer than that of securing for the people of the United States much greater freedom of religion, expression, assembly, and petition than the people of Great Britain had ever enjoyed.[102]

Of course, Black J was the pre-eminent First Amendment absolutist steeped in the writings of Madison and the British dissenters who more than any other Supreme Court judge conferred a broad (and literal) reading to the protection offered by the First Amendment.[103]

Early indications of a robust judicial attitude towards speech emerged in a series of challenges to the constitutionality of states' contempt powers in the 1940s. Thus, in *Nye v United States* the Supreme Court opted for a narrow construction of the power conferred in a federal statute allowing judges to punish conduct (in this case a letter written to a district judge) which obstructed the administration of justice.[104] This test had first been applied to out of court publications concerning matters pending before a judge in *Bridges v California* in 1941 when Bridges, a union leader, had criticised the ruling of a judge in an inter-union dispute and predicted while a motion for a new trial was pending that, unless the original ruling was reversed, a strike affecting Pacific Coast ports would follow.[105] Also cited for contempt was the *Los Angeles Times* which

[99] E S Corwin, *The Constitution and What It Means Today* 14th edn (revised by H W Chase and C R Ducat, 1978), (Princeton University Press, New Jersey) 302.

[100] See Lewis at n 98 at ch 6.

[101] (1941) 314 US 252, 264. The quote is taken from *VI Writings of James Madison 1790–1802*, 387

[102] *Ibid*, at 265. The absence of contrary indications may however be explained by the fact that formal records of Senate debates were not kept at this time. See Lewis at n 95 above at 50.

[103] See his article 'Bill of rights' (1960) 35 *New York University Law Review* 866, 874 in which he states 'The phrase "Congress shall make no law" is composed of plain words easily understood . . . Neither as offered nor as adopted is the language of this Amendment anything less than absolute . . .' See further Lewis, n 98 at 97. Note however his dissent in *Cohen v California* (1971) 403 US 15 where he denied that Cohen's expletive was properly speech at all.

[104] (1941) 313 US 33, overturning *Toledo Newspaper Co v United States* (1918) 247 US 402.

[105] (1941) 314 US 252. Bridges' comments were made in a telegram to the Secretary of State for Labour which later found their way into newspapers in Los Angeles and San Francisco.

had warned of a 'serious mistake' if a judge about to sentence two members of union for assault imposed a lenient punishment. Both parties had been punished for contempt by state courts. Holding that the punishments had violated the appellants' First Amendment rights, Justice Black for the majority noted how the 'clear and present danger of substantive evil' test from *Schenck*[106]—a case concerned with the scope of First Amendment protection for anti-conscription speech in wartime—had in recent times provided a workable standard to determine the constitutionality of restrictions across a number of free speech settings[107] and sought not only to apply it in a novel context but also to invest it with substance by arguing that only where:

> the substantive evil was extremely serious and the degree of imminence extremely high . . .

might speech be punished.

Subsequent indications of a more vigorous approach to speech protection occurred shortly after *Bridges*. In *Pennekamp v Florida*, contempt findings by a Florida state court in respect of editorials and cartoons alleging that judicial rulings were obstructing the effective prosecution of rape and blackmail cases were held unanimously to have violated the petitioners' First Amendment rights even though some of the comments were aimed at pending proceedings.[108] Likewise, in *Craig v Harney*, the contempt conviction of an editor for stating that a trial judge's handling of a civil law matter in front of a jury was a 'travesty of justice' while a motion for a new trial was before the impugned judge was also ruled unconstitutional.[109] Both *Pennekamp* and *Craig v Harney* applied the 'clear and present danger' test to establish that the state courts had violated the respective petitioners' First Amendment rights.

'Clear and Present Danger' as an Emanation of 'Preferred Freedoms'.

Although falling short of the absolute degree of protection for First Amendment freedoms he desired,[110] Justice Black's novel application of *Schenck* to

[106] See also the speeches of Holmes and Brandeis JJ in *Abrams v US* (1919) 250 US 616; *Gitlow v New York* (1925) 268 US 652; *Whitney v California* (1927) 274 US 357 where in the period prior to *Bridges* the two judges urged (unsuccessfully as it turned out) the adoption of this standard on their more conservative colleagues.

[107] These included where the substantive evil to be avoided included the destruction of life or property or the invasion of privacy *Thornhill v Alabama* (1940) 310 US 88, for breach of the peace at common law; *Cantwell v Connecticut* (1940) 310 US 296.

[108] (1946) 328 US 331.

[109] (1947) 331 US 367.

[110] 'Those cases do not purport to mark the furthermost constitutional boundaries of protected expression, nor do we here. They do more than recognise a minimum compulsion of the Bill of Rights.' (1941) 314 US 252, 263. See further his dissent with Douglas J in *Brandenburg v Ohio* (1969) 395 US 444, 450–57. Lewis at n 98 above asserts that Black felt compelled to settle for 'clear and present danger' in *Bridges* in order to carry a bare majority of his colleagues with him.

speech impacting on the administration of justice has been of enduring force.[111] Initially, the doctrine gathered momentum during the ascendancy of the wider 'preferred freedoms' approach to governmental conduct. Associated with Justices Cardozo and Stone,[112] under this approach interference with core freedoms such as those contained in the First Amendment is presumed to be unconstitutional either because the statute authorising the conduct itself was deemed unconstitutional or because the particular application of a broadly drafted statute was unconstitutional. Corwin reports that between the period 1937–1948, a majority of the Court applied this method in 14 cases.[113] The demise of the 'preferred freedoms' approach and its supplanting by the 'balancing' approach occurred as the personnel of the Court changed and as a further set of subversive advocacy cases reached the Court.[114] As implied in its title, 'balancing' requires the Court to weigh the individual and social interest in freedom of expression and the social interest which the regulation of speech seeks to advance. It is exemplified in judgments throughout the 1950s by Chief Justice Vinson and Justices Frankfurter and Harlan.[115] Unlike 'preferred freedoms', the 'balancing approach' did not presume constitutional invalidity but was characterised by a more deferential stance towards legislative enactments with the result that restrictions on speech might more easily pass constitutional muster:

> [It] is not for us to decide how we would adjust the clash of interests which this case presents were the primary responsibility for reconciling it ours. Congress has determined that the danger created by the advocacy of overthrow justifies the ensuing restriction on freedom of speech. The determination was made after due deliberation, and the seriousness of the congressional purpose is attested by the volume of legislation passed to effectuate the same ends.[116]

Since this time, neither 'balancing' nor 'preferred freedoms' has 'completely won out.'[117] What is significant for present purposes however is that 'clear and present danger'—an emanation of the preferred freedoms approach—has

[111] The variable standard of consitutional review of speech restrictions depending on speech type has been discussed in numerous places. For analyses, see W Brennan, 'The Supreme Court and the Meiklejohn Interpretation of the First Amendment' (1965) 79 *Harvard Law Review* 1; and TI Emerson, *The System of Free Expression* (Random House, New York, 1970). For a vigorous defence of the constitutionality of states' powers to punish for contempt see the dissents by Frankfurter J in *Bridges* (supra) and *Craig v Harney* (supra).

[112] *Palko v Connecticut* (1937) 302 US 319, 326–27 (Cardozo); *US v Carolene Products Co.* (1937) 304 US 144, 152(fn) (Stone). See further HJ Abraham and B Perry, *Freedom and the Court* (Oxford University Press, Oxford, 1998) ch 2.

[113] Eg *Thomas v Collins* (1945) 323 US 516; *Saia v New York* (1948) 334 US 558. See also Corwin at n 99 above at 306.

[114] See the Smith Act prosecutions in cases such as *Dennis v US* (1951) 341 US 494.

[115] *American Communications Association v Douds* (1950) 339 US 382 (Vinson); *Dennis ibid* (1951) (Frankfurter); and *NAACP v Alabama* (1958) 357 US 449 (Harlan). For a critique of the test see TI Emerson, 'Towards a General Theory of the First Amendment' (1963) 72 *Yale Law Journal* 877.

[116] Justice Frankfurter in *Dennis v US* (1951) 341 US 494, 550–551.

[117] See for example Corwin at n 99 above at 308.

remained relatively unchallenged as the standard by which the constitutionality of speech deemed to obstruct the administration of justice is adjudged. Despite the fact that the rulings in *Bridges*, *Pennekamp* and *Craig v Harney* relate entirely either to criticisms of judges or attempts to put pressure on judges to rule a particular way in a pending case,[118] the broader application of the 'clear and present danger' test to publicity concerning matters pending before juries in criminal cases does not appear to have been successfully questioned. On the rare occasions when states have brought contempt proceedings against allegedly prejudicial media speech, any convictions secured in the lower courts have not been sustained on appeal.[119] Chesterman has written of:

> *[t]he constitutional principle* that the media may not be punished for publishing material on the ground that it might prejudice a criminal jury trial in the absence of 'clear and present danger' (very narrowly defined) to the administration of justice. . .[120] (emphasis added)

The second edition of the American Bar Association's manual for journalists *The Reporter's Key* published in 1999 appears to go further by denying the existence of any circumstances in which prejudicial reporting could be met with a contempt finding:

> Question: Do reporters get in trouble if news stories cause the court to change the place of the trial or delay the trial because of adverse pretrial publicity?
> Answer: No legal penalty or obligation may be imposed on reporters to avoid publicity about a case. No legal penalty may be imposed for even the most intense, exaggerated, biased or 'hyped' coverage of any criminal case (except the remedies provided by successful libel suits).[121]

Of course, the paramountcy accorded to First Amendment freedoms has major implications for participants in the criminal justice system. The right of defendants under the Sixth Amendment to a fair and impartial trial need to be considered here alongside the interests of witnesses, victims and the state.

The Sixth Amendment—a Lower Order Constitutional Value?

> In all criminal prosecutions, the accused shall enjoy the right to a speedy and public trial, by an impartial jury of the State . . .

[118] See also *Wood v Georgia* (1962) 370 US 375.

[119] In *Maryland v Baltimore Radio Show Inc.* (1950) 338 US 912 the Supreme Court refused to grant *certiorari* in respect of an appellate court's quashing of a conviction for contempt in the trial court. Reversal of a contempt conviction at appellate level occurred in *Worcester Telegram & Gazette Inc v Commonwealth* (1968) 238 NE 2d 861.

[120] 'OJ and the Dingo: How Media Publicity Relating to Criminal Cases Tried by Jury is Dealt With in Australia and America' (1997) 45 *Am Jo Comp Law* 109, 126. For support, see Rehnquist CJ in *Gentile v State Bar of Nevada* (1991) 501 US 1030.

[121] American Bar Association, *The Reporter's Key—Access to the Judicial Process* ABA Standard 8–3.3—available electronically at http://www.abanet.org/media/nclm991c833.html

The width afforded to media comment about pending litigation under the prevailing 'clear and present danger' test has meant that the Sixth Amendment guarantees of fair trial and jury impartiality require to be safeguarded using means which do not entail curbs on speech generally and media freedom in particular.[122] One exception to this general rule examined below are the sets of restraints imposed on members of the legal profession and court officials in codes of professional conduct which regulate the making of statements which might have a prejudicial impact on pending cases. As Chesterman notes, the emphasis in the main however is upon 'remedial techniques' whereby the criminal process and its participants are required to endure prejudicial publicity and seek to minimise any resultant adverse impact on proceedings. On occasions, the failure of the trial court once proceedings have commenced to place limits on media coverage of particular proceedings has been criticised. The Supreme Court in *Sheppard v Maxwell* famously excoriated the trial judge for allowing Dr Sheppard's trial for the murder of his pregnant wife to take place in a 'carnival atmosphere.'[123] Measures typically employed to remedy adverse pre-trial publicity range from—at the lower end of the scale of seriousness—questioning of jury members (more or less detailed according to the degree of previous media comment),[124] issuing clear judicial directions to disregard published comment through to more drastic remedial techniques such as delaying and/or altering the venue of the trial or ordering the sequestration of jury members,[125] discharging an empanelled jury and culminating in the quashing of a conviction on appeal as occurred in *Estes v Texas*,[126] *Irwin v Dowd*[127] and *Sheppard v Maxwell*[128] The possibility exists in extreme cases that a re-trial or permanent stay of proceedings may be ordered.[129]

Not surprisingly, principles governing the use of the various remedial techniques have evolved. Thus, for example, less drastic measures must be considered and found wanting before resort to more far-reaching solutions is considered proper. In addition, the use of remedial devices in particular proceedings has come under close scrutiny forcing the Supreme Court to take a general stance on the reviewability of trial judges' decisions. Consider for instance the form of the *voir dire* sanctioned by the trial court in *Mu'Min v Virginia*[130] where the defence

[122] For a critical account of diminished Sixth Amendment protection see S Krause, 'Punishing the Press: Using Contempt of Court to Secure the Right to a Fair Trial' (1996) *Boston University Law Review* 537.

[123] (1966) 384 US 333, 358.

[124] For detailed consideration of the *voir dire* examination under Federal Rules of Criminal Procedure see RP Eclavea, 'Voir Dire Examination of Prospective Jurors under Rule 24(a) of Federal Rules of Criminal Procedure' (1976) 28 ALR Fed 26; G Knapp, 'Scope of Voir Dire Examination' (1990) 114 L Ed 2d 763.

[125] This was used in the OJ Simpson case.

[126] (1961) 366 US 717.

[127] (1965) 381 US 532.

[128] (1966) 384 US 333.

[129] As in *Sheppard v Maxwell ibid.*

[130] (1990) 500 US 415.

were not allowed to have prospective jurors questioned about the content of specific news items published in the pre-trial period. A majority in the Supreme Court refused to intervene with the trial court's ruling, holding that the defendant's right to a fair trial had not been violated and confirming previous Supreme Court decisions which had conferred a wide degree of discretion on trial courts to determine what questions may be asked in the *voir dire*.[131]

Of course, even assuming that resort to these remedial measures succeeds in curing prejudicial media coverage,[132] questions legitimately arise about the economic costs entailed in the various cures and, perhaps more importantly, the adverse impact on those caught up in the criminal process, whether as defendants spending more time in custody, or as witnesses and victims enduring their own distinct burdens as justice is delayed. The State as prosecutor also clearly suffers an injury to its interest in effectively prosecuting crime when proceedings are stayed whilst the whole community in addition suffers when guilty persons cannot be successfully prosecuted. These costs have naturally led some to question the wisdom of permitting media comment such latitude.[133] However, none of these critics have claimed that a significant proportion of criminal trials are irremediably tainted by publicity. Cases such as *Sheppard* do not, it seems, occur regularly.[134] Indeed, when set alongside evidence of more generic jury prejudice resulting from racial, class and gender stereotyping, pre-trial publicity would appear to pose a relatively minor threat to the fair administration of justice.[135]

One consequence of the scope of First Amendment protection for prejudicial media comment has been that defence lawyers stung by publicity adverse to their clients have on occasion made extra-judicial comments in an attempt to redress the balance of reporting. The disciplining of lawyers' speech in such circumstances under professional conduct rules has been challenged as violating attorneys' First Amendment freedoms. In *Gentile v State Bar of Nevada* a majority of the Supreme Court led by Rehnquist CJ held that the speech of lawyers representing clients in pending cases could be regulated in accordance with the First Amendment under a less demanding standard (substantial likelihood of material prejudice) than the 'clear and present' danger test applied to

131 *Rosales-Lopez v United States* (1981) 451 US 182; *Aldridge v United States* (1931) 283 US 308.

132 The empirical evidence produced by psychologists is considered in more detail in ch 3. For statements of judicial confidence in the ability of jurors to disregard prejudicial material see in the US, *inter alia*, Kennedy J in *Gentile v State Bar of Nevada* (1991) 501 US 1030, 1054–1055; and in the United Kingdom Taylor LCJ in *Ex parte Telegraph* [1993] 1 WLR 980, 987; Denning MR in *R v Horsham JJ ex parte Farquharson* [1982] 1 QB 762, 794–795; Lawton LJ *R v Kray* (1969) 53 Cr App R 412, 415–416.

133 Chesterman at n 120 above and Krause, at n 122 above.

134 See Kennedy J in *Gentile v State Bar of Nevada* (1991) 501 US 1030, 1054.

135 For evidence of racial bias in jury determinations see J Baldwin and M McConville, *Jury Trials* (Clarendon Press, Oxford, 1979); J Levine, M Musheno and D Palumbo, *Criminal Justice in America* (John Wiley & Sons, New York, 1986) at 413 *et seq* for evidence of race and gender influences.

the media.[136] The basis of the majority's preference lay in a distinction which was drawn between participants in court proceedings and strangers to courtroom litigation. The former could be made subject to greater speech restrictions because of the state's legitimate and substantial interest in preventing officers of the court from imposing serious costs on the judicial system and on litigants which would follow if, in the absence of such a prohibition, remedial measures were needed to cure prejudice arising from lawyers' comments.

V THE REGULATION OF COURT-RELATED SPEECH UNDER ARTICLES 6 AND 10 OF THE EUROPEAN CONVENTION ON HUMAN RIGHTS—AN OVERVIEW

The extent of the freedom to engage in court-related expression under the Convention can only be understood in the context of the limiting provisions in Article 6 and 10(2).

Article 6(1) states:

> In the determination of his civil rights and obligations or of any criminal charge against him, everyone is entitled to a fair and public hearing within a reasonable time by an independent and impartial tribunal established by law . . .

Convention jurisprudence regarding the importance of the unqualified right to a fair trial in Article 6(1) is unequivocal. It ranks among the most fundamental guarantees for the individual in democratic society. The Strasbourg Court has stated that the right to a fair trial 'holds so prominent a place in a democratic society that there can be no justification for interpreting Article 6(1) of the Convention restrictively.'[137] Harris, O'Boyle and Warbrick have stated that Article 6 enjoys a pre-eminent position in the Convention.[138] The requirement to be 'impartial' includes the fact that the court must not allow itself to be influenced by information/material outside the courtroom, especially where there is a marked political background to legal proceedings.[139] The Commission has also recognised that the threat posed by external publication will be greater in cases where lay jurors determine issues of guilt and innocence.[140]

The safeguarding of the trial process from extraneous influences also features as a legitimate purpose of derogation in respect of freedom of expression under Article 10(2). The freedom conferred in Article 10(1) may be lost where it is necessary to protect countervailing societal interests including that of maintaining

[136] (1991) 501 US 1030. In 1991 the vast majority of states adopted the 'substantial likelihood of material prejudice' test in their Rules of Professional Conduct. Only one state, Virginia, had explicitly adopted a standard of 'clear and present danger'.
[137] *Moreira de Azevedo v Portugal* (1990) 13 EHRR 721, 737.
[138] *Law of the European Convention on Human Rights* (Butterworths, London, 1995) at 164.
[139] See for example *Crociani et al v Italy Appls* 8603, 8723, 8729/79 D and R 22 (1981) 147.
[140] *X v Austria*, Coll. 11 (1963) 31, 43; *X v Norway* Yearbook XIII (1970) 302, 324.

the authority and impartiality of the judiciary. 'Authority' has been taken to refer to the general acceptance of the court system as the proper forum for dispute settlement.[141] 'Impartiality' in this context relates to the confidence which the courts inspire in accused persons and the wider public.[142] In cases brought by journalists and publishers to test the legality of contempt convictions, the breadth of the notion of 'impartiality' has obviated the need for States to mount an alternative defence of the conviction under the 'rights of others' exception which would encapsulate the right to a fair trial enshrined in Article 6(1) of the Convention. The Commission has gone so far as to indicate that limitations imposed upon expression aimed at preventing trial by media are a legitimate means of bolstering confidence in the courts.[143] Although it would also be possible for a convicted person to argue that domestic proceedings were tainted by prejudicial media comment with the consequence that the right to a fair trial was breached, no criminal case has been admitted on the merits on this basis and some commentators read into this fact the suggestion that some media comment on matters of public interest must be expected.[144] The idea of some leeway for media comment particularly in cases where any criminal trial remains some months away was endorsed by the Court in *Wloch v Poland*.[145] Here the applicant complained that, immediately after his arrest in September 1994, numerous newspaper articles were published in which, inter alia, spokepersons for the prosecuting authorities had told the media that the applicant was guilty of trading in children for adoption. These articles, the applicant argued, prevented him from receiving a fair trial and enjoying the presumption of innocence. The Court rejected this claim, stating that there was no evidence that the presumption of innocence to which the applicant was entitled under Article 6(2) had been violated. As of March 2000, the prosecution had yet to lodge a bill of indictment with the court authorities, and, consequently, the panel of judges which would preside over any future trial had not been determined. This aspect of the application was dismissed as manifestly ill-founded.

In the case of matters already before the courts, the *Sunday Times* case had, it will be recalled, positively encouraged media comment on matters before the courts in the following terms:

> whilst the mass media must not overstep the bounds imposed in the interests of the proper administration of justice, it is incumbent upon them to impart information and ideas concerning matters that come before the courts just as in other areas of public interest.[146]

141 *Chorherr v Austria* (1994) 17 EHRR 358; *News Verlags GmbH v Austria* (2001) 31 EHRR 8.
142 *Fey v Austria* (1994) 16 EHRR 387; *Worm v Austria* (1998) 25 EHRR 454, 473.
143 *Crociani et al v Italy Appls* at n 139 above.
144 DJ Harris, K O'Boyle, and C Warbrick, *The Law of the European Convention* (Butterworths, London, 1995) at 216 where they also state that if a national appeal court does not consider that a trial has been unfair, the Commission is unlikely to do so either.
145 European Court of Human Rights (March 2000) Information Note No 16.
146 (1979–80) 2 EHRR 245, 280.

Such views are of course consonant with the requirement in Article 6(1) that hearings be held in public. In *News Verlags GmbH v Austria* the Court clarified the outer limits of the media's duty in this regard by stating that it did not permit the publication of statements which were likely (whether intentionally or not) to prejudice the chances of a fair trial or public confidence in the courts.[147] On the facts in *News Verlags GmbH* however, the Vienna Court of Appeal's blanket order made under copyright law prohibiting the publication of photographs of a suspect accused of sending letter bombs to politicians and other public figures in connection with reports on the criminal proceedings against him was considered to be a disproportionate means of protecting the presumption of innocence. The Strasbourg Court clearly preferred the less stringent order imposed in the lower court which had prevented the publication of the suspect's photograph only if the suspect was referred to in the accompanying text as the perpetrator of the offences. In this way, the legitimate public interest in learning about the suspected activities of political extremists already in the public eye because of their political views is safeguarded.[148]

VI A MORAL READING OF ARTICLE 10

What Does a Moral Reading Entail?

Ronald Dworkin's moral reading of constitutions provides an interpretative tool for understanding abstractly stated constitutional propositions such as 'the right to free speech' or 'freedom of expression.' Central to any search for the moral reading of such clauses are first the intentions of the drafters *as expressed in the language they chose* and, second, the requirement of constitutional integrity. In the case of the drafters' intentions in respect of the First Amendment, what is stressed is the abstract nature of the language chosen. Unlike the Third Amendment with its very concrete prohibition ('No Soldier shall, in time of peace, be quartered in any house, without the consent of the Owner, nor in time of war, but in a manner prescribed by law.') the drafters of the First Amendment have opted for the broad *concept* of free speech, in preference to particular *conceptions* of that freedom.[149] According to Dworkin, this preference places responsibility for developing particular applications of the concept on successive generations of judges. It also lessens the importance of the precise situations the drafters had in mind at the time or those situations which they would have deemed to violate the Amendment had their attention been drawn to them. Instead, as each new free speech dispute comes before the courts for

147 (2001) 31 EHRR 8.
148 *Ibid* at 259–60.
149 *Taking Rights Seriously* n 3 above at 134–136.

resolution, the judges must apply their minds afresh to the question of how the concept of free speech is to be applied. The scope of the right is given a dynamic quality because it is not fixed by reference to conceptions which prevailed at the time of their formulation. Where, conversely, constitutional protections take the form of particular conceptions of free speech, the rights in question have a specific and fixed quality which do not require re-interpretation. The difference in approach is neatly illustrated by Dworkin in *Taking Rights Seriously* in respect of the concept of fairness when he states:

> When I appeal to fairness I pose a moral issue; when I lay down my conception of fairness I try to answer it.[150]

Perhaps somewhat surprisingly, Dworkin's dynamic vision of the judicial role finds support in the extra-judicial writing of William Rehnquist, then Justice of the Supreme Court:

> The framers of the Constitution wisely spoke in general language and left to succeeding generations the task of applying that language to the unceasingly changing environment in which they would live.[151]

At this point, a second feature of the moral reading comes into play. The requirement of constitutional integrity prevents judges from giving effect to their own convictions when construing the Constitution but rather charges them with elaborating and developing a moral stance which is coherent with what has gone before and will produce a 'best fit' solution. Dworkin puts it thus,

> [J]udges are like authors jointly creating a chain novel in which each writes a chapter that makes sense as part of the story as a whole.. the moral reading asks them to find the best conception of the constitutional moral principles . . . that fits the broad story of America's historical record.[152]

This dynamic aspect of the judicial role accords with Convention jurisprudence too. Van Dijk and Van Hoof put it thus:

> The standards of the Convention are not regarded as static, but as reflective of social changes. This evolutive approach towards interpretation of the Convention implies that the Commission and the Court take into account contemporary realities and attitudes, not the situation prevailing at the time of drafting of the Convention in 1949–50.[153]

The moral reading may not however generate universally accepted solutions to particular problems. Dworkin has been at pains to acknowledge that intelligent

[150] *Ibid* at 135.
[151] 'The Notion of a Living Constitution' (1976) 54 *Texas Law Review* 693, 694.
[152] *Freedom's Law* n 2 above at 10–11.
[153] P Van Dijk and GJ HVan Hoof, *Theory and Practice of the European Convention on Human Rights* 3rd edn (Kluwer, The Hague, 1998) at 77–78. See also P Mahoney, 'Judicial Activism and Judicial Self-Restraint in the European Court of Human Rights: Two Sides of the Same Coin' (1990) 11 *Human Rights Law Journal* 57.

persons may disagree over rival conceptions of a constitutional principle whereby each conception may be shown to 'fit' with aspects of the language, practice and precedent of the constitution. In these circumstances, all that judges can do is decide for themselves which conception does 'most credit to the nation.'[154] In the following section the question of what conception of the free speech/fair trial conflict best fits with a moral reading of Article 10 of the Convention is now addressed.

An Interpretative Scheme for Article 10 and Court-Related Expression

As was noted earlier, a textual analysis of the right to freedom of expression under the Convention reveals it to be both more inclusive and more heavily qualified than its US equivalent. The language of the drafters of the Convention requires the Court to balance the right to freedom of expression against competing individual and societal interests in a manner that is plainly distinct from the absolutist language of the First Amendment. In addition, it is clear that Convention jurisprudence does not prioritise expression interests above guarantees relating to fair trials as occurs in the United States. Nothwithstanding these differences, the first part of this article highlighted some general points of common ground between the narratives on freedom of expression found on both sides of the Atlantic concerning rationales for speech/expression, the preeminence of political speech, the hostility towards prior restraints and resort to doctrines of proportionality/overbreadth to control excessive interference with expression. This degree of commonality in turn lends support to the conclusion that freedom of expression under the Convention also enjoys a special status. Turning to the discrete issue of court-related expression, it can also be seen that the true reading of the language, practice and precedent of the Article 10 freedom *in this context* is one which requires national authorities to tolerate a fairly broad spectrum of media reporting and comment and which, accordingly, entails that national restrictions on such expression be subject to a particularly intense level of scrutiny. This proposition would appear to follow from a number of established features of Convention reasoning. First, court-related expression will frequently (though clearly not always) fall within Barendt's definition of political speech entitling it to an enhanced level of protection from interference by national authorities. Second, where a restriction is grounded on the legitimate need under Article 10(2) to maintain the authority and impartiality of the judiciary, *Sunday Times* makes clear that the Court will treat this as an objectively determinable interest.[155] Consequently, states' contempt restrictions will be subject to a more searching review than would occur where the restric-

[154] *Freedom's Law* at n 2 above.
[155] (1979) 2 EHRR 245, 276.

tion is justified say for the protection of morals as in *Handyside*[156] or national security as in *Leander v Sweden*.[157]

The requirement on national authorities to satisfy the Court of both the existence of a pressing social need and the selection of a proportionate means of defending that interest would seem natural points of focus within which the Court could conduct intense scrutiny of the impugned decision. In these terms, the ruling of the majority of the Court in *Worm v Austria* constitutes a poorly constructed next chapter in the narrative of Article 10 jurisprudence. A more intense level of scrutiny of Austrian law (and therefore a 'better fit' reading) is apparent in the minority judgment which manages more successfully to reconcile fair trial and media freedom interests.

Worm v Austria—The Unconvincing Triumph of Administration of Justice Interests

At the Vienna Court of Appeal, Worm, a journalist was convicted under section 23 of the Austrian Media Act for having exercised a prohibited influence on criminal proceedings. His offence consisted in having written a two page article in *Profil*—a political periodical—about the criminal trial of Hannes Androsch a former Minister of Finance on tax evasion charges. Worm had been investigating Androsch's activities for several years by the time of the latter's trial and was well known on this account. He had clearly formed an unfavourable impression of his subject—a fact evidenced by a number of highly opinionated statements made in the July 1991 issue of *Profil* as the Androsch trial was on-going. Androsch was said to be someone who took 'refuge in lapses of memory' and attempted to 'shift the blame onto others.' More specifically, the article asserted that it had been known since 1980 that Androsch had been evading taxes and that the investigative judge had proved long ago that Androsch was lying on this point. The fact that Androsch had a previous conviction for perjury was also mentioned, although this merely reported what the public prosecutor had said in open court. Androsch's trial was heard by two professional and two lay judges and in October 1991 he was convicted of having evaded taxes between 1973–1981.

Worm was later charged under section 23 of the Media Act. This states:

> Anyone who discusses, subsequent to the indictment . . . and before the judgment at first instance in criminal proceedings the probable outcome of those proceedings or the value of evidence in a way capable of influencing the outcome of proceedings shall be punished . . .

[156] (1979–80) 1 EHRR 737. Illustrating the point that national authorities are best placed in the first instance to determine what restrictions should be imposed on expression. See n 79 above.
[157] (1987) 9 EHRR 59.

The Vienna Court of Appeal took the view that, in respect of the lay judges at least, the article was capable of influencing proceedings and had been written with a view to so doing. It was no defence to argue that no prejudice to Androsch's trial had in fact occurred.[158] Worm was convicted and sentenced to pay a fine of 48,000 Austrian schillings[159] or face 20 days imprisonment in default of payment.

Both the Commission and the Court accepted that Worm's freedom of expression had been restricted by the conviction and that this restriction was prescribed by law for the legitimate purpose of maintaining the authority and impartiality of the judiciary. The decisive inquiry concerned the 'necessity of the restriction in a democratic society.' A majority of 7–2 in the Court held that the interference sanctioned under section 23 was necessary and that the conviction did not violate Article 10. Much hinged upon whether the Austrian Government could show that its reasons for restricting expression were 'relevant' and 'sufficient'. The Vienna Court of Appeal's finding that Worm's article was objectively capable of influencing Androsch's trial and its inference that Worm intended to influence proceedings was accepted by the majority as establishing the relevance of the interference. As to the sufficiency of the reasons behind restriction, the majority pointed to the different methods employed across Europe to protect the administration of justice, something which indicated that member states remained free to choose which measures they felt appropriate. Moreover, Austrian law did not seek to restrict Worm's freedom to inform the public about the Androsch trial 'in an objective manner'.[160] What was prohibited were publications like the present one which sought to convince its readers of the ex-minister's guilt. It was for the Vienna Court of Appeal to assess the likelihood that the article would be read by the lay judges hearing the Androsch case and to ascertain what Worm's intent was in writing it. The fact that domestic law did not require any actual prejudice to be established in the Androsch trial was not significant since, apart from these particular proceedings, section 23 also protected the long-term interests of the administration of justice by bolstering the notion that the courts be accepted as the proper forum for determining the guilt/innocence of accused persons. To allow 'pseudo trials' in the news media 'might in the long run have nefarious consequences' for public confidence in the criminal justice system.

Thus stated, the latitude conferred upon the Austrian authorities seems to run counter to a number of established themes in Article 10 jurisprudence and as such offers a flawed conception of the 'best fit.' Commentary on the Androsch case was without doubt political expression. Consequently, any restriction on that speech should normally have been made subject to a relatively strict level of

[158] Worm had been acquitted at first instance by the Vienna Regional Criminal Court.
[159] About £2,400 sterling.
[160] (1998) 25 EHRR 454, 477.

scrutiny by the Court. Here, after all, was a public figure and former Minister accused by the state of certain serious crimes including misleading an agency of the state. Moreover, where the state relies upon the 'authority and impartiality of the judiciary' category of permitted derogation, the extent of the interference required to protect this interest is treated as 'objectively determinable.' Even though differences across Europe exist as to how to protect the authority and impartiality of the judiciary, the Court's supervisory role in respect of this important freedom according to *Sunday Times*, is not thereby limited to ascertaining whether the respondent state exercised its discretion reasonably, carefully and in good faith. Instead, a sincere commitment to the crucial function played by political expression (especially expression which the state disapproves of) would seem to require states to show a sufficiently serious threat either to particular proceedings or the administration of justice generally before a proportionate curtailment of expression under this enumerated category was justified. This might call for evidence relating to the actual impact of the publication complained of (ie how much prejudice did it seem likely to cause at the time of publication?),[161] and further, consideration of alternatives short of proceedings for contempt (such as the issuing of clear directions to ignore prejudicial material, the empanelling of other lay judges, delaying the trial etc) to insulate the trial process where particular proceedings appeared threatened. In these regards, much could be learnt from the pro-active approach of the US courts. By contrast, section 23 of Austria's Media Act which employs a non-assessed 'potential impact' standard allows conviction in the case of a publication which in reality causes only a slight risk of minor prejudice. This constitutes an over-broad restriction on freedom of expression, one which the dissenting judges (Casadevall and Jungwierts JJ) rightly condemned as not corresponding to a pressing social need. As to any long term adverse effect upon public confidence in the Austrian Courts, the majority's failure to assess first the precise impact of Worm's article and thereafter the reasonableness of the relationship between his conviction and the objective behind it merely confirmed a more general absence of critical scrutiny on the part of the majority.[162]

Stricter Scrutiny—An Objection

The argument made in this chapter for Strasbourg to adopt a quasi-US style strict standard of supervision of national authorities' restrictions on court-related speech may be objected to on the ground that it fails to take account of one

[161] See by contrast the Contempt of Court Act 1981, s 2(2) and the pro-media freedom interpretations thereof in *AG v ITN* [1995] 1 Cr App R 204; *AG v MGN Ltd* [1997] 1 All ER 456 discussed further in ch 3.

[162] The minority concluded that this justification was ex post facto. Certainly it does not appear to have been relied upon by the Austrian Court of Appeal.

crucial difference in the respective roles of the Supreme Court and the European Court of Human Rights. According to this view, the latter is not in the position of a national supreme court with prime responsibility for protecting the rights of citizens against unconstitutional conduct but is rather a supra-national body operating under an international agreement which, under Article 1, entrusts Contracting States in the first place with the task of securing the rights and liberties conferred upon individuals. The Strasbourg Court is charged with supervising Contracting States' compliance with this task and only becomes involved upon the exhaustion of domestic remedies. Moreover, in cases involving trade-offs between competing interests, the Strasbourg Court has said that the Contracting States may be best placed to determine where the correct balance lies. There are several points that may be made in reply. First, as Gearty noted in 1993 as the volume of case-law to come out of Strasbourg over the years has grown, so the jurisdiction of the European Court has come to approximate to that of a national supreme court as a final arbiter of the rights and freedoms of individuals.[163] Secondly, whilst national authorities are indeed charged with the initial responsibility to secure the rights guaranteed under the Convention, it is also clear that the precise nature of the supervisory role undertaken by the European Court varies depending upon the nature of the right involved, and the purpose of the restriction on the exercise of that right. In respect of court-related speech, a higher level of scrutiny might be expected where national restrictions curtail the fundamental (not culture-specific) interest comprised in freedom of expression and debate about matters of genuine public concern. It will also be recalled that where the purpose of a restriction is the maintenance of the authority and impartiality of the judiciary, this is treated as an objectively determinable interest with a correspondingly diminished margin of appreciation afforded to national authorities. At bottom, strict scrutiny of restrictions on court-related speech may be justified because of the strong individual and public interests in unfettered reporting and comment.

VII CONCLUSION

> Democratic society does not stand still, and neither does the way in which democratic society upholds its cherished fundamental values. The drafters must be deemed to have realised this when they made democratic society one of the governing elements of the Convention.[164]

At some level, the majority's ruling in *Worm* may be likened to the 'balancing approach' in state versus individual liberty disputes which prevailed in the US

[163] C Gearty, 'The European Court of Human Rights and the Protection of Civil Liberties: An Overview" (1993) 52 CLJ 89, 93.
[164] Mahoney n 153 above.

Supreme Court in the 1950s. Both are characterised by a deferential stance towards legislative/judicial restriction of speech at state/domestic state level which effectively allows the outer limits of freedom of speech/expression to be laid down by a state/national body in accordance with its calculations (or more accurately, untested assumptions) regarding the prejudicial impact of publicity. The latitude so conferred sits uneasily alongside the Court's general commitment to an intense level of scrutiny required where a restriction on political expression is deemed necessary to maintain the authority and impartiality of the judiciary and which was shown to display similarities with US jurisprudence. A re-assessment of the treatment in *Worm* of court-related expression is now called for. Whilst the variety of regulatory stances encountered across Europe make it unlikely that post publication sanctions per se would be deemed to violate the guarantee of freedom of expression (as is the case under the First Amendment), a genuine commitment to this core freedom would seem to demand a more searching level of inquiry of national authorities' attempts to criminalise aspects of media reporting than was evident in *Worm*. Therein lies a route towards a plausible 'best fit' next chapter of Article 10 jurisprudence.

3

Speech and Criminal Jury Trials

I INTRODUCTION—TWO MODELS OF COURT-RELATED SPEECH REGULATION

THIS CHAPTER LOOKS at how speech which relates to matters before, or shortly to be put before, criminal juries in a number of jurisdictions (England & Wales, Scotland, United States, Canada and Australia) is constrained by the *sub judice* rule. In making sense of the regulatory stances of the various legal systems visited in this chapter, two ideal types or models may be set down.[1] The value of these models lies not in the fact that they correspond exactly to a pre-existing legal system but rather that they represent exaggerated versions of reality which allow both comparison to be made with actual legal systems and yield up insights about the real world.[2] The various legal systems considered in this chapter will be seen to lie at various points across a spectrum between the two models, sharing some or more features with either model.

The first model—the scrutiny of government model—proceeds from the assumption that the courts, the police and prosecutorial agencies ought, in a democratic society, to be subject to the widest possible levels of open discussion and comment. Public access to, and comment concerning, court proceedings and pre trial processes are required to facilitate informed discussion about the performance of criminal justice agencies and the courts. Restrictions contained in the *sub judice* rule and prior restraints inhibit discussion of these matters and contribute to a deficit of wider understanding. This deficit is undesirable not simply because it impedes informed democratic control, but also on account of its tendency to diminish public confidence in the administration of justice. In this model, media threats to the administration of justice are treated with scepticism. Instead, the virtues of judges and jurors as independent, robust individuals capable of laying to one side any previously held impressions about trial participants are emphasised. Where any prejudice is considered to have been caused to pending proceedings, the scrutiny of government model seeks not to punish the party causing prejudice but rather to employ remedial techniques

[1] The term is used in the Weberian sense to indicate an abstract or pure construct formed from real phenomena. See M Weber, *Methodology of the Social Sciences* Reprinted in Farganis J *Readings in Social Theory* 2nd edn (McGraw-Hill, New York, 1993) ch 5, pp 120–32.

[2] This understanding of ideal types is found in R Keat and J Urry, *Social Theory as Science* 2nd edn (Routledge & Kegan Paul, London, 1982) at 112.

(including re-trials and permanent stays on proceedings in extreme cases) to diminish the effect of adverse publicity.

By contrast, the second model—which I have called the administration of justice model—is characterised by an absence of principled commitment to free speech and/or the values served by the open administration of justice. Indeed, it is denied that *sub judice* restrictions throw up any constitutional issues whatsoever. Here, individual and societal interests in unimpeded, unprejudiced trials are paramount. Media threats to the fairness of proceedings are taken extremely seriously. Judges, jurors and witnesses are all considered vulnerable to varying degrees to being influenced by external comment/information not laid before the court in evidence. Accordingly, penal laws are promulgated restricting the publication of material which speculatively is thought to pose a risk to the fairness of proceedings. A low threshold of liability is set in which the prosecution need not show an intent to cause prejudice to proceedings. Little or no concession is made to the countervailing public interest in the contemporaneous discussion of matters raised in the trial. Moreover, injunctive relief to prevent threatened breaches of the *sub judice* rule is readily granted.

II THE JURY IN ANGLO-AMERICAN LEGAL SYSTEMS

The systematic introduction of juries in twelfth century England is usually credited to Henry II. The 'presenting jury' recognised in the Assize of Clarendon 1166 (and from which the trial jury would later evolve) consisted of persons with knowledge of persons and events concerned in the proceedings.[3] According to Cornish, the jury spread quickly from England to Scotland, albeit in an altered guise.[4] Centuries later, colonisation by the British saw the establishment of the jury system as an 'essential part of common law procedure'[5] in a number of its overseas possessions, including what are now the United States, Canada and Australia.[6] Although representing a small proportion of all criminal trials, the continuing vitality of lay jury trial as fact-finder in more serious criminal offences is reflected in constitutional guarantees and other legal provisions.[7] Thus, the Sixth Amendment of the United States Constitution guarantees right to a jury trial, although does not differentiate between types of criminal proceedings to which the guarantee applies.[8] It has fallen to the Supreme Court to

[3] The 'presenting jury' thus began to replace trial by ordeal. See further RC Van Caenegem, *The Birth of the English Common Law* 2nd edn (Cambridge University Press, Cambridge, 1988) ch 3; HG Richardson and GO Sayles, *The Governance of Mediaeval England* (Edinburgh University Press, Edinburgh, 1963) at 205–10.

[4] WR Cornish, *The Jury* (Allen Lane, London, 1968) at 15.

[5] *Ibid.*

[6] N Vidmar (ed), *World Jury Systems* (Oxford University Press, Oxford, 2000) ch 1.

[7] In Scotland for example a jury of 15 persons sits in cases under the solemn procedure brought before the Sheriff Court or High Court. See the Scottish Courts web site at http://www.scotscourts.gov.uk/html/main.htm.

[8] See also Article III, s 2 of the US Constitution.

hold that the right to a jury trial in federal and state courts exists where the maximum sentence authorised by law exceeds six months.[9] Under section 11(f) of the Canadian Charter of Rights and Freedoms, any person (other than a member of the military) has the right to trial by jury for offences carrying a sentence of imprisonment of five years or more. In Australia, the 1901 Constitution confers the right to a jury trial for indictable offences against the Commonwealth.[10] In England and Wales, jury trial is available in respect of indictable and triable either-way offences.[11] The present Government appears determined however to reduce the range of offences for which jury trial is available.[12] An attempt to remove the defendant's right of jury trial for either-way offences such as theft, possession of drugs and actual bodily harm in the Criminal Justice (Mode of Trial) Bill encountered cross-party opposition in the House of Lords and lapsed in the run up to the June 2001 General Election.[13] It is likely, however, that similar measures will be proposed during the current Parliament.

Although the juries encountered in different jurisdictions possess distinct features in respect of composition, functions and procedure,[14] the legal systems to which they belong all profess a profound commitment to the importance of fair trials. Again, this is reflected in the US[15] and Canadian Constitutions.[16] In Australia, whilst the right to a fair trial is not expressly protected in either the Commonwealth or State Constitutions, it is an implied constitutional right at least as far as federal offences are concerned.[17] Likewise in Scotland, England and Wales, cardinal importance is attached to safeguarding the interest of defendants and society in fair trials.[18]

[9] *Baldwin v New York* (1970) 399 US 66.

[10] S 80.

[11] This classification of offences is laid down in the Magistrates' Courts Act 1980 (as amended). See further Archbold, *Criminal Pleading and Practice* (Sweet & Maxwell, London, 2001) at paras 1.11 *et seq*.

[12] See further S Lloyd-Bostock and C Thomas, 'Decline of the "Little Parliament": juries and jury reform in England and Wales' (1999) 62 *Law and Contemporary Problems* 7. For earlier considerations of pressures to reform jury trials, see S Enright and J Morton, *Taking Liberties* (Weidenfeld and Nicolson, London, 1990): M Findlay and P Duff, *The Jury under Attack* (Butterworths, London, 1988).

[13] The Bill proposed to give magistrates and, on appeal, Crown Court judges the choice of venue in this class of offence. According to the Government, the change would reduce Crown Court trials by 12,000 annually, with net result savings of about £105m to the criminal justice system.

[14] See the account of differences between the US and Australian juries in M Chesterman, *Freedom of Speech in Australian Law; A Delicate Plant* (Ashgate, Aldershot, 2000) 254–5.

[15] The Sixth Amendment states 'In all criminal prosecutions, the accused shall enjoy the right to a speedy and public trial, *by an impartial jury* . . .'(emphasis added).

[16] S 11(d) of the Charter of Rights and Freedoms states that any person charged with an offence has the right to be presumed innocent until proven guilty according to law in a *fair* and public hearing by an independent and *impartial* tribunal. (emphasis added)

[17] *Dietrich v R* (1992) 177 CLR 292. See further J Hope, 'A Constitutional Right to a Fair Trial?' (1996) 24 *Federal Law Review* 173

[18] See previously at common law in Scotland *Stirling v Associated Newspapers Ltd* 1960 SLT 5, 8. The fair trial guarantee in Article 6(1) of the ECHR is now given greater domestic status by virtue of the Human Rights Act 1998.

In sharp contrast to the members of presenting jury of the Middle Ages,[19] the modern juror is expected not to have formed opinions about the guilt or innocence of the accused which are so firmly held that they could not altered by consideration of the evidence given in court. Persons with prior knowledge of events or individuals concerned in the proceedings must usually declare this fact and allow the court to assess whether they are capable of deciding the case solely on the evidence presented in court. Those unable to do so may expect to be excused from jury service.

III SCOTS AND ENGLISH APPROACHES TO PREJUDICIAL MEDIA COMMENT: FROM DIVERGENCE TO RAPPROCHEMENT?

In this section an account of Scots and English strict liability contempt law is offered. After highlighting aspects of the distinctive approaches in each jurisdiction and seeking possible explanations for the same, it will be asked whether more recent pronouncements from the High Court of Justiciary herald an era of greater concord between the two systems. One theme in this section of materials is the different pace at which the respective legal systems have assimilated the constitutional dimension of speech claims which occurred after *Sunday Times v United Kingdom* and the consequent passing of the Contempt of Court Act 1981 into domestic law. Ironically, after providing the initial stimulus for domestic change, recent ECHR jurisprudence is unlikely to prompt renewed introspection. The failure of the Strasbourg Court in *Worm v Austria*[20] to adopt an appropriately rigorous standard of scrutiny of Austrian contempt laws was discussed in chapter two. In consequence, the greater status given to Convention jurisprudence in national law under section 2(1) of the Human Rights Act 1998 is unlikely to usher in an era of heightened speech protection.[21]

The Nature of Divergent Positions in Scots and English Law

Scots strict liability contempt law (in both its pre- and post-Contempt of Court Act 1981 forms) has long been widely perceived as being both less tolerant of media comment regarding pending or current litigation than its English counterpart and also less willing to interfere with the criminal proceedings to which the comment relates. Thus Bonnington has written,

[19] The royal justices sent to preside over trials would of course have lacked this knowledge. See further N Vidmar, 'A Historical and Comparative Perspective on the Common Law Jury' in N Vidmar (ed) *World Jury Systems* (Oxford University Press, Oxford, 2000) ch 1.
[20] (1998) 25 EHRR 454.
[21] Conversely, it may encourage domestic authorities in the belief that greater restraints on court-related speech will be immune from an Article 10 challenge.

> In Scotland, newspapers are virtually guaranteed to be found in contempt for anything which is in the least prejudicial, while an accused (defendant) invariably fails in his attempt to stop the prosecution against him. So working from the one statute, the English and Scottish courts have managed to take two diametrically opposed approaches to this issue.[22]

Another guide for journalists warns that, despite the attempt to harmonise substantive aspects of Scots and English law in the 1981 Act 'several stories which would have seen an editor in Scotland at least heavily fined have passed without adverse comment in England.'[23] This view is also held by English commentators:

> In the years since the Act came into effect it has become clear that the provisions relating to strict liability contempts, and particularly with reference to media coverage to pending criminal proceedings, have been applied rather differently in England and Scotland.[24]

It is difficult to dissent from this view. As will be seen below, Scots law shares a number of characteristics associated with the administration of justice model of speech regulation. However, in as far as the quote implies a uniformly more liberal attitude to media freedom south of the border, it is an over-simplification. More accurately, it may be claimed that different interpretations of the same provision in the two jurisdictions have suggested some deep-level disagreement about media freedom to report and comment about matters before the courts. At a practical level, such variance has placed media organisations with cross-border audiences and readerships in an extremely difficult position. In the following sections, a closer look at the nature and extent of the distinct approaches to *sub judice* contempt law are considered.

Interpreting Section 2(2), Contempt of Court Act 1981

A strict liability contempt occurs when a publication:

> creates a substantial risk that the course of justice in particular proceedings will be seriously impeded or prejudiced.[25]

[22] 'Cross borders: cross purposes' (1996) 146 *NLJ* 1312. For an example of the English courts' willingness to quash a conviction in a high profile trial, see *R v McCann, Cullen and Shanahan* (1991) 92 Cr App Rep 239.

[23] B McKain, AJ Bonnington and GA Watt, *Scots Law for Journalists*, 6th edn (W Green & Sons, Edinburgh, 1995) See further AJ Bonnington, 'Contempt of Court: A Practitioner's Viewpoint' 1988 SLT 33, 38; 'Press and Prejudice' (1995) 145 *NLJ* 1632, 'Cross Borders: Cross Purposes' (1996) 146 *NLJ* 1312.

[24] Sir David Eady and Professor ATH Smith, *Arlidge, Eady & Smith on Contempt*, 2nd edn (Sweet & Maxwell, London, 1999) at 1000. The Divisional Court in England has been less circumspect, declaring the variance to be 'extremely undesirable' in *Attorney-General v Sport Newspapers Ltd* [1991] 1 WLR 1194, 1227 per Hodgson J.

[25] Strict liability only arises in respect of 'active' proceedings. In the context of criminal proceedings, this is defined in Schedule 1 of the 1981 Act para 4 as the period starting from the initial steps of arrest without warrant; the issue (or grant in Scotland) of a warrant for arrest; the issue of

Divergent attitudes in Anglo-Scots approaches to statutory contempt centre in a large part upon contrasting judicial interpretations of when a publication satisfies the standard laid down in the strict liability rule of substantial risk of serious prejudice. To a significant degree, this difference may be attributed to the willingness with which the courts have been prepared to embrace a constitutional dimension to the regulation of speech touching upon the administration of justice. In contrast to their Scottish counterparts, the English courts appear to have recognised relatively quickly the sea-change effected in criminal contempt law by the European Court of Human Rights in *Sunday Times v United Kingdom*.[26] In the 1987 ruling *AG v Newspaper Publishing Ltd*, Lloyd LJ remarked that:

> . . . the statutory purpose behind the 1981 Act was to effect a permanent shift in the balance of public interest away from the protection of administration of justice and in favour of freedom of speech. Such a shift was forced on the United Kingdom by the decision of the European Court of Human Rights in *Sunday Times v UK* . . .[27]

Certainly, it is difficult, for example, to imagine that, even a few years ago, the High Court of Justiciary would have shared the relaxed attitude towards media coverage of a high profile terrorist incident apparent in the Court of Appeal's decision in *Attorney-General v ITN and others*.[28] A national news programme broadcast details concerning the arrest of two men for the murder of a special police constable and stated that one of the men, Paul Magee, was a convicted terrorist serving life for the murder of an SAS officer who had escaped from the Maze Prison in Belfast. A photograph of Magee was included in the broadcast. Shortly afterwards, several newspapers also reported Magee's links to the IRA, his earlier conviction for murder and subsequent escape from prison. In respect of the ITN broadcast, Lord Justice Leggatt held that the ephemeral nature of news broadcasts and the background context of continuing terrorist activity coupled with the fact that the likely start date of Magee's trial was some nine months away at the time of the broadcast (the 'fade' factor) meant that there was no substantial risk of serious prejudice as required under section 2(2) of the 1981 Act. As for the newspaper coverage, the relatively small circulation of the publications in question and the nine month gap between publication and likely trial starting date also argued against the creation of a section 2(2) risk.[29] A

a summons to appear (or grant of a warrant to cite in Scotland); the service of an indictment or other document specifying the charge; oral charge. Criminal proceedings cease to be active under para 5 upon acquittal, or as the case may be, by sentence; by any other verdict, finding, order or decision which puts an end to proceedings; by discontinuance or by operation of law.

26 (1979) 2 EHRR 245.

27 [1987] 3 All ER 276, 310.

28 [1995] 2 All ER 370.

29 See also *AG v Sunday Newspapers Ltd and others* (1998) January 20 (LAWTEL) where the low level sales of a national Sunday newspaper meant that there was a very small risk that someone who had read the allegedly prejudicial material would be a juror at a related trial.

similarly relaxed view of pre-trial media comment emerged in *AG v MGN Ltd* in the context of a cumulative build-up of adverse publicity over a number of years. After the arrest on assault charges of Geoff Knights, the boyfriend of a well-known actress, a number of media outlets published stories detailing the extent of the injuries suffered by his alleged victims, revealing how they were inflicted, the stormy relationship between Knights and his girlfriend and Knights' violent background. The trial of Knights some six months later was stayed on the ground that the defendant could not receive a fair trial. On an application by the Attorney General to have the media organisations punished for strict liability contempt, the Queen's Bench Division found against the Attorney General. Taken individually, none of the *post*-arrest publications were deemed to have met the section 2(2) standard.[30] They did not add significantly to the long-established prejudicial climate surrounding Knights and the relationship with his girlfriend created by a number of separate publications going back some six years before his arrest.[31] Schiemann LJ in the Divisional Court distilled some general principles from leading English and Canadian authorities. He emphasised that a contempt conviction would only lie where the court was sure that the publication had created a substantial risk of serious prejudice. In assessing whether this level of risk had been created, relevant factors included whether publication had occurred in an area from which jurors were likely to be drawn and the number of copies of the offending publication which were circulated. On the crucial question of the residual impact of the publication on the notional juror at the time of trial, criteria which were relevant included:

> (a) the length of time between publication and likely trial date, (b) the likely focusing effect of listening over a prolonged period to evidence in the case, and (c) the likely effect of the judge's directions to the jury . . .[32]

A differently constituted Divisional Court in *AG v Sunday Newspapers Ltd* later developed criterion (b) above by holding that where a trial is lengthy and complex, prejudicial pre-trial publicity is likely to be overwhelmed.[33]

The pro-media stance of the English authorities detailed above extends only so far however and there remain traces of attitudes more commonly associated with the media-unfriendly administration of justice model. Thus, in the case of material published contemporaneously with the trial, the courts are quite prepared to find not only that any such publication will come to the attention of jurors but also that it will irremediably impair their ability to a try a case upon

[30] [1997] 1 All ER 456.
[31] These reports had referred, inter alia, to his prison record for violent conduct Cf National Heritage Committee's response to *AG v MGN* in *Press Activity Affecting Court Cases* (1996–97) HCP 86, paras 32–36 suggesting that the cumulative impact of media reporting ought to be criminalised under s 2(2).
[32] [1997] 1 All ER 456, 461.
[33] (1998) January 20 (LAWTEL).

the evidence solely.[34] Moreover, where the words used are 'strikingly prejudicial' and uttered by well-known public figures to describe other, well-known persons, the Divisional Court has held that it is less likely that the passage of time will diminish their adverse impact.[35]

By contrast with the predominantly media friendly nature of rulings in cases such as *ITN*, *MGN* and *Sunday Newspapers* cases, references to an accused person's criminal convictions and the publication of his photograph when proceedings were active north of the border in *HMA v The Daily Record*[36] were conceded by counsel for the newspaper to constitute a contempt and resulted in fines of £2,500 and £250 for the publisher and editor respectively. The High Court was unwilling to follow *MGN*, distinguishing it on the basis that the latter did not concern the publication of photographs where identification could have been a live issue at the trial.[37] Thus, apart from concerns over the impact of certain material on jury members, Scots law has also shown itself more alive to the possibility that the publication of photographs linking the accused to the offence may also cause prejudice in as far as it affects witness recollection. In *HMA v Caledonian Newspapers*,[38] following the escape of an accused person from custody prior to trial, the publication of the accused's photograph alongside an article in which mention was made of the armed robbery charge he was facing was held to have created a section 2(2) risk in respect of witnesses. The closeness in time between the date of the alleged armed robbery and the date of the publication complained of (20 days) may well have affected the witnesses' identification evidence.[39]

One explanation which has been advanced to explain differing attitudes between Scots and English authorities draws on differences in criminal procedure. Section 65(4)(b) of the Criminal Procedure (Scotland) Act 1995 which is designed to prevent delays in solemn proceedings requires that after full committal, the trial of accused persons held in custody must commence within 110 days. Failure to do so will normally mean that the accused cannot be tried for that offence ever again.[40] One consequence of the 110 day rule is that, in assess-

[34] *AG v Unger* [1998] 1 Cr App R 308; *AG v Birmingham Post and Mail Ltd* [1998] 4 All ER 49.

[35] In *AG v BBC* [1997] EMLR 76 the Maxwell brothers were described as 'scheming heartless bastards'during an edition of *Have I Got News for You* at a time when the Maxwell brothers' trial was some six months away.

[36] (1997) Part 9 *Media Lawyer* 28.

[37] *Arlidge, Eady & Smith on Contempt* 2nd edn, n 24 above, at 1004.

[38] 1995 SLT 926.

[39] See also *HMA v Whaldon and others* (1998) 3 Communications Law 155. Before the 1981 Act, Scots law had tended to take a strict stance on the publication of an accused person's photograph particularly where identification could well have been an issue at the trial itself. See *Stirling v Associated Newspapers* 1960 SLT 5; *Atkins v London Weekend Television Ltd* 1978 SLT 76. Note however that there is little empirical support for the idea that witnesses are influenced by media publicity. See New South Wales Law Reform Commission Discussion Paper No.43 *Contempt by Publication* (Sydney, 2000).

[40] S 65(7) allows for an extension to this period in specified circumstances.

ing whether a section 2(2) risk has been made out, the High Court of Justiciary may not able to make a similar allowance for the fade factor given weight in recent English rulings. However, the rule's explanatory force may have been overstated for several reasons. First, the limit of 110 days only applies to cases where the accused is held in custody after an initial appearance on petition. A longer period of one year is permitted in respect of cases where the accused is liberated on petition bail.[41] Second, the Scottish judiciary has shown on occasion that it is prepared to make allowance for diminishing prejudicial impact over time even within the 110 day period. In *HMA v Caledonian Newspapers Ltd*, Lord Hope—the Lord Justice General—relied upon the fact of a three month time lapse between the date of publication and date of likely trial to hold that the Crown had failed to show that an article which mentioned a charge facing the accused without going into details had by itself created a section 2(2) risk.[42] Moreover, as the 110 day rule does not start until the initial appearance of the accused on petition, it is plainly possible for media organisations to run contempt risks with their coverage prior to this moment. In cases where the accused has been set free on bail therefore, it might be expected that the longer gap between the date of publication and the likely starting date of the trial would permit greater scope for deployment of the fade factor argument. Consider for example in *HMA v Scottish Media Newspapers Ltd and others*[43] an actor known for various roles in situation comedies had appeared on petition before Glasgow Sheriff Court on several charges. He was bailed pending further examination and the Procurator Fiscal was still considering the case when the allegedly prejudicial newspaper report appeared. As the start of his trial was thought to be some nine months away, the High Court of Justiciary had little difficulty in dismissing the Lord Advocate's petition for strict liability contempt. The Lord Justice General Lord Rodger of Earlsferry delivering the opinion of the court stated that it was:

> rather unlikely indeed that anyone cited to serve as a juror would even recall the article.

Finally, according to *HMA v Caledonian Newspapers Ltd*, the gap between date of publication and date of trial is not relevant to an assessment of the prejudicial impact of a publication upon witnesses. Accordingly, in theory at least, media organisations in Scotland and England ought to run similar types of risk upon the publication of material affecting witness recollection close upon the heels of the incident itself. In practice however, the Scottish courts have shown themselves more concerned with this issue than their English counterparts. In conclusion therefore, the existence of the 110 day rule would not appear to take us very far in explaining differing outcomes on section 2(2) applications.

[41] Criminal Procedure (Scotland) Act 1995 s 65(1) as amended by the Crime and Punishment (Scotland) Act 1997 Sch 1 para 21; Criminal Procedure and Investigations Act 1996 s 73.

[42] *HM Advocate v Caledonian Newspapers* 1995 SLT 926.

[43] Available on Scottish Court Service web site at http://194.128.11.201/opinions/84_99.html

Relationship Between Section 2(2) Strict Liability Contempt and the Actual Adverse Impact On Criminal proceedings

> It seems to me important in these cases that the Courts do not speak with two voices, one used to dismiss criminal appeals with the Court roundly rejecting any suggestion that prejudice resulted from media publications, the other holding comparable publications to be in contempt, the Courts on these occasions expressing grave doubts as to the jury's ability to forget or put aside what they have heard or read.[44]

In recent times, English judges have indicated their unease with something which, to the lay onlooker, seems like a convenient double standard. Technically speaking however, as the weight of prejudicial material needed to make a conviction unsafe is greater than that for establishing a more than minimal risk of serious prejudice, the same judges have been at pains to stress that it does not follow that a contempt finding cannot lie consistently with the dismissal of a criminal appeal.[45] The position currently pertaining south of the border might be summarised thus: In high profile cases where considerable adverse, pre-trial publicity has occurred, the routine warning to juries to focus exclusively on the evidence presented in court is usually deemed sufficient to ensure that the defendant receives a fair trial.[46] Beyond this however, resort to other curative measures will be significant for subsequent *sub judice* contempt proceedings. Thus, the moving/delaying of a trial or the issuing of a special direction from the bench may render publishers vulnerable to contempt proceedings.[47] The imposition of a stay on proceedings, whilst not determinative, will also be a 'highly telling pointer' in a section 2(2) contempt application.[48] Curiously however, in *McCann*[49] and *Taylor*[50] where seriously prejudicial material was published *contemporaneously* with the trial which led the Court of Appeal to conclude the respective convictions were unsafe, no strict liability proceedings were brought against media organisations.

In Scotland, the High Court of Justiciary has not shared the Divisional Court's unease with the juxtaposition of contempt findings on the one hand and untainted verdicts of trial courts. The ruling in *Stuurman* made clear that a finding of contempt prior to an accused's trial would not sustain a plea in bar of trial since jurors could be assumed to behave properly and exclude from their deliberations any material which was not given in evidence at the trial.[51]

[44] *Attorney General v Unger* [1998] 1 Cr App R 308, 318 per Simon Brown LJ.
[45] A criminal conviction will only be set aside under Criminal Appeals Act 1995, s 2 if it is actually unsafe. For an attempt to avoid the double standard, see *AG v Guardian Newspapers* [1999] EMLR 904.
[46] See the remarks of Lord Justice Taylor in the appeal of Rosemary West at [1996] 2 Cr App R 374, 386.
[47] *Attorney-General v Unger* [1998] 1 Cr App R 308, 318–319.
[48] *Attorney-General v Birmingham Post and Mail Ltd* [1998] 4 All ER 49.
[49] *R v McCann, Cullen and Shanahan* (1991) 92 Cr App R 239.
[50] *R v Taylor and Taylor* (1994) 98 Cr App R 361.
[51] [1980] JC 111.

Stuurman has been criticised for sanctioning both the contempt conviction of journalists and their publishers whilst, at the same time, denying that the accused has not had a fair trial.[52]

As to the significance to be attached to jury directions for the purposes of section 2(2) liability, Scots law adopts an essentially similar approach to that prevailing in England. In *HMA v The Scotsman Publications Ltd,* the High Court implicitly accepted the idea that a publisher of material charged with strict liability contempt is entitled to rely in defence upon routine directions given to juries to ignore material not presented in evidence.[53] Where, by contrast, a trial judge issues particular directions to deal with specific publications, a publisher would be more likely to be found in breach of section 2(2).

The Role of the Prejudiced Party in Contempt Proceedings

Respect for the separate procedural traditions of Scots law resulted in the retention post-1981 of distinctive mechanism, north of the border, for the prosecution of allegedly contumacious material.[54] Thus, unlike England and Wales where the Attorney-General's consent to the bringing of proceedings under the strict liability rule is required under section 7 of the 1981 Act,[55] Scots law has allowed interested parties such as accused persons to petition the High Court directly, provided the Lord Advocate is notified of the petitioner's action. This procedural difference may explain why certain cases which reach court in Scotland fail to do so in England but cannot throw light on differences in substantive outcomes in section 2(2) applications between Scotland and England which rest ultimately upon differences in judicial attitudes. Using the example of the murder convictions of Lisa and Michelle Taylor whose trial was covered by elements of the press in a highly sensationalised manner which led to the quashing of the convictions, Bonnington comments that had the sisters been tried in Scotland, they would at least have had the opportunity to launch contempt proceedings themselves against certain national newpapers, instead of which they found themselves unable even to secure a judicial review of the Attorney-General's decision not to initiate strict liability contempt proceedings.[56] Any advantage gained from a successful petition would surely however

[52] B McKain, A J Bonnington and G A Watt, *Scots Law for Journalists*, 6th edn (W Green, Edinburgh, 1995) at 108.

[53] See also *Cox and Griffiths Petrs* 1998 SCCR 561.Cf *HMA v Whaldon* (1998) 3 Communications Law 155.

[54] *Robb v Caledonian Newspapers Ltd* 1995 SLT 631, 634 per Lord Justice General Hope.

[55] S 7 also provides that a court having jurisdiction to deal with the matter may act on its own motion. The Attorney-General's consent does not appear to be needed where injunctive relief is sought to prevent future publication. See for example *General Medical Council v BBC* [1998] 3 All ER 426.

[56] *R v Solicitor-General ex parte Taylor* [1995] COD 61. See also B Naylor 'Fair Trial or Free Press:Legal Responses to Media Reports of Criminal Trials' (1994) 53 *Cambridge Law Journal* 492.

have been more than offset by the almost negligible chances of securing a quashing of the convictions. In no single case north of the border has there been a successful appeal on the basis of prejudicial publicity.[57]

Injunctive Relief Under the 1981 Act

There are few reported attempts by the Attorney-General or private citizens with a 'special interest over and above that enjoyed by all members of the public in the due administration of justice in criminal proceedings'[58] to seek an interim injunction in respect of an anticipated breach of the strict liability rule and accordingly even fewer granted. In those cases where an injunction has been sought, it is accepted that the respondent publisher/broadcaster is entitled to resist the application on the basis that publication will, under the terms of section 5 of the 1981 Act, 'form part of a discussion of public affairs or other matters of public interest.'[59] It is also clear from the few cases that have been brought that the English courts have been reluctant to restrain future publication/broadcast on the basis of a likely breach of section 2(2), demanding as they have that claimants show a strong level of supporting evidence.[60] In *Leary v BBC*, a former member of the West Midlands Serious Crimes Squad sought to prevent the broadcast of a programme detailing events leading up to the disbanding of the West Midlands Serious Crimes Squad in view of a number of pending prosecutions against former members of the unit (although these did not include the plaintiff whose likely involvement in these proceedings would have been as a witness only). His application failed initially for want of *locus standi*, although the Court of Appeal went on to comment on its merits. The Court of Appeal noted the speculative, unevidenced nature of the application and strongly deprecated being invited to act as censor.[61]

In Scotland, the ease with which prior restraints on publication have been granted is characteristic of the administration of justice model of speech regulation. In *Muir v BBC*[62] it was held that in deciding whether to grant an interdict to prevent a threatened breach of the strict liability rule, the High Court of Justiciary need not take account of arguments based on section 5 of the 1981 Act. Even more significantly, the same court held that, absent a finding that the proposed programme/publication would create a section 2(2) risk, the High Court of Justiciary retains the power under the *nobile officium* to grant an

[57] A Bonnington, 'Press and Prejudice' (1995) 145 *New Law Journal* 1623.
[58] The phrase belongs to Lord Donaldson MR in *Leary v BBC* (1989) LEXIS.
[59] *Leary v BBC* (1989) LEXIS 29 Sept. In *Attorney-General v English* [1983] 1 AC 116, it was held that the onus fell on the Attorney-General to show that the defendant was unable to take advantage of the protection in s 5.
[60] See for example *General Medical Council v BBC* [1998] 3 All ER 426.
[61] On seeing a rough-cut version of the proposed programme, all three Court of Appeal judges held that it did not in any event create a s 2(2) risk.
[62] 1997 SLT 425.

interdict if, in the words of Lord Sutherland, the court considers in respect of a person who has been charged 'that there is *a risk* of prejudice to the trial of such a person.'[63] The ease with which injunctive relief is granted by the Scottish courts is further indicated by the fact that the petitioner need not aver that repetition of an offending statement is likely, nor the circumstances of the case disclose a risk of repetition, for an injunction to be granted under the *nobile officium* jurisdiction.[64] From a media perspective, the harshness of Scots law in this area is somewhat tempered by the ruling in *Lord Advocate v Scotsman Publications Ltd* that interdicts cannot be enforced against third parties.[65]

Discussion of Public Affairs

Not all speech which causes a substantial risk of serious prejudice to active proceedings results in criminal liability. UK law recognises a limited measure of protection for speech advancing the interests of an informed citizenry under section 5 of the Contempt of Court Act 1981. This states:

> A publication made as or part of a discussion in good faith of public affairs or other matters of general public interest is not to be treated as a contempt of court under the strict liability rule if the risk of impediment or prejudice is merely incidental to the discussion.[66]

Thus, in *AG v Times Newspapers and others* this section was seen to confer a broad freedom on the media to report the details and background of an intrusion into Buckingham Palace.[67] One description of the accused as a 'rootless neurotic with no visible means of support' which went on to suggest a homosexual relationship between the accused and the royal bodyguard was held to be protected by section 5 because the publication concerned the Queen's safety, a matter of clear public interest. On the other hand, the publication of a statement that the accused had assaulted his stepson did not raise any issue of public concern and could not come within the protective ambit of the section.

Of critical importance in determining the width of section 5 is the notion of an 'incidental' risk of serious prejudice. English law tends to distinguish between publications that cause the requisite degree of prejudice as an unplanned consequence of expounding their main theme and those whose subject matter relates so closely to proceedings that any risk of prejudice is considered more than incidental. This would explain the different outcomes

[63] Emphasis added *ibid*, at 427. The Court stated that authority for this view was provided by *Smith v Ritchie* (1892) 20 R (J) 52. On petition by either the accused or the prosecution, the High Court can invoke its *nobile officium* jurisdiction to prevent injustice.
[64] *Atkins v London Weekend Television* 1978 SLT 76, 78.
[65] 1989 SLT 705, 711.
[66] As Lord Diplock pointed out in *AG v English* [1983] 1 AC 116 the section does not strictly operate as a defence. The Attorney General must show that the section is not available to the defence.
[67] (1983) *The Times* 12 February.

in *AG v English* and *AG v TVS and Southey*. In the latter, a programme about Rachman-style landlords in the south of England focused on the conduct of Reading landlords and broadcast a still photograph of the defendant in Reading where he was on trial for conspiring to defraud the Department of Health and Social Security. The Divisional Court ruled that the risk of prejudice which had been created was more than incidental.[68] In *AG v English*, the publishers of the *Daily Mail* were able to rely on section 5, because the article in praise of a handicapped, pro-life candidate at a by-election contained no reference to the on-going trial of a doctor for the murder of Down's Syndrome baby and pursued an issue already in the public domain, namely the practice of euthansia. The article had been critical of what it perceived to be a practice of letting newly born, handicapped babies die and, although this was deemed to cause a substantial risk of serious prejudice to the doctor's trial, the article did so in an incidental way as a result of expounding its main theme about the morality of euthanasia. As *English* shows, it may be easier for a publisher to take advantage of this section where something is contributed to an on-going debate. Although this is not a prerequisite for section 5 protection, it may be more difficult for publishers to rely on this provision when they discuss matters which have become newsworthy on account of criminal proceedings.

It would be easy after *English* and *Southey* to reach the mistaken conclusion that in order for the media to take advantage of section 5, care must be always taken to avoid referring to persons involved in, or events at issue in, legal proceedings. This is an overly restrictive reading of the case law as *AG v Times Newspapers* shows. Giving 'incidental' its proper meaning of 'secondary' or 'subsidiary' permits such references provided these matters do not become the central focus of a programme/publication. It is important to emphasise this point otherwise the ability of investigative journalists and programme makers to illustrate and evidence themes in their work is compromised, alongside the wider public interest in receiving the product of informed journalism. In *Southey*, the contempt conviction might have been avoided had the reference to on-going proceedings formed an illustrative part only of a broader discussion about the misappropriation of public funds by private landlords across the South of England and the effectiveness of state responses to the problem.

The reluctance of Scots law to recognise a public interest dimension in speech relating to court proceedings was noted in an earlier section on injunctive relief. Unsurprisingly, its record on this point in respect of post publication contempt proceedings is hardly any more enlightened. Take *Muir v BBC* [69] where the High Court of Justiciary preferred a much narrower view of this section than laid down by Lord Diplock in *Attorney-General v English*.[70] In *Muir*, it was

[68] The trial was aborted at a cost of £215,000, although a subsequent re-trial resulted in a conviction.
[69] 1997 SLT 425.
[70] [1983] 1 AC 116.

suggested that where a respondent is warned that a future publication is adjudged to cause more than a minimal risk of prejudice to proceedings (presumably upon a petition to prohibit publication), (s)he would be in considerable difficulty in trying to invoke section 5 in any proceedings for contempt of court. Not only a *non sequitur*, this remark is difficult to reconcile with Lord Diplock's observation that, in addition to establishing a section 2(2) risk, the prosecution must overcome the *additional* hurdle laid down by section 5.

Enhanced Media Freedom and the Rapprochement of Scots and English Contempt Law

Recent High Court of Justiciary rulings in strict liability contempt cases indicate however that a re-assessment by senior judges of earlier, self-interested media-hostile attitudes has begun in Scotland. This development is attributable in part to a greater receptiveness towards English pro-media freedom authorities (accompanied by forthright criticism of certain media-hostile decisions south of the border) and in part to a greater awareness of the significance of rights in general and media freedom in particular engendered by Scotland Act 1998 and Human Rights Act 1998.[71]

An early indication of a more tolerant stance towards media comment is to be found in the remarks of the Lord Justice General, Lord Rodger in *Cox and Griffiths Petrs* concerning the significance of the 1981 Act which he declared:

> was designed to regulate the boundary, which had always, of course, existed between freedom of expression and the requirements of the due course of justice. That boundary may have been displaced from the familiar place where once it ran: Parliament may not have redrawn the boundary at a point which would not have been chosen by people looking at the matter primarily from the standpoint of the administration of justice.[72]

These remarks cannot have been lost on Lord Bonomy who, in the course of a trial of 11 men on drugs charges, had found the petitioners (a deputy editor and journalist employed by the Daily Record) guilty of contempt for referring to the accused as 'heavy-duty guys' and 'high-risk prisoners.' On petition to the *nobile officium* of the High Court, the contempt findings were recalled by a unanimous court on the basis that the article had fallen far short of the section 2(2) standard. Significantly, Lord Rodger's observations have been cited with approval subsequently by others including the Lord Justice Clerk, Lord Cullen and Lords Caplan and Coulsfield in *Abdelbasset Ali Mohamed Al Megrahi and another v Times Newspapers Ltd and others*.[73]

[71] Previously, Scots law considered the European Convention on Human Rights to have no status in domestic law, see *Surjit Kaur v Lord Advocate* [1980] 3 CMLR 79.
[72] 1998 SCCR 561.
[73] See the official Scottish Courts web site at http://www.scotcourts.gov.uk/opinions/104.99.html.

It also apparent that the High Court of Justiciary is showing greater willingness to pay attention to English pro-media freedom authorities. The list of pointers laid down by Scheimann LJ in the *MGN* case was described by Lord Marnoch in *HM Advocate v Scotsman Publications Ltd* as providing a 'particularly useful index of the various matter which should be borne in mind in a case of this sort.'[74] Similarly, the distinction advanced between the susceptibility of ordinary jurors and professional judges by Lord Bridge in *In re Lonhro*[75] was cited with approval by the High Court of Justiciary in *Abdelbasset Ali Mohamed Al Megrahi and another v Times Newspapers Ltd and others.*[76] As far as ordinary jurors are concerned, the courts' attachment to the earlier model of lay persons' vulnerability to media comment evident in cases such as *Atkins v LWT* is now being replaced in more recent times[77] by a clear preference for Lord Justice Lawton's more robust 'fellow-countryman' in *R v Kray* who has got the media 'sized-up.'[78]

Further evidence of a re-assessment of the appropriate balance between media freedom and the administration of justice is provided by *Abdelbasset Ali Mohamed Al Megrahi and another v Times Newspapers Ltd and others*. The High Court was critical of the Court of Appeal in *Attorney-General v Channel 4* for granting an injunction to prevent the transmission of a daily re-enactment on national television of proceedings in the contemporaneous appeal proceedings brought by the Birmingham Six.[79] Analysing the basis of the injunctive relief, the High Court of Justiciary concluded that it must have been based on the sort of general considerations laid down in *Attorney General v Sunday Times* relating to the administration of justice and the desire to prevent usurpation by others of the function of the court once a dispute had been placed in judicial hands.[80] However, as the House of Lords ruling in *Sunday Times* had been found in breach of Article 10 of the European Convention of Human Rights by the Strasbourg Court as not necessary in the interests of a democratic society; a unanimous High Court was unable to see how the injunction granted by the Court of Appeal in *Channel 4* case could be compatible with Article 10. Moreover, sections 1 and 2 of the 1981 Act, which were intended to bring domestic law into line with the European Court's ruling, tied contempt liability to the situation where a threat to particular proceedings arose. The provisions did not envisage liability in the more general sense where, irrespective of the

[74] 1999 SLT 466.
[75] [1990] 2 AC 154, 209.
[76] 1999 SLT 466.
[77] See for example the judgments of Lord Prosser in *Cox and Griffiths* 1998 SCCR 561 and the Lord Justice General in *HM Advocate v Scottish Media Newspapers Ltd and Others* http://194.128.11.201/opinions/84_99.html.
[78] (1969) 53 Cr App R 412, 414.
[79] Unreported. The case was later heard by the European Commission of Human Rights and is reported at (1989) 61 DR 285. The injunction was relied upon by the petitioners in *Al Megrahi*.
[80] See speech of Lord Diplock [1974] AC 273, 309.

position in relation to particular proceedings, it was asserted that the courts' function was being usurped.

Finally, in a further criticism on English dicta narrowing media freedom, Lord Coulsfield in *Al Megrahi* expressly doubted whether Lord Diplock's 'technical' interpretation of the term 'substantial risk' in section 2(2) of the 1981 Act in *Attorney General v English* as embracing any risk which is more than minimal was in accordance with Parliamentary intentions. Until this criticism, Lord Diplock's interpretation had enjoyed uncritical support in Scottish authorities.[81] It will be interesting to see whether in fact a narrower interpretation of the term does subsequently emerge to permit greater media freedom to report on active proceedings.

IV FREE PRESS AND FAIR TRIAL IN THE UNITED STATES

> The country's interest in the trial is so great that newspapers all over the United States are devoting many columns to it daily. Some sensational ones have been doing it for weeks past and have even gone so far as to try Hauptmann on their own account, employing writers of mystery stories to marshall evidence—real and conjectural—and enlisting their readers as juries . . .
>
> *The Times* 3 January 1935 on the opening day of the trial of Bruno Hauptmann in New Jersey

Getting and Holding Public Attention—Trials That Become Media Events

In a nation where indictments for murder and other serious criminal offences are relatively common, few trials manage to arouse, let alone sustain, intense levels of national media attention for the duration of criminal proceedings. More commonly, coverage of the vast majority of criminal investigations and proceedings is left to local/regional print and broadcast media. This factor is significant in terms of the constitutional guarantees of a fair trial and due process embodied in the Sixth and Fourteenth Amendments in that proceedings may usually be transferred outside the immediate locality where local media outlets may have contributed to a partisan climate of opinion about a suspect's guilt or innocence.[82]

Those comparatively rare instances of alleged criminal wrongdoing which do capture and retain national media attention even beyond their legal conclusion have tended to combine a variety of factors which allow the trial to serve as the

[81] See for example, Lord Justice General Lord Emslie in *HM Advocate v News Group Newspapers Ltd and Scottish Express Newspapers Ltd* 1989 SCCR 156.

[82] By contrast, the dominance of the national media in the UK makes trial transfer a less useful remedial device.

forum for a wider debate about societal institutions. In his analysis of the period between 1935 and 1995, Hunt argues that only the proceedings involving Bruno Hauptmann, Sam Sheppard, Charles Manson, Claus Von Bulow and OJ Simpson can properly be seen as belonging to this category.[83]

The trial of Bruno Hauptmann in 1935 for the abduction and murder of the Charles Lindberghs' 20 month old son in New Jersey provides an early example of saturated and partisan media coverage in the era of mass communications. The case had a number of ingredients which ensured the trial would grip public attention: the abduction and murder of the child whose father was a national hero; a defendant of German origins who fought against the United States in the First World War; the issue of ransom notes; a rendezvous at a cemetery and, finally, the prospect of the death penalty in the event of a conviction. In advance of the trial, a number of the media had decided that Hauptmann was guilty. All these features combined to ensure a massive media and public presence outside the Hunterdon County Courthouse, Flemington, New Jersey as the trial commenced. According to one police estimate, some 16,000 cars went to Flemington (population 2,500) on the first weekend of the trial. As well as 700 reporters and thousands of curious onlookers (including print and radio celebrities such as Damon Runyon, Jack Benny and Walter Wichell), street traders gathered outside the court, offering to sell miniature kidnap ladders, hair strands purporting to be locks of the victim's hair and photographs of his famous father. At the end of the trial, Hauptmann was convicted and sentenced to death.[84]

More recently, media coverage of the arrest and trial of OJ Simpson for the murder of his ex-wife and her friend was of an extent and partisan nature which would almost certainly have prompted the Attorney General in England and Wales to launch contempt proceedings either at common law or under the strict liability rule or both. Here too, the reasons for the national (and indeed international) coverage are not hard to discern. The defendant was black and enjoyed celebrity status as a former American football star while his alleged victims were white and slayed in circumstances of extreme violence. Added to this, the case contained the elements of secret sexual liaisons, glamorous lifestyles, suggestions of domestic violence and a racist police officer. Moreover, there was a body of forensic evidence at the scene of the crime and elsewhere which needed to be interpreted. Prior to the trial, the *New York Times* alleged that, in common with other sports stars, Simpson had physically abused his ex-wife.[85]

[83] D M Hunt, *OJ Simpson Fact and Fictions—New Rituals in the Construction of Reality* (Cambridge University Press, Cambridge, 1999) ch 1.

[84] For the view that Hauptmann was wrongly convicted see L Kennedy, *Crime of the Century: The Lindbergh Kidnapping and the Framing of Richard Hauptmann* (Collins, London, 1985).

[85] *New York Times* 22 June 1994. For details of this and other aspects of the coverage, see S Krause, 'Punishing the Press: Using Contempt of Court to Secure the Right to a Fair Trial' (1996) 76 *Boston University Law Review* 537. See also M Chesterman, 'OJ and the Dingo: How Media Publicity Relating to Criminal Cases Tried by Jury is Dealt With in Australia and America' (1997) 45 *American Journal of Comparative Law* 109.

Television programmes probed the state of Simpson's relations with his ex-wife and children and included interviews with the latter. A number of books were also published in the pre-trial period. During the trial itself, a seasoned trial reporter, Theo Wilson, noted how a number of reporters were convinced of Simpson's guilt. She recorded her dismay at:

> the hype, the manipulation of unseasoned media, the bias shown by commentators even before they heard evidence from the courtroom, the publication of rumors and gossip and leaks that violated every principle of trial reporting my colleagues and I practiced.[86]

Hunt's case study of the respective coverage offered by the *Los Angeles Times* and *KTLA*—a local Los Angeles television station which broadcast live during the trial—concludes that both news outlets in their distinct ways endorsed the prosecution's version of events. Although more 'understated' than the bias shown by *KTLA*,[87] the *Los Angeles Times*, according to Hunt,'routinely constructed and circulated news narratives that privileged prosecution accounts of the facts.'[88] Though Simpson was eventually acquitted of the criminal charge, it left some US commentators wondering whether the adoption of stricter, UK style contempt laws might represent a step forward.[89] Others proposed the banning of cameras from courtrooms where they had hitherto been permitted.[90] The fact that no contempt proceedings were brought against any media organisations in the aftermath of the Simpson case seemed at the very least to offer powerful endorsement of the conclusion in the American Bar Association's manual for journalists—*The Reporter's Key*—that:

> No legal penalty may be imposed for even the most intense, exaggerated, biased or 'hyped' coverage of any criminal case (except the remedies provided by successful libel suits).[91]

The Constitutional Standard—'Clear and Present Danger of Immediate Substantial Harm' and Resort to Remedial Devices

How did the US arrive at such a position? In chapter two it was observed that the extension of the 'clear and present danger of immediate substantial harm'

[86] *Headline Justice: Inside the Courtroom—The Country's Most Controversial Trials* (Thunder's Mouth Press, New York, 1996) 12.

[87] A fact which Hunt ascribes to the time afforded print journalists to reflect upon and edit news stories which was obviously not available to a live broadcaster. See n 83 above at 140 *et seq*.

[88] *Ibid* at 154.

[89] See for example Krause at n 85 above.

[90] See Wilson at n 86 above on the post-trial reaction of the Governor of California and certain judges at 18.

[91] American Bar Association, *The Reporter's Key—Access to the Judicial Process* ABA Standard 8–3.3—available electronically at http://www.abanet.org/media/nclm991c833.html.

standard beyond the early cases involving criticisms of judges to pre-trial publicity in criminal proceedings with juries effectively prevented successful prosecution of the media.[92] In 1960, Justice Frankfurter did question whether those who had created the prejudicial climate should always enjoy constitutional protection,[93] but his obvious unease did not receive any significant support in the Court's subsequent rulings. Instead, the Court in *Sheppard v Maxwell* put the onus squarely upon the trial court to diminish factors having a prejudicial impact on the fairness of proceedings.[94] Trial courts were actively encouraged to consider a range of remedial measures including restricting the number of reporters in the courtroom itself at the first sign that their presence would disrupt the trial. In addition, witnesses might be prevented from reading or hearing interviews with prospective witnesses. The various parties to the trial ought to be stopped from releasing information, accusations and rumours to the media.[95] Reporters who published material during the trial but not used in evidence before the court could be admonished by the trial judge. As regards prejudice caused in advance of the trial, the Court noted that the trial judge had conducted a *voir dire* to assess the extent of actual influence upon jury members. Other measures which the Court urged trial courts to consider included adjourning proceedings, transferring the trial to another county 'not so permeated with publicity',[96] jury sequestration and, where publicity during the trial continues to threaten the fairness of proceedings, the possibility of ordering a new trial.

Rules to regulate the circumstances in which the various curative devices may be invoked have been developed at statute and common law. The federal courts, for example, have provided guidance as to the circumstances in which particular remedial devices may be utilised. In *US v Abello-Silva* the 10th Circuit of Federal Appeals stressed the value of the *voir dire* to eliminate the effects of prejudicial pre-trial media coverage in cases where it was 'not overwhelming' and held that it would be improper for a judge to grant a change of venue where the less drastic corrective offered by a detailed *voir dire* would suffice.[97] Federal

[92] See for example *Maryland v Baltimore Radio Show Inc* 338 US 912 (1950) where the Supreme Court refused to grant *certiorari* in respect of an appellate court's quashing of a conviction for contempt in the trial court. Reversal of a contempt conviction at appellate level occurred in *Worcester Telegram and Gazette Inc v Commonwealth* 238 NE 2d 861 (1968).

[93] *Irwin v Dowd* (1960) 366 US 717, 730 'The Court has not yet decided that, while convictions must be reversed and miscarriages of justice result because the minds of jurors or potential jurors were poisoned, the poisoner is constitutionally protected in plying his trade.'

[94] (1966) 384 US 333.

[95] There must however be some doubt whether, consistently with First Amendment standards, a trial judge does in fact possess this power. See further W LaFave, JH Israel, *Criminal Procedure* (West Publishing Co, St Paul Minn, 1985) 855.

[96] *Ibid* at 363.

[97] At the same time, the Court has been less prescriptive about the form any *voir dire* should take, *Mu'Min v Virginia* (1990) 500 US 415. Cf the requirement in *Silverthorne v US* that, in cases where all jurors have prior knowledge of the case and there has been voluminous, inflammatory pre-trial publicity, the trial court should conduct extensive questioning. (1968) 400 F.2d 627 (9th Circuit). See further G Knapp, 'Scope of *Voir dire* Examination' (1990) 114 L Ed 2d 763.

Rules of Criminal Procedure also impact in this area. For example, under Rule 21(a) upon motion of the defendant, the trial court:

> shall transfer the proceeding as to that defendant to another district whether or not such district is specified in the defendant's motion if the court is satisfied that there exists in the district where the prosecution is pending so great a prejudice against the defendant that the defendant cannot obtain a fair and impartial trial at any place fixed by law for holding court in that district.

State laws making venue transfer impossible in certain categories of offence have also been declared unconstitutional by the Supreme Court.[98]

One option which will rarely meet the demanding standards of the First Amendment however is a pre-publication ban on the disclosure of trial-related material. In *Nebraska Press Association v Stuart*, the Court held that prior restraints could not normally be employed to safeguard a defendant's Sixth Amendment rights.[99] The trial court there had sought to preserve the fairness of a murder trial by prohibiting the publication of 'any testimony given or evidence adduced at trial.' The prohibition was invalidated by the Supreme Court. Stopping short of holding that orders restraining media coverage could never be constitutionally valid,[100] the Court did rule that such restraints were presumptively unconstitutional and that a trial court would be under a very heavy burden of showing that the order was necessary to avoid the prejudice. Moreover, it would need to be shown that other, less intrusive, but equally effective means of securing the same end were considered and properly rejected.

The most drastic of all curative measures open to an appellate court is to reverse a conviction imposed by the lower court. In such cases, there has been some dispute as to whether a defendant must establish actual prejudice to secure a reversal or whether the lesser standard of probable prejudice is sufficient. In *Irwin v Dowd* the Court appeared to favour the actual proof of prejudice test.[101] Here, the defendant's criminal record was published to potential jurors as well as stories asserting that Irvin had confessed to six murders and his offer to plead guilty if given a 99 year sentence instead of the death penalty. Of a panel of some 430 potential jurors, 90 per cent (370 jurors) expressed the opinion that Irwin was guilty of the murders. Eight of the 12 who finally served as jurors expressed the opinion that the defendant was guilty although claimed that they could still be impartial. Unsurprisingly, the Supreme Court found the necessary evidence to reverse Irwin's conviction. Nonetheless, since *Irwin* the Court has retreated from insistence upon proof of actual prejudice as a pre-requisite for

[98] *Groppi v Wisconsin* (1971) 400 US 505.
[99] (1976) 427 US 539.
[100] But see the opinion of Brennan J (joined by Marshall and StewartJJ) which held that prior restraints issued to safeguard the trial process could *never* be constitutional.
[101] (1960) 366 US 717. See also *United States ex rel Darcy v Handy* (1956) 351 US 454 and MD Bunker, *Justice and the Media—Reconciling Fair Trials and a Free Press* (Lawrence Erlbaum Associates, New Jersey, 1997) ch 3.

reversing convictions, preferring to infer the probability of prejudice where the totality of circumstances so allow. This lesser standard has been advanced by the Court in cases such as *Rideau v Louisiana*[102] where the defendant has alleged a breach of the due process entitlement under the Fourteenth Amendment.[103] Prior to the defendant's trial on murder, kidnap and robbery charges, a local television station broadcast on three separate occasions footage of the defendant's confession to a sheriff. The broadcast was seen in the locality where the trial was due to take place. At the trial itself, a defence request that the trial venue be changed was rejected by the presiding judge, as were challenges for cause against three members of the jury who admitted having seen the broadcast. The Supreme Court held that the judge's rulings violated Rideau's due process rights and the latter's conviction was reversed. No specific evidence of actual bias was required by the Court.[104] Later in *Sheppard v Maxwell*, the Court found that 'bedlam' and a 'carnival atmosphere' existed inside the Cuyahoga Court of Common Pleas, Ohio where Sheppard was tried. It rebuked the trial judge for the fact that 'newsmen took over practically the entire courtroom, hounding most of the participants in the trial, especially Sheppard.'[105] The probable prejudice test once more allowed the Court to hold that the defendant had been denied the judicial serenity and calm which due process required without a need to show proof of actual prejudice.[106]

V CANADA—RECONCILING FREE SPEECH AND FAIR TRIAL CONCERNS UNDER THE CHARTER

Pre-Charter regulation

> The right to a fair trial can never be compromised, in any way; and anyone who publishes remarks which it could reasonably be feared might affect the outcome of a trial, is guilty of 'contempt of court' and should be punished.[107]

Unsurprisingly given Canadian law's reliance upon English precedents, the pre-Charter period was characterised by the subordination of media free speech concerns in favour of fair trial and other administration of justice concerns. In

[102] (1962) 373 US 723.
[103] Whether a higher standard of proof is needed where breach of the Sixth Amendment right to an impartial jury is alleged is an interesting point.
[104] See however the joint dissent of Clark and Harlan JJ who clearly favoured a factually proven test of prejudice under the Fourteenth Amendment. *Ibid* at 729.
[105] *Ibid* at 355. Needless to say, intense media interest and speculation had already occurred in the pre-trial period. For vigorous criticism of the Supreme Court's assessment of the atmosphere inside the courtroom, see Wilson at n 86 above at 74 *et seq*.
[106] In this respect the Court was merely following its ruling a year earlier in *Estes v Texas* (1965) 381 US 532, 536.
[107] *L'Imprimerie Populaire Ltee et al v Leclerc* [1960] Que QB 923, 929 (translation).

criminal cases the *sub judice* rule applied from the moment of arrest or the issue of a summons or warrant for arrest.[108] According to a leading authority—*Steiner v Toronto Star Ltd*—liability was incurred whenever a publication tended to interfere with the right to fair trial.[109] Thus the publication of a story by the *Toronto Star* which attributed an alleged admission of guilt to the defendant then awaiting trial on fraud charges was held to be a contempt.[110] Subsequently, in *Re A-G for Manitoba and Radio OB Ltd* the revelation in a radio broadcast that a youth charged with murder had been diagnosed as psychotic and had confessed to police was deemed to have the necessary tendency to prejudice potential jurors.[111] It was irrelevant that, at the time of publication, it was uncertain whether the youth would be tried as a juvenile by a judge sitting alone or as an adult before a jury.[112] Other aspects of pre-Charter case law confirm the weak state of speech protection. For example, the publication of an accused person's past criminal record would usually be treated as tending to cause prejudice.[113] Moreover, there was no recognition (and hence no evaluation) of the countervailing value in the discussion of matters of legitimate public interest. In *Re A-G for Manitoba and Radio OB Ltd* it did not matter that the offending material was broadcast as part of a wider discussion of the facilities in Manitoba to house mentally disordered young persons. Finally, in the assessment of a publication's tendency to interfere with particular proceedings, no attention was paid to the curative possibilities offered by various remedial devices. The radical idea that a reasonably available and practicable alternative means of diminishing prejudice might go to the issue of a publisher's liability would however subsequently feature in Charter jurisprudence.

Resetting the Balance—Accommodating Free Speech and Fair Trial Interests Under the Charter

Although some commentators expressed the hope that the Charter would dramatically curb the reach of the *sub judice* rule,[114] early indications showed that

[108] SM Roberston, *Courts and the Media* (Butterworths, Toronto, 1981) at 48.

[109] (1955) 114 CCC 117—a decision of the Ontario High Court which referred expressly to the ruling of Lord Goddard CJ in *R v Evening Standard Co* [1954] 1 QB 578. See further the observations of Smith J on the pre-Charter position in *Re Southam Inc* (1983) 70 CCC (2d) 264, 267.

[110] See further McRuer CJ writing extra-judicially 'Criminal Contempt of Court Procedure. A Protection of the Rights of the Individual' (1952) 30 *Canadian Bar Review* 225, 227.

[111] (1977) 70 DLR (3d) 311, 316.

[112] See also *R v Carrochia* (1973) 43 DLR (3d) 427.

[113] *Re Murphy and Southam Press Ltd* (1972) 9 CCC (2d) 330, 334. Comments favourable to the accused were also thought capable of causing prejudice to the prosecution *R v Bryan* (1954) 108 CCC 209, 210.

[114] See MD Lepovsky, *Open Justice: The Constitutional Right to Attend and Speak about Criminal Proceedings* (Butterworths, Toronto, 1985) who argued that the Charter would 'confer immunity in most cases from prosecution under the *sub judice* contempt rule' at 240. See further his update

this view was not shared among Canadian judges. For example, in *R v Vairo and CFCF Inc* the Quebec Superior Court blithely asserted that media claims to free expression would continue to yield as they had in the past at common law.[115] The paramountcy of fair trial interests was re-iterated the following year by the Ontario High Court in *Re Southam Inc and The Queen*.[116]

The first signs that the common law might fall short of according court-related expression its enhanced constitutional status emerged in the ruling of Berger J in *Re AG of Alberta and Interwest Publications Ltd*.[117] Broad generalisations concerning the impact of prejudicial publicity upon judges and jurors were, he stated, to be discarded in favour of a particularised analysis of the factual circumstances of each case. The importance of the Charter right to freedom of expression would have to be assessed within context in order to determine whether, when balanced against the competing interest in a fair trial, a publication was in contempt.[118] For example, the revelation of a prior criminal record might not constitute a breach of the *sub judice* rule where a dangerous suspect was at large. Berger J further ruled that anecdotal opinions of neighbours and acquaintances regarding the character of the accused person and his/her alleged victim ought to be treated as 'idle gossip and rumour' and thus less likely to influence a trier of fact than, say, the publication of a past criminal record.[119] The time interval between publication and trial would also be relevant given the ephemeral nature of published comment.[120] Significantly, the *actus reus* of *sub judice* contempt was reformulated to be the publication of material which, beyond a reasonable doubt, constitutes a real and substantial risk of prejudice to a fair trial. When compared alongside the looser pre-Charter standard, Berger J's comparatively stringent test of liability appeared to enlarge the scope of protected expression. The suggestion of a more tolerant attitude towards court-related expression was confirmed by his remark that, *in any assessment of whether such a risk of prejudice was present*, the courts would need to be mindful of the array of remedial devices available to courts to safeguard the administration of justice from prejudice.

'Open Justice 1990: The Constitutional Right to Attend and Report on Court Proceedings in Canada' in *Freedom of Expression and the Charter* (ed D Schneiderman) (Thomson Professional Publishing, Canada, 1991).

115 (1982) 4 CCC (3d) 274, 276–8.

116 (1983) 70 CCC 264, 269.

117 (1991) 73 DLR 4th 83.

118 See further *Edmonton Journal v Alberta* [1990] 1 WWR 577, 584 *per* Wilson J.

119 (1991) 73 DLR 4th 83, 101–2.

120 The point was earlier recognised in *Guest v Knowles* (1908) 17 OLR 416, 424. Cf *A-G for Manitoba v Groupe Quebecor Inc* (1988) 45 DLR (4th) 80 where, despite the fact that publication of arrested persons' past criminal records occurred 'many months' in advance of trial, the publishers were nonetheless convicted of creating a real risk of prejudice to the trial.

Dagenais and Its Aftermath

The Canadian Supreme Court was provided with its opportunity to assess the impact of the Charter on the boundary between expression and fair trial interests in the context of a common law publication ban in *Dagenais v Canadian Broadcasting Corporation*.[121] The ban imposed by the Ontario Court of Justice restrained the appellants' broadcast of a fictional account of physical and sexual abuse of children at a Catholic orphanage. Two two-hour programmes were scheduled to be broadcast as jury trials involving members and former members of the Christian Brothers who had taught in Catholic training schools on charges of physical and sexual abuse of children had begun or were shortly about to begin. Although more directly concerned with the constitutionality of discretionary prior restraints imposed to safeguard the right to a fair trial, the Supreme Court's decision has implications for speech restraints advanced to protect the administration of justice in other contexts.

A clear majority of Justices started from the premise that the automatic priority accorded in the common law to fair trial interests was no longer sustainable. Chief Justice Lamer who gave judgment for the Court declared:

> The pre-Charter common-law rule governing publication bans emphasised the right to a fair trial over the free expression interests of those affected by the ban. In my view, the balance this rule strikes is inconsistent with the principles of the Charter in particular, the equal status given by the Charter to ss.2(b) (freedom of the press and other media of communication) and 11(d) (fair . . . hearing by an independent and impartial tribunal). It would be inappropriate for the courts to continue to apply a common law rule that automatically favoured the rights protected by s.11(d) over those protected by s.2(d).[122]

It followed that before a ban might be lawfully issued, common law principles must be revised to reflect the equal status of expression interests. In particular, the party seeking restraint would have the burden of showing first that the ban is necessary to avoid a real and serious/substantial risk to the fairness of a trial; second that no reasonably available and effective alternative means of securing a fair trial exists; third that the ban is as limited in time, scope and content as possible. Finally, it would also need to be shown that the deleterious effects of the ban are not disproportionate to its salutary effects.[123] On the facts in *Dagenais*, although the ban was aimed at preventing a real and substantial risk to the fairness of particular criminal proceedings, alternative means of safeguarding this interest (including adjournment, jury sequestration, judicial direction) were available. The failure of the Ontario Court of Justice to consider

[121] (1995) 4th DLR 12,
[122] *Ibid* at 37. Sopinka, Cory, Iacobucci and Major JJ concurring. See also La Forest J for concurrence on this point.
[123] Lamer CJC at 47–8.

and evaluate the utility of these devices meant that the publication ban violated the appellants' Charter right to freedom of expression.

What implications for *sub judice* contempt may be drawn from *Dagenais*? At the outset, it seems clear that the paramountcy of fair trial interests can no longer provide a constitutionally legitimate basis for restrictions on court-related expression. Instead, the requirement to accord equal status to expression must, it is contended, narrow the range of circumstances in which a publication may be held criminally liable. There are a variety of means through which this narrowing may occur. As to the *actus reus* of the offence, more robust protection of expression interests might entail that, as part of any judicial assessment of the nature and extent of the risk of any resulting prejudice, due account be taken of remedial devices. Assuming that a real risk of substantial prejudice has been created, the existence of an appropriate and reasonably available remedial device for correcting such prejudice might call into question the necessity of imposing a criminal penalty upon a publisher in order to safeguard the fairness of any trial. In such a case, a conviction might be thought to lack a rational connection to its objective under section 1 of the Charter as interpreted in *R v Oakes*.[124] On the issue of defences, it might be thought important to recognise the legitimate public interest in the unencumbered discussion of matters of public concern coincidentally before the courts. A further argument (albeit not one prompted by dicta in *Dagenais*) which might be made is that the vagueness inherent in the *sub judice* standard is violative of the 'prescribed by law' requirement in section 1 of the Charter. As Lepovsky has observed, outside of the most obvious cases, it is extremely difficult for media organisations and their lawyers to be sure in advance whether a particular publication will fall foul of the *sub judice* rule.[125] As such the rule may chill more speech than is absolutely necessary for the protection of fair trial interests.

At the time of writing, it is by no means clear that provincial courts are ready to embrace the brave new world of reconciling expression and fair trial interests. One of the few reported, *post*-Dagenais rulings on *sub judice* contempt *R v CHBC Television* has a decidedly pre-Charter media-unfriendly feel about it.[126] Despite frequent warnings from the trial judge in a murder trial held in British Columbia that the reporting of matters disclosed in *voir dire* proceedings was an offence under section 648 of the Criminal Code, the second defendant, a newspaper, published details of a mistrial application made by the defence and the

[124] [1986] 1 SCR 103. For a *pre-Dagenais* assertion that the *sub judice* rule complies with s 1 of the Charter, see *R v Robinson-Blackmore Printing and Publishing Co. Ltd* (1989) 47 CCC (3d) 366, 375–6.

[125] *Open Justice: The Constitutional Right to Attend and Speak about Criminal Proceedings* (Butterworths, Toronto, 1985) at 246–7. Lepovsky contrasts the uncertainty of the *sub judice* rule with the plainly defined parameters of the ban in the Criminal Code s 542(2) on publishing confession evidence at preliminary hearings. See further his attack upon the summary process by which the *sub judice* rule is enforced *ibid et seq*.

[126] (1998) 121 CCC (3d) 266.

judge's decision to postpone making a ruling on the application until later in the trial. The first defendant broadcast material raised in a *voir dire* concerning the accused's transfer to a correctional centre at one weekend during the trial and the delay this would cause to the start of proceedings on the following Monday. In addition, the first defendant broadcast accounts of the trial proceedings which contained other material not put before the jury. This included describing the accused as the 'prime suspect' and revealing that he was being held in police custody during his trial. A *Crime Stoppers* video which had been made of the incident was also transmitted which depicted a 'night' scene of the location where the victim's body was found. The video was not before the jury in evidence. Video footage was also shown of the nightclub door where an incident in issue in the trial occurred. The jury had been shown a still photograph only of this door.

In view of this accumulated material, Davies J acceded to a renewed defence application for a mistrial. A re-trial was ordered to take place in Vancouver eight months later. The same judge then presided over the subsequent summary proceedings in the Supreme Court of British Columbia where both media defendants were convicted of having created a substantial risk to the administration of justice. Apart from the obvious infringement of natural justice in having the same judge determine the mistrial application and the summary contempt proceedings, the case is also striking on account of its failure to engage with *Dagenais*. It is defective because, at bottom, it ignores the Canadian Supreme Court's edict in cases where expression and fair trial interests conflict to achieve a balance that 'fully respects the importance of both sets of rights.'[127] Indeed, Davies J remarkably asserted that the CBC broadcast raised no freedom of expression issue.[128] It is certainly difficult to agree his finding that, *individually* the *Crime Stopper's Video*, the nightclub door footage or even the revelation that the accused was in police custody tended to substantially interfere with the course of the trial.[129] It is equally hard to accept that these findings show an equal measure of respect for the countervailing and legitimate public interest (derived from the argument from democracy) in receiving information about the state's investigation and prosecution of serious crime. In respect of reports of matters arising in the *voir dire* hearings, the trial judge did not ascertain whether jury members felt able to disregard the published material. In any event, given the large degree of media interest in this one trial, ought he not to have given more urgent consideration to sequestering the jury?

[127] (1995) 120 DLR (4th) 12, 37 *per* Lamer CJC.

[128] (1998) 121 CCC (3d) 260, 289.

[129] Only the reference to the accused being a 'prime suspect' did not constitute the *actus reus* of contempt. On the separate question of *mens rea*, the taking of legal advice by the broadcaster in respect of the decision to include the extract from the *Crime Stopper's* video meant that the necessary mental element was absent. However, the revelations concerning the accused's custodial status and his whereabouts were held to show the broadcaster's reckless disregard for avoiding interference with the murder trial. As for the newspaper, its failure to supervise an unexperienced reporter indicated a lack of care sufficient to establish criminal recklessness.

It may be as well that the automatic bar in section 648 of the Criminal Code on reporting matters raised in the *voir dire* designed to safeguard an accused person's fair trial is itself unconstitutional. There are situations in which fairness will not in fact have been threatened by the publication of material raised in the *voir dire*.[130] For example, if the accused is ultimately acquitted, then no actual unfairness will have occurred. Furthermore, the bar is plainly more extensive than is strictly needed to safeguard trial fairness. At present, it catches material relating to *voir dire* proceedings in Nova Scotia which is published in a low circulation newspaper in the Yukon Territory.[131] Finally, section 648 may prevent the timely disclosure of claims relating to police/prosecutorial impropriety, which, under the argument from democracy, the public have a strong interest in receiving.

Remedial Devices to Protect Fair Trial Rights

As was seen from *Dagenais* above, Canadian law recognises a range of remedial devices which may be deployed to safeguard the right to a fair trial under section 11(d) of the Charter. These include the use of challenges for cause to eliminate partisan jurors upon empanelment,[132] venue changes,[133] delay and judicial warnings.[134] In general, the courts have expressed confidence in the ability of jurors to abide by clear judicial directions to disregard all material other than that laid as evidence before the court.[135] Recourse may also be had to a re-trial.[136] Only in the most exceptional circumstances of highly prejudicial media comment, would a permanent stay of proceedings be granted under section 24(1) of the Charter as an 'appropriate and just' remedy for a Charter right infringement.[137] One pre-condition for such a stay is that the applicant establish as a matter of fact after jury selection has occurred that an impartial trial is impossible.[138]

[130] Lepovsky makes a similar point in relation to the bar on publishing confession evidence in preliminary hearings under s 542(2) of the Code but the point remains valid for the *voir dire* as well, MD Lepovsky, *Open Justice: The Constitutional Right to Attend and Speak about Criminal Proceedings* (Butterworths, Toronto, 1985) 240 *et seq*.
[131] *Ibid* at 243.
[132] Criminal Code, s 638(1)(b) allowing the prosecution and defence 'any number of challenges' see further *R v Hubbert* (1975) 29 CCC (2d) 279.
[133] Criminal Code, s 599(1)(a) permits a venue transfer if it appears expedient to the ends of justice.
[134] *CBC v Keegstra* (1986) 35 DLR (4th) 76, 78 *per* Kerans JA.
[135] *R v Corbett* [1988] 1 SCR 670.
[136] *R v CHBC Television et al* (1998) 121 CCC (3d) 260.
[137] For judicial discussion of less drastic alternatives aimed at curing prejudice which results from reports of a public inquiry, see *Phillips v Nova Scotia (Westray Inquiry)* (1995) 124 DLR (4th) 129.
[138] *R v Vermette* (1988) 50 DLR (4th) 385.

VI AUSTRALIA

The Common Law Heritage

As with pre-Charter regulation in Canada, the Australian law of criminal contempt adopted and adhered to the prioritisation of fair trial interests derived from English common law.[139] Accordingly, the *sub judice* rule was rigorously enforced to punish factual disclosures[140] and commentary relating to pending cases[141] thereby deterring other would-be publishers. Over time, the Australian courts have fashioned a distinctive jurisprudence in this area, including rules concerning the point at which the *sub judice* rule is operative, the scope of certain defences and custodial penal sanctions.[142] In 1987, the Australian Law Reform Commission recommended the abolition of the common law and its replacement by a statutory offence.[143] Statutory reform was not forthcoming however and *sub judice* remained on a common law footing.[144] Elements of the current rules will be explored in the following section. Later, I devote space to considering some possible impacts of the implied freedom of political communication on *sub judice* rules.

Key Features of Australian *Sub Judice* Law

In line with the rhetoric of English common law and for much the same reasons, Australian judges too proclaim a firm commitment to the ideal of the open administration of justice.

> It is the ordinary rule of the Supreme Court, as of the other courts of the nation, that their proceedings shall be conducted 'publicly and in open view' (Scott v. Scott [1913] AC 417, at p 441). This rule has the virtue that the proceedings of every court are fully exposed to public and professional scrutiny and criticism, without which abuses may

[139] For a vigorous, though unsuccessful attempt to inject a US style 'clear and present danger' standard (albeit in the context of scandalising the court), see Murphy J in *Gallagher v Durack* (1983) 152 CLR 238.

[140] See *Packer v Peacock* (1912) 13 CLR 577 where the defendant was deemed to have implied an accused person's guilt.

[141] Eg *Davis v Baillie* [1946] VLR 486.

[142] Unlike English law's tendency to impose large fines on those responsible, the Australian courts have been known to send contemnors to prison. See the 1980s cases of *Gallagher v Durack* (1983) 152 CLR 238 and *Hinch v AG* (Vic) (1987) 164 CLR 15.

[143] ALRC Report No 35 Contempt (Australian Government Publishing Service, Canberra, 1987) paras 44, 299. The Report recommended that certain categories of statement should, subject to some exceptions and defences, be treated as capable of creating a substantial risk. The list included statements to the effect that the accused was innocent or guilty of the offence, that he/she has one or more criminal convictions, that he/she has confessed to the offence or made an admission in relation to the offence.

[144] For an explanation, see S Walker, 'Freedom of Speech and Contempt of Court: The English and Australian Approaches Compared' (1991) 40 *International Comparative Law Quarterly* 583.

> flourish undetected. Further, the public administration of justice tends to maintain confidence in the integrity and independence of the courts. The fact that courts of law are held openly and not in secret is an essential aspect of their character.[145]

Freedom to comment upon proceedings enshrined in the principle is, however, subject to a number of exceptions aimed at upholding the public interest in the proper administration of justice. Thus, in relation to the media, publishing material with a view to influencing or putting pressure on a litigant[146] or undermining the authority of a judge[147] is penalised under the law of contempt, as is breaching the terms of a properly made reporting restriction.[148] The fairness of pending trials is safeguarded by the *sub judice* rule.

The test under the *sub judice* rule is that the publication must create a real risk of serious prejudice to the administration of justice.[149] A fairly recent example of a contempt considered sufficiently serious to warrant a custodial sentence alongside a monetary fine occurred in *Hinch v AG* (Vic).[150] A Roman Catholic priest who organised children's camps in his capacity as governing director of a youth foundation was arrested and charged on child sex abuse charges. Prior to his trial, the defendant, a local radio broadcaster, referred to the case on three separate occasions. He commented upon the priest's prior convictions for similar offences and hinted that other offences may have been committed in which the Aboriginal victims were too frightened to come forward. The defendant also questioned how the priest had been able to run a foundation for young people given his criminal record. Although the trial was estimated at the time of the broadcast to be some two years away,[151] the High Court of Australia found that the memorable features of the case meant that it was unlikely that the prejudicial impact of Hinch's broadcasts would be blunted sufficiently over time. The Court refused to interfere with the Supreme Court of Victoria's penalty of 28 days imprisonment and a fine of $15,000.[152]

The *sub judice* rule comes into play once any of the following have occurred: arrest; arrest upon warrant; the laying of charges or the issue of summons.[153] This appears more generous to publishers than the notion of 'imminent' pro-

[145] *Russell v Russell* (1976) 134 CLR 495, *per* Gibbs J 520; See further *Raybos Australia Pty Ltd v Jones* [1986] 2 NSWLR 47, 50 et seq.

[146] *AG v Times Newspapers Ltd* [1974] AC 273.

[147] *R v Dunbabin ex parte Williams* (1935) 53 CLR 434.

[148] *John Fairfax & Sons Ltd v Police Tribunal of New South Wales* (1986) 5 NSWLR 465, 477.

[149] *Hinch v AG* (Vic) (1987) 164 CLR 15, 27 *per* Mason CJ. Other formulations used by the judges in this case include 'a clear tendency to prejudice the administration of justice' *per* Deane J at 46, 'a real and definite tendency' *per* Toohey at 70, and 'a real risk to the administration of justice' *per* Gaudron J at 87. It is generally thought that these amount to semantic differences only, see Walker at n 144 above 593.

[150] (1987) 164 CLR 15.

[151] In fact, the priest's trial commenced some five years after the third and final broadcast.

[152] The owners of the radio station were also fined $15,000.

[153] *James v Robinson* (1963) 109 CLR 593; *Packer v Peacock* (1912) 13 CLR 577.

ceedings at common law in England,[154] though is in line with the starting point for 'active' proceedings under Schedule 1 of the Contempt of Court Act 1981. Proceedings cease to be pending until acquittal, the time for an appeal has expired or all possible appeals have been exhausted. Unlike the UK equivalent, the Australian notion of pending also catches comment published after the conclusion of proceedings at first instance but before the commencement of appellate hearings.[155] As with statutory contempt in the United Kingdom, it need not be shown that the publisher intended to interfere with specific proceedings,[156] only that the publication was intentional.[157] The strict liability nature of this form of contempt has been criticised. A former President of the New South Wales Court of Appeal (now a High Court judge) Michael Kirby, has argued that normal rules of criminal liability should apply to *sub judice* contempt cases by requiring the prosecution to show an intention to interfere with particular proceedings. Given the especial difficulties facing publishers in federal jurisdictions, he maintained that it was unrealistic to expect media organisations to be aware of every trial in progress throughout the entire country.[158] The harshness of the strict liability rule is compounded by the fact that a publisher may not argue that reasonable precautions were taken to avoid the inclusion of prejudicial material.

Two Attempts to Reconcile Free Speech and Fair Trial Interests

An early attempt to accommodate both fair trials and the free speech interest in the scrutiny of governmental institutions is found in *ex parte Bread Manufacturers; Re Truth and Sportsman Ltd* where the value of certain forms of public discussion of matters was judicially recognised:[159]

> The discussion of public affairs and the denunciation of public abuses, actual or supposed, cannot be required to be suspended merely because the discussion or denunciation may, as an incidental but not intended by-product, cause some likelihood of prejudice to a person who happens at the time to be a litigant.

154 *R v Savundranayagan and Walker* [1968] 3 All ER 439, 441 *per* Salmon LJ; AG *v Times Newspapers* [1974] AC 273, 301 *per* Lord Reid.

155 Criminal proceedings in the UK cease to be active upon acquittal, discontinuance or sentence. See Sch 1 para 5 of the 1981 Act. Prior to the lodging of any formal notice of appeal or application for leave (when the strict liability rule is then re-activated, Schedule 1 para 15), the media are free to comment on the outcome of the case.

156 *John Fairfax & Sons Ltd v McRae* (1955) 93 CLR 351.

157 *Registrar of the Supreme Court of Equity Division v McPherson* [1980] 1 NSWLR 688.

158 *Registrar,Court of Appeal v Willesee* (1985) 3 NSWLR 650, 652; In the UK, the Contempt of Court Act 1981, s 3(1) does provide a defence to a publisher etc who can show that, at the time of publication, he did not know and had no reason to suspect that proceedings were active. For a view that Australian law also requires this see *Ex parte Bread Manufacturers Ltd; Re Truth and Sportsman Ltd* (1937) 37 SR (NSW) 242, 250–251.

159 (1937) 37 SR (NSW) 242, 249 *per* Jordan CJ, later endorsed by the High Court of Australia in *John Fairfax & Sons Pty Ltd v McRae* (1955) 93 CLR 351. The Chief Justice's remarks were also approved in *AG v Times Newspapers* [1974] AC 273, 296 (Reid), 321 (Simon).

Provided that a publication discussed a pre-existing question of public concern and that any prejudice resulting to particular proceedings was an incidental consequence of that discussion, the *Bread Manufacturers* principle gave publishers and others a degree of certainty that, no matter how strong the tendency to cause prejudice, a publication would be protected.

As Walker notes, the rule in *Bread Manufacturers* rendered critical the court's characterisation of the subject matter of publication and the motivation behind it.[160] In *AG NSW v Willesee No.1*[161] a programme was broadcast which dealt with the impact of a strike of prison staff. The strike occurred following the death of an officer. In the programme, it was stated that a prisoner accused of murdering the officer had previously assaulted two other officers. It was submitted for the broadcasters that any prejudice to the prisoner's trial was not actionable under the *Bread Manufacturers* principle since the programme dealt with the pre-existing issue of prison administration. The argument failed. The programme had been prompted by the officer's death and its subject matter, according to the court, was the consequences of the officer's death. The outcome in this case is to be contrasted with *AG NSW v Willesee No.2* where the New South Wales Court of Appeal took a more media-friendly approach to the characterisation of the subject matter of, and motivation behind, a programme broadcast on the evening before a jury retired to consider its verdict against a defendant charged with theft. The programme contained statements which alleged variously that the defendant had killed a man, that he routinely used his fists and gun to sort out trouble and that he gave in excess of $5 million to politicians and police officers. Whilst these statements were held to be likely to prejudice the trial, the broadcasters were able to point to previously published newspapers articles and Hansard reports on police corruption and the political response to it in New South Wales to establish an issue of prior public concern. The Court of Appeal accepted that the programme had been motivated by the issue of police corruption and the government's response to it and that these, rather than the defendant's trial, constituted the subject matter of the programme.

Although there may be epistemological difficulties inherent in showing that a matter is *already* one of public concern (what level of pre-discussion must there have been? where must it have been aired? by whom? to whom?),[162] *Bread Manufacturers* was clear that no protection existed where the media discussed matters of public concern which became newsworthy *on account* of their being raised in the context of legal proceedings as say in *Hinch* where the proceedings prompted concerns about the safety of children entrusted to the care of volun-

[160] S Walker, 'Freedom of Speech and Contempt of Court: The English and Australian Approaches Compared' (1991) 40 *International Comparative Law Quarterly* 583.

[161] [1980] 2 NSWLR 143.

[162] It is thus arguable that uncertainty over the application of *Bread Manufacturers* principle in practice would have chilled a degree of media comment on court-related matters.

tary organisations. Why free speech arguments are seen as less compelling here is not clear. In contrast, it should be noted that section 5 of the United Kingdom's Contempt of Court Act 1981 does not formally impose a requirement of previous public airing, although it may be more difficult for a publisher to claim the statutory protection when discussing matters which have become newsworthy on account of being raised in court proceedings.

The *Bread Manufacturers* principle was considered by the High Court of Australia in *AG v Hinch* where it was reformulated in a manner intended to reflect more fully the nature of competing public interests at stake in each case.[163] In particular, the principle in *Bread Manufacturers* that the incidental causing of prejudice was automatically protected where it occurred in the course of continuing discussion of matters in public affairs was rejected. In its place, the Court proposed a more flexible formula—balancing the competing public interests in fair trials and freedom of expression—for determining whether an infringement of the *sub judice* rule had occurred. Revealingly, the Court's guidance as to the factors relevant to any balancing exercise expends more column space on instances when the interest in freedom of expression must yield to administration of justice interests than *vice versa*. Thus, it is stated that the balance will tend to lie in favour of administration of justice concerns and the punishment of expression where a publisher reveals an accused person's previous criminal record for offences similar/identical to that with which he/she is currently charged.[164] This remains so even where, as in *Hinch,* countervailing considerations relating to the local community interest in protecting its young people and the broader public interest in discussing state supervision of child sex offenders would both favour publication.[165] Any implication that an accused person has committed offences other than those being prosecuted is also likely to constitute a contempt.[166] Under *Hinch*, reference to issues in pending cases which form a central part of the published discussion will also make it easier for the Attorney General to show a real risk of prejudice whereas an incidental reference to the litigation is less likely to meet this test.[167] Other relevant factors include the timing of the publication—the nearer in time the publication is to the start of a trial the greater will be the tendency to prejudice;[168] and the extent to which the account is memorable—the more unusual the circumstances of the

[163] (1987) 164 CLR 15.

[164] *Per* Mason CJ, Deane J.

[165] Mason CJ argued that disclosure of past convictions was unnecessary to alert the community to the risk posed by an individual. However, he neglects to consider that this information, whilst detrimental to offender's re-integration, allows the community to respond in an informed way to the particular threat posed by a convicted person.

[166] *Per* Toohey J.

[167] *Per* Mason CJ. However, it is not entirely inconceivable that an incidental reference could be held to have created a strong tendency to prejudice, as where the incidental reference occurs during the trial itself.

[168] *Per* Toohey J.

case, the greater the tendency of prejudicial material to remain in the minds of potential witnesses and jurors.[169]

The High Court was less forthcoming about the circumstances when a court might come down on the freedom of expression side of the balance. Mason CJ suggested somewhat unhelpfully that, apart from fair and accurate reports of the proceedings of Parliament and the courts, the discussion of a constitutional crisis or imminent threat of nuclear disaster which caused prejudice to proceedings might have an overriding claim for protection in the face of competing fair trial interests. Deane J for his part considered it neither 'practicable nor desirable' to give guidance in this area.

In summary, *Hinch* does enlarge media freedom in the sense that it does not insist on the subject matter of discussion being a pre-existing topic of public concern. It is thus possible for discussion to be protected when sparked off by an issue raised for the first time in litigation. On the other hand, where a publication continues a public controversy and incidentally causes prejudice to legal proceedings, *Hinch* ends the automatic protection for publishers afforded under the *Bread Manufacturers* principle. In the final analysis however, the requirement to balance imports greater, not less, uncertainty into the application of the law with result that some degree of media comment on matters related to pending proceedings is in all probability chilled.[170]

The Use of Remedial Devices

The continuing vitality of the *sub judice* rule in cases like *Hinch* has meant that the Australian courts have been less preoccupied than the US courts with the issue of remedial devices and that, accordingly, rules regulating their use are less developed.[171] Nonetheless, a variety of curative procedures may be invoked to diminish the prejudicial impact of media coverage including judicial warnings to ignore publicity, delaying the trial, questioning jury members to ascertain degree of influence, venue transfer, trial severance and re-trial. Very exceptionally, where there is no possibility of a fair trial at some point in the future, a conviction may be set aside and a permanent stay of proceedings granted.[172] It should be stressed however that, as with England and Scotland, the mere fact that there has been a prior finding of contempt against the media, does not lead automatically to the finding that the defendant failed to receive a fair trial.[173]

[169] *Ibid.*

[170] Walker at n 160 above.

[171] Chesterman has commented that the deterrent strategy is 'usually reasonably effective' in preventing prejudice to pending trials. *Freedom of Speech in Australian Law; A Delicate Plant* (Ashgate, Aldershot, 2000), 266.

[172] *Tuckiar v R* (1934) 52 CLR 335.

[173] See the criticism made by the majority in *R v Glennon* (1992) 173 CLR 592 of Nathan J sitting in the Victorian Court of Criminal Appeal for asserting that a prior finding of contempt automatically

Current practice would appear to put considerable faith in remedial devices such as judicial warnings to cure prejudice in all but the most extreme circumstances. An application to quash a conviction and grant a permanent stay of proceedings was heard by the High Court in *R v Glennon*.[174] The defendant was the Roman Catholic priest whose previous criminal record was broadcast by Hinch at a time when Glennon faced charges for child sex abuse. Hinch's subsequent contempt case received considerable media attention and ensured, according to the defendant, that the substance of the broadcasts remained fresh in the public mind. An application was made for a permanent stay of proceedings on the ground that the defendant would be unable to receive a fair trial due to ineradicable prejudice. This was refused and the full trial finally commenced more than five years after the third broadcast by Hinch. As the jury was being empannelled, the trial judge questioned prospective jurors about prior knowledge about the case and excused two persons on this basis.[175] After being empannelled, jury members were told to decide the case according to the evidence and to put out of their minds any 'prejudice, sympathy or bias or any other emotive consideration.' Upon hearing the evidence the jury convicted the defendant on five counts of indecent assault, buggery and attempted buggery. On appeal against the earlier refusal to order a stay, the Victorian Court of Criminal Appeal quashed the convictions as unsafe and unsatisfactory. On further appeal to the High Court, a majority of four to three held that the Victorian Court of Criminal Appeal had been in error and set aside the acquittals. In particular, the majority criticised the Court of Criminal Appeal for failing to have regard to the trial judge's efforts to safeguard the fairness of proceedings as well as its neglect of the community's expectation that a person accused of a serious crime will be brought to trial.[176]

Possible Impact of the Implied Freedom of Political Communication

As was seen in Chapter One, the High Court's power to review statute and common law for compatibility with the implied freedom of political communication establishes a means by which the constitutionality of restrictions on political speech may be gauged. One High Court judge, Michael Kirby, has questioned whether the *sub judice* rule does conform to the essence of the

meant that a fair trial was impossible. For an empirically-based discussion of the Australian legal system's responses to prejudicial material published during a trial, see M Chesterman, 'Media Prejudice During a Criminal Jury Trial: Stop the Trial, Fine the Media, or Why not Both?' [1999] *University & Technology Sydney Law Review* 5.

174 *Ibid.*

175 One had read an article about circumstances relating to the case whilst the other revealed that he had been taught by the defendant.

176 For a unique example of a successful application for quashing and the entering of an acquittal on ground of prejudicial publicity, see *Tuckiar v R* (1934) 52 CLR 335.

implied freedom.[177] A number of features of the current law do appear to inhibit discussion of governmental matters. Walker has argued that the very uncertainty of the 'balancing' exercise may well chill court-related expression.[178] As Schiemann LJ has shown in *AG v MGN*, it is possible for the courts to give greater guidance to editors and journalists about when speech will be protected and it will be interesting to see whether the High Court does go on to provide greater clarity in this area.[179] The departure from the normal *mens rea* requirement for criminal liability may also come under closer scrutiny, enlarging as it does the scope of the penal law. In addition, the extended period for which proceedings are pending may be seen as excessively protective when compared alongside the more narrowly defined notion of 'active proceedings' in the United Kingdom. Finally, the imposition of custodial sentences in cases where the trial adversely affected has later been deemed fair might also be thought excessive and difficult to reconcile with a robust commitment to unfettered discussion of public affairs.

More fundamentally, the implied freedom throws into doubt the constitutionality of the law's primary reliance upon preventative, penal means of securing the unimpeded administration of justice. A principled approach to the freedom of political communication might question whether the application of penal laws is consistent with the implied freedom in those cases where a reasonably available and practicable remedial measure would restore a defendant's right to a fair trial. A radical suggestion here would be to postpone any *sub judice* proceedings until the conclusion of the affected trial so that a publisher might only be punished where it was known that the material in question *did in fact prevent a fair trial*. If, on the contrary, speech is still to be punished on the speculative basis of damage it may cause at some point in the future to criminal proceedings, courts should be pressed to make a reasoned finding about the type and extent of the risk of prejudice caused by a particular publication. Such a finding ought to avail itself of relevant empirical evidence as to the likely prejudicial impact of certain forms of published information/comment. At this point a court should be required to consider the range of remedial devices and examine whether an alternative, less drastic and reasonably practicable means of securing a fair trial is available. Only in those cases where no such alternative means exists would a role for *sub judice* be constitutionally permissible.

Whatever merit may lie in this line of argument, it is perhaps unrealistic to expect the current High Court to engage in an immediate major rethink of *sub judice* law. Changes in personnel during the 1992–98 period have seen the High Court retreat from the high-water mark of judicial activism associated with Chief Justice Mason's tenure of office. Under his successor, Sir Gerrard

[177] Albeit in his capacity as President of the New South Wales Court of Appeal in *Civil Aviation Authority v Australian Broadcasting Commission* (1995) 39 NSWLR 540, 560.
[178] Walker, 'Freedom of Speech and Contempt of Court', n 160 above.
[179] [1997] 1 All ER 456.

Brennan, the Court cut back on the scope of the implied freedom in a number of significant respects. The category of 'political speech' was narrowed down from Barendt's definition accepted in *Theophanous* as comprising all speech which is:

> relevant to the development of public opinion on the whole range of public issues which an intelligent citizen should think about.[180]

to that in *Lange* of speech which 'enables the people to exercise a free and informed choice as electors'[181]—a re-definition which may cast *sub judice* speech restrictions outside the scope of speech protected by the implied freedom altogether. *Lange* is unlikely, however, to be the final word on this point. Immediately after the decision, Gaudron and Toohey JJ both of whom were advocates of the broader approach in *Theophanous* restated their support for this position in *Kruger v Commonwealth*.[182] Gaudron J for example declared that the implied freedom extended to:

> information, ideas or opinions with respect to matters which may fall for consideration in the political process.[183]

The exact boundaries of political speech look like remaining in a state of flux for some time to come.

Assuming, for the sake of argument, that the *sub judice* rule does impinge upon a constitutionally protected area of political expression, it must then be asked whether the rule would constitute a constitutionally impermissible interference with the implied freedom. Here again, battle lines between radical and conservative opinions on the Court have been drawn. At the outset, all appear to agree that the implied freedom is not absolute and that the administration of justice constitutes a lawful objective in respect of which speech may be restricted. However, a crucial area of disagreement emerges as to when a law infringing the implied freedom might nonetheless be deemed constitutionally valid. Under the 'compelling justification' standard adopted by Mason CJ, McHugh, Deane and Toohey JJ in *Australian Capital Territory v Commonwealth*[184] a US-style distinction is drawn between laws which regulate the contents of political speech and laws regulating time, manner and place of communications. For contents-based restrictions to be lawful, a compelling case for interference must be made out. Less stringently, time manner and place restrictions affecting how expression is communicated would be valid on this view provided that the restriction was not a disproportionate

[180] *Freedom of Speech* (Clarendon Press, Oxford, 1985) 152. See *Theophanous v The Herald and Weekly Times Limited* (1994) 182 CLR 104.

[181] (1997) 189 CLR 520, 560. See further M Chesterman, *Freedom of Speech in Australia—A Delicate Plant* (Ashgate, Aldershot, 2000) at 50 *et seq*.

[182] (1997) 190 CLR 1.

[183] *Ibid* at 114.

[184] (1992) 177 CLR 106, 143 (Mason), 234 (McHugh), 174 (Deane and Toohey).

means of advancing the competing public interest which lay behind the law. More recently, Gaudron and Kirby JJ have both advocated the compelling justification test in respect of restrictions on communications which are contents-based.[185]

Brennan J's rival account of permissible restrictions in *Australian Capital Territory* is more deferential to the will of Parliament and judge-developed restraints on speech. In *Lange* he stated that the courts should only intervene where the restriction is not 'reasonably appropriate and adapted to serve a legitimate end . . .'[186] In making this assessment, the legislature was to enjoy a margin of appreciation within which curtailment of political communications would remain free from judicial control.[187] In respect of common law restrictions on the implied freedom such as the *sub judice* rule, Brennan again favoured a loose test. Only those rules which 'unnecessarily or unreasonably impair the freedom of communication' are invalid.[188]

Brennan's adoption of the Strasbourg Court's doctrine overlooks the fact that the margin of appreciation is a supra-national doctrine used by the Strasbourg Court to determine those instances where the national authorities are best placed to weigh the competing interests at issue in the dispute. It is not considered relevant where a national court is asked to rule on the constitutionality of national law. Furthermore, as was noted in chapter two, the doctrine recognises the special status of political speech under the Convention so that national authorities enjoy a comparatively narrow margin of appreciation where restraints on political expression are subject to more critical oversight by the Strasbourg Court than is applied in the case of restraints on commercial or artistic expression.[189]

The looser standard of constitutional review in the Brennan approach does not therefore suggest an immediate dismantling of the *sub judice* rule. The 'compelling justification' criterion does however offer the prospect of a more critical review. Even then, it is not entirely inconceivable that a conservative-led court might treat the rule as going merely to issue of the *time* at which a publication occurs rather than its content, thereby bringing the less stringent proportionality test into play. Such a characterisation would of course be in error. The speech which offends under the *sub judice* rule is not speech *per* se about pending court proceedings. Rather, it is that speech whose actual content is alleged to be partisan and on this account, is criminalised.

[185] *Levy v State of Victoria* (1997) 189 CLR 579, 618 (Gaudron), 647 (Kirby).
[186] (1997) 189 CLR 520, 567.
[187] *ACTV* (1992) 177 CLR 106, 159.
[188] (1997) 189 CLR 520, 568.
[189] Contrast *Lingens v Austria* (1986) 8 EHRR 407 with *Casado Coca v Spain* (1994) 18 EHRR 1.

VII TAKING SPEECH TOO SERIOUSLY?

Chesterman has argued the commitment under the First Amendment to open and robust discussion of governmental matters and the hostility to government-imposed restraints on speech that this entails impose heavy and unnecessary costs in the arena of criminal justice administration. In support of some version of a *sub judice* rule, he argues that the media can perform their watchdog function 'without publishing the most obviously prejudicial material specifically relevant to a case.'[190] In any event, losses to speech incurred under any *sub judice* rule of the sort found in the UK, Australia and Canada are only of a temporary nature. By contrast, the costs of a pecuniary and non-pecuniary nature entailed through delays in the commencement of US trials occasioned by lengthy *voir dires*, adjournments, venue transfers, jury sequestration and re-trials which impact variously on defendants, jurors, witnesses, victims, the prosecution and taxpayers are significant. In those cases where a permanent stay of prosecution is granted, the state, victims and wider community suffer through the failure to punish those defendants who have in fact engaged in criminal conduct.[191]

Linked as it is to the broader argument from democracy, Chesterman's contention that media freedom to report and comment should be tied to those occasions where the scrutiny of the courts and associated public bodies and officials is enhanced is clearly attractive.[192] It is difficult for example to see how the sensationalist reporting in the Knights/Taylforth case advanced informed control over governmental institutions. Even here however, before we can properly criminalise such speech, we ought to be clear that it would, or is extremely likely to have a seriously prejudicial impact on proceedings. Recalling Schauer's point that self-regulation has tended in the past to produce overly aggressive restrictions upon speech,[193] it would seem appropriate to take a sceptical view of claims made in the name of administration of justice. Empirical evidence supporting some common assertions about the prejudicial effects of media publicity are examined in the next section of this chapter. For the time being, it can be noted that the case for *sub judice* rules is undermined by a lack of consistent

[190] 'OJ and the Dingo: How Media Publicity Relating to Criminal Cases Tried by Jury is Dealt With in Australia and America' (1997) 45 *American Journal of Comparative Law* 109, 137.

[191] It may also be historically significant that the clutch of conviction reversals on due process grounds in the United States between 1960 and 1966 (and the shift away from an actual prejudice to assumed prejudice standard) occurred just as new technology—television—was reaching a mass audience. In the cases of Rideau, Estes and Sheppard, fears about the prejudicial impact of television coverage at the pre-trial and/or trial stages are to the fore in the Court's reasoning.

[192] In ch 2 it was conceded that media commentaries which clearly do not advance informed public opinion have a less obvious claim to receive protection.

[193] F Scharer, *Free Speech: A Philosophical Enquiry* (Cambridge University Press, Cambridge, 1982) discussed in ch 1.

empirical support. Moreover, whichever version of the *actus reus* is adopted (Chesterman suggests 'most obviously prejudicial') the imprecise outer boundaries of the rule would mean that some speech of a non-harmful/beneficial nature is inevitably chilled. Even after judicial elaboration of the meaning of the standard, areas of doubt are likely to remain which cautious editors and publishers will be anxious to avoid. A further issue which must be addressed is whether speech which is 'obviously prejudicial' should nonetheless be protected if it was relevant to the scrutiny of public institutions and officials?

For Chesterman, the virtual absence of *post*-publication sanctions in the US is ultimately too costly a means of reconciling free speech and fair trial interests. But what precisely are these costs? How much delay is caused by *voir dires*, adjournments, transfers necessitated by advance publicity? How often do juries have to be sequestered in order to avoid prejudicial trial coverage? How many re-trials are ordered as a result of breaches of the Sixth and Fourteenth Amendments? How frequently is a permanent stay on proceedings granted? When totalled together, how do these costs compare alongside the costs of racial, class and gender prejudice in the criminal justice system? If we are serious about curtailing certain kinds of speech about governmental institutions, ought we not to be clearer about the savings/benefits that will result?

Chesterman's position also underplays the fact that some potentially prejudicial speech in the United States *is* regulated by way of post-publication sanction consistent with First Amendment standards. Rules of professional conduct limit the speech of those whose status and connection to on-going proceedings might ordinarily result in greater credence being placed in their opinions. In *Gentile v State Bar of Nevada*, a majority of the Supreme Court ruled that a 'substantial likelihood of material prejudice' standard used in the Nevada Supreme Court's disciplinary rules to reprimand the attorney petitioner for remarks made about a pending case did not violate his First Amendment rights, even though it represented a less demanding standard than the 'clear and present' danger test applied to the media.[194]

VIII THE EMPIRICAL EVIDENCE CONSIDERED

Much of the preceding discussion has rested upon assumptions about the likely impact of publications upon jury members. As has been seen, most legal systems considered in this chapter credit jurors with a limited ability to withstand prejudicial coverage and rely upon versions of the *sub judice* rule as a principal means of safeguarding the fairness of particular criminal proceedings. Nonetheless, even within these legal systems, judges differ among themselves in

[194] (1991) 501 US 1030.

their assessments of juror robustness and independence.[195] What does the empirical evidence on this issue reveal?[196]

The probative value of earlier psychological studies of the impact of pre-trial publicity has tended to be downplayed not simply because the research yields few consistent findings,[197] but also on account of perceived defects in research methodology. Simon for example has pointed to a number of problematic features, including the fact that the subjects used to measure prejudicial impact are usually drawn from an unrepresentative group (such as undergraduate psychology students) as opposed to real jurors.[198] In addition, surveys have tended to rely in the main upon fictitious cases and exposed subjects to stimuli such as audio-tapes, videos, written material etc which bore little relation to patterns of evidence presentation in real trials.[199] Finally, the research setting was typically somewhere other than a jury room, usually a university or someone's house, a factor which would have reinforced participants' awareness that their verdict could have no impact on an actual defendant. In result, it seems reasonable to suppose that these mock juries may well have been under less pressure than actual jurors to remain objective and to base their verdicts upon the evidence presented in court only. The artificiality of the research setting involving mock jurors is compounded by two further factors; the unreal nature of the focused exposure to prejudicial material in mock juror surveys; and the absence of what would be a normal time lag between exposure to media coverage and the commencement of any actual trial. Jurors in the real world do not normally know at the moment they are exposed to pre-trial publicity that they will be called upon at some unspecified time in the future to serve as jurors. In these circumstances, the purportedly prejudicial coverage is just one broadcast item among many others—one which the juror has no reason to pay especial attention to and remember a number of months afterwards. By contrast, a number of the research studies expose mock jurors to prejudicial material by itself, that is out of the normal context in which it is received by actual jurors and then, with little or no break, require the subjects to read/listen/view trial proceedings. In these

[195] Contrast the robust approaches to juror susceptibility expressed by Lawton J in *R v Kray* (1969) 53 Cr App Rep 412, 414 and Mason CJ in *Hinch v AG* (1987) 164 CLR 15, 31 with the more protective attitudes evident in remarks by Lord Diplock in *AG v Times Newspapers Ltd* [1974] AC 273, 309 and the New South Wales Court of Appeal in *DPP v Wran* (1986) 7 NSWLR 616, 639–40.

[196] Lack of space prevents discussion of the impact of publicity on witnesses. See however the tentative conclusion of the New South Wales Law Reform Commission that, as of 2000, little by way of empirical evidence supports the notion of influence on witnesses by media publicity. Discussion Paper No 43 *Contempt by Publication* (2000, Sydney).

[197] See Chesterman's remark that the research has 'produced little by way of conclusive answers' in *Freedom of Speech in Australian Law:A Delicate Plant* (Ashgate, Aldershot, 2000) at 290.

[198] RJ Simon, 'Does the Court's Decision in *Nebraska Press Association* Fit the Research Evidence on the Impact on Jurors of News Coverage?' (1976–77) 29 *Stanford Law Review* 515.

[199] This point is expressly conceded by researchers at the Centre for Socio-Legal Studies, University of Oxford in a study carried out for the Home Office in 1995 and reported as Law Commission Consultation Paper 141 *Previous Misconduct of a Defendant* (HMSO, London, 1996) Appendix D.

circumstances, it is to be expected that the prejudicial impact of media coverage would be greater in surveys of mock jurors than occurs in the real world.

Notwithstanding these criticisms, it is important to record what various empirical studies have found. Much of the research confirms a link between increased exposure to a case and a tendency to be pro-prosecution, although a number of studies stop short of ascertaining whether the pro-prosecution bias among the mock jury persists through the trial itself.[200] Studies which have followed pre-trial publicity through to its impact subsequently upon jury decision-making suggest that, after listening to both the trial judge's admonition to decide the case according to the evidence in court only and the evidence itself, the percentage of mock jurors who subsequently believed the defendant to be guilty dropped dramatically from its pre-trial level.[201] Another study by Padawer-Singer and Barton suggested contrariwise that pre-trial prejudice did influence mock jury verdicts,[202] although the authors failed to specify whether, after having gone through a *voir dire* examination, the tendency to be prejudiced remained or was diminished. Given the importance of the *voir dire* in actual criminal jury trials where there has been a high level of prior media coverage, it is difficult to draw too many conclusions from this survey.

Other research has sought to differentiate between the prejudicial effects of different types of pre-trial publicity and the curative impact of remedial measures. Thus, a survey by Kramer et al showed that delaying the start of the trial, whilst effective in remedying the prejudice caused by the pre-trial disclosure of factual information (for example the defendant's past criminal record), was ineffective in respect of more obviously emotive material (an oblique hint that a defendant may be linked in some way to an unrelated, though especially abhorrent crime such as rape or child abuse).[203] In a survey conducted by Otto, Penrod and Dexter, mock jurors comprising 262 psychology students watched a video of an actual trial.[204] Some of the jurors had been exposed to purposely created newspaper articles which contained adverse statements relating to the

[200] This is true in respect of the studies undertaken by RJ Simon and T Eimermann, 'The Jury Finds Not Guilty: Another Look at Media Influence on the Jury' (1971) 48 *Journalism Quarterly* 343 and E Costantini, J King, 'The Partial Juror: Correlates and causes of prejudgment' (1980/1) 15 *Law and Society Review* 9.

[201] Simon, 'Does the Court's Decision in *Nebraska Press Association* Fit the Research Evidence' n 198 above 520–23. The idea that judicial instruction might counter the effects of pre-trial prejudicial publicity is supported by the study of Kline and Jess, 'Prejudicial Publicity: Its Effects on Law Schools Mock Juries' (1966) 43 *Journalism Quarterly* 113, and research in England by WR Cornish and AP Sealy published as 'Juries and the Rules of Evidence' [1973] *Criminal Law Review* 208; and 'Jurors and their Verdicts' (1973) 36 *Modern Law Review* 496.

[202] 'The Impact of Pretrial Publicity on Jurors' Verdicts', in RJ Simon (ed) *The Jury System in America* (Sage, Beverley Hills Cal, 1975).

[203] GP Kramer, NL Kerr and JS Carroll, 'Pretrial publicity, judicial remedies and jury bias' (1990) 14 *Law and Human Behavior* 409.

[204] AL Otto, SD Penrod and HR Dexter, 'The Biasing Impact of Pre-Trial Publicity on Juror Judgments' (1994) 18 *Law and Human Behavior* 453.

defendant's character; a 'weak' inadmissible opinion from a neighbour;[205] the defendant's prior criminal record; a reference to the defendant's low status job; and a 'strong' inadmissible statement from a neighbour.[206] The researchers found that whilst some of the pre-trial publicity did affect the jurors' initial assessments of guilt/innocence,[207] none of the five pre-trial statements had a significant direct effect on the post-trial verdicts.[208] This finding was consistent with the suggestion that the introduction of trial evidence diminished the prejudicial impact of pre-trial publicity.[209] Only negative information about the defendant's character was shown to have a slight effect on final verdicts, a finding which prompted the researchers to advocate the issue of a judicial instruction prior to the presentation of trial evidence emphasising the presumption of innocence.

Arguably the most significant research into the working of the jury to emerge in recent years has been that conducted by the Law Commission of New Zealand.[210] Unlike earlier research, the New Zealand study drew on the experiences of 312 actual jurors sitting in 18 High Court and 30 District Court jury trials over a nine month period in 1998. The offences tried in these cases ranged from murder through fraud to attempted burglary. Trials in the sample lasted between half a day and five and a half weeks. High profile trials were deliberately chosen for inclusion in the sample. The juror sample did not vary significantly from the socio-demographic characteristics of New Zealand jurors reported by the Department of Justice in 1995.

Assessments were made of the impact of pre-trial publicity and publicity occurring during trials. Jurors were often told in the judge's opening instructions to ignore pre-trial publicity or other material which they believed to be connected to the trial. Where there was publicity during a trial, jurors were again reminded to ignore media accounts.[211] These warnings served to reinforce

205 'I would not live with (the defendant).'

206 In which the defendant was said to be a drug user.

207 The 'strong' inadmissible neighbour statement did incline the jurors to believe that the defendant was guilty. Conversely, the 'weak' inadmissible statement lead 'jurors' to think the defendant was not guilty. Interestingly, the disclosure of a past criminal record did not influence initial assessments of guilt/innocence.

208 Two English studies have found on this point that disclosure of previous similar convictions makes a mock jury more inclined to convict whilst disclosure of dissimilar convictions makes a conviction on the whole less likely, WR Cornish and AP Sealy published as 'Juries and the Rules of Evidence' [1973] *Criminal Law Review* 208; and 'Jurors and their Verdicts' (1973) 36 *Modern Law Review* 496; Centre for Socio-Legal Studies, University of Oxford in a study carried out for the Home Office in 1995 reported as Law Commission Consultation Paper 141 *Previous Misconduct of a Defendant* (HMSO, London, 1996) Appendix D. Cornish and Sealy also found that a judicial direction to disregard a defendant's previous conviction managed to avert any prejudicial effect.

209 See also JL Freedman and TM Burke, 'The effect of pretrial publicity: The Bernardo case' (1996) *Canadian Journal of Criminology* 253 for subsequent confirmation of this point.

210 New Zealand Law Commission Preliminary Paper 37 *Juries in Criminal Trials* (NZLC Wellington, 1999).

211 *Ibid* vol 2 para 7.46.

advice previously given to jurors on arrival at the jury assembly area in a video and booklet.[212]

In a conclusion with serious implications for the *sub judice* rule, the New Zealand Law Commission stated:

> The research shows that the impact of media publicity both before and during the trial is minimal . . . Jurors seemed quite able to recognise when media coverage of their trial is inaccurate and to put media coverage aside.[213]

Key findings thrown up by the research into pre-trial publicity included the fact that, despite the inclusion of high profile cases in the sample, very few jurors (16 out of 312) recalled anything of the case beyond a hazy recollection.[214] Of these, only a handful recalled material in terms which indicated prejudgment. Among this sub-class, some acknowledged their preconceptions and claimed to make a deliberate effort to discount them. As for others inclined to prejudgement, the study reports that when confronted with evidence in the trial which contradicted their initial opinions, these jurors had little difficulty in dropping earlier views.[215]

In the case of publicity during the trial, it was reported that some jurors had let media coverage affect their approach to the case in three of the 48 trials. In each case, these jurors were told by other jurors that the information was neither relevant nor wanted.[216] In other cases where jurors saw/heard media coverage of their trial, they stated that such coverage was put to one side in jury deliberations because it was seen as partial and inaccurate.[217]

It is of course impossible to discount the notion that the jurors, being aware of the research project, tailored their responses so as to appear conscientious and objective. It may also be differences in legal culture should make us wary of extrapolating the results across other jurisdictions. Nonetheless, the New Zealand research offers empirical support for the sceptical stance taken by the scrutiny of government model regarding actual media influence on jury trials. What is not clear from the research is the extent to which, in those minority of cases where jurors do carry prejudicial material into the trial, the warnings in the booklet, video and those issued by the trial judge manage to diminish such prejudice. Further research is needed into the precise remedial impact of particular devices and would be instructive to judges and policy-makers alike.

[212] It seems however that a 'significant' number of jurors in the sample did not read the booklet whilst 22% reported not having seen the video. *Ibid* vol 2. paras. 2.12–2.18.

[213] *Ibid* vol 1 para. 287.

[214] *Ibid* vol 2 para. 7.51.

[215] *Ibid* vol 2 para 7.52.

[216] *Ibid* vol 2 para 7.56.

[217] *Ibid* vol 2 para 7.55.

IX CONCLUSION: RETURN TO ERA OF JURY AS PERSONS WITH KNOWLEDGE OF MATTERS AT ISSUE IN THE TRIAL

> The objective of finding twelve jurors who know nothing of the facts of a highly publicized case is, today, patently unrealistic.
>
> —Cory J in *Phillips v Nova Scotia*[218]

Juries as originally constituted in the early Middle Ages came to a dispute with personal knowledge of events and persons involved in the proceedings and acted upon that knowledge in reaching their verdict.[219] Only in the later Middle Ages when the limitations about jurors' prior knowledge of events in cases were acknowledged were witnesses admitted to assist in fact finding. It was not however until the eighteenth century that a formal rule was established barring jurors with previous knowledge of a case. Today, as the quotation from Justice Cory acknowledges, most jurors in cases in high profile cases will have heard something which relates to the trial proceedings and, whilst a trial proceeds, be able to read/see/hear further such material. The question posed in this chapter is how should the legal system react to such levels of publicity?

One response is to hold up the spectre of ever greater numbers of collapsed trials to justify further restraints on court-related speech. Domestically, this might entail expanding the reach of section 2(2) of the 1981 Act. This development is not entirely fanciful. In the aftermath of the collapsed trial of Geoff Knights, the National Heritage Committee and the previous Labour Government agreed that the media enjoyed an excessive degree of freedom to report matters *in advance* of criminal proceedings and that ways of tightening up the law in respect of cumulatively caused prejudice needed to be examined.[220] In the case of material published *during* trials, we might adopt the approach of Poole J at the trial of several well-known professional footballers for assault at Hull Crown Court in April 2001. Whilst the jury were considering their verdict, a Sunday newspaper published an article with the father of the alleged assault victim in which it was claimed that the attack was racially motivated. The next day, on being told that one or more jurors was 'aware' of the article, Poole J halted the trial at no small expense to the taxpayer (and other non-pecuniary 'costs' to trial participants) and ordered a re-trial. He referred the matter to the Attorney General to see whether the newspaper should face strict liability contempt proceedings.[221]

By way of comment, it is submitted that the response of the judge was a dramatic and disproportionate response to the newspaper article. The jurors appear to have been credited with little ability to follow the judge's instructions

[218] *Phillips v Nova Scotia* (1995) 124 DLR (4th) 129, 181 *per* Cory J.
[219] WR Cornish, *The Jury* (Allen Lane, London, 1968) at 10–12.
[220] See the National Heritage Select Committee Report *Press Activity Affecting Court Cases* (1996–97) HCP 86 in the aftermath of *AG v MGN* and the Government's response promising a review at HL Debs (1999–2000) Written Answers 9 Feb.
[221] The newspaper was later fined £75,000 by the Divisional Court for breaching 52(2).

to focus solely on the evidence before the court. No factual finding was made about the article's impact on jury deliberations. The New Zealand evidence suggests after all that jurors can be trusted not to let partisan accounts published during a trial to affect their deliberations. If, conversely, the judge did fear that the media might be tempted to publish such accounts and that jurors would be influenced by them, why did he not consider sequestering jurors in a hotel until such time as they could reach a verdict?

This chapter has argued for an alternative approach to publicity which seeks to reconcile the core legal entitlement to a fair trial with media freedom. It starts from the premise that the freedom to speak about court proceedings may no longer be treated as a residual liberty which may be interfered with lightly by the courts who come to these disputes as a self-interested party. The enhanced constitutional status of speech requires courts and legislators to think more creatively about possible means of reconciling speech and fair trial interests, especially in an era of mass communication systems where jurors may well come to trials with some pre-conceived opinions about an accused's guilt. Clearly, whilst claims to media freedom are strongest where the impugned speech can claim to advance informed democratic control over agencies of government, not all court-related speech will fall within this category. However, before bringing the full weight of the criminal law to bear on speech which is less obviously beneficial, acceptance of the idea that contempt restrictions exist to protect the courts from outside interference would seem logically to require that punishment be confined to those instances where speech does actually have a seriously detrimental impact on the fairness of an accused's fair trial. At present, there is a speculative (not to say arbitrary) assessment of likely or threatened damage based upon factors known at the time of publication which catches inter alia speech which does not actually result in prejudiced proceedings. The New Zealand research suggests a possible explanation for this state of affairs. The susceptible juror upon which some judicial thinking is predicated looks to be some way off the mark.

4

For the Sake of the Children? Young Persons, Reporting Restrictions and Open Justice[1]

I INTRODUCTION

THE PREVIOUS CHAPTER considered the role played by *sub judice* rules in safeguarding the fairness of criminal proceedings before juries and the impact of constitutional norms in this area. This chapter takes as its focus legislative and judicial restraints imposed to protect the privacy interests of children and young persons involved in criminal proceedings. In recent years, media freedom in England and Wales to identify children and young persons involved in criminal proceedings has been both enlarged and diminished. On the one hand, the media have benefitted from parliamentary and judicial moves to end the anonymity of certain classes of young offenders. To this end, amendments to section 49 of the Children and Young Persons Act 1933 inserted by the Crime Sentences Act 1997, allow for restrictions on the identification of a child/young person convicted of an offence in the Youth Court to be lifted where 'a court is satisfied that it is in the public interest to do so.'[2] Guidance from the Home Office and Lord Chancellor's Department has stated that the intention behind this provision is to allow a young person to be named upon conviction either where a serious offence has been committed or where the offending is of a persistent nature or has impacted on a number of people in the community.[3] The amendment seeks to make young offenders accept responsibility for their wrongdoing and thereby reduce the chance of offending in the future. This change has mirrored a tendency on the part of Crown Court judges to lift young persons' anonymity upon conviction in cases of serious and/or repeat offending tried in the adult court.[4]

[1] An earlier version of part of this chapter appeared as 'Children, Young Persons, Criminal Proceedings and Open Justice—A Comparative Perspective' in E Barendt and A Firth (eds) *The Yearbook of Copyright and Media Law* (Oxford University Press, Oxford, 2000) at 141.

[2] Crime Sentences Act 1997, s 45 inserting s 49(4)(A) into the 1933 Act. Legal representatives for the child/young person are entitled to make representations prior to any such order, s 49(4)(B).

[3] Home Office/Lord Chancellor's Department Circular published in June 1998.

[4] See further I Cram, 'Publish and Damn' (1998) 148 *New Law Journal* 1748, 1787. There are signs however that well-publicised threats to the *post* release physical safety of the murderers of James

In contrast, other changes—albeit prompted in part by developments at the level of international law—appear to strengthen rules concerning juvenile privacy. The ruling of the European Court of Human Rights in *T v United Kingdom*[5] and *V v United Kingdom*[6] concerning the fair trials rights of two boys convicted at Preston Crown Court of killing James Bulger was followed by the issue of a Practice Note designed to safeguard the right of young persons to effective participation in trials under Article 6. Other recent domestic reforms have sought to confer greater privacy on young persons who come into contact with criminal justice agencies. Thus, under the Youth Justice and Criminal Evidence Act 1999,[7] new restrictions attach to media reporting of alleged criminal incidents which prevent the identification of certain classes of young persons once a criminal investigation has begun.[8]

A number of the restrictions considered in this chapter are prior restraints, understood in the rather narrow sense of judicial orders which prevent a publication seeing the light of day and which are issued after due consideration of factors for and against restriction in individual cases.[9] A further set of controls—automatic reporting restrictions—also restrict media reports in advance but here the constraints are laid down in statutory form and apply to a whole class of criminal proceedings regardless of the strength of particular privacy interests raised in any given case. Automatic restrictions may be defended as expressing the clear legislative preference of a democratically elected assembly for limited media reporting of cases involving young persons. As has been argued elsewhere however,[10] the routine imposition by the UK Parliament of fresh sets of reporting restrictions to a variety of sets of criminal proceedings has become an incidental feature of criminal justice reform, occurring frequently without regard to countervailing freedom of expression interests. Additionally, automatic restrictions may be thought controversial in light of the fact that they apply without an evaluation of alternative and less drastic forms of restraint. As such, there may be merit in treating automatic restraints as deserving of the level of scrutiny usually reserved for prior restraints.

Bulger—Robert Thompson and Jon Venables—have made judges more nervous about using this power. See *The Times*, 26 June 2001.

[5] (2000) 30 EHRR 121.

[6] *Ibid.*

[7] For the background to the Act see *Speaking up for Justice*, Report of the Working Group on the treatment of Vulnerable or Intimidated Witnesses in the Criminal Justice System (Home Office, London, 1998) and subsequent Parliamentary debates at HC Debs (1998–99) Vol 329, c 385 *et seq* (2nd Reading) and Standing Committee E (1998–99) cc 227–46.

[8] S 44(2). The Act reimposes the old sets of restrictions upon the identification of young persons involved in criminal proceedings (s 45, hitherto in s 39(1) of the Children and Young Persons Act 1933) and also imposes further sets of restrictions on the identification of vulnerable adult witnesses and sexual offence complainants. See generally Part II Chapter IV of the 1999 Act discussed below.

[9] See further *Alexander v United States* (1993) 509 US 544, 550. The lack of consensus on what constitutes a prior restraint is apparent from cases such as *Near v Minnesota* (1931) 283 US 697.

[10] I Cram, 'Automatic Reporting Restrictions in Criminal Proceedings and Article 10 ECHR' [1998] *European Human Rights Law Review* 742.

Indeed, they may be considered more objectionable because of the mandatory manner in which they apply. The purpose of this chapter is to consider the nature and range of restraints imposed to safeguard the privacy interests of young persons involved in criminal proceedings (whether as offenders, accused persons, witnesses or victims) across a variety of jurisdictions. As was noted previously, a number of restraints which the media find themselves subject to when reporting criminal proceedings involving young persons are the result of judicial orders. Accordingly, this chapter considers some objections to Alexander Bickel's general argument that prior restraints constitute an especially serious curtailment of media freedom. The cogency of privacy arguments invoked in the case of children and young persons are then examined. Later, the nature and influence of international legal norms in protecting children's privacy claims are then outlined. In the second half of the chapter, access rules and reporting restrictions in three federal jurisdictions—Australia, Canada and the United States are detailed. Of central importance here is the impact of constitutional norms upon closed proceedings (whether partial or wholly closed) and publication bans. The article concludes by considering some domestic implications of *T v United Kingdom* for the juvenile trial process as well as the compatability of the latest set of pre-trial reporting restrictions contained in the 1999 Act with the European Convention on Human Rights.

II DOMESTIC PROVISIONS GOVERNING ACCESS TO AND REPORTING OF CRIMINAL PROCEEDINGS INVOLVING YOUNG PERSONS IN ENGLAND AND WALES

Youth Court Proceedings

Apart from certain serious offences reserved for the adult courts, the Youth Court enjoys jurisdiction to try offences in respect of persons under 18 years of age at the time of the alleged offence. Unlike members of the public who are excluded from attending youth court proceedings, *bona fide* representatives of the media are permitted to be present and report these proceedings.[11] However, section 49 of the Children and Young Persons Act 1933 limits without the need for an express judicial order that which may be reported about Youth Court proceedings.[12] The section provides that:

[11] Children and Young Persons Act 1933, s 47(2). For judicial discussion on the general issue of when the media should be permitted to remain in court when members of the public have been removed, see *R v Waterfield* [1975] 1 WLR 711; and *Re Crook* (1991) 93 Cr App R 17.

[12] As amended by the Criminal Justice and Public Order Act 1994, s 49; the Crime (Sentences) Act 1997, s 45 and the Youth Justice and Criminal Evidence Act 1999, Sch 2 para 3. The restrictions apply to publications in Scotland and also cover appeals in England and Wales from youth court proceedings (although to be valid the court must announce that s 49 restrictions apply to the appeal proceedings, Children and Young Persons Act 1969, s 10(2)) and under ss 15 and 16 of the Children

> (1)(a) no report shall be published which reveals the name, address or school of any child or young person concerned in the proceedings or includes any particulars likely to lead to the identification of any child or young person concerned in the proceedings; and
> (b) no picture shall be published or included in a programme service as being or including a picture of any child or young person concerned in the proceedings.

The reference to a child or young person 'concerned' in proceedings refers to persons against whom proceedings are taken as well as witnesses in such proceedings.[13] This prohibition may be lifted by the court[14] in three sets of circumstances laid down in section 49(5) as amended. First, for the purpose of avoiding injustice to a child or young person.[15] Second, where a child/young person having been charged with or convicted of either a violent offence or a sexual offence; or an offence punishable in the case of a person over the age of 21 with fourteen years of more, that child/young person is unlawfully at large and publicity is needed for the purpose of apprehending him/her.[16] Under an amendment inserted by the Crime Sentences Act 1997, restrictions may also be lifted in respect of a child/young person convicted of an offence where 'a court is satisfied that it is in the public interest to do so.'[17]

Adult Court Proceedings

Children and young persons under 18 years may appear before the adult criminal courts as co-defendants with an accused adult,[18] or witnesses. Furthermore, children and young persons charged with an offence of homicide must also be committed to the Crown Court for trial[19] as may young persons charged with certain extremely serious offences.[20]

and Young Persons Act 1969 (varying/revoking supervision orders) and appeals arising from ss 15 and 16 proceedings. See further the Children and Young Persons Act 1933, s 49(2).

[13] Children and Young Persons Act 1933, s 49(4) as amended.

[14] The discretion which formerly vested in the Home Secretary to lift the prohibition was removed by s 49(5) of the Criminal Justice and Public Order Act 1994.

[15] *Ibid*, s 49(5). This might be the case where a mistaken belief gains ground to the effect that a child who is in fact a witness in youth court proceedings is the defendant. Publication of the defendant's name would then prevent stigma wrongly attaching to the witness.

[16] Children and Young Persons Act 1933, s 49(5)–(7) (as amended).

[17] Children and Young Persons Act 1933 s 49(4A).

[18] See further Children and Young Persons Act 1933, s 46(1) which also expressly denies jurisdiction to the Youth Court in respect of the following offences: where an adult is charged with aiding abetting, causing, procuring, allowing or permitting the offence by the child/young person; where the child/young person is charged with aiding and abetting, causing, procuring, allowing or permitting the offence by the adult.

[19] Magistrates' Court Act 1980, s 24(1).

[20] Known as 'grave' crimes under the Children and Young Persons Act 1933, s 53(2). See further T Moore and T Wilkinson, *Youth Court: A Guide to the Law and Practice* (Longman, London, 1992) 47–51.

The general rule in such proceedings is that, in the absence of an express judicial order to the contrary, the media are at liberty to identify the parties concerned in the proceedings.[21] Under the Youth Justice and Criminal Evidence Act 1999 however, section 45(3) which is yet to brought into force provides that:

> The court may direct that no matter relating to any person concerned in the proceedings shall while he is under the age of 18 be included in any publication if it is likely to lead members of the public to identify him as a person concerned in the proceedings.

This provision largely replicates the power of criminal courts under section 39 of the 1933 Act to confer anonymity on young persons. Restrictions imposed under section 45(3) may be dispensed with in part or whole to the extent that it is necessary in the interests of justice,[22] or where the court is satisfied that the restrictions impose a 'substantial and unreasonable restriction on the reporting of proceedings and that it is in the public interest to remove or relax the restriction.[23] In each case, the court must have regard to the welfare of the person to whom the restriction relates.[24]

Reporting Criminal Investigations

Under a novel addition which, at the time of writing, is yet to be brought into force, Parliament has extended backwards in time the point in time at which anonymity protection for young persons kicks in to the moment at which a criminal investigation has begun. Under section 44(2) of the Youth Justice and Criminal Justice Act 1999,

> No matter . . . shall while he is under the age of 18 be included in any publication if it is likely to lead members of the public to identify him as a person involved in the offence.

The restrictions will endure until the start of any court proceedings.[25] The term 'matter' above is stated to include reference to a young person's name, address, school, place of work and still/moving pictures of him.[26] It will be open to a magistrates' court or Crown Court to lift restrictions either in whole or part where satisfied that it is 'necessary in the interests of justice' to do so[27] after having regard to the welfare of the young person concerned.[28] Breach of section 44(2) will render newspaper proprietors, editors and publishers and those with

[21] The onus is on the applicant to show why restrictions should be imposed, *R v Central Criminal Court ex parte W, B and C* (2001) 1 Cr App R 7.
[22] Youth Justice and Criminal Evidence Act 1999, s 45(4).
[23] *Ibid*, s 45(5).
[24] *Ibid*, s 45(6).
[25] *Ibid*, s 44(3). Whether the restrictions remain permanently in force if, after a police investigation is concluded, no court proceedings follow is not clear.
[26] *Ibid*, s 44(6).
[27] *Ibid*, s 44(7).
[28] *Ibid*, s 44(8).

editorial control over broadcast programmes liable on summary conviction under section 49 to a fine not exceeding level five on the standard scale.[29] The Act lays down three defences to a section 49 charge. First, no liability will be incurred if it can be proved that at the time of publication the journalist/editor etc. was not aware, did not suspect and had no reason to suspect that the criminal investigation in question had begun.[30] Two further defences are provided by section 50(3) in the case of witnesses and alleged victims involved in a criminal investigation although these will only be needed once a separate affirmative resolution bringing these additional restraints into force has been passed by both Houses of Parliament.[31] Under the first defence, it must be proved to the satisfaction of the court that publication of the prohibited matter was in the public interest in that prohibition amounted to a 'substantial and unreasonable restriction on reporting of matters connected with that offence.'[32] A second defence permits identification where written consent has been given by the parent/guardian of a young witness/alleged victim aged below 16 years or the young person himself if aged 16 or 17 to identification unless the peace or comfort of the parent/guardian or that of the young person was interfered with.[33] This defence is lost if the consent is later withdrawn in writing and this withdrawal is communicated in sufficient time to prevent the publication of the prohibited matter.[34]

III PRIOR RESTRAINTS—A FREEZE ON SPEECH? BICKEL AND HIS CRITICS

> Free society prefers to punish the few that abuse rights of speech *after* they break the law than to throttle them and all others beforehand.[35]

From the Supreme Court ruling in *Near v Minnesota*,[36] carrying through to the *Pentagon Papers* case,[37] *Nebraska Press Association v Stuart*[38] and beyond, the

[29] Youth Justice and Criminal Evidence Act 1999, s 49(2), (3) and (5). The prohibition extends to publication in Scotland under s 68(6).
[30] *Ibid*, s 50(2)(b).
[31] The first defence is not available in respect of the identification of witnesses in investigations under the Sexual Offences (Amendment) Act 1992, s 1 while the consent defence is not available in respect of such witnesses where they are under the age of 16. See Youth Justice and Criminal Evidence Act 1999, s 50(3)(b)(ii), (4)(b)(ii).
[32] *Ibid*, s 50(3).
[33] *Ibid*, s 50(5),(6) and (8). In the case of consent by a parent/guardian, written notice must first be given to the parent/guardian drawing the latter's attention to the need to consider the welfare of the young person when deciding whether to give consent on his/her behalf.
[34] *Ibid*, s 50(6).
[35] *Southeastern Promotions Ltd v United States* (1975) 403 US 713.
[36] (1931) 283 US 697.
[37] *New York Times v United States* (1971) 403 US 713. Though Smolla has argued that upon closer analysis of the individual judgments it is incorrect to view this ruling as erecting an impregnable barrier against prior restraints. see RA Smolla, *Free Speech in an Open Society* (Alfred A Knopf, New York NY, 1997) at ch 9.
[38] (1976) US 427 US 539, 'Prior restraints on speech and publication are the most serious and least tolerable infringement on First Amendment rights.'

notion that prior restraint constitutes a particularly serious threat to freedom of speech has been an enduring theme of First Amendment jurisprudence. [39]As was noted in chapter two, the European Court of Human Rights has taken a similarly critical line. Thus, in the case of prior restraints affecting news coverage where judicial hostility tends to be most pronounced, the Strasbourg Court has reminded national authorities that these restrictions would be viewed with the most careful scrutiny.[40] Domestically, Parliament too has been uneasy at judicial readiness to grant interlocutory injunctions against media defendants in breach of confidence actions. This unease led to an amendment to the Human Rights Act 1998 making it more difficult for the courts in certain cases to restrain publication before the main trial.[41]

Central to the case against prior restraints is the idea that they constitute a uniquely destructive force on speech. In the oft-quoted remarks of Alexander Bickel, prior restraints cause

> a loss in the immediacy of speech, the impact, of speech . . . The violator of a prior restraint may be assured of being held in contempt; the violator of a statute punishing speech criminally knows that he will go before a jury and take his chance, counting on a possible acquittal . . . A criminal statute chills, prior restraint freezes.[42]

Bickel's thesis is that a system of prior restraints constitutes an excessive interference with freedom of speech when compared to alternative, *post*-publication sanctions. Two decades previously, Thomas Emerson, another First Amendment scholar, had pointed to increasing resort to preventative controls which, he argued, were beginning to jeopardise freedom of expression and whose origins he argued were attributable in part to the desire to control people's minds.[43] The conventional hostility to prior restraints wisdom has not commanded universal support however. Commentators have queried the orthodox position via two main lines of argument. The first of these asserts that *generalised* opposition to prior restraints amounts to a misreading of the English jurist Blackstone's original objection. Secondly, and more significantly, Bickel's critics deny that prior restraints entail especially heavy costs for speech. On the contrary, the 'reflexive rhetoric'[44] surrounding prior restraints obscures the fact that *post*-publication

[39] Cf *In re Cable News Network* 18 Media Law Reporter 1358 (Nov 10, 1990, 11th Circuit) where the Supreme Court refused to review the 11th Circuit's decision to affirm an order restraining the broadcast of tapes containing conversations between General Manuel Noriega and his lawyers. For criticism of the Supreme Court's non-intervention, see Smolla at n 37 above.

[40] *The Observer and Guardian v UK* (1992) 14 EHRR 153.

[41] Section 12(3) of the Human Rights Act 1998 requires a court which is considering the granting of interlocutory injunctive relief which might affect the Convention right to freedom of expression not to grant that relief 'unless satisfied that the applicant is likely to establish that publication should not be allowed.'

[42] *The Morality of Consent* (Yale University Press, New Haven Conn, 1975) at 61.

[43] 'The Doctrine of Prior Restraint' (1955) 20 *Law and Contemporary Problems* 648, 649. Emerson had in mind developments such as the non-Communist oath of the Taft-Hartley Act.

[44] M Redish, 'The Proper Role of the Prior Restraint Doctrine in First Amendment Theory' (1984) 70 *Virginia Law Review* 53.

sanctions may, in fact, pose a greater threat to freedom of expression. Accordingly, it is argued that such generalised hostility must be abandoned and replaced by a more particularistic analysis.[45] These lines of argument will now be considered in more detail.

In chapter two, it was seen that the especial hostility shown to prior restraints under First Amendment jurisprudence owes much to the influence of Blackstone. On closer examination however, it is clear that his specific target in the *Commentaries on the Laws of England* was the system of state licensing developed under various Regulation of Printing Acts designed to prevent seditious libel and other perceived evils. Subsequently however, the 'doctrine of prior restraint' came to be invoked against a much wider range of speech limitations including judicial orders and legislative bans.[46] There are however clear substantive and procedural distinctions between state licensing of expressive activity and prior restraints by judicial order which justify differential levels of judicial scrutiny. Licensing schemes for their part are characterised by the application of vague standards by an administrative body concerned to act somewhat narrowly in pursuance of its legislative purpose. Court-imposed restraints on the other hand are issued after consideration of a range of societal interests and in a forum which is fully aware of the importance of constitutional rights, including those of free speech. On a procedural point, it is further contended that administrative bodies rarely operate in an adversarial manner whereas, in respect of judicial orders, the case for suppression is usually tested in open, adversarial proceedings.[47]

The second main argument used by those sceptical of the generalised hostility is that judicially imposed publication bans do not entail greater social costs to free speech than *post*-publication criminal sanctions.[48] The precisely defined nature of prior restraints which impact upon specific material and identified parties means that minor speech losses only are incurred. By contrast, the reliance in penal statutes upon vaguely phrased standards such as 'clear and present danger' means that *post*-publication criminal sanctions deter a range of

[45] See thus P Freund, 'The Supreme Court and Civil Liberties' (1951) 4 *Vanderbilt Law Review* 533, cited with approval by Frankfurter J in *Kingsley Books, Inc v Brown* (1957) 354 US 436. Significantly in this regard, it is worth recalling Madison, the author of the First Amendment, who remarked that it would 'seem a mockery to say that no laws should be passed preventing publications from being made, but that laws might be passed for punishing them in case they should be made.' Quoted in L Levy, *Legacy of Suppression—Freedom of Speech and Press in Early American History* (Belknap Press (part of Harvard University Press), Cambridge Mass, 1960) at 274.

[46] (1765, Book IV) 151–52. 'The liberty of the press is indeed essential to the nature of a free state; but this consists in laying no previous restraints on publications and not in censure for criminal matter when published. Every free man has an undoubted right to lay what sentiments he pleases before the public; to forbid this is to destroy the freedom of the press; but if he publishes what is improper, mischievious or illegal, he must take the consequences of his own temerity.'

[47] See further WT Mayton, 'Toward a Theory of First Amendment Process: Injunctions of Speech, Subsequent Punishment, and the Costs of Prior Restraint Doctrine' (1982) 67 *Cornell Law Review* 245.

[48] See Mayton *ibid*, and JC Jeffries, 'Rethinking Prior Restraint' (1983) 92 *Yale Law Journal* 408.

speech activities in which a risk-averse public and cost-conscious publishers act as self-censors even though some of these activities will in the end be entirely lawful. This results in costs not only to the speaker but also the audience who are denied access to the suppressed material. Conversely, it is the state which benefits from low cost enforcement as self-censorship minimises the numbers who decide to publish and face the risk of prosecution.

One instance where Bickel's opponents concede that injunctions may bite more on free speech interests than *post*-publication sanctions occurs where the constitutionality of an injunction may not be challenged after disobedience to its terms in subsequent contempt proceedings—the so-called collateral bar rule.[49] According to the Supreme Court in *Walker v City of Birmingham* the rule ceases to apply where the order is 'transparently invalid' or with 'only a frivolous pretence to validity'.[50] In the context of the reporting of open court proceedings, the rule was applied in *US v Dickinson* where two reporters breached a federal district judge's order not to report details of evidence taken in court that day.[51] The two were later held by the same judge to have been in contempt and the convictions were allowed to stand by the Fifth Circuit Court of Appeals even though the initial order was found by the same court to have been unconstitutional. The ruling in *Dickinson* leaves media organisations with the option of taking an appeal against the injunction although the latter will remain in force unless/until it is set aside during which time the newsworthiness of the hearing may well have diminished. It is interesting to speculate whether, as Barnett has urged, the striking down of prior restraints in cases such as *Nebraska Press Association v Stuart*[52] and *Oklahoma Publishing Co v District Court*[53]—where the injuncted matter was already made public in open court proceedings or through documents available to public inspection—means that this type of restraint is 'transparently invalid' or possesses 'only a frivolous pretence to validity' with the consequence that the collateral bar rule ceases to apply.[54] If correct, then two elements in Bickel's objection to prior restraints—those of the loss of immediacy of speech and the certainty of punishment—begin to fall away. Publishers (or at least the bolder elements among them) would on this view have the option of breaching the terms of an injunction and relying upon the unconstitutionality of the restraint in later contempt proceedings. The major difficulty with Barnett's argument is that it involves a direct challenge to judicial authority which few, if any legal systems will readily tolerate. Certainly, as far as the UK is concerned, Arlidge, Eady and Smith are of the

[49] See further SR Barnett, 'The Puzzle of Prior Restraint' (1977) 29 *Stanford Law Review* 539, 551.
[50] (1967) 388 US 307, 315.
[51] (1972) 465 F 2d 496.
[52] (1976) 427 US 539.
[53] (1977) 430 US 308.
[54] See Barnett at n 49 above at 553–58. For an example of a transparently invalid prior restraint, see *Matter of Providence Journal Company* (1986) 820 F 2d 1342.

view that, in cases where an order is ultimately held to have been wrongly obtained, the 'fundamental principle' is that the order must be obeyed until such time as it is stayed or set aside.[55] Support for this view is to be found in Canada in the context of Charter violations in *Canada (Human Rights Commission) v Taylor*. There, Dickson CJ adopted the reasoning of the lower court in stating that:

> The duty of a person bound by an order of a court is to obey that order while it remains in force regardless of how flawed he may consider it or how flawed it may, in fact, be.[56]

The rationale behind the rule is the preservation of public order. As McLachlin J put it,

> If the people are free to ignore court orders because they believe their foundation is unconstitutional, anarchy cannot be far behind.[57]

The retention of a collateral bar goes some considerable way to bolstering Bickel's original objections. Not only is the immediacy of some court related speech lost (it being assumed that even an expedited appeals system will incur some loss to the newsworthiness of speech), the bar also ensures that a finding of contempt follows inexorably from the fact of publication. It is difficult then to disagree with Smolla when he argues that the collateral bar rule by itself 'is stringent enough to supply a cogent rationale for treating prior restraints as more onerous than post-publication criminal prosecutions.'[58] But what of the claim that loosely defined ordinary penal laws entail greater speech costs than prior restraints?

Focusing on the comparative costs to court related speech resulting from *sub judice* rules on the one hand and judicially ordered reporting bans on the other, it is by no means clear that the former necessarily produce a greater curtailment of speech. Bickel's critics have argued that uncertain standards of liability which characterise *sub judice* rules induce greater levels of media self-censorship. Whilst vaguely defined versions of these rules do exist, uncertainty of application is not an inherent attribute of *sub judice* restraint in practice. Consider for example the 'clear and present danger' standard in the US. In chapter two it was noted that the constitutional hurdles in the way of sustaining a *sub judice* conviction are so great that the American Bar Association's manual for journalists, *The Reporter's Key*, ruled out the existence of any circumstances in which prejudicial reporting could be met with lawful subsequent punishment. Even in jurisdictions where *sub judice* rules have been more readily invoked against the

[55] D Eady and ATH Smith, *Arlidge, Eady and Smith on Contempt*, 2nd edn (Sweet & Maxwell, London, 1999) at paras 12.131–133.
[56] (1990) 75 DLR (4th) 577.
[57] *Ibid*, at 635.
[58] Smolla at n 37 above at 287.

media, careful judicial interpretation and guidance may eliminate elements of uncertainty. The ruling of Schiemann LJ in *AG v MGN Ltd* for example which was discussed in chapter three clarified a number of matters relating to the assessment of the risk of prejudice under section 2(2) of the Contempt of Court Act 1981.[59] Thus, on the crucial question of the residual impact of a publication on a notional juror at the time of trial, Schiemann LJ in the Divisional Court stated that any assessment should consider:

(a) the length of time between publication and the likely date of trial,
(b) the focusing effect of listening over a prolonged period to evidence in a case,
(c) the likely effect of the the judge's directions to a jury.

The court also rejected the Attorney-General's proposition that the cumulative impact of a number of respondents' publications could be considered when ascertaining whether the statutory test was satisfied. Rather it is for the prosecution to show that an individual respondent has made a contribution which by itself creates the necessary risk. This requirement alone is likely to pose a major evidential difficulty for the prosecution in future cases. In consequence, the judgment will have diminished the tendency to exercise self-censorship.

Bickel's critics have further claimed that judicially-imposed prior restraints are less costly to speech interests because they target narrowly defined aspects of speech. Whilst certain powers of restraint are closely circumscribed, again this does not hold true in general. An obvious counter-example is provided by section 4(2) of the Contempt of Court Act 1981 which gives judges the power to postpone publication of

> any report of the proceedings, or any part of the proceedings . . . for such period as the court thinks fit.

It is not uncommon for section 4(2) orders to be made preventing reports of any aspects of one trial until the conclusion of a second, related trial. A glance at the width of discretionary powers of courts to restrict reporting of court proceedings considered later in this chapter serves only to throw further doubt upon the claim of prior restraints to precision. Of course, in most Youth Courts automatically applicable statutory restrictions preventing the identification of children/young persons involved in the proceedings obviate the need for further judicial orders. Where conversely the entire proceedings are in principle freely reportable such as the Northern Territory in Australia, a magistrate may issue a banning order in respect of all or part of the proceedings.[60] Even where *the subject matter* of an order is narrowly defined (say as to cover solely the identity of a person before the court), it does not follow that the *range of circumstances* in which that protection may issue is similarly confined. The Canadian Criminal Code for example confers a discretion on judges in adult courts to issue

[59] [1997] 1 All ER 456.
[60] Juvenile Justice Act 1983, s 23(1) (NT).

reporting restrictions to prevent the identification of adult/young person victims and witnesses under section 486(4.1) of the Code where the judge is satisfied that the order is 'necessary for the proper administration of justice.' Moreover, non-identification orders usually carry a permanent ban on publication.

Finally, the adversarial nature of the proceedings in which an order is made may not amount to a significant safeguard for speech interests since the prosecution/defence may simply acquiesce to the other side's request for reporting restrictions. Whilst the judge on such occasions ought to be especially mindful of the need to hear media representations opposed to the making of any order, it is not clear that this is common practice.[61]

In conclusion, Bickel's critics may have overstated the deleterious impact of *sub judice* rules whilst neglecting some speech-unfriendly aspects of court-issued prior restraints. The belief that prior restraints are particularly inimical to speech interests has especial force in the arena of court reporting as the restrictions strike at the very newsworthiness of information and comment.

IV YOUNG PERSONS' PRIVACY INTERESTS—ARGUMENTS AND COUNTERARGUMENTS

The Young Offender

The publication of true information about young persons involved in criminal proceedings has long been considered harmful. In 1927 the *Report of the Departmental Committee on the Treatment of Young Offenders* declared that it was:

> obviously undesirable that the names and addresses of the children (appearing in youth court proceedings) or any other matter should be published that can lead to their identification.[64]

Accordingly, section 49 of the Children and Young Persons Act 1933 prohibited the publication of matters calculated to lead to the identification of young persons involved in youth court proceedings. Past practice by itself however is not a sufficient reason to sustain limitations on the principle of open justice. It is important to examine the cogency of arguments which underpin juvenile anonymity. [65]

[61] In the context of statutory postponement orders under s.4(2) of the Contempt of Court Act 1981, see *AG v Guardian Newspapers (No 3)* [1992] 1 WLR 874, 886–87; *R v Clerkenwell Metropolitan Stipendiary Magistrate, ex parte The Telegraph* [1993] QB 462, 471. See further I Cram, 'Section 4(2) Postponement Orders: Media Reports of Court Proceedings under the Contempt of Court Act 1981' in E Barendt, S Bate, J Dickens and T Gibbons (eds) *Yearbook of Media and Entertainment Law*, Vol 2 (Clarendon Press, Oxford, 1996) at 111.

[64] Cmnd 2831 (HMSO, London). The Ingleby Report Cmnd 1191 (HMSO, London, 1960) also rejected the idea of publicity for juvenile offenders though more ambivalently, para 254.

[65] See SR Moody 'Publicity in Criminal Cases Involving Children' [1999] *Juridical Review* 1; KM Laubenstein 'COMMENTS, Media Access to Juvenile Justice: Should Freedom of the Press Be Limited to Promote Rehabilitation of Youthful Offenders?' (1995) 68 *Temple Law Review* 1897;

The principal fears associated with publicity are 'labelling', 'recidivism', the encouragment of others' lawlessness and the negative impact upon the offender's schooling and relationships with his/her family and peers.[66] In 'labelling' it is asserted that the public identification of a person through the media as an offender will create a self-perpetuating cycle in which the offender alters his/her conduct in order to reflect community perceptions of him/her. It is also claimed that publicity provides delinquent youths with sought-after recognition and thereby encourages recidivism in that the offender is more likely to engage in further criminal conduct.[67] The attention received via media coverage of juvenile proceedings may also encourage others to commit offences in order to secure public attention. Advocates of confidentiality also point to the adverse consequences upon an offender's family and peer group relationships which may follow from such publicity as well as diminished employment opportunities. A further argument against publicised proceedings is that the public nature of a trial may make it more difficult for young offenders to accept the seriousness of their acts and their own responsibilities and thereby hinder their re-integration into society.[68]

Those favouring greater openness of juvenile proceedings contest the validity of a number of the claims made above for offenders' anonymity. Thus, for example, it is pointed out that 'labelling' theory does not command universal acceptance as an explanation of criminal conduct (a point conceded by advocates of confidential juvenile proceedings).[69] Reference is also made to the view of some social psychologists that the stigmatising consequences of being labelled a delinquent have been exaggerated. A survey in 1972 found that only a small proportion of juvenile offenders felt seriously handicapped by their contact with the police and court system. The group reported no significant change in relationships with family and friends.[70] Crucially, critics further argue that the *incremental* effect of publicity (as opposed to any 'labelling' impact of the legal proceedings in themselves) has never been isolated and measured in a statistically significant way.[71] As to the dangers of publicity-induced recidivism,

J Michael 'A Child's Right to Privacy or Open Justice?' in G Douglas and L Sebba (eds) *Children's Rights and Traditional Values* (Dartmouth, Aldershot, 1998).

[66] See Laubenstein, *ibid* above, 1902–08.

[67] As the Earl of Mar and Kellie put it in the House of Lords debate on the Crime (Sentences) Act 1997, 'The risk is that the child or young person will bath in notoriety and enjoy the confirmation of his outlaw status.' HL Debs (1996–7) Vol 578 col 1325. See previously the *Report of the Committee on Children and Young Persons* Cmnd 1191 (1960 HMSO, London) at para 254.

[68] See the evidence of Sir Michael Rutter, Professor of Child Psychiatry at the University of London relied upon by the applicant in *V v United Kingdom* (2000) 30 EHRR 121.

[69] Laubenstein at n 65 above at 1902.

[70] JD Foster, S Dinitz and WC Reckless , 'Following Public Intervention for Delinquent Behaviour' (1972) 20 *Social Problems* 202.

[71] Research by Howard *et al* examined the impact of publicity on a single juvenile offender only. See 'Following Public Intervention for Delinquent Behaviour' (1977) 11 *Clearinghouse Review* 203. There is an issue about whether the impact of publicity alone is capable of being measured.

Geis writing in 1958 could find no empirical support for this assertion.[72] Moody—an advocate of juvenile anonymity who relies in part upon recidivism some 40 years later—is also unable to provide any corroborative data. Moreover, it is by no means clear that publicity (rather than the fact of conviction) diminishes an offender's employment opportunities. In the United States, the Supreme Court recognised in *In re Gault* that many courts routinely provided information about convictions to the FBI and the military while doing the same on request to government agencies and even private employers.[73] In England and Wales, Part V of the Police Act 1997 has created a statutory framework for the disclosure of criminal records for employment purposes and voluntary sector work in place of the largely unregulated police checks on behalf of employers, charities and other voluntary groups. It has been predicted that many employers will as a matter of course now require prospective employees to produce a 'criminal conviction certificate' prior to any offer of employment.[74] The National Association for the Care and Resettlement of Offenders and recruitment agencies have stated that Part V of the 1997 Act will create a pool of unemployable persons and hinder efforts at re-integration into society.[75]

Critics of juvenile anonymity also point to some adverse consequences to young offenders and their families of proceedings held in secret. Commenting on the closed state of Dutch juvenile proceedings, Van Nijnatten noted that procedural abuses such as the absence of a right to legal representation and to a rigorous examination of the evidence against the accused which were commonplace survived because of the absence of public scrutiny of proceedings.[76] Trasen has made similar criticisms of closed juvenile proceedings in the United States arguing that closure prevented the public from learning about dysfunctional aspects of the system.[77]

Apart from doubts concerning the empirical bases of claims made in support of juvenile confidentiality and the tarnished reality of closed door proceedings, a number of positive benefits are claimed to flow from openness. Thus it is argued that publicity can have a deterrent effect on offenders and would-be offenders and further that it might shame their respective families into preventative action—a view subscribed to by judges here[78] and in the United States.[79]

[72] 'Publicity and Juvenile Court Proceedings' (1958) *Rocky Mountain Law Review* 101.

[73] (1967) 387 US 1, 24.

[74] B Emmerson and D Friedman, *A Guide to the Police Act 1997* (Butterworths, London, 1998) at 89. For a statement of disclosure policy prior to the Act see Home Office Circulars 13/92; 47/93 and 42/94.

[75] *The Observer* 5 January 1997.

[76] (1989) 3 *International Journal of Law and the Family* 177 and G Van Bueren *The International Law on the Rights of the Child* (Martinus Nijhoff, Dordrecht, 1995) at 182.

[77] JL Trasen, 'Privacy v. Public Access to Juvenile Court Proceedings: Do Closed Hearings Protect the Child or the System' (1995) 15 *Boston College Third World Law Journal* 359.

[78] *R v Lee* [1993] 1 WLR 103, 109 and *R v Central Criminal Court ex parte Simpkins; R v Same ex parte Plummer The Times* 28 October 1998.

[79] In *United States v Three Juveniles* 862 F Supp 651, 658–59 it was stated that juveniles may 'benefit, in a rehabilitative way, from the public opprobrium attached to these charged acts.'

Little evidence exists however in support of this claim.[80] Another argument for publicity has as its premise the essential similarities between adult criminal trials and juvenile proceedings and concludes that just as the former recognises the benefits of open criminal trials as a principle of general application, so too ought juvenile proceedings. Publicity on this view might result in the correction of procedural deficiencies noted above and ensure at the same time a measure of accountability of court officials whilst informing the public more fully about judicial responses to youth crime. This latter point goes to the issue of public confidence in the administration of justice generally.[81] In response, privacy advocates counter that the demands of courtroom accountability can be met without disclosure of the offender's identity[82]—a response which does not address the question of public confidence in those cases where it is suspected (whether rightly or wrongly) that particular offenders are treated differently on class, race or other grounds.

A further positive argument for publicity concerns the ability of community members to take precautionary measures against further criminal acts. This point was relied upon by the Conservative Government (and supported by the Labour Opposition)[83] during the passage of the Crime (Sentences) Act 1997 to justify greater disclosure of young offenders' identities in Youth Court proceedings. The hope was expressed that the lifting of repeat offenders' anonymity would alert members of the local community such as traders, retailers and neighbourhood watches who might then be especially vigilant against the activities of specific individuals.[84] The same argument had already been accepted by the Divisional Court in respect of adult offenders in *Hellewell v Chief Constable of Derbyshire*.[85] The practice of Derbyshire police of showing to local shopkeepers and their staff photographs of the plaintiff taken without his consent whilst in police custody was held not to afford the plaintiff any grounds for alleging breach of confidence. The use made by the police of plaintiff's photograph (who had 32 previous convictions, 19 of which were for dishonesty offences) was deemed lawful as it was in good faith, for the purposes of crime prevention/detection and to a limited class of persons who had a reasonable

[80] Indeed, a number of academic writers have questioned the whether any real deterrent effect is served by publicising the fate of offenders. See eg J Fortin, *Children's Rights and the Developing Law* (Butterworths, London, 1998) at 453; G Borrie and NV Lowe, *The Law of Contempt*, 3rd edn (Butterworths, London, 1996) at 313.

[81] Marjorie Jones noted in 1974 that restrictions on identification had the effect of 'hampering communication' to the public and that no alternative means of informing and educating the public about the work of juvenile courts had yet been devised. *Justice and Journalism* (Barry Rose, Chichester, 1974) at 122.

[82] Laubenstein (1995) 68 *Temple Law Review* 1897, 1906.

[83] See the remarks of Alun Michael MP for the Opposition at Standing Committee A (1996–97) col 312. 'There is no argument between us on the principle which is straightforward.'

[84] See the Home Office Minister David Maclean MP *ibid*, at cols 315–317 and subsequently the incoming Home Secretary Jack Straw MP at HC Debs (1998–99) Vol 329, col 395.

[85] [1995] 1 WLR 804.

need to learn of the plaintiff's identity.[86] Of course, where a convicted young person has been sentenced to a lengthy period of detention, this argument ceases to be relevant.

Other Young Persons During Criminal Proceedings

In contrast to the diminished protection for young offenders, the privacy claims of young persons caught up in criminal proceedings as witnesses, victims or as unconvicted defendants continue to be taken seriously. For example, the prohibition on identifying witnesses or victims involved in Youth Court proceedings may not be lifted at the conclusion of the trial unless it is for the purpose of avoiding injustice to a child or young person.[87] This may reflect the view that publicity adds in some unquantifiable way to the trauma and stress of a court appearance which immature and possibly vulnerable persons should not be forced to endure. In the case of witnesses and victims, anonymity is also consistent with the State's interest encouraging those affected by criminal conduct who would otherwise be too frightened to testify to come forward and assist the effective prosecution of crime, although, for anonymity to be justified, it needs to be shown that it is the publicity resulting from media reporting which intimidates or frightens rather than the fact of having to testify in front of the defendant, his/her family/associates or the court. The trauma of providing testimony in certain classes of offence is already recognised by the Children and Young Persons Act 1933, section 37 of which allows for the exclusion of the public from the adult court in a prosecution involving offences against decency or morality when a child or young person gives evidence as a witness.[88] Bona fide media representatives are permitted to remain however.[89] What seems crucial here however is not so much the age of the witness but the nature of the offence.

Outside of the intimidated witness/offence-related grounds for non-identification, it is difficult to see what other justification might be offered in

[86] See also *R v Chief Constable of North Wales and others, ex parte AB and another* [1998] 3 All ER 310 where disclosure by the police of the whereabouts of two convicted paedophiles to a caravan site owner on whose property the two were staying was deemed lawful. The site was used by families and since disclosure was prompted by a concern to protect the children using the site the disclosure was in the public interest.

[87] Children and Young Persons Act 1933, s 49(5).

[88] Provision is also made in s 32A of the Criminal Justice Act 1988 for the video recordings of the testimony of child witnesses to be admitted in evidence with leave in relation to sexual, violent or cruelty offences. The effect of which is to spare a child the examination-in-chief although he/she may still be cross-examined in open court at which point it might be expected that an order under s 45 of the Youth Justice and Criminal Evidence Act 1999 might be made. The precise rules governing the admissibility and use of s 32A material are laid down in the Crown Court Rules 1982, r *23C*.

[89] Interestingly the statute is silent about what, if any details, may be published on such circumstances.

support of youth witness/victim anonymity.[90] Certainly none of the harm-based rationales advanced in support of offender anonymity appear to be relevant. On the contrary, it is clear that a witness may actually want to be identified where false rumours are circulating in the local community that he/she is on trial. Of course where publication of the defendant's name was allowed this would of itself prevent any stigma wrongly attaching to the witness.

In the case of young accused persons, the automatic anonymity conferred in Youth Court proceedings by section 49 of the 1933 Act and the usual practice of making a non-identification order in respect of adult court proceedings reveal an enduring attachment to the notion that publicity equals harm, although by the standards of the European Court of Human Rights, public access to Crown Court proceedings in high profile cases may still breach young defendants' fair trial interests under Article 6.1 of the European Convention on Human Rights. In *T v United Kingdom*[91] and *V v United Kingdom*[92] the Court criticised the public's presence during the trial of two boys (aged 11 at the time of trial) after a highly publicized murder investigation as contributing to their inability to participate effectively in the proceedings.[93] This matter will be returned to in the section dealing with the impact of international law below.

Youth Justice and Criminal Evidence Act 1999, section 44—Anonymity after the Commencement of Criminal Investigation

As was seen earlier, the latest set of automatic statutory restrictions pushes back the starting point for young suspects' anonymity to the moment when a criminal investigation is commenced. Justifying the extension of reporting restrictions, the Home Secretary argued that the previous restrictions which were applicable only after court proceedings had begun had created an anomaly:

> (I)f the evidence against someone is extremely strong and proceedings begin quickly, that person receives greater protection than someone against whom the evidence might not be so strong and might later be dropped. Such a person might be the subject of press reporting, while someone against whom there is strong evidence will not.[94]

Although these remarks are addressed to the position of alleged offenders, elsewhere the Government stressed the harm/emotional damage which could result

[90] The accepted uses of the anonymity power recognised in the Contempt of Court Act 1981, s 11 include blackmail victims, police informants and other 'exceptional and rare' cases. See further *R v Evesham JJ ex parte McDonagh* [1988] 2 WLR 227, 233.
[91] See n 5 above.
[92] See n 6 above.
[93] Even though a number of special measures were taken to promote the boys understanding of the proceedings. See further below.
[94] H C Debs (1998–99) Vol 328, col 394. Had they been in place in December 1997, the restrictions would have made it unlawful to reveal the identity of the Home Secretary's son William who was arrested after selling cannabis to a reporter from the *Daily Mirror*. See further below.

to all young persons through involvement in the criminal process and intended that victims and witnesses might too be given anonymity automatically upon the commencement of a criminal investigation. At Committee Stage, an Opposition amendment which would have required an express judicial order restricting publication in place of these new restraints was withdrawn after the Government promised that restrictions relating to young alleged victims and witnesses would only be brought into force by draft order approved by the affirmative resolution procedure in both Houses. A factor which the Government said it would have regard to in deciding when a draft order might be laid before Parliament was whether Ministers continued to have concerns about children being damaged by media reporting of crime.[95] In the interim, the Government expressed the hope that the Press Complaints Commission would conduct a review of existing extra-legal protection for children and young persons laid down in Clause 6 of the Code of Practice.[96]

Leaving aside for the time being issues regarding the compatability of these new provisions with Article 10 of the European Convention on Human Rights and definitional problems surrounding the commencement of a criminal investigation,[97] these developments prompt several responses. At the outset, the reliance upon the unevidenced assertion that publicity harms those involved in police investigations *over and above* any identifiable harm resulting from contact with the investigative process *per se* is arguably a weak and unacceptable basis for imposing criminal liability on journalist and editors. The handful of anecdotal recollections advanced by its supporters does not make good this evidential lacuna.[98]

The imposition of blanket restrictions in the case of suspects prior to the commencement of any legal proceedings appears to rest on a 'mud sticks' view of crime reporting in general namely, that where an arrested suspect is not charged or, if charged is not later prosecuted in court, he/she will suffer some residual damage from having been publicly identified.[99] It may well be true in

[95] *Ibid*, (Paul Boateng MP).

[96] Clause 6 states inter alia, at paragraph (ii) 'journalists must not interview or photograph children under the age of 16 on subjects involving the welfare of the child or of any other child, in the absence of or without the consent of a parent or other adult who is responsible for the children' and (v) 'Where material about the private life of a child is published, there must be justification other than the fame, notoriety or position of his or her parents or guardian.' Clause 6 is however subject to a public interest override. See also the strong prohibition on identifying children involved in sex offence cases as victims or witnesses in Clause 7 which is not subject to the public interest override.

[97] For one definition see *R v Uxbridge Magistrates' Court ex parte Patel; R v City of London Magistrates' Court ex parte Cropper The Times* 7 December 1999.

[98] See Hilton Dawson MP for a sadly typical contribution to the Parliamentary debate at Standing Committee E (1998–99) col 236–37. From this and other contributions it seems clear that it was occasional instances of press rather than broadcasters' misconduct which was in the Government's sights.

[99] This view is to found in R Munday, 'Name Suppression: An Adjunct to the Presumption of Innocence and to Mitigation of Sentence' [1991] *Criminal Law Review* 680, 756 where the case for adult defendant anonymity to be exercised by judicial discretion is made.

this regard that acquittals receive less media coverage than information concerning the arrest, charge and prosecution of an accused person. However, as is well known for the purposes of defamation law (which is otherwise noted for its zealous protection of individual reputation), the mere fact that an individual is under investigation is not by itself capable of bearing a defamatory meaning.[100] The ordinary reader with general knowledge and experience of worldly affairs will not equate the announcement of a police inquiry with the guilt of those parties being investigated.[101]

Advocates of suspect privacy also claim that none of the justifications standardly offered in support of publishable proceedings is apposite in the case of suspects.[102] In particular, this view fails to recognise the tangible benefits of public accountability and confidence which flow from media dissemination of police and prosecution conduct in individual cases. It may be thought important in an open democratic society that agencies within the criminal justice system (including the courts) show no favours to suspects who are well-connected or powerful members of the community. The point was made by the New South Wales Supreme Court albeit in the context of court proceedings in *Raybos Australia Pty Ltd v Jones*.[103] The defendant, a solicitor, facing charges of having interfered with the administration of justice, sought to restrain the publication of his name and that of his firm and its partners and employees in any report of the proceedings. The Court refused the defendant's application. All accused persons, Kirby P held, come to criminal proceedings before the court as equals. It would be 'especially inappropriate' to confer on a lawyer accused of interfering with the administration of justice a privileged position regarding media reports of the hearing. To appreciate the force of the same point with respect to the investigation stage of criminal proceedings, an example closer to home is offered. In late December 1998 William Straw, the 17 year old son of the Home Secretary was arrested after supplying a reporter from the *Daily Mirror* with a small quantity of cannabis. Immediately before the story was about to break in the English national press, the Attorney General sought and obtained an injunction of dubious legality which prevented the naming of the Minister's son or anything likely to lead to his identification although it soon became widely known that a Cabinet Minister's son had been arrested in connection with a drugs dealing offence. The lack of a clear legal basis for name suppression (which stemmed from the fact that no court proceedings had begun and therefore no protective order under section 49 of the

[100] *Lewis v Daily Telegraph* [1963] 2 All ER 151.
[101] A conclusion which if anything looks more, not less, sound in view of the high profile miscarriage of justice cases which have undermined confidence in English criminal justice. See further CP Walker and K Starmer (eds.), *Miscarriages of Justice* 2nd edn. (Blackstone Press, London, 1999)
[102] See for example the remarks of Robin Corbett MP during the Report Stage of the Sexual Offences (Amendment) Act 1976 at HC Debs (1976) Vol 911 col 1927; and endorsed by Munday at n 99 above.
[103] [1985] 2 NSWLR 47.

Children and Young Persons Act 1933 was possible)[104] prompted the Shadow Home Secretary to write to the Director of Public Prosecutions seeking an assurance that there was no question of different rules being applied to the instant case on the grounds that a Minister's son was involved. By contrast, now that the media is prevented under threat of penal sanction from revealing the identities of suspects, it is not difficult to see how accountability and public confidence might be eroded. Moreover, the procedure laid down in section 44(7) of the 1999 Act whereby a court may later dispense with restrictions if, after having had regard to the welfare of the young person, it is considered necessary in the interests of justice seems unnecessarily burdensome on young suspects who wish to publicise their treatment at the hands of the police or to appeal for alibi witnesses.

V THE ADVANCEMENT OF CHILDREN AND YOUNG PERSONS' PRIVACY INTERESTS IN INTERNATIONAL LAW

Moves to protect the privacy interests of juveniles in domestic criminal processes have been given added impetus by developments in international law. Whilst neither the 1924 or 1959 Declarations on the Rights of the Child referred to standards in juvenile justice administration, the matter was addressed in the International Covenant on Civil and Political Rights in 1966.[105] Article 10(2)(b) requires the separation of accused juveniles from adults. Article 14(4) further insists that trial procedures take account of the age of juveniles and the desirability of promoting their rehabilitation. Subsequently, a more detailed statement of minimum rules of juvenile justice administration known as the Beijing Rules were adopted by the General Assembly of the United Nations in 1985.[106] The Beijing Rules focus on the rights of juvenile offenders rather than other young persons involved in criminal proceedings. They lack treaty status however and are therefore not binding on states *per se*.[107] Nonetheless, aspects of the

[104] It has been argued that the injunction was granted under the strict liability rule in ss 1–2 of the Contempt of Court Act 1981 but this too seems unlikely. Although theoretically available, any prior restraint would have to be shown to meet the demanding standards of Article 10 of the European Convention on Human Rights and, from October 2000, s 12(3) of the Human Rights Act 1998. A particular difficulty would lie in establishing the necessity for any such restraint. The minister's son was identified in Scotland prior to the eventual lifting of restrictions in England because the original injunction could not be enforced north of the border and the Lord Advocate made no move against the Scottish press presumably on the basis that anonymity in Scotland ceases to be an option once a young person reaches 16 years of age.

[105] G Van Bueren *The International Law on the Rights of the Child* (Martinus Nijhoff, Dordrecht, 1995).

[106] Resolution 40/33 *United Nations Standard Minimum Rules for the Administration of Juvenile Justice* which was adopted without a vote on 29 November 1985.

[107] It is interesting to note however that the Beijing Rules continue to set benchmarks for the reform of national juvenile justice systems. In 1997 the Australian Law Reform Commission's report *Seen and heard: priority for children in the legal process* (ALRC 84) expressly referred to the

Rules have become binding in international law however by virtue of having been incorporated into Article 40 of the United Nations' Convention on the Rights of the Child (1989).[108] Furthermore, states are invited to inform the Secretary General on the implementation of the Rules and to report on a regular basis to the Committee on Crime Prevention and Control on the results acheived. Specifically, Rule 8 of the Beijing Rules entitled 'Protection of Privacy' states:

> 1. The juvenile's right to privacy shall be respected at all stages in order to avoid harm being caused to him or her by undue publicity or by the process of labelling.
> 2. In principle, no information that may lead to the identification of a juvenile offender shall be published.

Article 40.1 of the United Nations Convention on the Rights of Child 1989 lays down some general obligations on States' treatment of children accused or convicted of criminal conduct to promote the child's sense of dignity and worth and which:

> takes into account the child's age and the desirability of promoting the child's reintegration and the child assuming a constructive role in society.

The essence of Rule 8 of the Beijing Rules is incorporated in Article 40(2)(b)(vii) which declares that where a young person is accused of having broken the criminal law States will guarantee that he/she will 'have his or her privacy respected at all stages of the proceedings.'[109]

The Council of Europe has also been active in this area. In 1987, the Committee of Ministers adopted Recommendation R (87) 20 which asked member states to review domestic law and practice to avoid committing minors to adult courts and to ensure that the right of juveniles to respect for their private lives was recognised throughout proceedings.[110] These provisions would appear to cast doubt on the legality in international law terms of disclosure of young offenders' identitities in the Youth and Crown Courts.

Reference to young persons' privacy protection in international law was made by the European Court of Human Rights in *T v United Kingdom* and

need to comply with Beijing standards at paras 18.8–9. (Australian Government Publishing Service, Canberra, 1997).

[108] The UK ratified the Convention in December 1991 although this fact only emerged by way of an answer to a written parliamentary question. No press release was issued nor was any Parliamentary time allocated to a discussion of the Convention's provisions. For further criticism see I Cram, 'Minors' Privacy, the Courts and Limits on Freedom of Expression' in E Barendt, S Bate, J Palca and T Gibbons (eds) *Yearbook of Media and Entertainment Law* (Oxford University Press, Oxford, 1997–98) at 38–40.

[109] For a review of UK compliance with the 1989 Convention see G Lansdown, 'Implementing the UN Convention on the Rights of the Child in the UK' (1995) 7 *Child and Family Law Quarterly* 122 and *Making the Convention work for Children* (Children's Rights Office, London, 1995).

[110] Paras 5 and 8 adopted 17 September 1987.

V v United Kingdom which was asked for the first time to consider how the guarantee of a fair trial under Article 6.1 of the Convention applied to criminal proceedings against children.[111] In particular, the Court had to ascertain whether the very public nature of the trial of two eleven year old boys on trial for the murder of a two year old boy at Preston Crown Court prevented their effective participation in the trial.[112] For the government, emphasis was laid upon the various arrangements were put in place prior to and during the trial to promote T and V's understanding of the proceedings. These included, in advance of the trial, visits to the courtroom and access to children's guides explaining trial procedures and personnel. During the trial, the accused sat in a raised dock next to social workers and close to their parents and lawyers. Ten minute intervals were taken every hour in which the accused could join their parents in a play area. The length of each day's proceedings was shortened to reflect the school day.

In the Court's view, where the trial occurred of a young person charged with a grave offence in a context of high levels of media and public interest,

> it would be necessary to conduct the hearing in such a way as to reduce as far as possible his or her feelings of intimidation and inhibition.[113]

Despite the special measures taken to assist the accused, the Court concluded that the applicants were unable to participate effectively in their trial. In support of this conclusion, the Court pointed to the formality of Crown Court proceedings,[114] the use of the raised dock which paradoxically had added to the boys' sense of discomfort[115] and psychological evidence obtained after the trial which revealed that V had been worried about what people were thinking about him and was unable to pay attention to the proceedings, passing the time instead by counting in his head or making shapes with his shoes. In the case of T, the psychological evidence appears more limited although the Court accepted that he too was prevented from following the trial and taking decisions in his best interest. Accordingly, the United Kingdom was held to have breached the applicants' Article 6 right to a fair trial. With one eye on Youth Court practice, the Court stated that the undoubted public interest in the open administration of justice could have been satisfied by a modified procedure providing for 'selected attendance rights and judicious reporting.'[116] Analysis of the Court's ruling and the United Kingdom's response occurs below.

[111] The applicants also argued that the Crown Court trial and surrounding publicity breached the guarantee in Article 3 outlawing inhuman or degrading treatment. The argument was rejected.
[112] *Stanford v United Kingdom* Series A vol 282 (1994)
[113] (2000) 30 EHRR 121 at para 87.
[114] Eg the Judge and counsel wore wigs and gowns.
[115] It had been designed to allow them to see proceedings more clearly.
[116] At para 87.

VI NATIONAL LEGAL SYSTEMS' TREATMENT OF PRIVACY CLAIMS

An Australian Perspective[117]

The regulation of the conflict between children's privacy claims and media freedom to report on juvenile justice matters in Australia is a matter which is handled primarily at state level although Commonwealth legislation also impacts more generally on the publication of material before the Commonwealth and state courts. In a jurisdiction where the general principle of justice openly administered laid down in *Scott v Scott*[118] is fully accepted, departure from the principle is permitted in exceptional cases only. It follows that statutory derogations from open justice are narrowly construed.[119] Moreover, an 'increased resolve' to defend the ideal of the open administration of justice has led to the repeal or modification of a number of those statutory derogations.[120] Thus, for example, the provision whereby Family Court proceedings were as a general rule heard in closed court was amended in 1975 to allow for open court proceedings unless an order is made to the contrary.[121] The following year rules which had hitherto prohibited public access to courts dealing with first-time female offenders were also relaxed.[122] In the case of states' Children's Courts, a clear trend towards greater openness is also evident as will now be shown.[123]

Children's Courts

The precise degree of restraint placed on the media in states' Children's Courts varies somewhat from state to state. Certain patterns do emerge however. Broadly speaking, states which give overriding status to the privacy claims of children and young persons close their Children's Court to the public and restrict entry to specific individuals. It is also common to find the imposition of automatic reporting restrictions which restrain reports of part or the entirety of proceedings. Elsewhere, the privacy interests of young persons are afforded less protection where a presumption in favour of open proceedings operates

[117] I am grateful to Professor Sally Walker, Hearn Professor of Law at Melbourne University for help in gathering materials for this section. See further her *Law of Journalism in Australia* (Sweet & Maxwell, London, 1989).
[118] [1913] AC 417. *Russell v Russell* (1976) 134 CLR 495; *David Syme & Co Ltd v General Motors-Holden's Ltd* [1984] 2 NSWLR 294.
[119] *Raybos Australia Pty Ltd v Jones* [1985] 2 NSWLR 47, 53.
[120] *Raybos ibid*, at 55 per Kirby P. See also Walker at n 117 above at 11.
[121] Family Court Act 1975 (Cth), s 97(1), (2) (as amended by the Family Law Amendment Act 1983 (Cth), s 52). See also the modification of the common court practice of ordering that the terms of settlement filed in court should not be disclosed in *S Hoffnung & Co Ltd v Hesky* [1977] 2 NSWLR 669.
[122] First Offenders (Women) Repeal Act 1976.
[123] See further ALRC Report No 18 *Child Welfare* (ALRC, Canberra, 1981).

together with provisions allowing the media to apply to the court to have any prohibition on naming those involved lifted.

As far as public and media access is concerned, it is clear that most states have in recent times moved towards allowing greater access to proceedings. Until the 1980s, Children's Courts in the Australian Capital Territory, New South Wales, Northern Territory, South Australia and Victoria were closed to media and public alike. Today, Children's Courts in Australian Capital Territory,[124] New South Wales[125] and South Australia[126] remain closed to members of the public but allow members of news organisations to attend proceedings much in the same way as Youth Courts in England and Wales. Children's Courts in the Northern Territory[127] and Victoria[128] are presumptively open to public and media alike, bringing these states into line with Western Australia[129] and Tasmania.[130] Closure of these presumptively open courts can occur for a variety of reasons which are sometimes indicated in the relevant statutory framework. In the Northern Territory, closure is ordered if it appears to the presiding magistrate that 'the ends of justice will be best served by him so doing'.[131] In Western Australia, persons may be excluded where this may prejudically affect the interests of a child,[132] whilst in Tasmania 'any person' may be ordered to remain outside the courtroom although the circumstances in which this power can be exercised are not indicated in the statute.[133]

As regards the publication of Children's Court proceedings (or their equivalent), the vast majority of States and Territories with the exception of the Northern Territory impose automatic bans prohibiting the publication of material likely to lead to the identification of young persons involved in such proceedings. Tasmania—one of the more restricted states—prohibits reports of proceedings and determinations in Children's Courts in their entirety.[134] More selectively, Western Australia[135] and New South Wales[136] impose automatic restrictions on the identification of children involved in the proceedings as defendants, victims or witnesses.[137] Queensland also imposes an automatic bar on the publication of material likely to identify a child against whom proceedings

[124] Children's Services Act 1986, s 169(1)(h).
[125] Children (Care and Protection) Act 1987, s 67(1).
[126] Youth Court Act 1993, s 24(1)(f)(ii).
[127] Juvenile Justice Act 1983, s 22(1).
[128] Children and Young Persons Act 1989, s 19(1).
[129] Children's Court of Western Australia Act 1988, s 31(1).
[130] Child Welfare Act 1960, s 17.
[131] Juvenile Justice Act 1983, s 22(1).
[132] Children's Court of Western Australia Act 1988, s 31(1).
[133] Child Welfare Act 1960, s 17(1).
[134] Child Welfare Act 1960, s 18(1).
[135] Children's Court of Western Australia Act 1988, s 35(1).
[136] Children (Care and Protection) Act 1987, s 68(1).
[137] Although the legislation in South Australia (Youth Court Act 1993, s 25(1) (b) (ii)) refers simply to a child 'concerned in the proceedings either as a party or witness.'

are taken[138] and, in cases where a child appears as a witness or alleged victim of a criminal offence, further empowers a court to make a non-identification order.[139] Legislation in Victoria and South Australia respectively bans the identification of defendants and witnesses without referring expressly to position of victims.[140] The same two states further allow for restrictions to be lifted by the court without indicating which criteria are relevant to such a decision.[141] Restrictions on identification in Western Australia may be lifted by the Supreme Court after consideration of the public interest and child's interests.[142]

Exceptionally, the Northern Territory allows proceedings in its Juvenile Court to be reported unless a magistrate issues a banning order in respect of all or part of the proceedings.[143]

In one of the few reported instances of litigation, a recent media challenge to the refusal of a senior magistrate in the Victoria Children's Court to lift reporting restrictions in respect of a child accused of murder failed. The Court of Appeal's unwillingness to find fault with the initial refusal indicated the considerable burden placed on media organisations seeking to reverse the legislative preference for anonymity.[144]

Other Proceedings

As in England and Wales, adult court proceedings in Australia are usually open to the public and media alike. Under statute, closure of these proceedings and the accompanying imposition of reporting restrictions most commonly occurs when this is deemed to be 'necessary in the interests of the administration of justice.'[145] The Federal Court of Australia considered the proper scope of this phrase in *Australian Broadcasting Commission v Parish*.[146] Exclusion of persons might lawfully occur for example where 'demonstrators or rioters would disrupt the proceedings.'[147] As to the ambit of the power in section 50 of the

[138] Juvenile Justice Act 1992, s 62.

[139] Children's Services Act 1965, s 138(2)(b). In the case of children alleged to be victims or witnessses to an offence of a sexual nature, an automatic bar on matters relating to the child applies, see s 138(2)(a).

[140] Children and Young Persons Act 1989, s 26(1)(a)(Vic) Youth Court Act 1993, s 25(1)(b)(ii) (SA).

[141] Children and Young Persons Act 1989, s 26(1)(b) (Vic). Youth Court Act 1993, s 25(2) (SA).

[142] Children's Court of Western Australia Act 1988, s 36A.

[143] Juvenile Justice Act 1983, s 23(1). This section is silent on the criteria justifying a non-publication order.

[144] *The Herald and Weekly Times Ltd v Levine* (1996) (Supreme Court of Victoria, Court of Appeal) (LEXIS).

[145] Other commonly encountered statutory restrictions include those made to protect national security and complainants in sexual offence cases. See for example Federal Court of Australia Act 1976, s 50 and at state level Magistrates' Court Act 1989, s 126 (Vic) and the Supreme Court Act 1986, s 19 (Vic).

[146] (1980) 29 ALR 228.

[147] Bowen CJ *ibid*, at 233 referring to the power of the Federal Court to exclude the public or persons where the court is satisfied under the Federal Court of Australia Act 1976, s 17(4) that their presence would be 'contrary to the interests of justice'.

Federal Court of Australia Act 1976 to prohibit reports of parties' names or particular evidence where 'necessary in order to prevent prejudice to the administration of justice', this was variously interpreted to authorise the suppression of material where a party to the proceedings would otherwise be 'seriously prejudiced'[148] or where 'legitimate claims of confidentiality' (arising particularly in a commercial context) would be undermined.[149] Another relevant factor according to Deane J was the wishes of the parties. The case for making a suppression order would be stronger if both parties to the proceedings consented to the restriction. Although the judge may have had a commercial context uppermost in mind, the notion of prohibition orders in criminal proceedings being more readily granted where the consent of prosecution and defence was present is somewhat disturbing and not easily reconcilable with the robust defence of open justice found in authorities such as *R v Evesham Justices ex parte McDonough*.[150] To recall Sir Christopher Staughton's observation in *ex parte P* it is precisely when both sides in a criminal case are *ad idem* on the need for reporting restrictions that the courts should be most vigilant in the defence of the freedom to report.[151] In this respect *Parish* stands in sharp contrast to the clear balance of authorities at Commonwealth and state level which stress the importance of open court proceedings.[152]

At state level, a particularly widely drawn suppression power formerly existed in South Australia whereby a court might prohibit the publication of material tending to identify an accused or other person in order to prevent 'undue hardship' to that person.[153] Under an amendment introduced in 1989, accused persons can no longer derive the benefit of this basis for suppression as it has now been confined to alleged victims of crime and witnesses in criminal and civil proceedings.[154]

Despite the variety of grounds on which suppression orders may lawfully issue, Walker has stated that in practice the courts use their statutory powers to restrict reports cautiously. [155] Recently granted access rights to the media in

[148] Franki J *ibid*, at 246.

[149] Deane J *ibid*, at 255.

[150] [1988] 2 WLR 227; See also *AG v Leveller* [1979] AC 440, 451 *per* Lord Diplock.

[151] *The Times*, 31 March 1999. See also the concurring views of Kirby P in *Raybos Australia Pty Ltd v Jones* [1985] 2 NSWLR 47, 59.

[152] *Ibid*, at 55 (Kirby P); *Russell v Russell* (1976) 134 CLR 495, 520 (Gibbs J). It is of course true that at common law *AG v Leveller* [1979] AC 440 authorises departure from the requirement to sit in public where to do so would frustrate or render impracticable the administration of justice, although the House of Lords rejected the view that courts enjoyed an express power to prohibit the publication of matters revealed in closed procedings so that breach of any such order is *ipso facto* a contempt.

[153] Evidence Act 1929 (SA), s 69(1)(b). See *G v The Queen* (1984) 35 SASR 349 where it was stated that prejudice to an accused person in his employment or, if not employed, his chances of obtaining employment would be sufficient to justify resort to the court's discretion.

[154] Evidence Act Amendment Act 1989 (SA); See now *Re F* (1989) 51 SASR 141.

[155] Walker, at n 117 above.

respect of Children's Courts and the retention in many states of automatic reporting restrictions points to an English-style compromise between the public interest in learning of judicial proceedings and the privacy interests of young persons involved in those proceedings. Just as elsewhere however, where unsupported by an actual finding of likely to harm to a young person, the use of court closures and reporting restraints to protect a young person's privacy interests raises legitimate doubts about the real level of commitment to the practice of open justice. It may be that the High Court's recognition of a constitutionally implied freedom of political discussion in cases such as *Australian Capital Television Pty Ltd v Commonwealth*,[156] *Theophanous v The Herald and Weekly Times Ltd*[157] and *Stephens v West Australian Newspapers Ltd*[158] will be taken up by broadcasters and the press at some point in the future to challenge the width of State and Commonwealth laws restricting media reporting of court proceedings involving young persons.[159]

Open Juvenile Justice—Canadian style[160]

In recent years, court proceedings involving children and young persons in Canada has become more open—a fact which owes much to the impact of the Charter of Rights and Freedoms. As such, developments in Canada support a more general argument advanced in this book; namely that the constitutionalisation of speech/expression interests invariably leads to a more rigorous examination of limitations on media freedom and, for this reason alone, is to be welcomed.

Previously, under section 12(1) of the Juvenile Delinquents Act 1970, the trials of young persons were always heard *in camera*. The constitutionality of this requirement was successfully challenged in *Re Southam Inc and The Queen (No.1)*[161] when the Ontario Court of Appeal held that automatic closure in section 12(1) did not constitute a reasonable limit[162] upon freedom of expression

156 (1992) 177 CLR 106.
157 (1994) 182 CLR 104.
158 (1994) 182 CLR 211.
159 HP Lee, 'The Australian High Court and Implied Fundamental Guarantees' [1993] *Public Law* 606; T Jones, 'Legal Protection for Fundamental Rights and Freedoms: European Lessons for Australia?' (1994) 22 *Federal Law Review* 57; S Walker, 'The Impact of the High Court's Free Speech Cases on Defamation Law' (1995) 17 *Sydney Law Review* 43; G Williams, '*Engineers* is dead, Long Live the Engineers!' (1995) 17 *Sydney Law Review* 62.
160 See generally in this area M David Lepofsky, *Open Justice: The Constitutional Right to Attend and Speak About Criminal Proceedings* (Butterworths, Toronto, 1985); P Anisman and AM Linden (eds), *The Media The Courts and The Charter* (Carswell, Toronto, 1986) esp ch 10 by Linden. On background youth justice issues, see RR Corrado, N Bala, R Linden and M Le Blanc, *Juvenile Justice in Canada—A Theoretical and Analytical Assessment* (Butterworths, Canada, 1992).
161 (1983) 41 OR (2d) 113.
162 See earlier discussion in chapter 1.

as required by section 1 of the Charter of Rights and Freedoms.[163] The Young Offenders Act later replaced blanket exclusion by conferring on Youth Court judges—who enjoy exclusive jurisdiction in respect of any offence alleged to have been committed by persons between 12 and 17 years old[164]—a discretionary power to exclude persons from part or all of proceedings where the evidence presented to the court would be 'seriously injurious or prejudicial' to a young defendant, a child/young person involved in the proceedings as a witness or victim.[165] In addition, the court may exclude persons where it would be:

> in the interest of public morals, the maintenance of order or of the proper administration of justice.[166]

The standards in the Youth Offenders Act supplement those in the Criminal Code.[167] The latter confers a more general discretion on judges to exclude any or all members of the public for part or all of the proceedings where he/she is of the opinion that such closure:

> is in the interest of public morals, the maintenance of order or the proper administration of justice.[168]

One of the chief beneficiaries of an exclusion order are child witnesses in ordinary proceedings. Section 486(1.1) of the Code clarifies this point by stating that 'the proper administration of justice' is to be understood as meaning that the interests of witnesses under 14 years of age are to be safeguarded in cases where the defendant is charged with a sexual offence or certain other designated offences. The discretion to exclude members of the public must be exercised on the basis of evidence submitted by the party seeking an exclusion order which is sufficient to overcome the presumption in favour of open proceedings.[169] The mere fact that the victims of an offence were young females has been held by the Supreme Court not to warrant, by itself, an exclusion order under section 486(1) where those victims would not be testifying as witnesses in proceedings and

[163] MacKinnon ACJO stating at (1983) 41 OR (2d) 113, 134 that 'Society loses more than it protects by the all-embracing nature of the statute.'

[164] S 5(1) Youth Offenders Act SC 1980–81–82, c 110. By virtue of s 16(1) where defendants having reached 14 year or over wish to be dealt with by the adult court (or the Attorney General so requests) the Youth Court may transfer proceedings to the adult court. In addition, certain offences must normally be tried in the adult court where the defendant was sixteen or seventeen years old at the time of the alleged offence. These include first and second degree murder, attempt to commit murder, manslaughter and aggravated sexual assault. S 16(1.01). On differences of implementation of the 1985 Act across the provinces, see N Bala in RR Corrado, N Bala, R Linden and M Le Blanc, *Juvenile Justice in Canada—A Theoretical and Analytical Assessment* (Butterworths, Canada, 1992) at ch 1.

[165] S 39(1)(a)(i)-(iii).

[166] S 39(1)(b).

[167] RSC 1985 C–46.

[168] *Ibid* at s 486(1).

[169] *R v Vandevelde* (1994) 89 CCC (3d) 161 (Sask CA), affirmed by the Supreme Court in *CBC v AG for New Brunswick* [1996] 3 SCR 480.

where their anonymity was already protected by a publication ban.[170] Following *CBC v AG for New Brunswick*, before any such order can be lawful, the presiding judge must be satisfied that other reasonable and effective alternatives are not viable, and that the order is as limited in scope as possible and that, having weighed the importance of the objectives of the order and its effects against the importance of openness and the particular expression that would be restricted by any order, the deleterious effects of the order do not outweigh its salutary effects.[171]

In addition to powers of exclusion under the Code, it should also be noted that a superior court of criminal jurisdiction further enjoys an inherent jurisidiction to regulate its proceedings, something which extends to control of those in attendance at the trial, provided any exclusion is exercised in accordance with Charter principles.

The privacy interests of young persons involved in criminal proceedings are additionally protected by the reporting restrictions at both Youth and adult courts. At the Youth Court, subject to some narrowly defined exceptions,[172] the identity of young persons concerned in the proceedings as a defendant[173] or a witness[174] may not be revealed.[175] However, if a young defendant is transferred to the adult court for trial (normally on the application of the prosecution where for example the maximum sentence available to the Youth Court is considered by the Crown to be insufficient),[176] rules regarding adult trial publicity will apply. Thus, unless an exceptional case can be made out in favour of a reporting restriction, the media will be at liberty to identify accused persons, even where this results in acute embarrassment to the accused and/or his family.[177]

At the adult courts, protection for young witnesses and complainants are laid down in the Criminal Code. In cases where an accused person is charged with a designated offence (including sexual assault, incest, prostitution)[178] a court is obliged to issue a non-publication order when requested to by a witness under the age of 18 or a complainant or the prosecutor.[179] Moreover, the presiding

[170] *CBC v AG for New Brunswick ibid.*
[171] *Ibid.*
[172] Including temporary publication where in cases prior to conviction where a youth deemed 'dangerous to others' is at large and publication is necessary to assist in that person's apprehension. S 38(1.2), (1.3) Young Offenders Act.
[173] S 38(1)(a) Young Offenders Act.
[174] S 38(1)(b) Young Offenders Act.
[175] Clause 110 of the Youth Criminal Justice Bill (which is before the Canadian Parliament at the time of writing) proposes an expansion of the range of circumstances in which the names of convicted young persons might be revealed.
[176] A young person can seek transfer in order, for example, to have a jury trial. See further N Bala in RR Corrado, N Bala, R Linden and M Le Blanc (eds.) *Juvenile Justice in Canada—A Theoretical and Analytical Assessment* (Butterworths, Canada, 1992).
[177] *Regina v P* (1978) 43 CCC (2d) 197.
[178] The full list of designated offences is provided by S 486(3) of the Criminal Code.
[179] S 486(3),(4) *ibid.*

judge must remind a young witness or complainant at the first reasonable opportunity of the right to make an application for such a non-publication order.[180] Outside of these categories, a more general residual discretion to issue reporting restrictions to protect victims and witnesses (adult as well as children and young persons) is provided by section 486(4.1) of the Code where the judge is satisfied that the order is 'necessary for the proper administration of justice.' Factors which the judge must consider when deciding whether to exercise this discretion include whether there is a real and substantial risk that the victim/witness would suffer significant harm if their identity were disclosed; the need for an order to prevent intimidation or retaliation; the societal interest in encouraging the reporting of crime. Charter-related freedom of expression considerations are addressed in this part of the Code by requiring the judge to explore effective alternative measures and consider the salutory and deleterious consequences of making an order.[181]

Access and Publicity in US Juvenile Delinquency Hearings

In a jurisdiction where state laws regulating access to, and reporting of, court proceedings raise fundamental questions of constitutional validity, it is perhaps surprising that juvenile proceedings have hitherto escaped scrutiny by the Supreme Court under First Amendment principles.[182] Instead, the Court's attention has been focused largely on the degree to which proceedings in the juvenile court ought to conform to notions of due process prevailing in the adult criminal court. In this section, the pattern of access to juvenile proceedings is described after which an analysis of the case for open juvenile proceedings grounded in First Amendment jurisprudence is offered.

State laws vary considerably in the degree of access granted to the public and representatives of the media. In those states where representatives of the media may lawfully attend juvenile proceedings, a clear line of Supreme Court rulings establishes that the publishing of information obtained lawfully at those proceedings may not subsequently be restrained.[183]

[180] S 486(4)(a) *ibid.*

[181] S 486(4.7) *ibid.*

[182] The matter has been discussed by academic commentators. See for example SS Greenbaum 'Conditional Access to Juvenile Court Proceedings: A Prior Restraint or a Viable Solution?' (1993) 44 *Washington University Journal of Urban and Contemporary Law* 135; S Jonas 'Press Access to the Juvenile Courtroom: Juvenile Anonymity and the First Amendment' (1982) 17 *Columbia Journal of Law and Social Problems* 287.

[183] *Cox Broadcasting Corporation v Cohn* (1975) 420 US 469; *Oklahoma Publishing Co. v District Court* (1977) 430 US 308.

[184] 'At the Crossroads of Richmond and Gault: Addressing Media Access to Juvenile Delinquency Proceedings Through a Functional Analysis' (1998) 28 *Seton Hall Law Review* 1155 for a stimulating argument in favour of open juvenile proceedings.

A survey by Dalton in 1998 revealed a highly varied pattern of access.[184] A few states require juvenile proceedings to be open to the media or press access in all cases (such as Illinios, Montana), while others impose this requirement when a juvenile is charged with a violent felony only (including California, Georgia, Kansas, Los Angeles, Massachussetts). Elsewhere, a number of states operate with a presumption of openness which may be rebutted upon a clear public and/or child interest in closure (including Arizona, Colorado, Florida, Indiana, Iowa, Michigan, New Mexico,Texas). In seven states no such presumption exists (Arkansas, Maryland, New Jersey, New York, North Carolina, Ohio, Tennessee). More restrictively, a presumption in favour of closed juvenile proceedings exists in 16 states. This presumption may be overturned in favour of access to parties with a 'direct' or 'proper' interest including the news media whose genuine interest in informing the public about how judicial power is exercised is recognised.[185] In New Hampshire access is denied to all but the 'immediately involved' parties. No discretion to widen access is conferred. In Connecticut persons whose presence in the opinion of the court is 'not necessary' are excluded although victims and their parents/guardians are permitted to attend hearings unless the court orders otherwise.

At federal level, the relevant provision of the Juvenile Delinquency Act 1988 states somewhat unhelpfully that juvenile proceedings

> may be convened at any time and place within the district in chambers or otherwise.[186]

This has been interpreted on two recent occasions as allowing media access.[187]

Although the constitutionality of wholly/partially closed juvenile proceedings has yet to be tested in the Supreme Court, a number of states have in recent years opted to make juvenile proceedings more open—a trend which Dalton attributes to raised public concern about violent juvenile crime and a desire on the part of states to enhance levels of public confidence in juvenile justice.[188] This has prompted discussion of whether the media has a right of access to juvenile proceedings in the same way as exists in respect of adult criminal proceedings. Of course, it remains open to an accused young person invoking the Sixth Amendment to insist upon a public trial. In order to understand why an access standard found in the adult criminal court may be applicable to the juvenile court, it is necessary to say something about the origins and subsequent development of the juvenile court and the treatment of juvenile offenders.

It is not disputed that the intention of the founders of the juvenile court system at the turn of the century was to remove children from the adult criminal court where they had previously been and place them in a non-adversarial

[185] *In re RLK* (1978) 269 NW 2d 367.
[186] 18 USC 5031–5042.
[187] *United States v Three Juveniles* 61 F 3d 86 (1st Cir 1995); *United States v AD (PG Publishing)* 28 F 3d 1353 (3rd Cir 1994).
[188] See n 184 above at 1206.

setting.[189] There the emphasis was to be upon rehabilitation in which the judge would act as a 'wise and merciful father' and treat the offender as an individual in need of protection rather than punishment.[190] In this rehabilitative environment child offenders were thought to be less in need of state protection in terms of the bundle of formal legal rights normally provided to criminal defendants in full criminal trials. Unfortunately, the reality of juvenile justice proved to be quite different. Children were incarcerated in overcrowded detention homes or even regular jails (where states had failed to provide separate juvenile facilties). Boys were kept for up to 32 days in confinement for punishment purposes where they were denied shoes and mattresses to sleep on. Some were handcuffed to iron pipes for extensive periods. In short, the rehabilitative ideal was not realised in practice.[191] Recognising the punitive realities of juvenile justice, the Supreme Court in a series of rulings commencing in the mid 1960s imposed a set of minimum standards akin to those operating in adult criminal trials including those of due process and fair treatment,[192] the rights to counsel and to confront witnesses and the privilege against self-incrimination.[193] In 1970 the Court insisted that delinquency be proved beyond reasonable doubt.[194] Five years later in *Breed v US* the Court held that deliquency proceedings constituted a form of jeopardy for the purposes of the double jeopardy clause of the Fifth Amendment.[195]

The imposition of standards of criminal procedure akin to those operating in adult criminal courts prompted consideration in turn of whether the rights of access enjoyed by the media and public in respect of adult criminal trials recognised in *Richmond Newspapers Inc v Virginia*[196]and pre-trial proceedings in *Press-Enterprise Co v Superior Court of California*[197] should apply to juvenile proceedings. Some commentators have argued that, in the absence of a meaningful distinction between a juvenile delinquency adjudication and an adult criminal trial, the media should have equivalent access rights to juvenile

[189] The first juvenile court was created by Illinois in a statute of 1899. By 1917, juvenile courts were to be found in all but three states. See further *Note* at (1982–83) 81 *Michigan Law Review* 1540, 1547.
[190] Mack (1909) 23 *Harv L R* 104, 106. A juvenile court judge in Indianapolis is quoted in another study as saying, '(I)f I could get close enough to him to put my hand on his head or shoulder, or my arm around him, in nearly every such case, I could get his confidence.' See RM Mennel, *Thorns and Thistles: Juvenile Delinquents in the United States 1825–1940.* (University Press of New England, New Hampshire, 1973) at p. 135. (cited by Dalton at n 184 above). This accords with the intention which lay behind the closure of Dutch Juvenile Courts. See further Van Nijnatten at n 76 above.
[191] See AM Platt, *The Child Savers: The Invention of Delinquency* (University of Chicago Press, Chicago, Ill, 1977).
[192] *Kent v US* (1966) 383 US 541.
[193] *In re Gault* (1967) 387 US 1. See in particular Justice Black's concurring opinion where he states that the exalted ideal of the juvenile justice system (the preference for rehabilitation over punishment and stigma) 'has failed of achievement since the beginning of that system.' *Ibid*, at 61.
[194] *In re Winship* (1970) 397 US 358.
[195] 421 US 519. The Fifth Amendment states, 'No person . . . shall . . . be subject for the same offence to be twice put in jeopardy of life or limb'.
[196] (1980) 448 US 555.
[197] (1984) 464 US 501.

proceedings.[198] Of course, as *Richmond Newspapers* and *Press-Enterprise* both recognise, media and public access under the First Amendment is not protected absolutely. Specifically, the Court in *Richmond Newspapers* noted that, although presumptively open, closure of a criminal trial may be justified if, in the words of the plurality opinion, there is 'an overriding interest articulated in findings.'[199] The right to attend proceedings is also regulated more generally by reasonable 'time, manner and place' restrictions applicable to all First Amendment freedoms.[200] It is also clear however that mandatory closure of courtrooms authorised by statute (as occurred in cases such as *Globe Newspaper v Superior Court for the County of Norfolk*)[201] will infringe First Amendment access rights since the closure is not based on assessment of the balance between the state's interest in closure and the public interest in access *as disclosed by the particular circumstances of the case*. For closure to be lawful, the state would need to show that closure was motivated by a 'compelling interest' and that the closure itself was narrowly tailored to serve that interest.[202] Before turning to consider whether in respect of juveniles a compelling interest is present and, if so, whether closure represents a narrowly tailored method of protecting that interest, it must be asked whether the classic access rationales developed by the Court in relation to adult criminal proceedings have any relevance to juvenile proceedings. In *Richmond Newspapers* Brennan J referred to the

> structural role of the First Amendment in securing and fostering a republican form of government.[203]

—that is, the ability of the citizens to exercise effective self-government (and the control this implies over the conduct of public officials) is dependent upon access being provided to all information relevant to this function.[204] As was noted earlier, opening up the courts to public access via media reporting provides citizens with the information they need to pass informed judgment on a variety of officials including judges, prosecutors and police who act on the public's behalf. In addition, publicity has a disciplining effect on these public officials and thus helps prevent abuses of public power. Moreover, public confidence in judicial processes is enhanced when observation is permitted, at least to the

198 See Dalton at n 184 above; and *Note* (1982–83) 81 *Michigan Law Review* 1540; Cf Laubenstein (1995) *Temple Law Review* 1897.
199 (1980) 448 US 555, 581.
200 'There is no constitutional right under the First Amendment to 'insist upon a street meeting in the middle of Times Square at rush hour as a form of freedom of speech or assembly.' *Cox v Louisana* (1965) 379 US 536, 554. See also *Cox v New Hampshire* (1941) 312 US 569 where the requirement placed on the holders of street parades to obtain a licence was held to be a constitutionally valid means of preventing the obstruction of streets and pavements.
201 (1982) 457 US 596.
202 *Ibid.*
203 (1980) 448 US 555, 587.
204 See also A Meiklejohn, *Free Speech and Its Relation to Self-Government* (Harper, New York, 1948).

extent that the proceedings in question are conducted properly. Finally, as Brennan J pointed out in *Richmond*, there are the prophylactic purposes served by publicity when, after a shocking crime occurs, an outraged community is made aware that the criminal processes have begun. Here, the open trial provides an orderly outlet for the outpouring of community feelings.[205] Secrecy, by contrast, entails the denial of information to citizens upon which to formulate views on the conduct of public officials and institutions. It allows for the possibility that failings in the conduct of public officials' remain unnoticed outside the courtroom. It may further engender public mistrust in the capacities and activities of officials and institutions whilst denying the community an measured outlet to express its emotions. In extreme circumstances, secrecy may foment self-help vigilantism.

If, as Dalton and others have argued with some force, all of the foregoing access rationales could apply equally to juvenile proceedings, it remains to be seen whether, in the first place, cases involving children and young persons disclose a compelling interest which might justify restrictions on access and second whether closure of the court represents a narrowly tailored restriction of the access right as demanded by First Amendment jurisprudence.

The Supreme Court has recognised the legitimacy of limits placed on First Amendment freedoms when prompted by a wish to protect the welfare of children and young persons. In *FCC v Pacifica Foundation* the issue of a warning to the owners of a radio station after the latter broadcast an admittedly offensive monologue entitled 'Filthy Words' at 2pm was upheld.[206] The State's interest in the well-being of its youth (who constituted part of the listening audience at such a time) provided a legitimate basis for the regulation of otherwise protected speech. Again, in *New York v Ferber* the Court upheld the constitutionality of a New York statute which prohibited the distribution of child pornography. Justice Brennan acknowledged:

> the State has a special interest in protecting the well-being of its youth . . . this special and compelling interest, and the particular vulnerability of children, afford the State the leeway to regulate pornographic material, the promotion of which is harmful to children.[207]

Of course, as neither of the putative First Amendment freedoms unsuccessfully advanced in *Pacifica* (freedom to broadcast offensive language during daytime) and *Ferber* (freedom to distribute child pornography) concerned speech relating to events in the criminal courtroom, they reveal little beyond the fact that the well-being of children and young persons (including presumably the rehabilitation of those that commit crime) can constitute a compelling interest.

[205] (1980) 448 US 555, 571.

[206] (1978) 438 US 726.

[207] (1982) 458 US 747. See also *Osborne v Ohio* (1990) 495 US 103 where the constitutionality of a statute making unlawful the possession of child pornography in one's own home was upheld by the Supreme Court.

Given the compelling nature of the state's interest in the well-being of young persons, and, assuming for a moment that juvenile hearings constitute part of a rehabilitative juvenile justice system, First Amendment arguments surrounding the closure of such hearings are likely ultimately to turn on two questions. First, the extent to which factual findings support the conclusion that a young person's interests would be harmed if closure did not occur. Second, whether, in the absence of adequate though less drastic alternative measures, closure conforms to the notion of a 'narrow curtailment'of First Amendment rights.[208] The lack of convincing empirical evidence that publicity alone causes harm to young offenders would appear to offer media organisations some encouragement on the first question at least. As to witnesses and victims, the Supreme Court has conceded the possibility that factors such as age and pyschological maturity might in an individual case point towards closure.[209]

VII LESSONS FROM EUROPE—(I) ACCESS TO CROWN COURT PROCEEDINGS POST T v UNITED KINGDOM; V v UNITED KINGDOM AND (II) THE (IN)COMPATABILITY OF REPORTING RESTRICTIONS UNDER THE YOUTH JUSTICE AND CRIMINAL EVIDENCE ACT WITH ARTICLE 10 OF THE EUROPEAN CONVENTION ON HUMAN RIGHTS

In domestic criminal proceedings involving young persons, the European Convention emerged in *T v United Kingdom; V v United Kingdom* as a force for less open justice, though not to an extent which is particularly troubling. Paradoxically, Strasbourg jurisprudence also holds out the prospect of a successful challenge to the recent set of reporting restrictions promulgated in the Youth Justice and Criminal Evidence Act 1999. In the following section, some domestic implications of Strasbourg-led regulation of the conflict between free expression and young persons' privacy interests are considered.

T v United Kingdom; *V v United Kingdom*

Within three months of the Strasbourg Court's ruling in *T v United Kingdom* and *V v United Kingdom*, the Lord Chief Justice announced changes to the treatment of young defendants in the Crown Court in a Practice Note.[210] As part of a package of measures aimed at facilitating the effective participation of young defendants in trial proceedings (principally by avoiding the intimidation, humiliation or distress of a young defendant), the Note takes up, somewhat

[208] Of course where the juvenile justice system offers no programme of rehabilitation, there ceases to be a compelling basis justifying closure.
[209] *Globe Newspapers Co. v Superior Court* (1982) 457 US 596.
[210] [2000] 2 All ER 285.

uncritically, the Court's conclusion that the public interest in open administration of justice could have been satisfied by 'selected attendance rights and judicious reporting'. Of course, media presence at, and coverage of, the trial was just one of several factors which the Court found contributed to the breach of the applicants' Article 6 rights to effective participation in their own trials. Other contributory factors included the formal procedure of the court, the wearing of formal attire by the judge and barristers, and the feelings of discomfort induced in the applicants by the raised dock used in those criminal proceedings.[211] However, the negative effect of a public trial *by itself* was never established or isolated. [212] It thus becomes pertinent to ask whether, if the judge and counsel had discarded their formal attire, the defendants had not been seated on a raised dock and proper account taken of the pre-trial mental state of the defendants, the fact that members of the public and the media attended trial proceedings was in itself of critical importance to the finding of no effective participation.

Whatever the force of this point, the new arrangements for the trial of young persons in England and Wales in the Crown Court set out in the Note stipulate at paragraph 14 that

> The court should be prepared to restrict attendance at the trial to a small number, perhaps limited to some of those with an immediate and direct interest in the outcome of the trial.

Specific guidance on media attendance is stated in paragraph 15:

> Faciltities for reporting the trial (subject to any direction given under s 39 of the 1933 Act or s 45 of the 1999 Act) must be provided. But the court may restrict the number of those attending the courtroom to report the trial to such number as is judged practicable and desirable. In ruling on any challenged claim to attend the courtroom for the purpose of reporting the trial the court should be mindful of the public's general right to be informed about the administration of justice in the Crown Court. Where access to the courtroom by reporters is restricted, arrangements should be made for the proceedings to be relayed audibly and if possible visually, to another room in the same court complex to which the media have free access if it appears that there will be a need for such additional facilities.

The new arrangements do not pose a serious threat to the practice of open justice. The combined effect of paragraphs 14 and 15 is the partial closure of Crown Court proceedings. Members of the public not directly connected to the proceedings (admittedly an imprecise formulation) may be excluded from the courtroom whilst media representatives will be able to remain—as currently occurs in Youth Court proceedings. In those rare cases of an unusually large

[211] Although it may be noted that the Court's interference with the national authorities here flies in the face of the earlier ruling in *Nortier v Netherlands* Series A No 267 (1993) conferring a wide margin of appreciation in such matters, see especially Judge Morenilla.
[212] This is apparent from paras 88–89 of the judgment in *V v United Kingdom* at n 6 above.

media presence, the provision permitting the relaying of proceedings to media organisations in another part of the court building seems an entirely appropriate way of meeting the legitimate interests represented by such bodies.

As far as reporting restrictions are concerned, courts are reminded of their discretion to issue an order under section 45 of the Youth Justice and Criminal Evidence Act 1999 at the plea and directions hearing. No attempt is made in the Practice Note to alter the practice of naming persistent and/or serious young offenders after sentence. It remains to be seen, however, whether the trend towards naming young offenders after conviction in the adult court evident in cases such as *R v Lee* will continue.[213] On one view, the use of the discretionary power to lift restrictions at the trial's conclusion does not go to the issue of the defendant's participation during trial. As such, no immediate revision to domestic practice in this area seems required. There are signs however that judges may have become more reluctant to use this power in the light of certain threats made to Robert Thompson and Jon Venables at the time of their release into the community.[214]

Reporting Restrictions under the Youth Justice and Criminal Evidence Act 1999

As he is obliged so to do under section 19(1) of the Human Rights Act 1998, the Home Secretary asserted that the provisions of the 1999 Act were compatible with the European Convention on Human Rights, a position he confirmed when pressed specifically about the novel extension of the restrictions imposed by section 44 once a criminal investigation has been commenced.[215] Nothwithstanding the Minister's confidence, media organisations might be justified in feeling optimistic about the chances of a successful challenge under Article 10 of the European Convention on Human Rights. The principal problem with section 44 (as for other automatically applicable sets of restrictions) is that its restrains the media in a blanket fashion without having identified a particular threat to specific rights of particular persons. That is to say it operates with a complete disregard for evidential matters. Even assuming that an infringement of the rights of others might be considered to be threatened by publication, the mechanism of automatic restraints leaves no scope for the evaluation of, and resort to, alternative and less drastic forms of media restraint. Accordingly, the proportionality of this latest set of automatically applicable restraints might be considered questionable, making early clarificiation from the courts on the point essential.[216]

[213] [1993] 1 WLR 103.

[214] See (2001) *The Times*, June 26. The matter is discussed further in ch 7.

[215] HC Debs. (1998–99) Vol 329, c 394.

[216] See further I Cram 'Automatic Reporting Restrictions in Criminal Proceedings and Article 10 ECHR'[1998] *European Human Rights Law Review* 742.

VIII CONCLUSION

Judicially-imposed prior restraints represent a significant limitation on the ability of media to report criminal proceedings/investigations involving young persons. They impact particulary severely because of the perishable quality of such reporting. In drawing some line between juvenile privacy and court reporting, this chapter has looked to an evidence-based approach to curtailment of media freedom which would require those seeking court closure and the suppression of juveniles' identities to establish a sound basis for deviating from the norm of justice administered openly. It may well be that for some young people individual susceptibility (on grounds of age, psychological maturity etc.) may necessitate some closure of trial proceedings to safeguard fair trial rights and that accompanying reporting restrictions would be crucial to a young person's subsequent rehabilitation. Less justified, by contrast, are the devices of routine closure and mandatory reporting restrictions authorised under statute which carry risks for the administration of justice and public acceptance of the same. Though well-intentioned, such restraints have typically failed to isolate specific harms resulting from public/published proceedings, as opposed to those which arise through contact with the processes of criminal justice generally. One obvious attraction of US regulation under the First Amendment is the demanding level of factual inquiry engaged in by the court before reporting restrictions pass constitutional muster. In view of the clearly-established countervailing benefits of openly administered justice, it may be time for similarly rigorous questions to be asked whenever and wherever access to criminal proceedings is denied.

5

The English Foolishness—Scandalising the Courts and the Limits of Constitutionally Protected Expression

I INTRODUCTION

SOME CONSIDERABLE TIME has elapsed since the last prosecution in England and Wales for scandalising the courts. A search through reported case law in England and Wales reveals that the last successful prosecution for this offence occurred in 1931.[1] So why devote space to consider something which Justice Frankfurter of the US Supreme Court called in 1941 the 'English foolishness'[2] and appears at the beginning of the twenty first century to have fallen into desuetude? By way of response several points can be made: First, lack of resort to the offence at present offers no guarantee of a continued state of abeyance. In an era of relative disrespect for our institutions, it is not inconceivable that some particularly vituperative piece of journalism might exceed the present limits of judicial tolerance. Christopher Miller, a leading authority on contempt, has suggested that the offence still has a role to play in respect of what he calls 'orchestrated campaigns which are aimed at seeking a reduction or increase in a sentence imposed in a particular case'[3] or where it is suggested that a court has bowed to outside pressure in reaching a verdict.[4] Secondly, the offence endures in other common law jurisdictions which have incorporated English common law contempt rules into their legal systems.[5] In Hong Kong for example the editor of a mass circulation newspaper—the

[1] See MK Addo (ed), *Freedom of Expression and the Criticism of Judges* (Ashgate, Aldershot, 2000) and C Walker, 'Scandalising in the Eighties' (1985) 101 *Law Quarterly Review* 359

[2] *Bridges v California* (1941) 314 US 252, 287.

[3] CJ Miller, *Contempt of Court* 3rd edn. (Oxford University Press, Oxford, 2000) at 596. He cites an example from *The Sun* newspaper in December 1994 under the headline 'NO JUSTICE FOR NIKKI' where the paper opined, 'Judges never fail to amaze us. Today they disgust us too . . . It's clear the judges don't give two hoots about the victims.'

[4] Eg *Gallagher v Durack* (1983) 152 CLR 238.

[5] For a recent Privy Council case upholding a contempt finding of the Supreme Court of Mauritius see *Ahnee v DPP* [1999] 2 AC 294. See further G Borrie and N Lowe, *The Law of Contempt* 3rd edn by N Lowe and B Sufrin (Butterworths, London, 1996) 337. For New Zealand see *Solicitor General v Radio Avon Ltd* [1978] 1 NZLR 225.

Oriental Daily News[6] was convicted in 1998 of scandalising in respect of a series of articles which criticised judges and tribunal members who had ruled against the newspaper in earlier sets of proceedings.[7] Two judges were singled out for particular criticism, being called *inter alia* 'judicial scumbags', 'street rats' 'British white ghosts' and 'pigs.' The judges were said to have been biased and have shown animosity towards the defendants.

In the same year, scandalising proceedings were launched in Australia against a defendant in *Re Colina ex parte Torney* who demonstrated outside the Family Court building in Melbourne. Mr Torney was said to have made abusive remarks about the Family Court and its judges. He asserted that the court was to blame for the deaths of certain individuals and instances of child abuse. He accused the judges of being 'terrorised' by women's organisations and of 'destroying the lives of innocent children'. In a leaflet distributed outside the court, Mr Torney suggested that the Family Court was biased against men and claimed that there would in all likelihood be violent action towards the judges if people were alerted to what the Court was doing. Judges, he went on, made decisions 'based on their twisted morals' and were 'protected by . . . secrecy'.

A decade earlier, Harry Kopyto, a Canadian lawyer, faced a scandalising charge after a number of unsuccessful civil and criminal actions were brought against the Royal Canadian Mounted Police on behalf of Dowson, his client. Frustrated after the latest set of proeceedings were thrown out, Kopyto gave a press interview which was later accurately reproduced in a national newspaper—*The Globe and Mail*. The lawyer was quoted as saying:

> This decision is a mockery of justice. It stinks to high hell. It says it is okay to break the law and you are immune so long as someone above you said to do it. Mr Dowson and I have lost faith in the judicial system to render justice. We're wondering what is the point of appealing and continuing this charade of the courts in this country which are warped in favour of protecting the police. The courts and the RCMP are sticking so close together you'd think they were put together with Krazy Glue.

Outside the common law tradition, the main mechanism in European legal systems which protects persons including judicial figures from criticism which lowers the esteem within which he/she is held is the offence of criminal libel, buttressed by an ancillary civil law entitlement to compensation. In the last decade, the European Court of Human Rights has had to consider the compatibility of criminal libel convictions/civil law compensation with Article 10 of the Convention on three occasions—*Barfod v Denmark*, *Prager and Oberschlick v Austria* and *De Haes & Gisjels v Belgium*.

[6] At the time of publication, the newspaper had a circulation of 2.3 million readers and 53% of the daily market.

[7] Reported as *Wong Yueng Ng v Secretary for Justice* [1999] 3 HKC 143 (Court of Appeal) and *Secretary of State for Justice v The Oriental Press Group Ltd and others* [1998] 2 HKLRD 123 (High Court).

The focus of this chapter is a comparative assessment of the constitutionality of restraints upon criticism of courts and judicial figures. Given the importance attached to which speech/expression interests in liberal democracies and noting the especial weight accorded to speech on matters of clear public interest, this chapter considers whether scandalising and its European counterparts survive constitutional scrutiny and, if so, on what terms. A central issue here is the extent to which speech which is critical of courts/judges is judged differently to speech which is critical of other societal institutions/public figures. Should for example the judges and courts enjoy merely the same protection as politicians and other public officials/bodies? Or do free speech arguments which underpin the latitude conferred on speech about politicians and public institutions cease to apply in respect of speech about judicial matters? At the outset of this chapter, the key elements of the offence and its historical basis will be set down.

II THE OFFENCE OUTLINED

The essence of the common law offence of scandalising the court is a publication which is calculated to bring a court or judge (or decision(s)) of the court into disrepute, or to lower its authority.[8] It has to be established beyond a reasonable doubt that the publication has created a real risk that public confidence in the administration of justice would be undermined. The offence is one of strict liability in England and Wales,[9] Australia[10] and New Zealand.[11] Evidence of actual intention is however relevant to the issue of level of penalty.[12] In Canada[13] and South Africa[14] by contrast, *mens rea* must be shown. Criticism in the form of 'reasoned argument'[15] or even vigorously expressed comment that is within the bounds of 'reasonable courtesy and good faith' has not been treated as a contempt.[16] Finally, once the elements of a contempt have been

[8] 'Any act done or writing published calculated to bring a court or judge into contempt or to lower his authority, is a contempt of court.' Lord Russell of Killowen CJ in *R v Gray* [1900] 2 QB 36, 40. See further Borrie and Lowe's attempt to identify three main types of scandalising *viz* (i) scurrilous abuse of a judge; (ii) scurrilous abuse of a court; and (iii) allegations of impartiality. This suggests somewhat artificially that a clear division exists between each category. *The Law of Contempt* 3rd edn by Lowe and Sufrin (Butterworths, London, 1996) ch 9. In reality however, the same statement is capable of straddling across two or more of these categories.

[9] *R v Editor of New Statesman ex parte DPP* (1928) 44 TLR 301.

[10] *AG NSW v Mundey* [1972] 2 NSWLR 887.

[11] *Solicitor-General v Radio Avon Ltd and Another* [1978] 1 NZLR 225.

[12] Borrie and Lowe, *The Law of Contempt* 3rd edn by Lowe and Sufrin (Butterworths, London, 1996).

[13] *Re Ouellet* (1976) 72 DLR (3d) 95.

[14] *S v Van Niekerk* 1970 (3) SA 655 (T).

[15] *R v Gray* [1900] 2 QB 36.

[16] *Per* Lord Justice Salmon in *R v Commissioner of Police of the Metropolis ex parte Blackburn (No 2)* [1968] 2 QB 150, 155. *quaere* whether Lord Atkin's alternative formulation of 'respectful, though outspoken comments' in *Ambard v AG for Trinidad and Tobago* [1936] AC 322, 355 is any more enlightening.

established, a defence of fair comment may be available to the defendant,[17] although it is doubtful that justification may be likewise pleaded.[18]

Origins and Subsequent History

The origins of contempt of court lie in the desire to protect the institutions of the administration of justice, the reputations of those involved in its daily practice and, crucially, in medieval England, the sovereign in whose name judges dispensed justice. An attack on a judge was thus tantamount to an assault upon the Sovereign as the fountain-head of law and justice. As Wilmot J put it in *Almon's* case, criticism:

> excites in the Minds of the People a general Dissatisfaction with all Judicial Determinations, . . . and whenever men's Allegiance to the Laws is so fundamentally shaken, it is the most fatal and dangerous Obstruction of Justice.[19]

Acknowledgement of the offence in the eighteenth century is found in *Roach v Garvan* in 1742 when Lord Chancellor Hardwicke identified it as one of three forms of contempt known to the law.[20] Shortly thereafter, the offence was deployed against the supporters of John Wilkes who attacked Lord Mansfield, the Lord Chief Justice of England.[21] Thus, in *Almon's* case,[22] proceedings were laid against a publisher of a pamphlet which had accused Lord Mansfield of 'officiously, arbitrarily and illegally' amending a charge against John Wilkes out of court and further of intending to deprive John Wilkes of the benefit of the Habeas Corpus Act.[23] Two subsequent sets of proceedings followed in 1768

[17] *R v Commissioner of Police of the Metropolis ex parte Blackburn (No 2) ibid*, where Lord Denning MR stated, 'It is the right of every man, in Parliament or out of it, in the Press or over the broadcast, to make fair comment, even outspoken comment, on matters of public interest.' Subsequently, Salmon LJ in an extra-judicial capacity later assumed that the defence was available in English law. See his report '*The Law of Contempt as it affects Tribunals of Inquiry.*' (1969) Report No 35, para 421. For Australia, see *Nationwide News Property Ltd v Wills* (1992) 177 CLR 1; *R v Fletcher ex parte Kisch* (1935) 52 CLR 248.

[18] Borrie and Lowe maintain that as justification is not a defence for publications charged with causing prejudice to particular proceedings, it is unlikely to apply to scandalising. See n 12 above at 357. The Phillimore Committee argued for a defence of justification provided that publication could be shown to be for public benefit. *Report of the Committee on Contempt of Court* (1974, Cmnd 5794) (HMSO, London) paras 165–167.

[19] (1765) Wilm 243, 255 and see also JE Wilmot (ed), *Notes of Opinions and Judgments Delivered in Different Courts* (London, 1802).

[20] Sometimes referred to as the *St James Evening Post case* (1742) 2 Atk 468, 471.

[21] See for example the case of *William Bingley* described in Sir John Fox, *Contempt of Court* (Professional Books Ltd, London, 1972) at 35–36. Wilkes and others' dislike of Mansfield stemmed from the Lord Chief Justice's support of the Earl of Bute's administration and his Jacobite lineage. The judgment of Lord Hardwicke had not by this time been printed.

[22] Reported in the judge's own *Notes* n 2 above at 243 *et seq*.

[23] The pamphlet—*An Enquiry into the doctrine lately propagated concerning Libel, Warrants, and the Seizure of Papers . . . in a Letter to Mr. Almon from the Father of Candour*—was thought to have been written by a Master in Chancery at the behest of Lord Camden, the Lord Chief Justice

again in respect of libels on Lord Mansfield published on each occasion in the *North Briton*.[24]

Summary procedure

Aside from the insight these legal skirmishes give us into wider political conflicts in Hanoverian England, their enduring legal significance concerns the procedure by which the scandalising offence is tried. Justice Wilmot had asserted in *Almon's* case that the manner of proceeding by attachment (that is summarily without a jury) in cases where the authority of the court was threatened had existed from time immemorial. Doubtless, summary proceedings offered a clear advantage over the alternative of a charge of seditious libel which entailed the uncertainties of trial by jury. However, Sir John Fox writing in 1927 suggested that Wilmot may have oversimplified matters. Whilst it was clearly established that for contempts committed in the face of the court a power to try summarily had existed from the time of Edward I,[25] Fox maintained that the clear practice in the case of contempts committed outside the courtroom by a stranger was for trial by jury in the common law courts. Despite Fox's carefully argued refutation and other academic criticism, *Almon's* case has crystallised over time into an authority for the summary nature of proceedings against alleged offenders. It was endorsed by Holroyd J in *R v Clement* and, later, in the associated cases of *Onslow & Whalley*[26] and *Skipworth & Castro*.[27]

Apart from avoiding uncertainties inherent in jury trial, summary procedure also has the merit of being relatively expeditious, thereby limiting the supposed damage done by unchecked criticism. This would have been considered particularly valuable in an era when Wilkes' supporters included the London Mob whose members were not averse to physical intimidation of their opponents.[28] The value of fast-track justice was still being talked up some 100 years later by Blackburn J in *Skipworth & Castro* where he upheld the power to try summarily on the ground that this would avoid the 'great mischief' which might be done if the slower processes of trial by jury were employed.[29] Notwithstanding such

of Common Pleas who was an opponent of Lord Mansfield. On the circumstances surrounding the non-delivery of this judgment, see further Sir John Fox n 21 above at ch 2.

[24] The respective cases of *William Bingley* and *Steare*. The latter is reported at Howell's *StateTrials* viii, 60.

[25] Even then, Fox contends, there is evidence to show that some of these *in facie* contempts were tried in the ordinary manner before a jury. *Contempt of Court* (Professional Books Ltd, London, 1972) at 50–52.

[26] (1873) LR 9 QB 219.

[27] (1873) LR 9 QB 230.

[28] For background on this period, see *inter alia* PDG Thomas, *John Wilkes—A Friend to Liberty* (Clarendon Press, Oxford, 1996); R Postgate, *'That Devil Wilkes'* (Dobson Books Ltd, London, 1956).

[29] (1873) LR 9 QB 230, 233.

views, there is evidence that some trials at least proceeded by way of indictment in the presence of a jury.[30]

Scandalising in the nineteenth and twentieth centuries

In the early part of the last century, a clutch of successful prosecutions in England meant that journalists and their editors had to tread carefully when airing criticism of judges and courts. Thus, in *R v Gray* a journalist was convicted for publishing an article savagely critical of Justice Darling's conduct in an obscene publication trial. The article stated that there was 'not a journalist in Birmingham who has anything to learn from the impudent little man in horsehair, a microcosm of deceit and empty-headedness . . .'[31] Less personally offensive but nonetheless considered to be beyond the bounds of acceptable comment was the allegation of bias in the *News Statesman* which suggested that the birth control pioneer Dr Marie Stopes could not expect to receive a fair trial from a court presided over by Justice Avory, a Roman Catholic.[32] Abel Smith and Stevens have suggested that the climate created by these various successful prosecutions was one of 'almost unbroken sycophantic praise for the judges.'[33] Indeed, no publication has been held to be in contempt for scandalising the court in England and Wales since 1931.[34] In recent years however, the absence of successful prosecutions is attributable less to a sycophantic media and more to a relaxed attitude on the part of the judiciary towards published criticism, a point demonstrated by the Court of Appeal in *R v Commissioner of Police of the Metropolis ex parte Blackburn (No.2)*.[35] The Rt Hon Quintin Hogg QC, MP wrote an article in *Punch* in which he argued that gaming legislation had been rendered unworkable by the unrealistic, contradictory and erroneous decisions of the courts including the Court of Appeal. He further suggested that the Court of Appeal was suffering from 'blindness' and should apologise for the expense and trouble to which it had put the police. Notwithstanding the wrongful attribution of decisions of the Queen's Bench Divisional Court to the Court

30 See for example *HMA v Carr* (1854) 1 Irv 464.

31 [1900] 2 QB 36,

32 *R v Editor of New Statesman ex parte DPP* (1928) 44 TLR 301. The piece carried a more general allegation of pro-Roman Catholic bias on the Bench when it observed, 'and there are so many Avorys.'

33 *Lawyers and the Courts* (Heinemann Educational Books Ltd, London, 1967) 126–7.

34 *R v Colsey The Times* 9 May 1931. The rather innocuous remark which led to the conviction stated that 'Lord Justice Slesser, who can hardly be altogether unbiased about legislation of this type maintained that really it was a very nice provisional order or as good a one as can be expected in this vale of tears.' Slesser LJ had been Attorney-General in an earlier administration and had been involved in steering the legislation through Parliament. See also one year previously, *R v Wilkinson The Times* 16 July 1930.

35 [1968] 2 QB 150. This explanation is borne out by the Phillimore Committee at paras 160–161. The Committee cites the view of the then Lord Chief Justice that 'Judges backs have got to be a good deal broader than they were thought to be years ago.' Report of the Committee on Contempt of Court (1974, Cmnd 5794) (HMSO, London).

of Appeal and the accompanying invective, a unanimous Court of Appeal refused to find the writer in contempt. For Lord Justice Salmon, the writing had been rumbustious and wide of the mark, however,

> the authority and reputation of our courts are not so frail that their judgments need to be shielded from criticism, even from the criticism of Mr Quintin Hogg . . .[36]

More recently, the *Daily Mirror* was not prosecuted when, under the headline which exclaimed 'You Fools!', it published upside-down the photographs of three Law Lords who upheld the Crown's application for an injunction in the Spycatcher litigation.

It should not be inferred from the absence of prosecutions for scandalising that judges in England and Wales are averse to pursuing alternative means of remedying what they perceive as unjustified attacks upon their competence. Libel actions are initiated by judges from time to time although the majority appear to be settled in advance of trial or adjudicated by means of arbitration with published apologies from editors.[37]

North of the border, a similar pattern in recent times of non-prosecution for the equivalent offence of 'murmuring' is found. The last reported conviction for murmuring happened in 1870.[38] The statutory form of the offence created by the Judges Act of 1540 having been abolished in 1973,[39] the common law equivalent offence has in theory remained.[40] According to Gordon, proceedings under this head of contempt are unlikely unless clearly disrespectful to the courts or likely to interfere with the administration of justice.[41]

The state of desuetude into which the offence has fallen in the United Kingdom stands in sharp contrast to its continuing vigour elsewhere in the common law

[36] *Ibid*, at 155.

[37] Some examples are to be found at *The Times* 22 and 24 July 1992. (Popplewell J awarded £7,500 in the first libel action to be settled using arbitration after the *Today* newspaper had alleged that he had fallen asleep during a murder trial; *Sunday Times* 8 August 1993 and (1996) 146 *New Law Journal* 1070 where Garland J used the letters column of the *New Law Journal* to publicise the fact that he had taken legal action against, and obtained an apology from Channel 4 in respect of a programme in its *Trial and Error* series. In his letter the judge warned that the 'judiciary too can take action when the media go too far.'

[38] *Alex Robertson* (1870) 1 Couper 404. The case is discussed in G Gordon, *The Criminal Law of Scotland* (W Green & Son Ltd, Edinburgh, 1978) at para 51-03. In 1965 there was however an unsuccessful prosecution for sending slandering, threatening letters to a sheriff and prosecutor in the unreported case of *Walter Scott Ellis*. See Gordon *ibid*.

[39] By the Statute Law (Repeals) Act 1973. The existence of the Act did not prevent prosecutions at common law. See *Magistrates of Kirkaldy v Dougal* (1679) Mor 1984; *Lord Advocate v Hay* (1822)1 S 288 (N E 267) both cited in *Arlidge, Eady & Smith on Contempt* 2nd edn by Sir D Eady and ATH Smith (Sweet & Maxwell, London, 1999) paras 16-95–16-103.

[40] *Stair Memorial Encyclopedia* vol 6, Contempt of Court.

[41] G Gordon, *The Criminal Law of Scotland* (W Green & Son Ltd, Edinburgh, 1978 (Sweet & Maxwell, London, 1999) at para 51-03. Arlidge and Eady state that action against those whose abuse contains an element of real threat to the administration of justice. See n 39 at para 16–103. It is less implausible that the outburst of an angry litigant or defendant might reach this standard. Even there however, Lord President Normand in *Milburn* warned against an 'oppressive or vindictive use of the court's powers.' 1946 SC 301, 315.

world and beyond. In the next section, the impact of constitutional norms on laws criminalising criticism of judges and courts in the United States, Canada, Australia and at the supra-national level of the ECHR will be assessed.

III THE ENGLISH FOOLISHNESS ABROAD—THE CONSTITUTIONALITY OF SCANDALISING IN THE UNITED STATES, AUSTRALIA, CANADA AND UNDER THE EUROPEAN CONVENTION ON HUMAN RIGHTS

United States—An Informed Citizenry, Impolite Speech and Judicial Fortitude

As was noted earlier in chapter two, the First Amendment standard of clear and present danger of immediate substantive evil emerged in several cases involving contempt penalties for judge/court-critical speech in the 1940s where its application resulted in the quashing of convictions imposed in the lower courts. In applying this standard, the US Supreme Court appealed explicitly to the argument from democracy and self-government and the audience interest in vigorous and uninhibited debate on matters related to self-governance. Thus, in *Garrison v Louisiana* the appellant district attorney was convicted of criminal defamation after accusing eight district court judges of taking excessive vacations and undermining the enforcement of vice laws. The appellant had also speculated about the 'racketeer influence' over the judges.[42] The conviction was quashed by the Supreme Court. Following swiftly on the heels of his definitive ruling in *New York Times v Sullivan*, Justice Brennan declared:

> The First and Fourteenth Amendments embody our 'profound national commitment to the principle that debate on public issues should be uninhibited, robust, and wide open, and that it may well include vehement, caustic, and sometimes unpleasantly sharp attacks on government and public officials.' . . . The public-official rule protects the paramount public interest in the free flow of information to the people concerning public officials, their servants. To this end, anything which might touch on an official's fitness for office is relevant.[43]

Allied to this idea of self-government, the Supreme Court has also invoked the notion of judges as 'men of fortitude, able to thrive in a hardy climate'[44] as a reason for affording protection to critical speech. The law of contempt cannot be a refuge for judges who are sensitive to the 'winds of public opinion.'[45]

[42] (1964) 379 US 64.

[43] *Ibid*, at See further *Wood v Georgia* (1962) 370 US 375, 388–9 *per* Warren CJ.

[44] *Craig v Harney* (1947) 331 US 367, 376. See also Justice Holmes' reference to 'a mind of reasonable fortitude' in his dissent in *Toledo Newspaper Co v United States* (1918) 247 US 402, 425 cited with approval by Black J in *Bridges v California* (1941) 314 US 252, 278.

[45] *Craig v Harney ibid*. See the admonition of Frankfurter J in *Pennekamp v Florida* (1946) 328 US 331 'Weak characters ought not to be judges.' at 357.

Accordingly, contempt convictions for comments to the effect that judges were hindering prosecutions in rape and blackmail cases[46] and had acted in a 'high-handed manner' resulting in a 'travesty of justice'[47] were deemed to have been over-protective of judicial reputations and in violation of the First Amendment.

The width of free speech protection in the US is further demonstrated by the fact that criticism which diminishes the standing of a court/judge need not necessarily exceed the bounds of First Amendment protection.[48] Expression of a vitriolic and intemperate nature might not be lawfully punished except in those rare cases where it prevented a court from administering justice.[49] A relevant factor here concerns the timing of criticism. Both majority and minority opinions in *Bridges v California* accepted that criticism of concluded proceedings 'however unrestrained' would always be constitutionally protected.[50] Where, on the other hand, criticism is made of matters then under judicial consideration, there is support for the view that the threshold of the clear and present danger standard could be reached.[51] Even in these cases however a trial court may only convict where the factual record demonstrates that the publication did in fact cause a clear and present danger of immediate interference. An assumption of interference will not be sufficient.[52]

The elective nature of a number of US judicial posts has also figured as a factor in deciding how much latitude to allow published criticism. The issue was adverted to by Frankfurter J in his dissent in *Bridges v California* in support of narrowing the scope of the First Amendment freedom.[53] Conversely however (and in line with the argument from democracy), it seems more plausible to argue that the fact of election demands greater freedom to engage in critical commentary. In order to exercise an informed choice in any re-election, the voters should be free to weigh up the widest possible range of views about the judge's performance to date. As Douglas J put it:

> Judges who stand for re-election run on their records. That may be a rugged environment. Criticism is expected. Discussion of their conduct is appropriate, if not necessary. The fact that the discussion . . . (is) not in good taste falls far short of meeting the clear and present danger test.[54]

46 *Pennekamp v Florida* (1946) 328 US 331.
47 *Craig v Harney* (1947) 331 US 367.
48 *Ibid.*
49 *Pennekamp v Florida* (1946) 328 US 331.
50 (1941) 314 US 252, see Black J at 273 and Frankfurter J at 291, 300.
51 See thus the opinion of Reed (at 346) and Frankfurter (366 *et seq*) in *Pennekamp ibid* and Frankfurter in his earlier dissent in *Bridges v California* (1941) 314 US 252 at 291.
52 *Wood v Georgia* (1962) 370 US 375.
53 *Ibid.* See also Jackson J in *Craig v Harney* (1947) 331 US 367, 397.
54 *Craig v Harney ibid* at 377.

Australia—The Impact of the Implied Freedom of Political Communication

The ground-breaking assertion by the High Court of Australia in *Nationwide News Pty Ltd v Wills*[55] and *Australian Capital Television Pty Ltd v Commonwealth*[56] (*ACTV*) of a power to review the validity of Commonwealth statutes was noted in chapter one. Significantly, this development occurred in *Nationwide News Pty Ltd* in the context of a Commonwealth statute—the Industrial Relations Act 1988—which created the offence of using words 'calculated to bring the Industrial Relations Commission (or a member of the Commission) into disrepute'[57]—a statutory version of scandalising. The High Court ruled that the offence constituted an unlawful interference with the implied freedom of political communication because it conferred an excessive degree of protection upon the Commission, penalising not only true statements but also fair comment. Legitimate criticisms of this public institution were thus being stifled improperly.

What implications might the implied freedom have for the offence of scandalising? The narrowing of the category of 'political speech' in *Lange*, described in chapter one, may of course prevent a challenge to the constitutional basis of the offence getting to first base. The non-elective nature of judicial posts may be argued to mean that electors have no strong interest in receiving speech which is critical about judges/courts. Even within this narrowed category, there is a strong counter-argument to be made. It is only if electors can receive and evaluate such speech that they will be able to express a preference among electoral candidates for political representatives who maintain the most appropriate stance on administration of justice issues. After all, judges in Australia are appointed by the executive which is comprised of members of the ruling political party. By electing a government, Australians are also determining who selects the next generation of judges. Alternatively, Barendt's more generous formula which refers to speech which is 'relevant to the development of public opinion on the whole range of public issues which an intelligent citizen should think about' would capture most forms of judge-critical speech.[58] There is, in any case, some evidence that *Lange* may not prove the final word on the definition of political speech.[59]

Assuming that speech which scandalises is of a type protected under the implied freedom, it must then be conceded that safeguarding of the administration

[55] (1992) 177 CLR 1. See J Kirk 'Constitutional Implications from Representative Democracy' (1995) 23 *Federal Law Review* 37.

[56] (1992) 177 CLR 106.

[57] Industrial Relations Act 1988, s 299(1)(d)(ii).

[58] *Freedom of Speech* (Oxford University Press, Oxford, 1985) 152. Where the speech is predominantly abusive with little or no attempt to persuade others to the justness of the criticism, it is plainly more difficult to fit such speech within Barendt's definition.

[59] In *Kruger and Others v Commonwealth of Australia and Others* (1997) 190 CLR 1 an attempt to reinstate the majority view in *ACTV* was made by Toohey and Gaudron JJ.

of justice constitutes a lawful purpose of restricting political communication. The crux of the matter would then appear to hinge upon the reasonableness or proportionality of the restraint. The comparisons made by members of the High Court in *Nationwide News Pty Ltd* between the excessive width of the Industrial Relations Act offence and the more limited common law version indicate that the latter would not be found so readily to infringe the implied freedom. This view is likely however to come under closer scrutiny in the event that Mr Torney is convicted in the Family Court. He would however encounter the difficulty in showing that scandalising unnecessarily or unreasonably impairs freedom of political communication. Of relevance here is the fact that Australian law currently allows the defence of fair comment based upon an accurate factual basis. Arguably, Mr Torney's best hope is for the Court to assess scandalising by Mason CJ's 'compelling justification' standard and, then, to argue that the vagueness of the offence coupled with the fact that currently truth is not a valid defence render the offence an impermissibly wide restriction upon the implied freedom.[60]

Canada—Judge-critical Speech Under the Charter

In contrast to the Australian judges' efforts to protect political speech by means of constitutional implications, Canadian judges have enjoyed the luxury of an express guarantee of free expression. As was observed in chapter one moreover, such protection as exists is not limited to purely political speech.

Section 2 of the Charter states that:

> Everyone has the following fundamental freedoms:
> (a) . . .
> (b) freedom of thought, belief, opinion and expression, including freedom of the press and other media of communication;

The right in section 2(b) of the Charter is qualified by Section 1 which states that Charter Rights are subject:

> only to such reasonable limits prescribed by law as can be demonstrably justified in a free and democratic society.[61]

That the Charter has forced a far-reaching re-assessment of the constitutionality of laws restricting media freedom is beyond doubt. For example, pre-Charter common law discretionary publication bans designed to safeguard particular

[60] The Australian Law Reform Commission in 1987 favoured a defence based upon actual truth or honest and reasonable belief in the truth. ALRC Report No 35 *Contempt* (Australian Government Publishing Service, Canberra, 1987) para 460.

[61] See further S Woolman, 'Riding the Push-Me Pull-You; Constructing a Test that Reconciles the Conflicting Interests which Animate the Limitation Clause' (1994) 10 *South African Journal of Human Rights* 60.

legal proceedings from interference tended to prioritise fair trial interests over those of free expression. In order to reflect the enhanced status of expression interests under the Charter, the majority of the Supreme Court in *Dagenais* reformulated the common law rule in a manner consistent with the fundamental values of the Constitution.[62]

Turning to the structure of permissible restrictions on Charter Rights under section 1, it will be recalled that *R v Oakes* requires that the objective behind a restriction must be of 'sufficient importance'—a phrase equated with a democratic society's pressing and substantial concerns.[63] In the context of media reporting of court proceedings, safeguarding fair trials and the administration of justice more generally constitute legitimate purposes behind restrictions upon expression rights.[64] *Oakes* further requires that restraints on Charter rights be 'reasonably and demonstrably' justified. Thus, a limitation must be rationally connected to its objective and impair the Charter right as little as is necessary to meet its objective.[65]

How have restrictions on speech which is critical of courts and judges been received under the Charter? In *R v Kopyto*, the defendant lawyer's conviction for scandalising was the subject of an appeal in the Ontario Court of Appeal where a unanimous panel of judges agreed that the appeal should succeed, although for contradictory reasons.[66] Justices Dubin and Brooke allowed the appeal on the ground that the *actus reus* element of the offence of scandalising had not been made out. The prosecution had failed to show that the lawyer's 'preposterous' allegation would have caused a serious, real or substantial risk of interference with the administration of justice. Bizarrely however, Brooke and Dubin JJ refrained from discussing the compatibility of the offence with the Charter on the ground that neither scandalising, nor contempt of court more generally, constituted an infringement of freedom of expression![67]

The approaches apparent in the remaining three judges in the Ontario Court of Appeal—all of whom reversed the contempt finding of the lower court and all of whom embrace First Amendment norms—offer contrasting methods of protecting constitutionally entrenched freedoms.

For Justice Houlden, the offence of scandalising is inconsistent with the Charter and could not be redefined so as to be brought within the scope of the Charter. It required a publication to be punished whenever it was shown to be

[62] On the power to re-align the common law with the Charter, see further *RWDSU v Dolphin Delivery* [1986] 2 SCR 573.

[63] [1986] 1 SCR 103.

[64] *Edmonton Journal v Alberta* (1990) 64 DLR (4th) 577; *Canadian Broadcasting Corp. v AG (New Brunswick)* [1996] 3 SCR 480.

[65] For further discussion on this point see Lamer CJ in *Dagenais v Canadian Broadcasting Company* [1994] 3 SCR 835.

[66] (1987) 47 DLR (4th) 213.

[67] It is revealing to note that the Hong Kong Court of Appeal in *The Oriental Press Group* case thought the reasoning of Dubin and Brooke JJA was 'impressive'.

calculated to bring a judge or court into disrepute or lower his authority. Thus defined, the offence could not be said to be reasonably and demonstrably justified under the second part of the *Oakes* test. The Canadian judiciary was not so weak as to need the extensive protection conferred via the common law. Neither would Canadian citizens lose faith in the judicial system because such criticism was published. Reading an explicitly Millian rationale into the protection of speech in the Charter, Houlden AJ argued that the suppression of critical opinion was undesirable since its suppression in cases where the criticism is misguided, denied an opportunity to assert the truth and accrue the benefits which result from being forced to respond to unfounded criticism. In cases where the criticism was valid, suppression deprived the audience of an opportunity to exchange error for truth.

Cory and Goodman AJJ agreed that that the offence infringed the Charter and declared Kopyto's conviction to be unconstitutional. They took objection in particular to the *assumption* in the offence that the defendants' words would bring the court into disrepute (rather than a requirement on the prosecution to prove that the words have in fact had this effect). This meant that the offence was not carefully designed to achieve the objective in question and that in consequence the impairment of freedom of expression exceeded the minimal infringement standard in *Oakes*. Unlike Houlden AJ however, Cory and Goodman AJJ could see a way of reformulating the offence which would allow it to survive constitutional scrutiny in the future. That is, they were prepared to reformulate the common law to ensure compliance with the constitutional standard. Cory AJ laid down the following requirements in a revised form of scandalising: First, the defendant must be shown to have intended to cause disrepute to the administration of justice or be reckless as to whether such disrepute followed from his acts/words; Secondly, that the words themselves created a real, substantial and immediate danger to the administration of justice. This revision, he admitted would place a 'very heavy and difficult onus upon the Crown',[68] adding that it would be difficult to imagine factual circumstances in which the test would be satisfied. The judge did however accept the distinction drawn in *Bridges v California* between comment pertaining to concluded proceedings on the one hand and that related to pending proceedings. The circumstances in which liability arose in the latter case would, in any event be limited if, as Cory AJ preferred, a defence of truth could be advanced.[69]

Goodman J for his part would have upheld the constitutionality of a contempt conviction where the words in question bring the administration of justice into disrepute in the eyes of the reasonable person *and* resulted in a clear, significant and imminent threat to the fair and effective administration of justice. Interestingly, the assessment of whether a clear, present danger had been

[68] (1989) 47 DLR (4th) 213, 241.
[69] Cory J endorses a Millian justification for speech in his opinion. *Ibid* at 227.

created would involve consideration of the source and timing of the criticism. Where it came from a person of good reputation or standing in the community using mild language, the threshold may more easily be reached than when a person of 'ill-repute' or no standing in the community launched a vitriolic attack on the court. Goodman AJ too drew a distinction between pending and concluded cases stating that where the criticism related to a case still before the courts, this would be a telling though not necessarily conclusive factor.[70]

European Convention Free Speech Jurisprudence

In chapter two some central themes underscoring Article 10 freedom of expression jurisprudence were explored. These included the fact that owing to its fundamental role in the maintenance of democratic society and the development of the individual, freedom of expression enjoys 'core status' in Convention jurisprudence.[71] Limitations imposed on expression may only be imposed to further certain enumerated societal or individual objectives and, then, must pass a test of proportionality. In *The Observer and The Guardian Newspapers v United Kingdom* the Court reminded national authorities of the need to establish convincingly that the interference in question was necessary for a legitimate purpose.[72] Political speech is entitled to a greater level of judicial protection than other forms of speech, a position reflected in a variable margin of appreciation doctrine. Restraints on political expression are subjected to closer scrutiny than those concerning commercial[73] and artistic expression.[74]

The requirement to ensure the open discussion of political issues such as the conduct of politicians has led to the Court to find in both *Lingens v Austria*[75] and *Oberschlick v Austria*[76] that the convictions of journalists in the national courts for the defamation of politicians violated Article 10. Greater latitude exists to criticise politicians than private citizens.[77] In *Castells v Spain*, the Court was prepared to confer an even wider degree of freedom where govern-

[70] Cory J endorses a Millian justification for speech in his opinion. *Ibid*, at 263 echoing a theme in US case law.

[71] *Handyside v UK* (1979–80) 1 EHRR 737. The democracy enhancing function of free expression has tended to feature more prominently in Strasbourg jurisprudence. See inter alia *Lingens v Austria* (1986) 8 EHRR 407, 418; *Oberschlick v Austria* (1995) 19 EHRR 389, 421 and *Sunday Times v UK* (1979) 2 EHRR 245, 280.

[72] (1991) 14 EHRR 153.

[73] *Markt Intern Verlag and Beerman v Germany* (1990) 12 EHRR 161; *Casado Coca v Spain* (1994) 18 EHRR 1. *Jacubowski v Germany* (1995) 19 EHRR 64. The boundary between commercial and non-commercial expression was discussed in *Barthold v Germany* (1985) 7 EHRR 383.

[74] *Muller v Switzerland* (1988) 13 EHRR 212; *Otto-Preminger-Institut v Austria* (1995) 19 EHRR 34; *Wingrove v United Kingdom* (1997) 24 EHRR 1.

[75] (1986) 8 EHRR 407.

[76] (1995) 19 EHRR 389.

[77] S Tierney, 'Press Freedom and Public Interest: The Developing Jurisprudence of the European Court of Human Rights' [1998] *European Human Rights Law Review* 419.

ment *per se* rather than an individual politician was attacked.[78] As for other public officials/bodies, recognition of the importance of subjecting the activities of police officers to scrutiny was evident in *Thorgeirson v Iceland*.[79] After the conviction of a Reykjavik police officer for assault, unspecified members of the Reykjavik police were accused in an open letter to the Minister of Justice of brutality, bullying, forgery and other unlawful activities. The conviction of the writer in the domestic courts for criminal defamation was held by the European Court to have constituted a disproportionate interference with his Article 10 right to freedom of expression. In reaching this conclusion, the Court drew particular attention to the factual basis of the writer's concerns, his recounting in good faith of allegations made by others on a matter of public interest. It expressly rejected the Icelandic government's suggestion that the width of critical comment afforded in *Lingens* to expression concerning politicians ought to be more narrowly drawn in the case of other matters of public interest. In the next section, the record of the Court in cases of criticism of judges and courts is considered.[80]

Expression Critical of Judges and Courts Under the Convention

Given the promising commitment to robust protection of political speech, the Court's application of overarching principles to expression which is critical of courts and judges will seem unnecessarily cautious. Implicit in this jurisprudence is the notion of courts as somehow especially vulnerable to a collapse in public confidence resulting from critical commentaries, although, on closer inspection, the basis for such a belief is not clear. In any event, the case law here sits uneasily alongside the Court's rhetoric about the importance of tolerating a broad range of political speech in a democracy. In *Barfod v Denmark*, and *Prager & Oberschlick v Austria* it may also be argued that the Court has been unduly deferential to national courts' self interested condemnation of this type of expression and, further, that it has lost sight of the requirement for restrictions

[78] (1992) 14 EHRR 445. D Voorhoof, 'Defamation and libel laws in Europe—the framework of Article 10 of the European Convention on Human Rights' (1992) 13 *Journal of Medical Law and Practice* 254; S Coliver, 'Defamation jurisprudence of the European Court on Human Rights' (1992) 13 *Journal of Medical Law and Practice* 250.

[79] (1992) 14 EHRR 843. Cf *Schopfer v Switzerland* where a lawyer's criticism of conduct by the police as in flagrant disregard of human rights and the laws of the Canton of Lucerne resulted in a fine of 500 Swiss Francs being imposed by the Supervisory Board of the Lucerne Bar for a breach of professional ethics. Schopfer had been prompted to make his criticisms after learning that police officials had told a client's wife that her husband would not be released from custody as long as Schopfer acted for him. In holding that the lawyer's Article 10 freedom was not interfered with disproportionately, the Court (by 7–2) pointed to the pending nature of the proceedings involving his client, the importance of deferring to the judgment of the disciplinary findings of the professional body and the smallness of the fine. [1998] HRCD 560.

[80] See further MK Addo (ed.), *Freedom of Expression and the Criticism of Judges* (Ashgate, Aldershot, 2000).

upon expression to be *convincingly* established. The immediate consequence of this will have been to stifle open discussion on matters of legitimate public concern. Only in *De Haes & Gisjels v Belguim* has a more appropriately critical regard towards national authorities' regulation of speech been evident.

In *Barfod* two lay judges in the Greenland High Court were criticised by the applicant for 'doing their duty' in a tax case by finding for the respondent authority who happened to be their employer. The applicant's conviction under the Greenland Penal Code was deemed by 6–1 in the European Court to be a proportionate and hence lawful interference with his Article 10 freedom of expression.[81] Particular stress was laid upon the fact that the applicant could have questioned the composition of the High Court (which was conceded by the Danish authorities to raise doubts about the impartiality of the proceedings)[82] without going on to impugn the two lay judges personally. He had not, in any event, offered any proof that the two judges were in fact biased. The suggestion here that actual bias would need to have been proved for the applicant to be protected under Article 10 is however difficult to sustain. How might such proof have been forthcoming? Might it not have been preferable to argue that, as in *Lingens*, the applicant was advancing a personal opinion based upon undisputed facts (the employment relationship between a party to the taxation dispute and the two lay judges, the admitted unconstitutionality of their participation in its resolution) and that, where such an opinion is advanced in good faith, the applicant ought not to be expected to establish the 'truth' of such an opinion. It was left to Golcuklu J, the dissenting judge, to remind the Court of the importance of allowing a public debate about the functioning of the judiciary and to conclude that the acknowledged appearance of bias brought the published criticism within the ambit of protected expression under Article 10.

Barfod may plausibly be seen as a one-off. The unwillingness to protect the expression interests there being attributable to the peculiar circumstances of Greenland, namely scattered communities within a large territory where the administration of justice is dependent upon the active support of lay persons. The latitude to be conferred upon strong criticism of professional judges in less atypical circumstances was subsequently addressed in *Prager & Oberschlick v Austria*. In a series of character sketches of named members of the Vienna Regional Criminal Court published under the heading 'Danger! Harsh Judges!', it was alleged by the applicants (an author and his publisher) that the judges routinely assumed guilt at the outset of a trial and that sentencing was harsh. One particular judge J was accused inter alia of 'arrogant bullying' and of consorting with prostitutes.[83] Criminal defamation proceedings initiated by J in

[81] The Commission by contrast had found by 14 votes to one that the applicant's Article 10 rights had been violated.

[82] Article 62 of the Danish Constitution requires the administration of justice to remain separated from the Executive.

[83] Elsewhere it was said that J was 'rabid', 'cynical' and displayed 'pig-headedness'.

respect of five isolated passages resulted in the applicants' conviction in the Austrian courts. The convictions were challenged before the European Court as a disproportionate interference with the applicants' Article 10 freedoms. There, a bare majority inclined to a generous view of the margin of appreciation afforded to the national authorities in deciding not only which measures were necessary to protect public confidence in the judiciary, but also whether the statements complained of were value-judgements or allegations of fact. In practice, the categorisation of a number of the statements as ones of fact put the applicants under the added difficulty of establishing their truth according to strict conditions in domestic law, a burden which the Austrian courts had found could not be discharged. The unwillingness of the majority to intervene is attributable in part to their assessment that the applicant author had failed to engage in adequate research before launching upon his criticisms. Thus, despite doing research over a six month period during which time he had contacted lawyers, judges and academics and had sat daily in the Vienna Courthouse for three and half months, the author failed to sit in J's court or afford to J an opportunity to comment on the adverse findings. Finally, in sustaining the convictions the majority relied, as in *Barfod*, upon the undemonstrated causal connection between the publication of criticism of judicial figures and a consequent lowering of the esteem in which the same are generally held.

Consistent with a more rigorous approach to the incursions upon expression under Article 10, the minority led by Judge Martens started from the proposition that restrictions upon expression must be convincingly established. This meant inter alia that it was inappropriate for the national courts to have the final say over whether the allegations contained in the publication were ones of fact or value-judgements. In the minority's view, four out of the five allegations were properly classified as value-judgements—a finding which in their view meant that, however 'impudent, curt or uncouth' the remarks might have been, the failure of the Austrian courts to consider the availability of a fair comment defence violated Article 10.[84] In respect of the remaining allegation of fact, the strictness of Austrian law on the adducing of proof cast further doubt on its compatibility with Article 10.

The minority in *Prager & Oberschlick* would doubtless have welcomed the less deferential approach adopted by the Strasbourg Court to the civil law penalties imposed by the Belgian courts in respect of critical comments made about three judges and an advocate-general of the Antwerp Court of Appeal in *De Haes & Gisjels v Belgium*.[85] The author and publisher of *Humo* had claimed that the decision of the court to award custody to a father in a custody dispute

[84] The minority denied that Prager had been guilty of 'glaring carelessness' and that the only possible interpretation of his article was that he was maliciously motivated. Another reading of the piece was that he was advancing in good faith an honestly held opinion based upon detailed research.

[85] (1998) 25 EHRR 1.

against whom incest allegations were levelled was biased because the court shared the father's extreme right-wing political views. Once more, the issue for the European Court centred upon the necessity for the restriction on the applicants' freedom of expression.[86] On this occasion however, the Court found that the Belgian authorities had failed to establish the need for interference. It pointed to the fact that, at the time the impugned articles were published, the issue of incest in Flanders and judicial responses to individual cases were already both matters of media comment. There was thus a strong public interest in the fate of young children and the level of protection accorded to them by the courts. Moreover, no accusation of professional carelessness in the preparation of the comments could be made against the applicants.[87] Indeed, the articles in *Humo* cited expert medical and psychiatric evidence supporting the allegation of sexual abuse against the father. The Court also took a more interventionist line on the categorisation of factual statements and value-judgements than it had done previously in *Prager & Oberschlick*, holding the allegations of bias to be value-judgements whose truth did not need to be established, provided there was, as here, a factual basis upon which the opinion or comment might be based.[88] Accordingly, the applicants' Article 10 freedom had been violated.[89]

IV CONCLUSION

Justice Frankfurter's rejection of the 'English foolishness' in *Bridges v California* was echoed in the same case by an even doughtier defender of First Amendment speech interests—Justice Hugo Black.

> The assumption that respect for the judiciary can be won by shielding judges from published criticism wrongly appraises the character of US public opinion . . . an enforced silence, however limited solely in the name of preserving the dignity of the bench, would probably engender resentment, suspicion, and contempt much more than it would enhance respect.[90]

Closer to home Judge Martens' dissent in *Prager & Oberschlick* opted for much the same sceptical line:

[86] The national courts had ordered the applicants to pay nominal one franc damages to each of the plaintiffs, to publish the judgment of the Brussels tribunal de premiere instance in *Humo* and to pay for that judgment to be published in six daily newspapers.

[87] The applicants had engaged in 'thorough research' and had furthermore recognised the limits of media commentary on the matter when they wrote 'it is not for the press to usurp the role of the judiciary, but in this outrageous case it is impossible and unthinkable that we should remain silent.'

[88] *Humo* had detailed links between judges involved in the custody hearing, right-wing political groupings and the father's family.

[89] The applicants also established a breach of Article 6(1) 'equality of arms' principle in respect of the Belgium courts failure to admit expert evidence relied upon by the applicants.

[90] *Bridges v California* (1941) 314 US 252, 270–71.

> I agree that public confidence in the judiciary is important . . . but rather doubt whether that confidence is to be maintained by resorting to criminal proceedings to condemn criticism which the very same judiciary may happen to consider as 'destructive'.[91]

In modern democratic societies, resort to the offences of scandalising and criminal libel seems a clumsy and archaic means of bolstering public confidence in the judiciary. In the United Kingdom, we live in an era of relative disrespect for societal institutions including Parliament, the monarchy and the police. Tabloid campaigns against what is perceived to be misguided judicial conduct have replaced the London Mob as the supposedly popular expression of outraged opinion. In these circumstances, it is right to ask whether any good reasons exist for giving the courts/judges a privileged position over other public bodies or persons when it comes to criticism.

The arguments from truth and democracy offer no reason to provide special protection for the courts and judges. Indeed, Mill's argument for example would seem to permit a very broad range of truthful and false assertion about judicial conduct, even where this related to pending cases and could be shown to be damaging to public confidence in the judiciary. It is interesting in this regard to see the Ontario Court of Appeal's use of Millian arguments to establish the unconstitutional nature of scandalising, although this was tempered by the recognition for two of the Appeal Justices that, where a real, substantial and immediate danger to the administration of justice had been intentionally or recklessly created, the competing societal interest in safeguarding the administration of justice ought to prevail.[92] Although it has yet to figure explicitly in judicial analyses, Schauer's distrust of speech regulation as notoriously partisan appears particularly relevant to the *self-interested* nature of judge-developed restraints referred to in the quotation from Judge Martens above and suggests why these restraints ought to be subject to particularly close scrutiny.[93]

The extent to which critical comment is permitted is arguably a reliable indicator of a state's confidence in its legal system. Outside of the US, the legal system which discloses most confidence in its judicial system to withstand the assaults of critics and offer a principled defence of speech interests in this area is the Canadian system. Apart from its resort to Millian theory, confidence is evident in the scepticism the Ontario Court of Appeal in *Kopyto* expressed about the causal link between critical speech and damaged public confidence in the judiciary. In Australia, the doctrine of the implied freedom of political communication does not look like sweeping away the common law offence in the immediate future. Not only is it not clear whether criticism of courts and judges is protected political communication, the existence of a fair comment defence

[91] (1996) 21 EHRR 1, 24 at fn 47

[92] Even then Justice Cory would have allowed a truth defence. Earlier, the Phillimore Committee had suggested that for a defence of truthful allegation to succeed, the defendant would also have to show that it was made for the public benefit. Cmnd 5794 (1974) at paras 164, 167.

[93] F Schauer, *Free Speech: a philosophical enquiry* (Cambridge University Press, Cambridge, 1982).

may shield the offence from constitutional attack. The Strasbourg Court for its part sends conflicting signals to those tempted to risk the wrath of municipal legal systems by criticising judicial figures.

In the past, defenders of scandalising in England and Wales pointed to the fact that judges were precluded from replying under the Kilmuir Rules.[94] In recent times however, there has been a move away from the model of judicial reticence endorsed therein.[95] Increasingly, judges are being encouraged to engage with the media in an effective manner in order to communicate with the public. Thus, the Lord Chancellor's Department in England and Wales issued guidance in 1997 to judges on speaking to the media in order to avoid media misreporting of sentencing matters. Under the guidance, judges are encouraged to produce a written note of their sentencing remarks for distribution to the media at the close of any trial.[96] The Lord Chief Justice and Master of the Rolls make regular extra-judicial contributions to public debate on criminal and civil law issues. Lord Woolf has been vocal in the debate over the prison system.[97] Support for increased judicial participation in public debate is not confined to England and Wales. The Canadian Supreme Court judge, Justice Sopinka in an address to the Empire Club, Toronto in April 1992 stated that:

> . . . a judge should be able to comment on matters relating to the administration of justice and any reforms to that system.

In 1998, the Chief Justice of South Australia John Doyle wrote that the time for judges to accept a responsibility for informing the public about their work in partnership with the media had arrived.[98]

In those cases where the media is considered to have overstepped the boundary of acceptable criticism of an individual judge, the option of suing to vindicate reputation remains, and is resorted to from time to time.[99] Thus in 1992 Mr Justice Popplewell successfully sued the *Today* newspaper for suggesting that he had fallen asleep during a murder trial. In Australia, a special magistrate brought an action against a litigant after the latter questioned the magistrate's

[94] In a letter to the Director General of the BBC written in 1955, the Lord Chancellor had said: '. . . the overriding consideration . . . is the importance of keeping the Judiciary in this country insulated from the controversies of the day. So long as a Judge keeps silent his reputation for wisdom and impartiality remains unassailable: but every utterance which he makes in public, except in the actual performance of his judicial duties, must necessarily bring him within the focus of criticism . . .'

[95] Relaxation of the rules was announced in a letter from the Lord Chancellor Lord Mackay of Clashfern to the Lord Chief Justice, Lord Lane on 16 October 1989. Lord Mackay stated that it would be left to judges to decide 'whether, and on what conditions, they should give interviews to journalists or appear on radio or television.'

[96] Press Notice 57/97 issued on 26 March 1997.

[97] See his address to the Prison Reform Trust 'The Woolf Report: a Decade of Change?' in London 31 January 2001 in which he argued in favour of more effective community-based methods of tackling offending instead of custodial sentences.

[98] See http://www.jc.nsw.gov.au/FB/fbdoyle.htm

[99] In the US, the rule in *New York Times v Sullivan* would cut off a large number of suits.

mental fitness in a letter to the judicial authorities.[100] The argument in this chapter has not been that these defamation actions are to be discouraged.[101] Rather, it has been to suggest that the archaic offence of scandalising has no place in a modern democratic society which is committed to robust exchanges on matters of public interest more generally. In the case of unfounded criticism, the answer to critical speech lies in more judicial (and other) speech. Where the criticism has force, it is surely better to direct energies at reforming the administration of justice than to apply the prosecutorial forces of the state against its critics.

[100] *Mann v O'Neill* (1997) 191 CLR 204.

[101] Although there could be disagreement about the degree of constitutional protection for speech concerning public officials such as judges.

6

A Civil Law Comparison: Freedom of Expression and the Administration of Justice in Spain

1 INTRODUCTION

THIS COMPARATIVE TREATMENT of laws regulating media freedom to report and comment upon matters before the courts has focused exclusively until now upon the common law world where affinities of inductive legal method and varying degrees of procedural and substantive overlap may be detected. In chapter one, it was argued that the trend in common law jurisdictions towards the constitutionalisation of speech claims would result in greater interest in comparative freedom of expression jurisprudence so that, accordingly, it might be expected that judicial and academic discussion of expression issues would come to draw upon and critique a wider range of materials.

Of course, common law jurisdictions are not unique in having to regulate the conflict between freedom of expression and the administration of justice. In civil law jurisdictions too, public access to criminal proceedings and media freedom to report and comment upon them have been thought to pose a threat to the administration of justice. However, few scholars based in common law jurisdictions have ventured to consider the regulation of court-related expression under civil law systems. An exception to this is Michael Chesterman who has contrasted common law contempt rules with their equivalents in the French legal system.[1] In the case of Anglo-Hispanic legal scholarship, little appears to have been written in English about the regulation of expression under Spanish law and yet Spain would seem to offer an attractive case study for a variety of reasons. The relatively recent emergence of Spain as a social democracy committed to the underlying values of political pluralism and fundamental rights would merit study of the development of legal regulation of expression and fair trials/administration of justice in its own right. What makes this material more compelling however is the wider political context in which this regulation is situated. The enduring nature of the Basque struggle for independence, the

[1] Michael Chesterman 'Contempt: In the Common Law, but not the Civil Law' (1997) 46 *International Comparative Law Quarterly* 521.

responses of the Spanish state to terrorist activities of ETA activists, a failed military coup and allegations of corruption at the highest levels of public office have required the *Tribunal Constitucional* as guardian of the constitutional settlement of 1978 to elaborate upon the meaning of a range of constitutional guarantees, among which number freedom of expression and the right to a fair trial. The resulting jurisprudence is detailed in this chapter.

A significant influence operating on the *Tribunal Constitucional* since 1979 has been the European Convention on Human Rights which enjoys a superior status in domestic law over inconsistent domestic law. The impact of these European norms on domestic Spanish law is also considered. The chapter begins however in 1970 with the infamous Burgos trial of Basque activists and the moment when the fascist regime of Francisco Franco Bahamonde gambled on freely reported criminal proceedings to broadcast to the whole of Spain its determination to crush the regime's opponents.

II BURGOS 1970 AND AFTER

On 3 December 1970, 16 persons were put on trial before a military court in Burgos, Spain charged with various offences including murder, incitement to murder, causing explosions and belonging to an illegally armed group. Although a law terminating aspects of the prior censorship of published materials had been enacted in 1966,[2] press freedom had not been relaxed to the point where proceedings in the military courts were, as a matter of course, open to the public and freely reportable. Indeed, under a Concordat between Franco's regime and the Vatican in 1953, the Catholic Church retained a special power to request that certain classes of trial be held *in camera*. However, on learning that two priests were among the accused, the Apostolic administrator of Bilbao interceded with the Vatican for the trial to be held in public—a fact which by itself spoke to the Catholic Church's growing disaffection with the regime. In the weeks before the start of the trial, signs of growing tension within the country were apparent. Prominent opposition leaders were arrested whilst preparing a letter protesting about the trial. In response, a hundred Madrid lawyers staged a sit-in at the Palacio de Justicia. Universities in Madrid and Barcelona also closed down. Students and workers clashed with police. Then, on 1 December, an ETA-grouping kidnapped the West German Honorary Consul in San Sebastián. By the start of the trial, the Basque struggle was now high up on the international news agenda. Journalists from a number of different countries

[2] *Ley 14/1966 de Prensa e Imprenta*. Publishers were, it seems, still subject to suspension or closure on a variety of grounds although mild criticisms of the Franco regime could be made. The 1966 law also permitted regional languages such as Catalan to flourish after a period of repression. See further R Gunther, G Sani, and G Shabad, *Spain after Franco—The Making of a Competitive Party System* (University of California Press, Los Angeles, 1986) at 31–32.

attended the proceedings. It was clear from the outset that both the prosecution and defence shared the view that it was not only the accused who were on trial but Basque nationalist aspirations more generally. For the state authorities, the decision to prosecute so many Basques in one showcase trial for offences—some of which were capital crimes—could only be interpreted as a determined and very public attempt to inflict a deep blow upon Basque nationalism. Defence lawyers for their part sought at some considerable personal peril to focus attention of the world's media on Francoist oppression of the Basque people. This they did through their questioning of the accused and by lodging frequent objections to the military court's handling of the trial. Outside the courtroom, press conferences were held with foreign journalists to ensure their clients' grievances reached a wide audience[3]

On 4 December, a state of emergency was declared in Guipuzcoa—one of the most nationalist of all Basque provinces—in response to the general strike called the previous day by outlawed trades unions. House searches, unlimited detention and censorship of mail all served to link in a most graphic way the ongoing trial and the wider persecution of the Basques.

In a surprise opening to the trial, some of the accused were allowed to give detailed accounts of police torture and the wider oppression of the Basque people by the Francoist state. The military judges did not however take long to realise that this opportunity for propaganda would have to be closed off. After an adjournment on 7 December, the Presiding Judge announced that the defendants must in future confine themselves to responding to the questions put to them. From this time onwards, submissions from the accused and their lawyers were frequently interrupted. The trial descended into chaos on 9 December when one of the accused—Mario Onaindia Nachiondo—gave a detailed defence of ETA's position in the Basque struggle. Refusing an order from the President of the Court to be silent, he jumped out of the witness box, attempted to grab an axe and moved towards the panel of judges singing *Eusko Gudariak* —the 'Basque Warrior.' Onaindia was overpowered but the anthem was taken up by the rest of the accused and members of the public at which point the court was cleared and proceedings suspended. After a delay, the trial resumed *in camera*. The proceedings never resumed in open court.

During the long wait before the verdicts were announced, the anti-regime feeling intensified across Spain. Demonstrations followed in Madrid, Barcelona and other cities. There were violent clashes between the police and the regime's opponents. The Benedictine monastery at Montserrat was occupied by 300 Catalan artists, writers and intellectuals with the approval of the Abbot and defied a siege from members of the Civil Guard. International protests followed.

[3] For a detailed account of the trial in English see J Sullivan, *ETA and Basque Nationalism—The Fight for Euskadi 1890–1986* (Routledge, London, 1988) ch 4. For accounts in Spanish see K Salaberri, *El proceso de Euskadi en Burgos. El Sumarisimo 31.69* (Paris, 1969) at 153–238. The regime's view may be discovered by reading F Artega, *'ETA' y el proceso de Burgos* (E Aguado, Madrid, 1971)

French and Italian dockers refused to load ships bound for Spain. The Vatican published an article in its daily newspaper asking that the prisoners be treated with clemency. The regime responded by denouncing anti-Spanish campaigns in the foreign media and suspending the guarantee of habeas corpus in Article 18 of the 1936 Constitution.

The verdicts were announced on 28 December. Three of the accused were each found guilty of two capital charges and were sentenced to death. Aware of the potential international and domestic repercussions of their implementation, Franco commuted the sentences two days later to lengthy terms of imprisonment.

Burgos—Its Significance and Aftermath

The Burgos trial is credited with being a pivotal moment in the decline of Francoism and the transition to democracy.[4] True, the regime had been spared immediate further international criticism and the Church's plea for clemency had been heeded. Unfortunately for Franco, his opponents were now more united than ever before at a time when factional strains in the regime were surfacing.[5] Three years later, his Prime Minister Admiral Carrero Blanco returning from daily mass was blown up by an explosive device placed under his car by ETA activists on the day that another show trial—this time of 10 leaders of an illegal trades union—*Proceso 1001* was due to commence.[6] The central elements of the final crisis of the Franco regime—labour militancy, Basque terrorism and internal schism within the government—were all now in place. The end of Francoism and a relatively peaceful transition to democracy were within sight.

In open justice terms, Burgos serves as a reminder that motives other than those of ensuring public scrutiny of judicial power may lie behind a decision to allow public access to the administration of justice. Franco's government perceived that an advantage was to be gained from public and pre-determined trials against political opponents in terms of a wider deterrence function. The success however of the defence in placing the repressive conduct of the state at the centre of this public trial revealed a serious miscalculation by the authorities on

[4] Preston comments that the trial 'altered the balance of forces within Spain. The opposition was more united than at any time since the Civil War. ETA had boosted the morale of the entire left and had united the Basque Country around its cause.' P Preston, *The Triumph of Democracy in Spain* (Routledge, London, 1993) at 36.

[5] See Preston *ibid* for a fascinating account of the terminal decline of Francoist state and the transition to democracy. Shortly before his death in 1975, the ailing Franco did confirm death sentences passed on two Basques for the murder of a Civil Guard and three members of a revolutionary Maoist group FRAP for the murder of two policemen. They were executed in September 1975. The contrast in outcomes between 1970 and 1975 is explained by Preston in terms of the grip exercised over the *Cuadillo* by ultra rightist elements immediately prior to his death. P Preston, *Franco* (Fontana Press, London, 1995) at 776.

[6] See further S Ellwood, 'The Working Class under the Franco Regime' in P Preston (ed), Spain in Crisis—*The Evolution and Decline of the Franco Regime* (Harvester, Sussex, 1976).

this point and demonstrated how, even in the most unpromising of circumstances, the reporting of court proceedings can exert a legitimate form of scrutiny on state activities by bringing information and opinion into the public domain.

In *post*-Franco Spain, high profile criminal proceedings remain a feature of the administration of justice although this is not simply on account of the enduring nature of the Basque conflict which continues to bring bloodshed to Spanish cities and towns. In the period from December 1999 (when ETA announced the end of its fourteenth month long ceasefire) to June 2001, elements associated with the organisation are estimated to have killed 31 persons. Those killed include politicians, judges, members of the *Guardia Civil*, journalists and businessman.[7] A number of assailants have themselves been killed whilst on active service. Naturally enough, criminal prosecutions against Basque separatists for acts of violence remain a focus of media attention. Increasingly of late, prosecuting authorities have focused their attention on Basque political propaganda and the economic structures which support their terrorist activities. For example, members of political parties such as *Herri Batasuna* (*People's Unity*—a Basque left nationalist party) have been charged with apologising for, or collaborating in, terrorism. Other legal moves have resulted in judicial orders temporarily closing down the Basque daily newspaper *Egin* and its subsidiary radio station *Egin Irratia* on the grounds that both were part of the economic and financial structures of a terrorist organisation.[8] In this context, it should be noted that two journalists on *Egin* had earlier been convicted of belonging to an armed group and of illegal possession of explosives and weapons. Even foreign-owned news networks have come under pressure albeit of an non-legal nature from the state as a result of their coverage of Basque activities. Shortly after the widely reported kidnapping and murder of a local *Partido Popular* politician in July 1997, the Spanish Government asked CNN—the US cable television network—to remove a hyperlink between its internet site and that belonging to ETA. CNN refused, stating that its policy was to link up its web sites with organisations mentioned in those sites. Two days later, CNN's web site was 'mail bombed' out of existence by a deluge of e-mails.[9]

[7] A particular feature of recent ETA activity has been the targetting of journalists. In addition to parcel bombs sent to journalists in Madrid, Bilbao and Seville, buildings owned by media organisations have also been bombed.

[8] ETA-KAS For qualified support of the closure order from an academic lawyer, see Prof M Carrillo, *A proposito de la clausura de 'Egin'* in *El País* 11 August 1998. A new daily newspaper *Euskadi Información* appeared quickly upon the closure of *Egin*.

[9] Mail bombing refers to a technique found more typically in a commercial context when a large number of recipients are deluged with unsolicited e-mail. Most of the costs in mail bombing is borne by the recipient or carriers of the mail in terms of time and money spent identifying and discarding this type of mail and of the disk space used to transmit and store this unwanted communication. In CNN's case the news corporation was the sole recipient of an avalanche of unsolicited e-mail that caused its server to crash.

The unofficial response of the Socialist Government to Basque terrorism in the early 1980s was the creation of *Grupos Antiterroristas de Liberación* (GAL) a secret paramilitary force comprised of members of the security forces and hired assasins whose function, it is now clear, was to harass, kidnap, torture and murder Basque nationalists. In the so-called 'dirty war' between 1983–1987 it is estimated that 28 persons were killed by elements associated with GAL. Somewhat belatedly, Spanish judicial authorities began investigations into allegations of serious criminal misconduct at senior governmental levels. In the first trial to take place concerning the activities of GAL, the former interior minister Jose Barrioneuvo and the former Secretary of State Security, Rafael Vera, were each sentenced in July 1999 to 10 years imprisonment for their involvement in the kidnapping and illegal detention of a French businessman and the illegal use of public funds in 1983.[10] Others, including national police officers, have been convicted of the torture of suspected Basque terrorists.[11] At the time of writing, judicial inquiries into the torture and deaths of other ETA activists are extant. Corruption scandals involving government ministers and other public figures from the Gonzalez era have also resulted in some high profile legal proceedings.[12] The Governor of the Central Bank of Spain between 1984–1992, Mariano Rubio, was found to have defrauded state revenues when he placed about £600,000 in secret accounts which were used for speculation and personal gain on international money markets. A former head of the Civil Guard—Luis Roldán Ibáñez—was imprisoned for 28 years after being convicted on counts of illegally amassing a personal fortune of over £8 million, bribery and tax evasion. His crimes included stealing from a fund which had been set up by the state for the orphans of victims of terrorism. Vicente Albero, Secretary of State for Agriculture, admitted defrauding the Revenue Authorities in the *Ibercorp* scandal. The scandal surrounding Roldán who had escaped from custody in April 1994 prior to his trial is generally thought to have played a significant part in bringing down the government of Felipe González in 1996.

An account of the norms which regulate media coverage of high-profile, politically charged criminal trials will be provided later in this chapter. In the next section, an outline of some key features of the 1978 constitutional settlement is set down. Attention here will focus on some general values given constitutional status and the nature of protection afforded to fundamental rights such as freedom of expression and the right to a fair trial. Turning to institutional arrangements, the role of the *Tribunal Constitucional* (Constitutional Court) in

[10] The sentences were later reduced on appeal.

[11] See *Annual Report on Spain* (Amnesty International, London, 1999).

[12] For an account of recent scandals in English see F Jimenez, *Political Scandals and Political Responsibility in Democratic Spain* in P Heywood (ed), *Politics and Policy in Democratic Spain* (Frank Cass, London, 1999); An earlier account is to be found in P Heywood, *The Government and Politics of Spain* (Macmillan Press, London, 1995) at 117–120. The same theme is tackled in numerous Spanish publications including J Sinova and J Tusell, *La Crisis de la Democracia en España* (Espasa Hoy, Madrid, 1997).

the protection of individual rights is then outlined. Later, the incorporation of these norms in Spanish criminal procedure is considered. Finally, some implications of the recent re-introduction of juries in certain criminal proceedings will be explored.

III THE 1978 CONSTITUTION—HUMAN RIGHTS IN A MODERN SOCIAL DEMOCRACY

Central Features of the 1978 Constitución Española[13]

The designers of the 1978 Constitution (hereafter *CE*) consciously sought to draw upon aspects of other European constitutional models.[14] In particular, aspects of the Italian Constitution of 1948 and the West German Constitution of 1949 were influential—a fact which may be attributed to these nations' experiences in moving from dictatorship to democracy.[15]

Article 1 of *CE* establishes Spain as a social democracy committed to the values of liberty, justice, equality and political pluralism.[16] Sovereignty is vested in the Spanish people.[17] The state assumes the form of a parliamentary democracy nominally headed by the monarch.[18] The real centre of political power however rests with the office of the President who heads the executive and who is required to have the confidence of the *Cortes* or Parliament.[19] Under Article 9 *CE* Spain is declared to be an '*estado de derecho*' or *Rechtstaat* under which laws passed by Parliament (an assembly which is representative of the popular will) provide the legal basis for the conduct of public bodies and persons.[20]

[13] For a general account of the 1978 Constitution and Spanish Legal System in English see E Merino-Blanco, *The Spanish Legal System* (Sweet & Maxwell, London, 1996); P. Heywood., *The Government and Politics of Spain* (Macmillan Press Ltd, London, 1995). In Spanish, see A Predieri, and E García de Enterría (eds) *La Constitución Española de 1978* 2nd edn (Editorial Civitas, Madrid, 1984); M Pulido Quecedo, *La Constitución Española* (Aranzadi Editorial, Pamplona, 1993).

[14] M Herrero y Rodríguez de Minon, *La elaboracíon de la Constitución in Cuenta y Razón* (Alianza Editorial, Madrid, 1988) 65, 72.

[15] A Nieto, *La Organización del desgobierno* (Editorial Ariel, Barcelona, 1984). Thus, on the difficult question of the distribution of powers between the centre and the regions for example the influence of the Italian Constitution is apparent.

[16] The precise wording of Article 1(1) *CE* states 'Spain constitutes itself into a social and democratic state of law which advocates liberty, justice, equality, and political pluralism as the superior values of its legal order.'

[17] Art 1(2) *CE*.

[18] Art 1(3) *CE* provides that 'The political form of the Spanish State is the parliamentary monarchy.' The monarch is however at the margins of political life being confined to largely symbolic functions such as expressing the unity and continuity of the Spanish state (Art 56(1) *CE*) including the approval of laws, the dissolution of Parliament and the appointment of members of the Government on the advice of the President (Art 62 *CE*).

[19] Comprising a Lower House (Congreso del Diputados) designed as a chamber of popular representation and Upper House (Senado) representing more concretely the distinct territorial areas in Spain.

[20] Art 9(1) *CE*. The citizens and public powers are subject to the Constitution and legal order.

Where disputes arise concerning the constitutional propriety of laws passed by Parliament or delegated legislation,[21] the *Tribunal Constitucional* is the supreme interpreter of constitutionality. The creation of an independent supreme court with the power of judicial review over legislative enactments of the *Cortes* reflected the prevailing view that parliamentary sovereignty alone might not suffice to ensure the longer term survival of the democratic state and that individual rights would be better safeguarded by an independent judiciary.[22] The record of the West German Constitutional Court in protecting individual rights after a period of fascist dictatorship was especially persuasive in this regard. As for the composition of the supreme judicial body, Herrero de Miñón, one of the drafters of the 1978 Constitution, has acknowledged that the method of selection employed for the *Conseil Constitutionnel* in France was influential.[23]

Fundamental Rights, Rights and Duties and Guiding Principles in the 1978 *CE*—A Typology[24]

The rights of Spanish citizens under the 1978 *CE* fall into one of three categories. The group of rights and freedoms listed in Article 14 and Chapter 2 of the Title 1 (Articles 15–29) (*Fundamental Rights, Public Liberties*) comprise many of the classic negative civil liberties of western liberal democracies including freedom of expression, religion, assembly and association and are accorded an enhanced constitutional status.[25] The rights protected include the right to a public trial without delay and 'with all the guarantees.'[26] The latter phrase has

[21] These may take the form of *decretos leyes* under Art 86.1 *CE* (which may be introduced in times of emergency and extreme need with the approval and ratification of the *Cortes* but lack the power to affect either the organisation of the basic institutions of the state or the fundamental rights and liberties of citizens protected in Title 1 of the Constitution) or *decretos legislativos* under Art 82*CE* (where the *Cortes* has conferred limited rule-making powers on the executive outside of urgent situations). *Decretos legislativos* cannot be used to alter fundamental rights and liberties.

[22] The notion of a body formally situated outside the judiciary to ensure compliance by the legislature to the Constitution can be traced to writings of Hans Kelsen. Previously, under the Second Republic's Constitution of 1931, a *Tribunal de Garantías Constituciónales* (Court of Constitutional Guarantees) had been established.

[23] Arts 159–160 *CE*.

[24] For general discussion of the protection of rights in Spain, see F Rubio Llorente, *Derechos fundamentales y principios Constituciónales* (Editorial Ariel, Barcelona, 1995) and, more specifically, on media freedom L de Carreras Serra, *Régimen jurídico de la información—Periodistas y medios de comunicación* (Editorial Ariel, Barcelona, 1996); M Carrillo, *Los Límites a la libertad de prensa en la Constitución española de 1978* (Promociones Publicaciones Universitarias, Barcelona, 1987)

[25] Expression is protected by Art 20 *CE*. Other rights and freedoms protected include the right to life (Art 15 *CE*), freedom from torture and inhuman or degrading punishment (Art 15 *CE*), freedom of religion (Art 16 *CE*), liberty of the person (Art 17 *CE*), personal honour and privacy (Art 18 *CE*), freedom of movement (Art 19 *CE*), assembly (Art 21 *CE*), association (Art 22 *CE*), participation in political affairs (Art 23 *CE*).

[26] Art 24(2) *CE*.

been taken by the *Tribunal Constitucional* in a 1988 ruling to include the right to an impartial trial. The Court was mindful on this occasion of the fact that the guarantee of an impartial trial is a key element of the administration of justice under the rule of law.[27] The special status of these rights is indicated by the fact that by Article 53.2 *CE* these rights may be invoked under a special summary procedure in front of the ordinary courts and, as a last resort, before the *Tribunal Constitucional* under the *recurso de amparo* procedure.[28] Moreover, where Parliament wishes to enact a law which touches in some way upon a fundamental right or public liberty in section 1 of Chapter 2, it may only do so by means of a *ley orgánica* under Article 81*CE* which is subject to the procedural requirement of needing an absolute majority of the *Congreso del Diputados* or Lower House.[29]

The second group of rights which are located in section 2 Articles 30–38 comprise economic and social entitlements such as the right to hold private property[30] and the right to marry.[31] Some important civic duties are also set down here, including the duty to undertake a period of military service,[32] and to pay taxes.[33] Section 2 further establishes Spain as a market economy committed to the principles of free enterprise.[34]

The third set of 'rights' are those laid down in Chapter 3 Title 1 under the heading 'Guiding Principles of Economic and Social Policy'. These fall short of conferring concrete entitlements on the part of citizens, constituting instead a looser statement of standards on social, economic and cultural matters. Thus, there are provisions relating to families and children, the elderly and unemployed which lay down obligations on public authorities.[35] Parliament, public authorities and the courts are thus enjoined to recognise, respect and protect these standards although failure to so does not *per se* afford a basis for impugning either the validity of a law otherwise validly enacted or an executive action which is otherwise lawful.[36]

[27] *Sentencia Tribunal Constituciónal* (hereafter *STC*) 145/1988. See also *STC* 60/1995 where the Court declared that 'without an impartial judge, there can be no proper trial.'.

[28] Art161(1)(b) *CE*. See further Arts 43(1) and 44(1) of the *Ley Orgánica del Tribunal Constitucional LO* 2/1979 October 12. The *recurso de amparo* is also available to persons seeking to avoid military call up on grounds of conscientious objection under Art 30(2)*CE*.

[29] *Leyes ordinarias* by contrast may be passed by a simple majority.

[30] Art 33.

[31] Art 32.

[32] Art 30.

[33] Art 31.

[34] Art 38.

[35] Herrero de Minon has stated that the origins of the distinction between guiding principles and fundamental rights was the Burmese Constitution of 1948 in *La elaboración de la Constitución* in *Cuenta y Razón* (Alianza Editorial, Spain, 1988) 65.

[36] Art 53(3)*CE*.

The International Dimension to Human Rights Protection in Spain

By virtue of Article 96 *CE*, international treaties are automatically incorporated into the Spanish legal system once they have been signed and ratified.[37] However, where a treaty confers authority on an international organisation,[38] Article 93 requires the enactment of a *ley orgánica* approving ratification of the treaty in question after which it only remains for the treaty to be published in the official state journal before incorporation into domestic law is completed.

Understandably, given the Francoist legacy, the framers of the 1978 Constitution moved quickly to import an international dimension to the domestic protection of fundamental rights and liberties.[39] This is evident in Article 10.2 *CE* which states that:

> the norms relative to basic right and liberties which are recognised by the Constitution shall be interpreted in conformity with the Universal Declaration of Human Rights and the international treaties and agreements on those matters ratified by Spain.[40]

The following year the European Convention on Human Rights was duly ratified by Spain and published, thereby acquiring the status of domestic law.[41] Validly concluded treaties may only be abolished, suspended or modified 'in the manner provided for in the treaties themselves or in accordance with general norms of international law'.[42] Accordingly, in the event of a conflict with domestic law, international law prevails. A right of individual petition to Strasbourg was subsequently recognised in 1981.

IV FREEDOM OF EXPRESSION JURISPRUDENCE OF THE TRIBUNAL CONSTITUCIONAL: SOME GENERAL FEATURES

In the previous section, freedom of expression was shown as belonging to that groups of rights and freedoms deemed fundamental in the new constitutional settlement and worthy of the highest level of protection. In this section, the freedom of expression jurisprudence of the *Tribunal Constitucional* is considered in terms of its underlying themes and values.

[37] Under Art 95 *CE*, international treaties are subject to the Constitution. The *Tribunal Constitucional* may therefore hear a challenge to a treaty on the ground that it conflicts with the Constitution under Art 95(2)*CE* by either the Government, the Lower or Upper House of Parliament.

[38] As is the case with the European Convention on Human Rights.

[39] M Delmas-Marty, *The European Convention for the Protection of Human Rights* (Kluwer, The Hague, 1992) see ch V by E Cavagna and E Monteiro.

[40] *STC* 36/1984.

[41] The Convention was ratified on 4 October, 1979 and announced officially in the *Boletin Oficial del Estado* of 10 October 1979. The requirements of ratification and publication are set down in Articles 94(1) and 96(1) *CE*. See further A Drzemczewski., *European Human Rights Convention in Domestic Law* (Clarendon Press, Oxford, 1983) at 158–162.

[42] Art 96(1) *CE*.

Article 20(1) *CE* recognizes and protects the rights:

> (a) to express and disseminate freely thoughts, ideas, opinions through spoken words, writing or any other means of communication,
>
> . . .
>
> (d) to communicate or receive freely truthful information through any means of communication. The law shall regulate the right to the protection of the clause on conscience and professional secrecy in the exercise of these freedoms.[43]

Moreover, under Article 20(2) *CE*:

> The exercise of these rights cannot be restricted through any type of prior censorship.

Notwithstanding the unconstitutionality of prior restraint, freedom of expression under Article 20 *CE* is not absolute. It is subject to certain limitations derived, in part from other individual rights and in conditions of national emergency or state of siege.[44] Thus, Article 20(4) *CE* states:

> These liberties find their limitation in the respect for the rights recognized in this Title, in the precepts of the laws which develop it and, especially, in the right to honour, privacy, personal identity, and protection of youth and childhood.

And Article 55(1) further provides that:

> The rights recognized in Articles . . . 20(1)(a) and (d) . . . may be suspended when a state of emergency or seige is declared under the terms provided in the Constitution . . .[45]

Rationales for Expression

Unsurprisingly given the Francoist history of state controlled presses, a dominant theme in rulings of the *Tribunal Constitucional* on Article 20 *CE* is the instrumental link between freedom of expression and the preservation of a democratic society. Thus, the Court has reiterated on a number of occasions that freedom of expression must not be seen solely in terms of a right pertaining to individuals but more broadly as a necessary pre-condition for maintaining political pluralism[46] and a democratic society.[47] Moreover, its ambit extends not simply to matters which the state considers inoffensive or is indifferent to, but also to those forms of expression which disturb the state or a section of its

[43] This is a reference to the protection of journalistic activity and information protected by professional privilege.
[44] Art 55 *CE*.
[45] As regulated by Art 116(1), (3) and (4) *CE*.
[46] See also in this regard Art 16(1) *CE* which guarantees 'freedom of ideology'—which comprises the freedom to hold and express one's views including the assertion of values which are contrary to those constitutional values enshrined in Art 1(1) *CE* and limited only on grounds of public order. On the nature of the relationship between Art 16(1) and Art 20(1), see *STC* 20/1990 (*Punto y Hora*).
[47] *STC* 121/1989; *STC* 51/1989 (*capitán de Caballería*).

people.[48] This is consistent with Strasbourg jurisprudence as developed in cases such as *Handyside v UK*[49] and *Oberschlick v Austria*.[50] In the latter ruling, it will be recalled that the European Court linked the tolerance of offensive or unpopular expression to the demands of pluralism, tolerance and broadmindedness 'without which there is no democratic society.'[51] The centrality of expression and communication to the maintenance of a democratic society in the 1978 Constitution is also indicated in the especial status accorded by the *Tribunal Constitucional* to Article 20(1) freedom in the hierarchy of fundamental freedoms recognised by the Consitution:

> The balancing of conflicting constitutional rights requires in respect of the established rights in Art 18.1[52] that account be taken of the especial position occupied by the freedom to impart and receive information and freedom of expression . . . given that the latter belong not only to each citizen but are also part of the guarantee of free public opinion which is inextricably linked to pluralism and democracy.[53]

This re-alignment of values did not occur overnight however. In one of the early freedom of expression disputes to come before the *Tribunal Constitucional*, Miguel Castells—a lawyer and member of the the Upper House representing *Herri Batasuna*—had his conviction for insulting the government upheld.[54] Castells had written an article in June 1979 in a magazine entitled 'Outrageous Impunity' in which he claimed that right-wing groups were roaming about the Basque country and murdering local people without facing the possibility of arrest or trial. No effort had even been made to seek information from the public about the identities of the perpetrators of these crimes. This lack of activity on the part of the state authorities, Castells argued, was explicable only on the ground that the Government itself was party to the killings. At his trial, he was denied the opportunity by the *Tribunal Supremo* and, subsequently on appeal, by the *Tribunal Constitucional*, to show the factual basis for his claims about the nature of the state's involvement in the murders. The *Tribunal Supremo* ruled that the defence of truth could not be pleaded where the words at issue had been directed at state institutions. The *Tribunal Constitucional* refused to re-consider the point as it related to a question of the interpretation of a provision of the *Código Penal* and was therefore outside of its jurisdiction. On application to the European Court of Human Rights, Castells' Article 10 right to freedom of expression was declared to have been violated by his conviction. The denial of an opportunity to establish the truth of his accusations had not been shown to be 'necessary in a democratic society.'

[48] *STC* 62/1982.
[49] (1979–80) 1 EHRR 737.
[50] (1995) 19 EHRR 389.
[51] *Ibid* at 421.
[52] These comprise the rights to honour, privacy and image.
[53] *STC* 240/1992.
[54] An offence under Art 161 of the *Código Penal* of 1983.

Since that time however, *Castells v Spain* has been accepted as a binding authority domestically, necessitating some reconsideration of laws impinging upon freedom of expression. For example, pre-existing laws relating to penal sanctions for defamation have had to be modified to reflect the preferential position accorded to freedom of expression and communication. In particular, it is no longer sufficient to show that an author intended to injure another person's reputation. Instead, the courts must now give appropriate weight to the interests in protecting expression as disclosed by the facts of the case.[55]

Article 20(1) *CE* makes distinct references to thought, ideas and opinions on the one hand and truthful information on the other, a fact which has led the *Tribunal Constitucional* to distinguish between the respective degree of protection accorded to each freedom. In *Objetor Navazo* for instance, the *Tribunal Constitucional* stated that, as the expression of thoughts, ideas and opinions (including value-judgements and beliefs) could not be made susceptible of proof, they were not intrinsically limited in the same way that the right freely to communicate and receive factual information was.[56] This accords with the jurisprudence of the European Court of Human Rights in cases such as *Lingens*[57] and *Thorgier Thorgierson*.[58] In respect of Article 20(1)(d), the requirement of factual information does not mean, however, that the speaker's right to communicate is always lost when that which is communicated is not completely accurate. Nonetheless, in a judgment signifying the importance which is attached to accurately informed public opinion in a democracy, the court in *STC* 40/1992 (*Televisión Española*) held that Article 20(4) *CE* protection will be lost when the speaker is negligent or irresponsible in publishing as true, unchecked rumours, mere inventions or insinuations. All the same, it may not prove easy to isolate which of the two freedoms is called into play in any particular dispute. The expression of opinion will frequently rely upon a factual basis whilst the presentation of news or other supposedly factual information will invariably be value-laden.[59]

The Court has recognised that free communication underpins the exercise of other constitutional rights such as the right to participate in public affairs (whether directly or via a representative).[60] In particular, the ability of citizens to form opinions on, and participate intelligently in, political matters will depend upon the extent to which they are free to weigh diverse opinions. The link between freedom to receive information, the freedom to form one's own opinions and a system of democratic governance was highlighted by the Court

[55] *STC* 15/1993.

[56] In places, the Court spoke even more narrowly of a right to communicate and receive factual information which is newsworthy. *STC* 107/1988 (*Objetor Navazo*), see also *STC* 6/1988 (*Crespo*), *STC* 171/1990 (*Patino-El País*) and *STC* 223/1992.

[57] (1986) 8 EHRR 407.

[58] (1992) 14 EHRR 843.

[59] *STC* 6/1988 (*Crespo*).

[60] Art 23; and see *STC* 6/1981 (*periodistas de San Sebastián*).

in *STC* 168/86 (*Tiempo*) in a passage which is resonant with the ideal of republican self-government discussed earlier in chapters two and three:

> The right to receive truthful information is an essential means of learning about matters of importance in the life of the community and allows the participation of all in the proper functioning of the democratic relations fostered by the Constitution as well as the effective exercise of other rights and liberties.

In this sense, freedom of information is ultimately fundamental to the concept of the sovereignty of the people which is guaranteed by Article 1(2) *CE*.[61]

As to observations on the role of the media, the Court has commented on the constitutional duty of the news media to disseminate information about the working of public institutions such as the courts which affect all citizens.[62] The reference to a duty on the media to inform (and a correlative right on the part of the public to receive) bears close resemblence to the remarks of the European Court of Human Rights in *Lingens v Austria*:

> Whilst the press must not overstep the bounds set, inter alia, for the 'protection of Others', it is nevertheless *incumbent* on it to impart information and ideas on political issues just as on those in other areas of public interest. Not only does the press have the task of imparting such information and ideas: the public also has a right to receive them.[63] (emphasis added)

and is entirely consistent with the notion of a self-governing citizenry exercising informed control over its institutions. Thus, in the context of publicising court proceedings, the *Tribunal Constitucional* has spoken of the media's key function in bringing reports of court proceedings to a wider audience than those physically present in the courtroom.[64]

Prior restraint

> The exercise of these rights cannot be restricted by any form of prior censorship
> —(Art 20(2) *CE*)

The exercise of rights to freedom of expression and communication in Article 20(1) *CE* may not be restricted by any form of prior restraint, a term defined in 1983 to include any means of limiting the production or distribution of material especially where the production or distribution is dependent on previous examination of content.[65] Accordingly, provisions of the Press Law of 18 March 1966 which required media organisations to submit copy for approval prior to

[61] Art 23; and see *STC* 6/1981 (*periodistas de San Sebastián*).
[62] *STC* 30/1982 (*Diario 16*).
[63] (1986) 8 EHRR 407 at para. 41. See also *Worm v Austria* (1998) 25 EHRR 454 and *News Verlags GmbH v Austria* (2001) 30 EHRR 8.
[64] *STC* 30/1982 (*Diario 16*).
[65] *STC* 52/1983.

publication were held to violate the prohibition on prior restraint.[66] Since this time, it appears that, with the exception of prior restraints designed to safeguard judicial proceedings, the Court has rigorously upheld the constitutional bar in Article 20(2) *CE* regardless of the purpose which may lie behind a restriction.[67] So stated, it goes further than the approach of the European Court on Human Rights which in *The Observer and the Guardian v UK*—a case concerned with injunctions affecting news coverage—reminded national authorities that prior restraints were to be viewed with the most careful scrutiny.[68]

The application of the prohibition on prior restraint to matters related to judicial proceedings was considered *STC* 13/1985 (*Última Hora*) in the context of an on-going criminal investigation where the Court adopted a strained interpretative approach. The case arose out of a judge's order prohibiting the publication of photographs taken by the newspaper *Última Hora* revealing the burnt remains of an apartment where a person had died. The basis of the order was that publication could affect the investigation into a possible crime. Rejecting the argument of the newspaper, the Court ruled somewhat bizarrely that the order could not be said to be a form of prior restraint since it had been made solely to safeguard the summary investigation (an initial part of a criminal investigation usually conducted in secret in order to clarify the facts surrounding any alleged offence and ascertain the identity of the offender) and had not been intended to operate as a prior restraint. The Court also noted that the order was expressed to be of limited duration, expiring on the conclusion of the summary investigation. *Última Hora* fails to convince in a number of respects. To begin with, it is difficult to agree with the Court's analysis that the ban was not a form of prior restraint *by virtue* of its underlying purpose! The essence of prior restraint is that material is prohibited on account of its content as occurred here. For some unarticulated reason(s) connected with the investigative procedure, the Court did not want the material in the photograph communicated to the general public. Less difficult to fathom is the Court's reason for not wishing to have the ban described as a prior restraint. Article 20(2) is quite plain. Its prohibition on prior restraints is absolute and unqualified. The framers of the 1978 Constitution did however envisage that rules of criminal procedure might wish to qualify access to certain aspects of criminal proceedings. Article 120(1) *CE* states that:

> Judicial proceedings shall be public, with the exceptions provided for by the laws on procedure.

Article 301 of the Law of Criminal Procedure (*LECr*)[69] does provide for the summary stage of an investigation to be conducted in secret. To maintain this

66 Arts 12 and 64 of *Ley 14/1966 de Prensa e Imprenta*.
67 L de Carreras Serra, *Régimen jurídico de la información—Periodistas y medios de comunicación* (Editorial Ariel, Barcelona, 1996).
68 *Observer and Guardian v UK* (1992) 14 EHRR 153, 191.
69 *Ley de Enjuiciamento Criminal*.

secrecy, it may be thought necessary to imply a power to prohibit the publication of material relevant to the summary procedure. On this reading, Article 301 *LECr* may thus be thought of as introducing an exception to the prohibition on prior restraint in Article 20(2) *CE*.

Other Restrictions on Freedom of Expression and Communication

Earlier, it was noted that Article 20(4) *CE* provides constitutional authority for restrictions on freedom of expression and communication for the purposes of protecting other rights and liberties in Title 1 and that limitations intended to safeguard the specific rights to 'honour, privacy, personal identity, and protection of youth and childhood' were expressly envisaged by the authors of the Constitution. Whilst a comprehensive account of Article 20 jurisprudence is beyond the confines of the present book, a glimpse of the Court's approach to the task of balancing some of the conflicting rights and freedoms may be gained from the following material which deals with restrictions on expression derived from claims to honour or reputation, privacy and the protection of youth and childhood.[70]

(i) Honour

The right to honour which is recognised in Articles 18 and 20(4) *CE* is restated in more detail in both the civil[71] and criminal law.[72] These laws offer protection against defamatory statements which are false and have been published to a third party. They have had to be reconstructed to reflect the constitutional preference for expression and communication interests. The principles developed by the Court seek thus to retain a measure of protection for reputation whilst reflecting the importance of expression interests where these function to bolster democratic government.

Although the ambit of constitutionally protected expression extends to criticism of others which is irritating or hurtful, the Court has frequently reminded journalists and publishers that Article 20 *CE* jurisprudence does not permit the use of insulting words.[73] Factors which are relevant to deciding whether in any particular case the limit of constitutionally protected expression has been exceeded include the status of the complainant (whether a public or private figure—the former must expect less protection from defamation law),[74] the tone employed by the author (the Court looks at, inter alia, whether the opinions were

[70] A useful account in Spanish is to be found in L de Carreras Serra., *Régimen jurídico de la información—Periodistas y medios de comunicación* (Editorial Ariel, Barcelona, 1996) chs 4–5.
[71] *Ley Orgánica* 1/1982
[72] Art 7.7 *Código Penal* (*Ley Orgánica* 10/1995).
[73] *STC* 105/1990; *STC* 85/1992; *STC* 76/1995.
[74] *STC* 165/1987.

expressed in humorous or scathing terms and the existence of any intention to cause injury), the impact of the words on the reputation of the complainant and, finally, the contribution made to the formation of public opinion on a matter of public interest.[75] An example of the interplay and resolution of some of these factors is provided by *STC* 76/1995. An open letter which was published in a local newspaper to the Rector of Salamanca University cast doubt upon the character and academic qualifications of the complainant—a prominent figure at Salamanca University and in the cultural life of the city—clearly concerned an individual in the public domain who was therefore less protected from critical comment than a private person. However, the description of the complainant in the letter which included claims that he was resentful of humanity, engaged in plagiarism and had risen in the academic world on account of his powers of persuasion and scheming was held by the Court to have transgressed beyond the limits of protected expression and violated the complainant's right to reputation.

The right to honour was held in *STC* 223/1992 to extend to protection against criticism made of a person's professional competency in a ruling which recognised that the concept of honour or reputation was a flexible one whose precise content fluctuated depending upon current values and norms. Unlike previously, a central element in personal reputation today was one's standing at work and, whilst not every attack on a person's professional skill could be considered to be an illegal interference with that person's right to reputation, words which criticised professional competency (as opposed to more personal characteristics) could well go to reputation in the eyes of others and might give rise to an action for breach of the right to honour.

Nonetheless, in the case of comment upon public institutions including the courts, a wider range of criticism is tolerated. In *Objetor Navazo*, a conscientious objector to military service gave an interview to a magazine in which he said that a large number of judges were incorruptible as absolutely nothing could make them do justice. The Court took this to be an attack on the institution of the judiciary itself rather than a denigration of individual judges and therefore protected by freedom of expression. A contrary result would have produced the wholly paradoxical result that a fundamental right (in this case to honour) had been conferred by the Constitution *on* an agency of the state enabling it to penalise a citizen. It is possible however for speech which is critical of individual judges to exceed the bounds of the protection in Article 20.1 *CE* and constitute the crime of *desacato* (a Hispanic form of scandalising). In his comparative survey of court-related speech, Barend Van Niekerk described *desacato* as 'the most important penal institution of control of free speech in the legal domain.'[76] This was considered to have happened in *STC* 46/1998 (*El Mundo del País Vasco*) when a lawyer gave an interview in which he criticised

[75] *STC* 15/1993. *STC* 76/1995.

[76] B Van Niekerk, *The Cloistered Virtue* (Prager, New York, 1987), 87.

the conduct of a judge as 'illegal' and 'lacking in knowledge of the law.' The lawyer was further quoted as saying that 'people should not have to suffer judges' who revealed such a poor grasp of the law. Someone had yet to explain to him why the judge continued working in a job about which she was 'ignorant.' Whilst recognising the importance of freedom of expression on matters of public interest, the Court placed greater emphasis on this occasion on the protection of the courts from what it described as 'baseless attacks'. After all, the courts had a fundamental role to play in a state under the rule of law and it was vital that public confidence in the judiciary was maintained, especially where the judges could not themselves respond.[77]

(ii) Privacy

The weight accorded to the freedoms in Article 20(1) *CE* in fostering and maintaining informed public opinion on the part of the electorate in public matters inevitably brings with it diminished levels of privacy protection for certain individuals. Persons who choose voluntarily to occupy positions or engage in activities which are in the public domain have to accept a lesser degree of privacy than those outside this category. In particular, those who enjoy public office must expect such publicity and attention.[78] Conversely, persons not in the public domain enjoy a greater degree of protection,[79] although even here privacy interests may legitimately be overridden when the dissemination of news stories relating to such persons is in the public interest.[80] Nonetheless, if trivial items of information are published or no element of public interest is present in a story, non-public figures will have a remedy for breach of their entitlement to privacy.[81]

(iii) Children and Young Persons

The protection of the moral and physical well-being of children and young persons may on occasions permit interference with another party's Article 20(1) freedoms especially where sexually explicit materials are concerned. Relevant factors will include the form of the publication in question, its intended recipients and the subjects depicted in any visual materials. Where children or young persons are the target audience or form the subject of photographic or textual material, the interest in protecting expression will yield to the more compelling state interest in the protection of young persons.[82]

[77] See further chapter five.
[78] *STC* 107/1988 (*Objetor Navazo*); *STC* 85/1992 (*concejal de Palencia*); *STC* 76/1995; *STC* 15/1993 (*Igualada*).
[79] *STC* 165/1987.
[80] *STC* 20/1992 (*Baleares*).
[81] *Ibid.*
[82] *STC* 62/1982.

In *STC 52/1995* (*Correos*), the *Tribunal Constitucional* considered the constitutionality of administrative resolutions adopted by the state-owned Post Office in Barcelona which were intended to prohibit the distribution of materials judged by the Post Office to be pornographic. The application was brought by a company which had been prevented from using the public mail system to distribute its magazines and was forced instead to contract with commercial carriers. The Court took the view that the application of the resolutions, whilst not actually preventing distribution, nonetheless did constitute a real obstacle to distribution and therefore did restrict the complainant's fundamental right to freedom of expression. Accordingly, the ruling turned upon the legality of this interference. The Court did not doubt that restrictions on the sending of pornographic or obscene mail might be imposed for a constitutionally valid reason such as the protection of children and young persons as was the case here. However, apart from disclosing a lawful purpose, a restriction which limited a fundamental right as here would need to have the status of a law (as opposed to an administrative rule) and be proportionate to the end objective which it sought to advance.[83] Not only did the administrative resolutions lack the status of a law (a conclusion which, by itself, would have been sufficient to uphold the application), they had not been shown to be tailored narrowly to protect the legitimate purpose which motivated them.[84]

(iv) Freedom to Communicate Intimidating Words

In *STC 136/99*, the *Tribunal Constitucional* recognised a further limit on the right to freedom of expression and right to communicate information where the expression or communication in question is presented in way which is judged to be intimidating. The ruling emerged in an appeal against conviction by 23 members of the executive of *Herri Batasuna* accused of collaborating with a terrorist group (ETA) in the production of a party election broadcast for *Herri Batasuna*. Three hooded figures wearing symbols associated with ETA spoke in the video of a 'democratic alternative' to establish peace in the Basque country in terms which had been outlined by ETA previously. Two of the figures were shown to be armed with guns. A poster displayed in the same video urged viewers to 'Vote for *Herri Batasuna*.' An audio tape was also made which was sent to the national radio station to be broadcast in one of the slots allocated to the political parties' election broadcasts. The text of the tape demanded that the Spanish State recognise the right of the Basque people to self-rule and claimed

[83] Obviously, these requirements would apply to restrictions on expression for the purposes of protecting honour, privacy and other constitutionally recognised rights.

[84] In the field of broadcasting, the *Cortes* has passed laws designed to implement European Union directives aimed at protecting children and young persons from images and messages which prejudice their moral or physical development, see *Ley de 25/1994* giving effect to EU Directive 89/552. See also *La Ley 4/1980* (del Estatuto de la Radio y Televisión) Art 4.

that ETA had shown that it would cease its armed struggle when certain conditions were met.

Aside from other alleged violations of the defendants' constitutional rights (dealt with below), it was also argued that the convictions breached the defendants' right to freedom of communication to inform the public of a possible solution to the violent conflict.

The *Tribunal Constitucional* rejected this claim, noting the intimidatory impact of the broadcasts upon electors—which it inferred from the images of guns and the reference to a viable ceasefire if ETA's conditions were met—which were not made as part of a piece of neutral reporting merely describing an existing situation but, on the contrary, were made in the context of attracting public support in forthcoming elections. As such, the expression in question fell outside the scope of protection in Article 20(1)(d).

V MEDIA FREEDOM AND IMPARTIAL TRIALS

Outline of Relevant Aspects of Spanish Criminal Procedure

Before looking at the principle of openness in Spanish criminal trials and associated issues of media freedom, it is necessary to provide a brief outline of some key aspects of criminal procedure.[85] The Spanish Criminal Code (*Código Penal*) distinguishes between three types of criminal offence. These are respectively *delitos graves* (serious crimes); *delitos menos graves* (less serious crimes) and *faltas* (minor crimes).[86] In the case of *delitos*, two distinct stages of criminal procedure may be identified after a formal complaint has been accepted by the courts.[87] The first stage is known as *La Instrucción* in which the investigating judge will order particular investigations and inquiries to be made in order to ascertain the circumstances surrounding the alleged crime and the identity of those involved. These proceedings are usually conducted without publicity, although it is clear from a glance at regional and national newspapers that some investigating judges do brief the media about developments and progress in individual *instrucciones*.[88] If, upon completion of the inquiry stage, the investigating judge is of the view that the available evidence indicates the commission of a *delito grave*, the papers are sent to the court with jurisdiction to try the offence—usually the *Audiencia Provincial*. Where satisfied that the *instrucción* is complete, this court has the power to order that the second or oral stage of proceedings should be commenced. After having determined pre-trial issues

[85] See further E Merino-Blanco, *The Spanish Legal System* (Sweet & Maxwell, London, 1996) ch 6.
[86] *Código Penal* Art 1 (*Ley Orgánica 10/95 de 23 de Noviembre*).
[87] This complaint or *querella* may be made by the prosecutor or, in certain types of offence, by the alleged victim. Another form of complaint is the 'denuncia'.
[88] The powers of the investigating judge are defined in the *Ley de Enjuiciamiento Criminal*.

relating to, inter alia, the admissibility of evidence, the trial of the accused can be commenced. The trial is conducted before three professional judges who determine both factual and legal questions by a simple majority if necessary. At the conclusion of the trial, the verdict and any sentence are announced in open court by the presiding judge (*el Magistrado Ponente*). Since May 1995 however, the enactment of the *Ley Orgánica del Tribunal Jurado*[89] has paved the way for the re-introduction of jury trials in Spanish criminal procedure for certain specific crimes. Aspects of this development are considered at the end of this chapter.

The Principle of Openness in Criminal Trials

Apart from the general right to receive and impart information in Article 20(1)(d) *CE*, a specific guarantee concerning the openness of court proceedings is provided by Article 120 *CE* which declares that:

> (1) Judicial proceedings shall be public, with the exceptions provided by the laws on procedure.
>
> . . .
>
> (3) The sentences . . . shall be pronounced in public.

In criminal cases, the *Tribunal Constitucional* has stressed the importance of the role played by the media in bringing the oral stage of such proceedings to the attention of those outside the courtroom.[90] In this way, public confidence in the administration of justice may be maintained.[91] The law of criminal procedure (*LECr*) reflects this constitutional commitment by requiring that, subject to narrowly defined exceptions (related to reasons of morality, public order or the respect owed to the victim of a crime or his/her family)[92] the oral stage of criminal proceedings must be heard in public. Failure to do so renders the proceedings a nullity.[93] An example of a lawful closure of the oral stage of proceedings on public order grounds occurred in *STC* 65/1992. During the summary stage of homicide proceedings, members of the victim's family and friends had been involved in incidents which led the police to fear that the oral stage of proceedings might be marked by disturbances. As a precaution, the court acceded to a defence request that the trial proceed in closed session. Despite this measure, four defence witnesses failed to appear. Their non-appearence subsequently formed the basis of an unsuccessful appeal by the

[89] *LO 5/95*.
[90] *STC* 30/1982.
[91] D Alfonso Arroyo de las Heras and D Javier Muñoz Cuesta, *Ley de Enjuiciamiento Criminal* (Aranzadi, Pamplona, 1993) at 369.
[92] *Ley de Enjuiciamiento Criminal* Art 680.2, 680.3. The exceptions are construed narrowly. See further F Ramos Méndez, *El proceso penal* (J M Bosch, Barcelona, 1999) at 156–157; and D Alfonso Arroyo de las Heras and D Javier Muñoz Cuesta, *ibid* at 367–370.
[93] *Ley de Enjuiciamiento Criminal* Art 680.1.

convicted defendant. Commenting on the closure of the oral stage, the *Tribunal Constitucional* found that, far from reducing the guarantees of the trial process, the decision allowed for the orderly progress of the trial, avoiding whatever intimidation might have been aimed at the trial participants. Nothing in the case indicated that the closed proceedings were motivated for reasons which were other than legitimate.

The withdrawal of the courtroom passes of a journalist and his editor by the Military Chamber of the Supreme Court (*Tribunal Supremo*) in *STC* 30/1982 (*Diario 16*) gave the *Tribunal Constitucional* an opportunity to examine the constitutionality of accreditation practices of that court. Following the failed coup attempt of Colonel Tejero and others in February 1981, the criminal trial of the coup participants naturally attracted much media attention. In order to ensure an orderly media presence within the limited confines of the courtroom, *Diario 16*—a national daily newspaper—in common with other news media—was allocated two passes. After the trial had begun, *Diario 16* published an article recounting the evidence of a coup member under the title 'How we stormed Parliament'. The defendants took objection to the article and refused to enter the courtroom thereby delaying the start of that day's session. As a consequence, the passes of the journalist and his editor were suspended by the court authorities. Later, the newspaper was re-accredited with two passes on condition that these be taken up by persons other than the journalist and his editor. These conditional passes were challenged before the *Tribunal Constitucional*. After emphasising the significance of media coverage of criminal proceedings in communicating information about trials to the public in a democracy (which was all the more compelling in instances where, as here, the trial concerned events with a special resonance for society), the Court ruled that the right to information could not be made to depend upon a system of accreditation. Moreover, whilst it was within the inherent power of the presiding judge to expel those who threatened the orderly conduct of a trial, this power could not be invoked to punish the journalist and his editor for conduct outside the courtroom in respect of which the court disapproved.[94]

Protection Against Trial By Media

> '*La Constitución brinda un cierto grado de protección frente a los juicios paralelos en los medios de comunicación*' *STC* 146/1999
>
> —*La Mesa de Herri Batasuna*

tr. The Constitution affords a certain degree of protection against trials by media.

[94] It should also be noted that under Art 463 of the *Código Penal* it is an offence to obstruct the oral stage of a criminal trial without just cause in such a way as to lead to the suspension of those proceedings. Moreover, any person who by means of violence or intimidation tries to influence proceedings directly or indirectly commits an offence under Art 464 of the *Código Penal*.

Although until recently criminal trials in Spain have not involved lay jurors, the *Tribunal Constitucional* has nonetheless been alive to a number of concerns about the impact of media coverage on the administration of justice. Thus for example the Court has observed that even professional judges might come under a degree of pressure or influence as a result of material published in the media. It has also acknowleged more general anxieties about the usurpation of judicial functions by the media and a consequential loss of respect or status which the administration of justice might suffer. The norms developed by the Court to regulate the outer boundaries of media freedom seek consciously to give effect to ECHR case law. Interestingly, the *Tribunal Constitucional* in *STC* 136/99 1999 (*La Mesa de Herri Batasuna*) was presented with an opportunity to consider the domestic application of *Worm v Austria*.[95] In chapter two, it was argued that this decision afforded an over-broad discretion to national authorities to impose criminal liability on court-related speech, one which was inconsistent with the European Court's rhetoric on the importance of court-related speech. Interestingly, it is possible in 1999 in *La Mesa de Herri Batasuna* to detect a more robust approach to such speech on the part of the Spanish judiciary, although as a cautionary note it should be remembered that this robustness emerges in the context of an appeal by defendants alleging breach of the constitutional guarantee of a fair trial, as opposed to a media appellant seeking to have a contempt conviction overturned.

As was detailed earlier in this chapter, the dispute in *La Mesa de Herri Batasuna* arose from proceedings against the 23 executive members of *Herri Batasuna* for having collaborated with a terrorist organisation (ETA) in the production of a video and audio tape made for broadcast on behalf *Herri Batasuna* in forthcoming elections.[96] Injunctions were granted preventing the broadcast of either tape and, in later criminal proceedings, all 23 executive members of *Herri Batasuna* were convicted of having collaborated with a terrorist organisation contrary to Article 174 of the 1973 *Código Penal* (hereafter *CP*). Each defendant was sentenced to seven years in prison and fined 500,000 pesetas.[97] The principal argument of the defendants on appeal to the *Tribunal Constitucional* was that permitting members of a terrorist organisation to appear in a party election broadcast did not constitute an act of collaboration. By a majority of 8 votes to 4, the *Tribunal Constitucional* upheld the appeal. The principle of *nulla poena sine lege* or punishment according to law in Article 25(1) *CE* required that no one could be punished for doing something

[95] (1998) 25 EHRR 454.

[96] The offence is to be found in Art174 of the *Código Penal* 1973.

[97] Or roughly speaking £2000. Interestingly, they were acquitted of the charge of apologising for terrorism brought by an association representing victims of terrorism. This charge which is laid down in Arts 571 and 573 of the *Código Penal* continues, however, to be deployed by state prosecutors against spokepersons of separatist Basque parties. See for example the charging of Arnaldo Otegi of *Euskal Herritarrok* in August 2000 for describing as 'young patriots' and 'comrades' four members of ETA killed on active service in Bilbao, see *Las Provincias* 10 August 2000.

which at that time did not constitute a criminal offence. This applied with especial force to cases where punishment was being imposed on the exercise of fundamental rights such as the freedom to engage in political debate during elections. The vagueness of Article 174 *CP* therefore breached the defendants' constitutional rights.

Although rendered somewhat academic by the success of the foregoing argument, the Court also considered the applicants' submission that their right under Article 24(2) *CE* to a trial 'with all the guarantees' had been violated. Analysis of the Court's treatment of this aspect of the appeal is instructive in terms of the robust attitude it adopts with respect to media coverage which in all likelihood would be regarded as having prevented any possibility of a fair trial before a jury in English law. It was alleged that widely reported statements during the trial had prevented the defendants receiving a fair trial before an impartial court. The evidence cited by way of support in this part of the appeal included a series of comments made in the national press while the trial was ongoing. One national magazine reported that Government ministers wished to see an exemplary sentence of five years. The same publication also reported that two named members of the court were inclined to convict the accused after a detailed study of the case. Other published statements included the reported remarks of the Chief Prosecutor of the *Audiencia Nacional*—a court seized with national jurisdiction in respect of certain crimes such as crimes against the Crown, and the high organs of state although with no jurisdiction in the present case—that the defendants were the 'actual leaders of ETA'. Even the Prime Minister, in a general interview talked about the responsibility of the security forces, the judges and prosecutors in the fight against terrorism and added that the Government's strategy against terrorism 'would contribute to an exemplary sentence in the matter of *la Mesa de Herri Batasuna*.' The Minister of the Interior was widely quoted elsewhere as saying that he was 'morally certain that the ringleaders of *Herri Batasuna* deserve eight years behind bars, all that is missing is the legal certainty.'[98]

In response, the Court acknowledged (or perhaps, more accurately, paid lip-service to the notion) that the Constitution did afford a certain degree of protection against parallel trials in the media. This was necessary to prevent the administration of justice generally from suffering a loss of respect and a usurpation of the judicial function which the Court noted, had been deemed a legitimate purpose of restraints placed on media coverage of legal proceedings by the European Court of Human Rights in *Sunday Times*[99] and *Worm v Austria*.[100] More importantly for present purposes, some protection was needed to safeguard the appearence and reality of the impartiality of the

[98] Cf *R v McCann, Cullen and Shanahan* (1991) 92 Cr App R 239.

[99] (1979) 2 EHRR 245.

[100] (1998) 25 EHRR 454.

judges. The publication of supposed or real states of public opinion about the trial could, for example, influence the judges and bring matters which might not have been admitted into court as evidence to the attention of the court. The pressure that might be brought in any particular case would be greater where, as here, the statements in the media are made by senior officials in government. In these circumstances, the constitutional right to a fair trial might be breached without the applicant having to show that the prejudicial coverage actually influenced the decision of the court. In accordance with *Worm*, the Court held that it would be sufficient to establish a probability of interference. At the same time, the Court pointed to the fact that in numerous rulings it had emphasised the 'extraordinary importance' which was attached to the maintenance of free public opinion in a democratic society, the scope of which included speech regarding the administration of justice. The courts did not operate in a vacuum. The mere fact that a matter was before a court ought not by itself to prevent discussion in media outlets or among the public in general. Provided that any discussion did not cross the boundary line whereby the administration of justice was impeded, information and commentaries in the media relating to legal proceedings could be said to contribute to public knowledge about trials and were perfectly compatible with the fundamental requirement of public proceedings in Article 24(2) *CE* and Article 6(1) of the European Convention on Human Rights. Correlatively, the constitutional entitlement of the public to receive information and commentaries served by media freedom in this regard was all the stronger where the proceedings concerned individuals in the public domain. Having laid down these guiding precepts, the Court then considered whether, as disclosed by the facts of the present appeal, objective grounds to support the allegation of a lack of impartiality on the part of the trial court did exist. Whilst it was true that statements declaring the voting inclinations of judges did not contribute positively to public confidence in the judicial function, the remarks cited by the defendants which revealed an opinion or a wish about the verdict did not appear to the Court to have produced a parallel trial in the media or the appearence of impartiality on the part of the judges.

VI CONCLUSION

The emergence of Spain as a modern social democracy under the rule of law committed to individual rights offers an interesting civil law comparison into the trade-offs which occur between speech and other individual and collective interests. This chapter has considered the expression-related jurisprudence of the *Tribunal Constitucional*, noting in particular the fundamental importance which is attached to freedom of expression in maintaining an informed, popular sovereignty.

The reintroduction of a lay jury in certain criminal proceedings before the *Audiencia Provincial*[101] will doubtless spark off renewed debate about permitted limits of media reporting and comment.[102] Juries now have jurisdiction across a range of offences including high profile crimes such as homicide, fraud, embezzlement of public funds and causing forest fires.[103] Until now, the relative impunity with which the media and others (including public officials) have in the past made partial comments relating to particular proceedings points up the absence in the pre-jury era of developed *sub judice* rules. Whilst the constitutional right to a fair trial continues to offer convicted persons an avenue for contesting verdicts in heavily publicised cases, those responsible for the administration of justice in Spain might soon be looking to amend the *Código Penal* in order to penalise the media and other speakers if threats to the fairness of particular proceedings before juries become commonplace.

[101] Provincial courts with jurisdiction to sit as first instance courts in cases of serious offences (*delitos graves*).

[102] The reintroduction of juries is provided for in Ley del Jurado (*Ley Orgánica* 5/1995 del Tribunal del Jurado). Historically, juries had existed at times of relative individual liberty (eg under the Constitution of Cádiz (1812) and during the Second Republic (1931)). Conversely, jury trial has been abolished or severely restricted during periods of repression of individual liberty.

[103] A full list of the offences triable by jury are found in Art 1 of the *Ley del Jurado*. For an official report into the operation of jury trial between April 1997 and March 1998 see http://www.cgpj.es/docs/informejurado97_99.doc

7

Conclusion: Court-Related Speech in the Electronic Age and Some Emergent Themes

I INTERNET SPEECH—AN INTRODUCTION

Irvine closes down 'anti-judge' website[1]

IT IS FAIR to say that in most discussions of the dangers of virtually unregulated, transnational expression through the Internet, threats to the administration of justice have not featured prominently. Instead, comment has tended to focus on the respective perils of pornographic material,[2] paedophile activity,[3] hate speech,[4] libel[5] and intellectual property issues.[6] The dissemination

[1] *The Independent*, 7 November 1999. This relates to the case of James Hulbert whose web pages containing criticism of judicial figures were deemed offensive by the Lord Chancellor's Office and subsequently removed from Mr Hulbert's internet service provider. The case is discussed below. Further details can be found at <http://www.cyber-rights.org/documents/hulbert.htm>. I am grateful to Yaman Akdeniz, Director of Cyber-Rights & Cyber Liberties <http://www.cyber-rights.org/> and a lecturer in the Department of Law, Leeds University for supplying me with this material.

[2] See A Hamilton, 'The Net Out of Control—A New Moral Panic: Censorship and Sexuality' in Liberty (ed) *Liberating Cyberspace* (Pluto, London, 1999) ch 9. Y Akdeniz, 'Governance of Pornography and Child Pornography on the Global Internet' in L Edwards and C Waelde (eds), *Law and the Internet* (Hart Publishing, Oxford, 1997).

[3] G Leong, 'Computer Child Pornography—The Liability of Distributors' in C Walker (ed), *Crime, Criminal Justice and the Internet* [1998] *Criminal Law Review*—Special Edition, Y Akdeniz, 'Child Pornography' in Y Akdeniz, C Walker, D Wall (eds), *The Internet, Law and Society* (Longman, Harlow, 2000).

[4] B Steinhardt, 'Hate Speech' in Y Akdeniz, C Walker, D Wall (eds), *The Internet, Law and Society* (Longman, Harlow, 2000); D Capitanchik and M Whine, 'The Governance of Cyberspace: Racism on the Internet' in Liberty (ed), *Liberating Cyberspace* (Pluto, London, 1999).

[5] I Cram, *SPTL Media Law Newsletter* No 3 available at <http://www.leeds.ac.uk/law/plrg/newslet3.htm>. See Opinion column 'The Hoaxer, The Demon, Their Victim, The Court-Case'; Y Akdeniz and H Rogers, 'Defamation on the Internet' in Y Akdeniz, C Walker, D Wall (eds), *The Internet, Law and Society* (Longman, Harlow, 2000).

[6] See C Waelde, 'Trade Marks and Domain Names: What's in a Name?' and H McQueen, 'Copyright and the Internet' in L Edwards and C Waelde (eds), *Law and the Internet* (Hart Publishing, Oxford, 1997).

of extremist political literature[7] has also tended to be given more prominence than 'cybercontempt' or 'cyberscandalising'. Prior to the development of Internet-based communication forms, the reach of satellite and cable broadcasting beyond specific national reception areas did prompt supra-national regulation from both the Council of Europe and the European Union.[8] Here again however, the regulatory emphasis in instruments such as the European Convention on Transfrontier Television lay not with administration of justice concerns but focused upon the threats posed by pornography and incitement to racial hatred. No reference in the Convention is to be found to either the individual right to a fair trial or the privacy interests of certain classes of trial participants. That said, Article 7 of the Convention does impose a general requirement on broadcasters to 'respect the dignity of the human being and the fundamental rights of others'—a phrase capable of being read as incorporating the rights to fair trial and privacy. In what follows, I turn to consider the nature of threats raised by internet speech forms and ask whether difficulties inherent in regulating electronic communication will force a re-evaluation of restrictions on court-related speech.

II THE INTERNET—DEFINITION AND CHARACTERISTICS

The Internet is commonly described as a network of computers through which data is transferred in 'packets' made readable by other computers which recognise the TCP/IP protocols[9] or specifications which standardise the exchange of information across different operating systems around the world.[10] To gain access to information held on other networked computers, a user requires an Internet Service Provider (ISP) which may entail payment to the ISP.

The facilities which are accessible via the Internet include e-mail (allowing messages and documents to be sent to individuals and larger groups via mailing lists); Usenet newsgroups (bulletin board style discussion groups organised according to subject matter and where postings are sometimes subject to prior approval by a 'moderator'); and Internet Relay Chat (synchronised conversation which develops between users in a virtual chatroom. The responses of other users appear directly on the screen. Graphics and other computer files may be

[7] J Craven, 'Extremism and the Internet (EMAIN)', Work in Progress, (1998) (1) *The Journal of Information, Law and Technology*.

[8] The Television Without Frontiers Directive 97/36/EU [1997] OJ L202/60; On the Council of Europe's Convention, see FW Hondius, 'Regulating Transfrontier Television—The Strasbourg Option' (1988) *Yearbook of European Law* 141, PJ Humphreys, *Mass Media and Mass Media Policy in Western Europe* (Manchester University Press, Manchester, 1996) ch 5.

[9] Transmission Control Protocol/Internet Protocol.

[10] Another common definition is a 'network of networks', see A Terrett, 'A Lawyer's Introduction to the Internet' in L Edwards and C Waelde (eds) *Law and the Internet* (Hart Publishing, Oxford, 1997).

exchanged), and the World Wide Web (a virtual library of information, comment, sound, and graphics available on pages stored on a host or server computer linked to the Web by an internet service provider. Web pages can be stored and accessed anywhere in the world at any time).[11]

Volokh has identified some important consequences of the era of 'cheap speech' ushered in by the Internet.[12] These include the wresting of power away from intermediaries such as proprietors, editors and vendors in the private sector and a consequent empowerment of speakers and listeners. Speakers with unconventional or unprofitable messages are freed from the censorship imposed by private parties and/or the market. Listeners too are liberated. They can access as much electronic information/comment on topics of interest as they wish especially since the space constraints of the print media don't apply to electronic speech. The absence of censorship on the Internet and the widened access it offers link in to broader libertarian/anti-censorship themes which lie at the core of much theorising about cyberspace.[13]

The loss of private sector power over what is written and read has however been overshadowed by the demise in the regulatory role played by the nation state. Put simply, the Internet is

> too widespread to be easily dominated by any single government. By creating a seamless global-economic zone, borderless and unregulatable, the Internet calls into question the very idea of a nation state.[14]

Although it is true that the sovereign state retains a presence in the governance of the Internet in the form of pre-Internet era laws regulating speech,[15] it is more sensible to refer to a largely non-state-based, multi-layered structure of internet governance.[16] Non-governmental regulatory bodies such as ISOC,[17]

[11] See further, Terrett *ibid.*

[12] E Volokh, 'Cheap Speech and What It Will Do' (1995) 104 *Yale Law Journal* 1805.

[13] JP Barlow, cited in H Rheingold, *The Virtual Community* (Secker & Warburg, London, 1994). Other commentators have pointed to the new technology's potential to enhance democratic decision-making, see C Walker and Y Akdeniz,'Virtual Democracy' [1998] *Public Law* 489.

[14] JP Barlow, n 13 above. See also BD Loader (ed), *The Governance of Cyberspace* (Routledge, London, 1997) 9–10. Cf P Hirst and G Thompson, 'Globalization and the Future of the Nation State' (1995) 24 *Economy and Society* 408.

[15] See thus in libel law, the application of the common law definition of 'publisher' to ISPs in *Godfrey v Demon Internet Ltd* [1999] 4 All ER 342. In relation to incitement to racial hatred, ISPs must be concerned that the posting of inflammatory material on a Usenet newsgroup or a web page would be caught by the prohibition on 'publishing' and 'distributing' in s 19 of the Public Order Act 1986. Some pre-existing laws have been amended to cover digitized computer imagery. See in the case of child pornography see the extension in s 84(4) of the Criminal Justice and Public Order Act 1994 of the definition of 'photograph' in s 7(4) of the Protection of Children Act 1978 to include photographs and pseudo-photographs in electronic form.

[16] See further the discussion by C Walker *et al*, 'The Internet, Law and Society' in Y Akdeniz, C Walker and D Wall (eds), *The Internet, Law and Society* (Longman, Harlow, 2000).

[17] Internet Society, a Virginia based international group of Internet enthusiasts, including among its members corporate telecomunications interests.

IAB,[18]IETF,[19] ICANN,[20] and ISPs[21] have played a major role in shaping the Internet and sit alongside supra-national regulation such as developed by the European Union to combat certain forms of harmful content,[22] in conjunction with specialist local police forces, pressure groups[23] and self-imposed regulation via software filters.

Finally, it is important to sound a cautionary note about the actual impact of advances in computer-mediated communications. The socio-economic context of access to the Internet means that the liberating/democratising effect of the Internet has yet to be experienced across all sections of society.[24] At the time of writing, most UK households remain unconnected to the Internet. Access is skewed towards high- to middle-income households, employed persons, males and younger age groups.[25] The poor, unemployed, women and the elderly remain on the fringes of the so-called 'information superhighway.' This fact is relevant to any assessment of the prejudicial impact of material posted onto the Internet.

III THREATS TO THE ADMINISTRATION OF JUSTICE

The publication of court-related speech via the new Internet-based technologies may be seen to threaten administration of justice interests in three respects. First, by undermining the fairness of individual jury trials. Secondly, by breaching the terms of prior restraint orders and bringing about 'jigsaw identification'.[26] Finally, by scandalising a judge or court. Whilst, legal systems have faced these threats previously from print, terrestrial and satellite broadcasters, the

[18] Internet Architecture Board which oversees the development of Internet protocols, standards and procedures.

[19] Internet Engineering Task Force—a community of network designers which formulates and then forwards standards to the ISOC for approval.

[20] Internet Corporation for Assigned Names and Numbers—responsible *inter alia* for domain name system management and allocating IP addresses.

[21] ISPs can be either commercial entites such as AOL, Demon etc or in the public sector as non-profit making see for example JANET (Joint Academic Network).

[22] For example the European Commission's *Green Paper on the Protection of Minors and Human Dignity in Audiovisual and Information Services* (COM (96) 483 final, Brussels-Luxembourg, 16 October 1996). See also 98/560/EC: Council Recommendation of 24 September [1998] OJL 270/48–55. See in addition more recent measures to protect the confidentiality, integrity and availability of computer data and systems in the *Draft Convention on Cybercrime* available at <http://conventions.coe.int/Treaty/EN/projets/FinalCybercrime.htm>.

[23] Such as the Internet Watch Foundation which enjoys the backing of the UK Government.

[24] This point is made by Loader in BD Loader (ed), *The Governance of Cyberspace* (Routledge, London, 1997) 7.

[25] Surveys collated by Nua.com—a leading source of information on Internet demographics available at <http://www.nua.ie/surveys/>. In July 2000, men in the UK constituted 61% of Internet users. Other empirical surveys reveal that income and age are the primary determinants of Internet access.

[26] Whereby separate pieces of information about an individual are published which when put together allow the individual to be identified.

Internet raises especially problematic issues relating to the identification of speakers who breach restraining orders and the enforcement of such orders where the party in breach is located outside the jurisdiction.

Speech Impacting Upon Particular Jury Proceedings

Facilities for the dissemination of information and comment on the Internet and via satellite and cable systems offer the possibility of cross-border, instantaneous flows of information and comment, both of which may be thought to undermine the prospects of a fair trial. The tendency of cable, satellite broadcasters to cover 'breaking' news stories is a particular concern here. As Bonnington has pointed out, this form of media coverage is often subject to incomplete legal checks when compared to those available to the print media sector.[27] What is more, in the case of a non-national live broadcaster with a possible reception area inside several jurisdictions, it is unlikely that due regard is had for the respective restrictions in each jurisdiction when deciding what to transmit.

At present, official responses to web sites, newsgroup postings and internet relay chatrooms suggests that the Internet is seen as posing a low-level threat to the fairness of particular proceedings, even where information/comment is posted during the currency of proceedings. The relative liberty which contributors and ISPs currently enjoy may nonetheless come under threat if, as is predicted, Internet access extends more widely beyond its current age/class/gender boundaries, making it more likely for potential jurors to encounter partisan accounts of proceedings. Even then, there is an interesting issue about whether, assuming that ISPs are treated under the Contempt of Court Act 1981 as 'publishers' of material breaching the strict liability rule,[28] they might nonetheless plead the defence of innocent publication under section 3(1) of the 1981 Act. To make good this defence, an ISP would have to show that having taken all reasonable care, it did not know and had no reason to suspect that at the time of publication, relevant proceedings were active.[29] In high profile criminal investigations, it would thus be extremely difficult for an ISP to run the defence successfully. For the time being however, the Attorney General's Office maintains a relaxed attitude towards internet material concerning active proceedings. During the recent trial of Jeffrey Archer on charges of perverting the course of justice,

[27] A Bonnington, 'News Without Frontiers: Pre-Trial Prejudice and the Internet' in L Edwards and C Waelde (eds), *Law and the Internet* (Hart Publishing, Oxford, 1997).
[28] ISPs were treated in *Godfrey v Demon Internet* [1999] 4 All ER 342 as publishers at common law for the purposes of a defamation action. There is no reason to suppose that this finding would not also apply in proceedings for contempt.
[29] The burden of proof is on the distributor for the purposes of this defence, s 3(3), Contempt of Court Act 1981.

perjury and forgery for example, it was possible using a search engine such as *Google* to find postings on the *soc.culture.british* and *alt.politics.british* Usenet newsgroup sites which were highly unfavourable to the accused. It was not suggested (officially, at least) that jurors might have been influenced by such sites.

Prior Restraints

In the case of prior restraints, legal establishments in England and Wales and elsewhere have shown a Canute-like determination to enforce suppression orders in the face of evidence that breaches of reporting restrictions on the Internet and by non-domestic broadcasters/publishers have occurred and will continue to occur. Early challenges to the enforceability of reporting restrictions occurred in the high profile proceedings against two (as then) unidentified boys for the murder of James Bulger and in the Canadian cases of *Homolka* and *Teale(Bernardo)*. In the former proceedings, a French satellite television news station whose output could be picked up by dish owners in England named the accused prior to the Crown Court's lifting of anonymity orders.[30]

Homolka and *Teale* concerned a husband and wife who were charged with the assault and killing of two girls in extremely gruesome circumstances. After plea-bargaining, Homolka was tried first for manslaughter. The trial judge, Kovacs J in the Ontario High Court, ordered that the public and non-Canadian news media be excluded from the courtroom and granted a postponement order sought by the Crown to restrain reporting by Canadian media organisations of Homolka's trial. The ban covered reports of the circumstances of the victims' deaths and details of the sentence handed down by the court. The postponement was to endure until the completion of a separate trial of Teale on two charges of murder. The purpose of the ban was to secure the fairness of the husband's trial at the Crown's request although, ironically, he had unsuccessfully opposed the ban. The husband had claimed that unfettered reporting of the evidence in his wife's trial would correct the widely held impression induced by the plea bargain that his wife was herself a victim of the husband's domineering conduct.

After the ban was imposed, practical difficulties of enforcement emerged in respect of the conduct of traditional media organisations from outside Canada and those with Internet access within Canada. It appears that while most members of the Canadian media grudgingly respected the ban, the foreign news media and others did not. The Sunday Mirror in this country ran a story in breach of the ban entitled 'Killer Ken and Barbie's Video Of Horror.'[31] The

[30] See reports at (1993) 14 *Journal of Media Law and Policy* 157 and *Guardian Unlimited* (1993) November 5.

[31] See the issue of 19 September 1993.

Washington Post also published banned material.[32] The offending edition was subsequently recalled from newstands, although when the Buffalo News and the Detroit Free Press reported details from the Washington Post, curious Canadians crossed the border to obtain their copies. It is reported that Canadian Customs allowed those returning home to keep one copy for personal use while confiscating excess copies.[33] In the broadcast sector, suppression of the case details was more successful. A United States television show *'A Current Affair'* which covered the case in three separate broadcasts could not be received in most Canadian homes because of a programme substitution imposed by Canadian border stations. Cable operators also 'blacked out' the same broadcasts on their networks. An American disc jockey did manage however to broadcast details of the trial from the middle of a bridge spanning the Canadian–US border. In other incidents, a retired Canadian police officer deliberately brought about his own arrest for mailing and distributing American and British newspaper cuttings so that the constitutionality of the ban might be tested.

Information about the trial contained in electronic media transmissions posed a greater threat to the ban. Students at Canadian universities created their own Usenet newsgroups which became the focus for exchanging information (both true and false) about the case.[34] Material from the banned newspapers and television programmes appeared in these newsgroups. Shortly afterwards, the authorities at a number of Canadian universities took action to delete some of the offending newsgroups.[35] In one incident, a bulletin board service carried by the Internet and traced to the University of Western Ontario was publishing information in breach of the ban. A student was visited and searched by police. Of course, had there been no identifiable local source, this action would not have been possible. In place of the deleted newsgroups, others sprung up in their place. The University of Toronto student newspaper printed a guide to finding information about the case on the Internet. It was said that one effective means of violating the ban was to place information in the newsgroup *rec.sports.hockey* because no Canadian government official would ever close down anything that had to do with hockey! Elsewhere, a server in Helsinki was used to anonymise e-mail, although the sheer volume of mail handled by this server caused the server's administrator to become nervous and the service was switched to another server operating from Texas.[36]

Notwithstanding the obvious failure of restriction orders in the *Homolka/Teale* cases, the English Courts have maintained the pretence that

[32] See the issue of 23 November 1993.

[33] This claim is made at <http://www.cs.indiana.edu/pub/canada/KarlaFAQ.v40>.

[34] One of the earliest appears to have been created by students at the Universities of Waterloo and Toronto at *alt.fan.karla-homolka*. Other newsgroups were formed including *alt.pub.ban*, *alt.censorship.canada.dumb* and *alt.fan.paul.bernardo*, however many of these were not available in Canada.

[35] The University of Minnesota also removed the alt.fa.karla-homolka newsgroup from its local site.

[36] At abdul@io.com.

national authorities can control the flow of information. As is widely known, indefinite injunctions against the whole world were recently granted in the cases of *Venables v News Group Newspapers Ltd and others* and *Thompson v News Group Newspapers Ltd and others* prohibiting the publication or solicitation of any information as to physical appearance of the killers of James Bulger, their whereabouts or movements, their new identities or present appearance and similar information.[37] Threats to the injunction emanate from both the traditional and new media sector. Prior to the defendants' release, a web site was set up in Florida to campaign against the defendants' release.[38] Others in the United States, Germany, Australia and New Zealand have followed.[39] Certainly for individuals and ISPs located outside the jurisdiction, in the absence of a bilateral/multilateral agreement giving mutual recognition to court injunctions, breaches which do occur, will go unpunished. For those within the jurisdiction determined to breach such orders, anonymous servers situated outside the jurisdiction offer the possibility that wherever material is posted, no-one will be able to discover the identity or whereabouts of the speaker.[40] Even where speakers take little or no trouble to conceal their identity, the sheer numbers of persons who post material (whether factually accurate or otherwise) in breach of the ban make enforcement in all cases unlikely. Domestic ISPs will have been reassured by the Family Division's decision to relax the terms of the original injunction. Under the revised arrangements, ISPs will not be liable for the publication of material covered by the injunction if they can show that they took all reasonable steps to prevent material being published or removed it when brought to their attention. The amended injunction was granted after Demon—a leading ISP—argued that there might be circumstances where it was impossible to prevent certain information being put on its servers.[41]

In the case of the traditional media sector, the virtual certainty of severe punishment did not prevent one regional newspaper—*The Manchester Evening News*—publishing information in their first edition on 22 June 2001 which, according to the Attorney-General, may have helped identify the whereabouts of Thompson and Venables. The paper was subsequently fined for this lapse.[42] On the continent, Dutch, French, Italian and Spanish magazines have all expressed a willingness to pay for closed-circuit television footage which allegedly shows Robert Thompson on a visit to a shopping centre.[43]

[37] [2001] 2 WLR 1038.

[38] See *Guardian Unlimited*, 28 June 2001.

[39] *Ibid*. *The Manchester Evening News* was prosecuted for breaching the terms of the High Court injunction, see below.

[40] Usenet.co for example offer this facility.

[41] *The Times*, 11 July 2001.

[42] *The Guardian*, 5 December 2001.

[43] *The Times*, 25 June 2001.

Bad-Mouthing the Judges/Courts

The attraction the Internet possesses for unconventional and anti-authoritarian expression naturally means that some of the speech encountered there is of a critical and sometimes hostile nature, assailing societal institutions and those who wield power within them. A characteristic of Usenet newsgroups sites for example is the practice of 'flaming'. This refers to sarcastic, disrespectful or abusive expression directed at others. In the case of criticism of judicial conduct in England and Wales, the Lord Chancellor's Office has already moved against one web site consisting of complaints from James Hulbert about the conduct of judicial figures and the police.[44] After government officials informed Mr Hulbert's ISP (Kingston Internet limited) that the web pages were considered 'offensive', the site was taken down by Kingston as it was concerned about the possibility of legal action in the aftermath of *Godfrey v Demon Internet*.[45] Subsequently, mirror copies of Mr Hulbert's web pages appeared elsewhere on the Internet (including some located on UK-based ISPs) following a message from Mr Hulbert.

It is not clear at the time of writing whether the Lord Chancellor's Office has taken further action against any ISPs. Whatever the outcome in this case, it would be niave to expect disgruntled parties to court proceedings and their supporters to deny themselves the opportunities for instantaneous and worldwide communication of their grievances against judicial systems offered by the Internet.

IV CONCLUSION

The purpose of this book has been to survey and critically assess a range of legal restraints impacting on media coverage of administration of justice issues. The right of individual defendants to receive a fair trial, the privacy interests of young persons and public confidence in the administration of justice are all said to have been put in serious jeopardy by the irresponsible actions of journalists, editors and media proprietors. In this comparative treatment of the constitutional protection afforded to the media, I have argued that, aside from ignoring positive benefits flowing from freely reported proceedings, this view (and its implication that media freedom must remain subordinated to administration of justice concerns) is no longer tenable for a number of reasons. First, freedom of speech no longer ranks as a residual freedom prone to legislative/judicial incursion at will. Formal recognition in constitutional documents (such has occurred in the European Convention on Human Rights and Fundamental Freedoms, the Canadian Charter of Rights and Freedoms, the Spanish Constitution of 1978

[44] See n 1 above.
[45] [1999] 4 All ER 342.

and the United Kingdom's Human Rights Act) or judicial activism in defence of the freedom to engage in political communication (as occurred in Australia) has quite recently marked speech out as an especially vital freedom in democratic societies. Whilst Madison and the other framers of the US Constitution were undoubtedly well ahead of other jurisdictions in recognising this fact, my contention in chapter two was that currently European and US free speech jurisprudence share a number of common features, including a commitment to the idea that freedom of speech in modern democratic society functions to ensure informed debate about public institutions. This commitment is apparent *inter alia* in the more intense level of scrutiny applied by both sets of judges to restrictions on political expression and, in Article 10 jurisprudence, in a diminished margin of appreciation for national authorities. The fact that the Strasbourg Court may have occasionally lost sight of the centrality of political speech (as I argued it did in the court-related speech cases of *Worm v Austria* and *Prager & Oberschlick v Austria*) should not be allowed to obscure these common features. Nor, incidentally, should it be assumed that the Court will in future uphold the unduly deferential approach adopted in *Worm* and *Prager & Oberschlick*.

An important consequence of the constitutionalisation of speech entitlements is that the priority traditionally afforded by the English common law to fair trial interests and other administration of justice concerns requires to be reassessed. As was seen in chapter three, having decided that the Charter of Freedoms and Fundamental Rights enshrined freedom of expression on an equal footing with the right to a fair trial, the Canadian Supreme Court in *Dagenais v Canadian Broadcasting Corporation* was compelled to reformulate common rules relating to publication bans to reflect the new parity of speech entitlements. For its part, the Scottish judiciary too shows willingness to discard earlier media-hostile precedents. This development stems in part from greater awareness of the significance of Convention rights to media freedom after the Scotland Act 1998 and the Human Rights Act 1998. It also reflects the High Court of Justiciary's greater receptiveness towards media-friendly Contempt of Court Act 1981 rulings south of the border.

Aside from the enhanced constitutional status of speech claims, a further reason why I claimed that restraints on court-related speech must be examined closely derives from the self-interested nature of governmental curtailment of political speech forms. In the case of court-related speech, nowhere is such close examination more warranted than in respect of the offence of scandalising. Although considered largely moribund in England, the United States and Canada, the offence continues to act as a real deterrent to those minded to criticise judicial figures in other jurisdictions, including Australia. Chapter five asked whether any good reasons exist for giving the courts/judges a privileged position over other public bodies or persons when it comes to criticism and concluded that resort to the offences of scandalising and criminal libel constituted heavy-handed means of bolstering public confidence in the judiciary. In any case, it is not unreasonable to expect a degree of fortitude from those who occupy judicial office. As Justice Frankfurter of the US Supreme Court pointed out in *Pennekamp v Florida* 'weak characters ought not to be judges.' I suggested in this chapter that judicial engagement with the media was a better response to criticism, bringing as it did an informed counter-perspective into the public arena.

The critical perspective adopted towards speech restrictions advanced elsewhere in this book was also brought to bear on varieties of *sub judice* laws encountered in the UK, Canada and Australia. In chapter three, I set out two models or ideal types of reporting regimes to gauge the extent to which individual jurisdictions possess attributes of each. One feature of less liberal systems was the largely unquestioning acceptance of a causal link between partisan media comment and the prejudicing of particular proceedings. This chapter examined whether assumptions of juror susceptibility which lie behind *sub judice* laws are supported by empirical evidence as well as exploring the curative possibilities offered by remedial devices in those instances where a clear threat to fairness of proceedings is demonstrably present. The empirical evidence uncovered to date tends if anything to undermine the basis of *sub judice* laws. The latest research published in 1999 by the New Zealand Law Reform Commission into pre-trial publicity in high profile cases disclosed that few jurors recalled anything of the media's presentation of pre-trial events of a case beyond a hazy recollection, and of those that did, the majority did not recall material in a way which indicated prejudgment. As to publicity during the trial, whilst a minority of jurors did let media coverage affect their approach to the case in three of the 48 trials in the study sample, a number of these jurors were sharply reminded by other jurors that media coverage was not relevant to their deliberations on the grounds that it was partial and/or inaccurate. In conclusion, the model of susceptible jurors which underpins *sub judice* laws was shown by the New Zealand study to lack credibility.

Media reporting and comment upon criminal proceedings is further hampered by the existence of a vast array of automatic and discretionary prior restraints. Despite coming under attack in recent years, Alexander Bickel's argument that prior restraints are particularly inimical to speech interests remains valid and carries especial force in the arena of court reporting where restrictions strike at the very newsworthiness of information and comment. In chapter four, I attempted a defence of Bickel's position before considering some sets of restraints commonly imposed to protect the privacy interests of young persons involved in criminal proceedings. Particular focus was given to the tendency of legislatures to impose mandatory sets of reporting restrictions. In light of the demonstrated benefits of openly administered justice—including in this respect the interests of local retailers, neighbourhood watches and householders in being made aware of the identities of offenders in their midst—my argument was that in order for privacy claims to triumph here, some particularly compelling evidence of specific harm resulting from media identification would be required, rather than reliance upon an empirically unsubstantiated presumption of harm as frequently occurs at present.

Chapter six sought to bring a civil law perspective to bear upon the regulation of media freedom. Spain's emergence as a social democracy committed to the underlying values of political pluralism and fundamental rights offered an interesting case study of one civil law system's efforts to reconcile conflicting fundamental freedoms. The highly politicised wider context in which the *Tribunal Constituciónal* has been called upon to elaborate upon the nature of core constitutional guarantees to freedom of expression and fair trials has comprised the Basque struggle for independence, responses of the Spanish state to terrorist activities of Basque activists, a failed military coup and allegations of corruption at the highest levels of public office. As indicated by its ruling in *La Mesa de Herri Batasuna* the *Tribunal Constitucional* has opted for a robust approach to court-related speech. The 'extraordinary importance' which the Court attached there to the maintenance of free public opinion in a democractic society prompted its finding that the fact that a matter was before a court ought not by itself to prevent discussion of that topic in the media. On the facts of *La Mesa de Herri Batasuna*, even though government ministers were reported as believing the defendants to be guilty, the Court denied that this attribution, or other revelations about the voting intentions of the judges had created a parallel trial of the defendants in the media. It remains to be seen whether this robust approach will survive the recent reintroduction of lay juries in certain criminal proceedings before the *Audiencia Provincial*.

Finally, newer internet-based forms of communication were seen in this concluding chapter to pose an urgent and qualitatively different set of challenges for national authorities minded to regulate expressive activity. In particular, the practical difficulties which ensue from seeking to control Internet expression may force a re-evaluation of the basis of some current restrictions.[46] This is generally to be welcomed. In the case of speech directed at ongoing proceedings for example, the virtual impossibility of enforcing *sub judice* laws may well lead to an abandonment of facile assumptions of prejudice and prompt instead a more critical approach to any assessment of damage caused to a particular trial. Where harm to particular proceedings is considered to have occurred, the absence of a corporeal defendant within jurisdiction against whom contempt proceedings may be brought may focus judicial minds on the curative value of specific remedial devices. It might be expected that the higher courts would over time develop rules about resort to particular devices and the degree of

[46] For evidence that this is already happening, see A Bonnington, 'News Without Frontiers: Pre-Trial Prejudice and the Internet' in L Edwards and C Waelde (eds), *Law and the Internet* (Hart Publishing, Oxford, 1997).

discretion retained by the trial judge in this process. In respect of criticism of courts and judicial figures, the lesson from the Hulbert case is that not even the Lord Chancellor can stop critical postings from overseas. Given the seriousness with which the Government views this matter, one wonders what thought has been given in official circles to issuing via the Internet a carefully argued refutation which, from a Government perspective, sets matters straight?

In those rare cases where a restriction is demonstrably needed to protect an overarching individual interest (such as the right to life as in *Venables* and *Thompson*), the new audio-visual sector and the Internet will remain a source of extreme anxiety. In the absence of injunctions enforceable on a worldwide basis, it is to be hoped that those charged with safeguarding the security of high profile individuals have contingency plans to deal with the anticipated breach of reporting restraints.

Index

administration of government model, 78
Article 6, court-related speech and, 66–8
Article 10:
  see also First Amendment
  administration of justice interests and, 71–3
  certainty 58–9
  commercial and artistic expression, 55–6
  construction of derogations from, 54–5
  core status, 174–5
  court-related speech expression and, 66–8, 70–1
  First Amendment and, structural differences, 43–4
  hostility to prior restraints, 56–7
  moral reading, 68–70
    administration of justice interests and, 71–3
    interpretative requirements, 70–1
    Strasbourg scrutiny and, 73–4
    Worm v Austria, 71–3
  political speech and, 55
  proportionality, 57–8
  rationales for freedom of expression, 51–3
  right to shock or offend, 53–4
  Strasbourg scrutiny and, 73–4
  Worm v Austria, 71–3
artistic expression, 55–6
assumption of infallibility argument, 7–8
Australia:
  constitutional guarantees, 31–3
  implied freedoms, 33–6
  prejudicial media comment:
    implied freedom of political communication, 111–14
    public discussion and, 107–10
    remedial devices, 110–11
    sub judice law, 105–10
  privacy claims:
    adult proceedings, 147–9
    children's courts, 145–7
  scandalising the courts, 170–1
avoidance of mistake arguments, 7

balancing freedoms, clear and present danger and, 61–3
Barendt, E, 7, 36, 55
Barnett, SR, 131
Bickel, A, 39–40, 49–50, 125, 128–34
Blackstone, W, 49, 59–60, 129, 130
Bollinger L, 9
Bonnington, A. 213

Canada:
  Charter of Rights and Freedoms, 26–9, 171–74
  Duff Doctrine, 25
  fair trial and free expression, 29–30
juvenile justice:
    adult court restrictions, 151–2
    openness, 149–51
  Oakes test, 27–9
  pre-Charter, 24–6
  prejudicial media comment:
    Dagenais effect, 101–04
    pre-Charter regulation, 98–9
    post-Charter regulation, 98–9
    remedial devices, 104
  scandalising the courts, 171–4
certainty, 51, 58–9
Chafee, Zechariah, 6
Chesterman, M, 115–16, 183
children:
  see also young persons
  privacy in:
    Australian courts, 145–7
    Canadian courts, 149–51
    Spain, 200–01
    US courts, 152–7
civil law jurisdiction *see under* Spain
clear and present danger standard:
  post-publication contempt and, 59–61
  preferred freedoms and, 61–3
collateral bar rule, 131–2
commercial and artistic expression, 55–6
constitutionalism, 2
constitutions, moral reading of, 68–70
constitutive basis of speech, 18–19, 46–7
contents-based restrictions, 45
courts *see* scandalising the courts
criticism of courts and judicial figures *see* scandalising the courts, *see also under* Internet

Dagenais effect, 101–04
deontological arguments for free speech, 15–19
Dworkin, RM, 14–15, 18–19, 41–2, 43, 46–47, 68–9

European Convention on Human Rights:
see also Article 6; Article 10
UK status, 36–9

free speech rationales, 6–19
assumption of infallibility argument, 7–8
avoidance of mistake, 7
from democracy, 10–15
from government incompetence, 19–21, 45
from self-determination, 15–17, 45
from truth, 7–10
instrumentalist, 7–14
marketplace of ideas, 10, 45, 52
Millian, 7–10, 45
First Amendment, 23–4
see also Article 10
clear and present danger and, 61–3
costs, 115–16
free speech rationales, 45–7
hostility to prior restraints, 49–50, 57
location-based distinctions, 48
overbreadth doctrine, 50–1
post-publication contempt and, 59–61
right to shock or offend, 47–8
speech type differences and, 48–9, 56
vagueness, 51

Gearty, C, 74
government incompetence, and freedom of speech, 19–21
Gunther, G, 46

Holmes, Wendell, 10, 45, 52
Human Rights Act 1998, 36–9

instrumentalist arguments for free speech, 7–14
international law, young persons' privacy interests and, 142–4
Internet, 209–10, 220–1
adminstration of justice and, 212–13
consequences, 211–12
criticism of courts and judicial figures, 217
facilities, 210–11
jury proceedings impact, 213–14
prior restraints, 214–16
regulation, 209–10

judicial proceedings, clear and present danger and, 61–3
judicial review, 39–42
jury system, 78–80
see also prejudicial media comment
Internet impact on proceedings, 213–14
jury as persons with knowledge, 121–22
pre-trial publicity effect, empirical effect, 117–20
juvenile justice:
see also children; young persons
Canada, 149–51, 151–2
United States, 152–7

Kirby, Michael, 33

Madison, James, 11, 46
marketplace of ideas argument, 10, 45, 52
media:
see also prejudicial media comment
duty to impart information, 52–3
prejudicial comment and Sixth Amendment, 63–6
Mieklejohn, Alexander, 11, 46
Miller, C, 161
Millian argument, 7–10, 45
moral reading of constitutions, 68–70

New Zealand Law Commission, 119–20
Niekerk, Barend van, 5

Oakes test, 27–9
offend or shock, right to, 47–8, 53–4
overbreadth doctrine, 50–1

post-publication:
contempt, clear and present danger and, 59–61
sanctions, 116
preferred freedoms, clear and present danger and, 61–3
prejudicial media comment:
see also under jury system
Australia:
public discussion and, 107–10
remedial devices, 110–11
sub judice law, 105–10
Canada:
Dagenais effect on *sub judice* rule, 101–04
empirical evidence, 116–20
pre-Charter regulation, 98–9
post-Charter regulation, 98–9
remedial devices 104
Scots and English divergencies, 80–1
contempt proceedings, prejudiced party's role, 87–8
injunctive relief, 88–9
public interest dimension 89–91
strict liability contempt, 81–5
strict liability contempt and adverse impact on proceedings, 86–7
Sixth Amendment and, 63–6
sub judice models, 77–8

United States:
clear and present danger and, 95–8
remedial devices, 95–8
trials as media events, 93–5
presenting jury, 78–80
press:
duty to impart information, 52–3
prejudicial comment and Sixth Amendment, 63–6
prior restraints:
collateral bar rule, 131–2
comparative costs, 132–3
cost arguments, 130–1
distinct from state licensing, 130
as freeze on speech, 49–50, 56–7, 128–30
Internet and, 214–16
precision of restriction, 133–4
Spain, 196–8
privacy:
Australia, adult courts, 147–9
Australia, children's courts, 145–7
Canada, adult courts, 150–1
Canada, children's courts, 149–50
international law and young persons' interests, 142–4
Spain, 200
United States, juvenile proceedings, 152–7
proportionality, 57–8

rationales for free speech:
see also free speech rationales, 6–7

scandalising the courts:
Australia, 170–1
Canada, 171–4
definition, 163–4
European Convention jurisprudence, 175–8
history of use, 165, 166–8
role of offence, 161–3, 178–81
summary procedure and, 165–6
United States, 168–9
Scanlon, T, 15–17
Schauer, F, 3, 19–21, 115
Scots and English divergencies under strict liability rule *see under* prejudicial media comment
scrutiny of government model, 77–8
shock, right to, 47–8, 53–4
Sixth Amendment, 23–4
prejudicial press comment and, 63–6
Spain:
1978 Constitution, 189–90
European Convention and, 192
fundamental rights, 190–2
Burgos trial, 184–6
significance, 186–9
children and young persons, 200–01
as civil law jurisdiction, 183–4, 207–08
criminal trials, 202–03
courtroom passes, 204
openness principle, 203–04
protection from trial by media, 204–07
expression jurisprudence, 192–3
democratic rationale, 193–6
intimidatory words, 201–02
prior restraints, 196–8
privacy, 200
right to honour, 198–200
strict liability contempt law *see under* prejudicial media comment
sub judice models, 77–8

Ten, CL, 7
Thayer, James Bradley, 40
Trasen, JL, 136

United Kingdom, human rights legislation and, 36–9
United States:
see also First Amendment; Sixth Amendment
Bill of Rights, 22–4
juvenile proceedings:
access patterns, 152–4
First Amendment jurisprudence and, 154–7
post-publication sanctions, 116
prejudicial media comment:
clear and present danger and, 95–8
remedial devices, 95–8
trials as media events, 93–5
scandalising the courts, 168–9

vagueness and validity of statute, 51, 58–9
Van Dijk and Van Hoof, 52, 54, 69
Volokh, E, 211

Walker, S, 145, 148
Wilkes, John, 164–5
Worm v Austria, 71–3

young persons:
see also children
adult court proceedings and, 126–7
commencement of criminal investigation, 139–42
criminal investigations, reporting restrictions, 127–8
European Convention challenges:
reporting restrictions, 159

young persons: *(cont)*
trial arrangements, 157–9
international law and, 142–4
prior restraints and, 123–5, 160
Spanish jurisprudence, 200–201
unconvicted defendants, 139
witnesses and victims, 138–9
youth court proceedings, 125–6
youth offender, 134–8